THE SEASCAPE PAINTER'S PROBLEM BOOK

THE SEASCAPE PAINTER'S PROBLEM BOOK

BY E. JOHN ROBINSON

WATSON-GUPTILL PUBLICATIONS, NEW YORK
PITMAN PUBLISHING, LONDON

To Kathy and Karen
Daughters can be the best critics

Copyright © 1976 by Watson-Guptill Publications

First published 1976 in the United States and Canada by Watson-Guptill Publications,
a division of Billboard Publications, Inc.
1515 Broadway, New York, N.Y. 10036

Published in Great Britain by Pitman Publishing Ltd.
39 Parker Street, London WC2B 5PB
ISBN 0-273-00972-9

Library of Congress Cataloging in Publication Data
Robinson, E   John, 1932–
    The seascape painter's book.
    Bibliography: p.
    Includes index.
    1. Marine painting—Technique. I. Title.
ND1370.R63 1976   751.4'5   76-17120
ISBN 0-8230-4737-7

Manufactured in U.S.A.

First Printing, 1976
Second Printing, 1977

ACKNOWLEDGMENTS

I wish to thank students of marine painting everywhere who purchased my first book, *Marine Painting in Oil*, with such enthusiasm. I would also like to thank Lee Burleson and my wife June for their darkroom photography; Nona Turbitt, for typing the manuscript; Don Holden of Watson-Guptill for encouraging me on a second book; and, of course, the staff at Watson-Guptill Publications.

CONTENTS

INTRODUCTION

I concluded my first book, *Marine Painting in Oil*, with these words: "There is no better way to develop your own approach than to begin with this book and progress completely beyond it! In the meantime, I'll be trying to do the same. We may both use this book as a beginning, for with art and artistry there should be no end."

This book is designed to follow *Marine Painting in Oil*, but there are more demonstrations included here, and less text. Some of the material here will be a review of basic steps. But I try to add a new twist to them so they don't merely repeat the information in my first book.

Most of the book is a step-by-step approach to painting such tricky or downright difficult passages as, for example, putting in the glitter of sunlight without speckling the entire painting, making water translucent, and showing rocks below the surface of the water. Most of the material in this book is entirely new and is the result of my own progress since writing *Marine Painting in Oil*.

I review the basic materials in Chapter One. Then, starting with Chapter Two and proceeding through Chapter Nine, I show "special problems" that are represented by closeup or detail shots of portions of my recent paintings. They show a passage that is difficult to paint or they present an aspect of the sea that, to my knowledge, was never observed or painted until now. Along with these special problems, I add

some variations on the same theme from other paintings of mine.

Next, I take these special problems and demonstrate how to paint them in three or four steps. Most
of these demonstrations are in black and white, but a
number of them are also in the color section.

You should have the basics in fair control before
attempting many of these problems. To use this book
properly, first read it carefully, then pick out the
problems or new ideas that most interest you, and
follow the instructions as they're written. I suggest
that you practice on scraps of canvas or paper or
cheap supplies that *won't become a painting*. My rea-
sons are sound: when you're trying to paint a new
idea, you shouldn't be hampered by the stigma of
having to paint a full painting or a masterpiece.

Try to approach this book as a student approaches
a teacher. You have questions and this book has an-
swers. Don't try to avoid the work by skipping it and
copying the paintings. This is neither creative nor
ethical. Worse, it robs you of the knowledge necessary to be your own creative artist.

If you follow *these* step-by-step lessons and study
the sea at every opportunity, you'll be able to compose your own compositions—and that means to be
your own artist! I can think of nothing that could be
more satisfying.

Happy painting!

CHAPTER ONE

MATERIALS AND EQUIPMENT

The materials discussed in this chapter are my personal choices after many years of experimentation. Although they may not be suitable for everyone who tries them, they should at least be tried. Advanced students will want to compare these materials to what they've already found comfortable, and beginning students will want a place to start.

Next to his talent, materials are the most important asset of any artist. They're the extension of his creative thoughts, the medium by which he communicates. They are, indeed, more important than his voice.

Because materials are so important, the artist should never be satisfied with anything but the best. This doesn't mean the most expensive or the most talked about. "Best" means materials of high quality that feel comfortable to the artist.

If you are having problems painting the sea, make doubly sure the problems aren't caused by such basic things as poor materials, dirty brushes, wobbly easels, etc. There are enough problems in painting a recognizable wave without compounding the problem further.

EASEL

My studio easel (below) cost less than $10.00 in scrap lumber, so it can't be termed expensive. However, it's so sturdy that it won't wobble, it's large enough to hold any size canvas I wish to place on it, and it's exactly the right height and size for my comfort. Naturally, to acquire these characteristics I had to build it myself; but it's exactly what I want.

Now when I paint, I won't be bothered by a wobbling easel. If I bump the easel or accidentally kick it, it won't fall over or splash paint thinner over the palette. So, in effect, it helps me to paint a better picture.

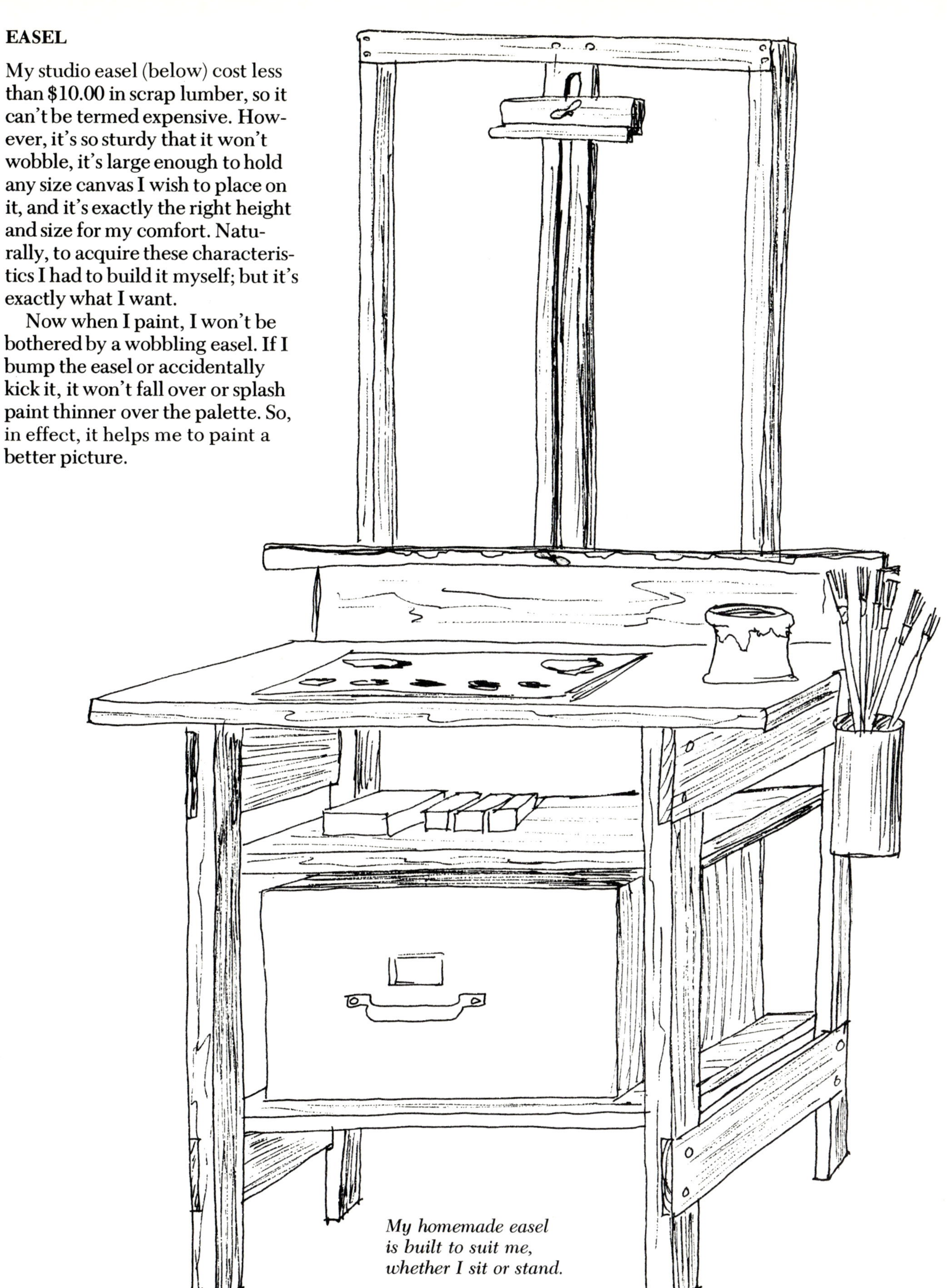

My homemade easel is built to suit me, whether I sit or stand.

PALETTE

I'm one of those lazy artists who dislikes cleaning up after myself. One way around that problem is to use a disposable kind of palette—use a sheet, tear it off, and a clean one is ready and waiting.

There are many other types of palettes that range from the old-fashioned wooden kind to pieces of glass, marble, pressed wood, enamel trays, and waxed paper.

The important thing is to choose the one that best suits your temperament and also does the job. A dirty palette is far more hazardous than one of the wrong color. If chunks of dried pigment find their way into fresh paint and destroy a delicate passage in a painting, then it's either time to do a better job of cleaning or change to the disposable kind, as I did.

COLOR ARRANGEMENT

While we're discussing palettes, you might also want to study my color arrangement (below). My arrangement may not suit you at all, but I find it convenient. Because I blend so much paint with white or a tinted hue, I like a large mixing area between the colors and the two areas of white.

The white on the right-hand side of the palette is for mixing with yellows only. The white at the left-hand side is for use with all other colors. Working in this manner, I always have clean yellows for sunlight; no other color touches them.

COLOR CHOICES

This book does not have a chapter devoted to color. (You'll find that in my first book, *Marine Painting in Oil.*) Here I will simply list my palette and give an alternate one for your consideration.

My palette consists of the following colors:

Permalba white
Alizarin crimson
Viridian
Ultramarine blue
Burnt sienna
Cadmium yellow
    (pale, medium, or deep)

As an alternate, I suggest:

Titanium white
Cadmium red deep
Cadmium green
Manganese or cerulean blue
Brown madder
Any yellow, including yellow
    ochre and raw sienna

Try these colors and experiment with others, but remember that no tubed paint can ever match nature exactly. Keep your selection of colors small and learn to mix. Do buy good-quality pigments if you can.

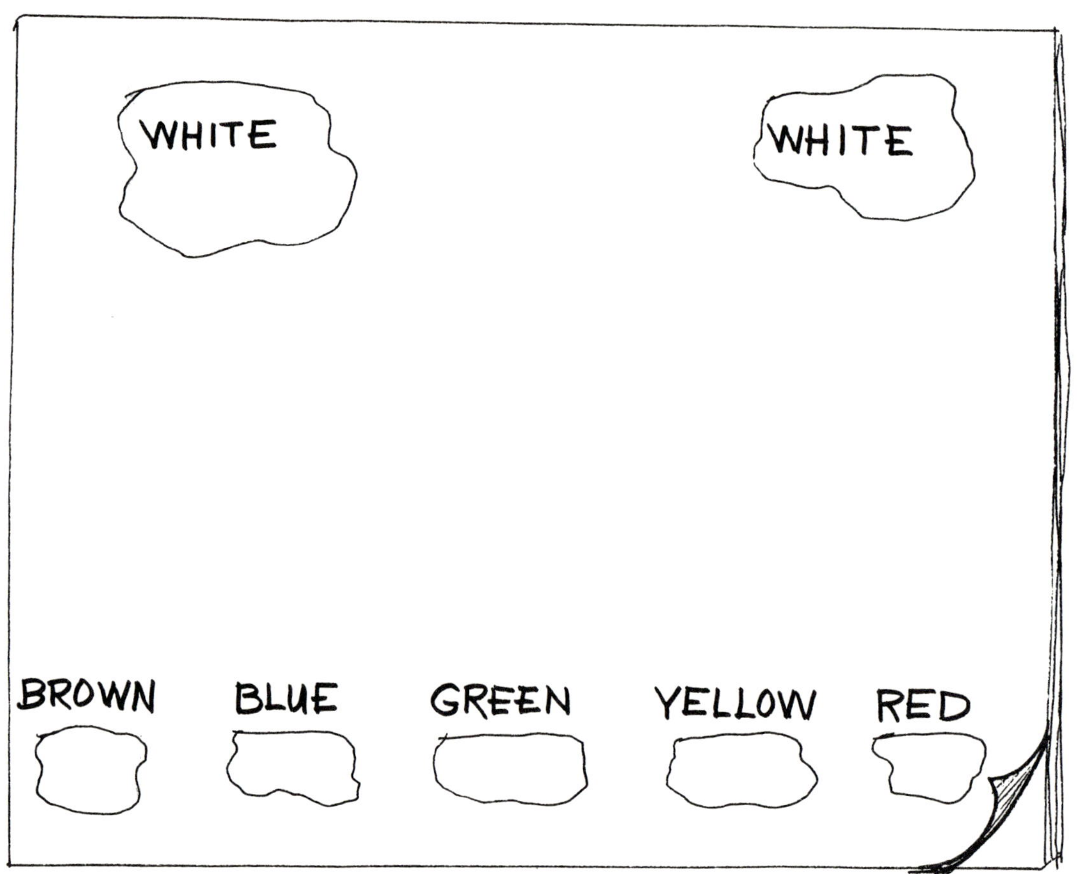

This is the color arrangement on my disposable palette.

MEDIUMS AND THINNERS

Modern pigments are ground in good-quality linseed or poppy oil, placed in airtight tubes, and sold ready to use. Unless you use a special technique, such as glazing, that requires adding varnishes, etc., to your paints, no additional mediums are necessary. Adding linseed oil only thins the pigment, gives it less tinting power, and makes it dry slower. Adding turpentine thins the pigment and should not be done unless your personal technique calls for it.

I use what is commonly called cleaning solvent, which is also sold in some places as paint thinner. In either case, it's much cheaper than turpentine, and I use it simply to clean my brushes. On occasion, I also use it to thin my paints, such as when I am drawing preliminary outlines on the canvas.

BRUSH WASHING

Enough can never be said for cleaning brushes. I've seen too many students spoil an otherwise successful painting by using dirty ones. Try painting a clean, crisp line of sunlight white with a brush containing some burnt sienna or blue. The result is mud.

I've found that the best way to solve this problem is to wash your brush thoroughly every time you lay it down, and probably a few times in between. For this purpose I use a commercial brush washer (below) filled with paint thinner or turpentine. (Make sure you have good ventilation, no matter what solvent you use.) The screen midway down permits residue to settle so the solvent stays clean.

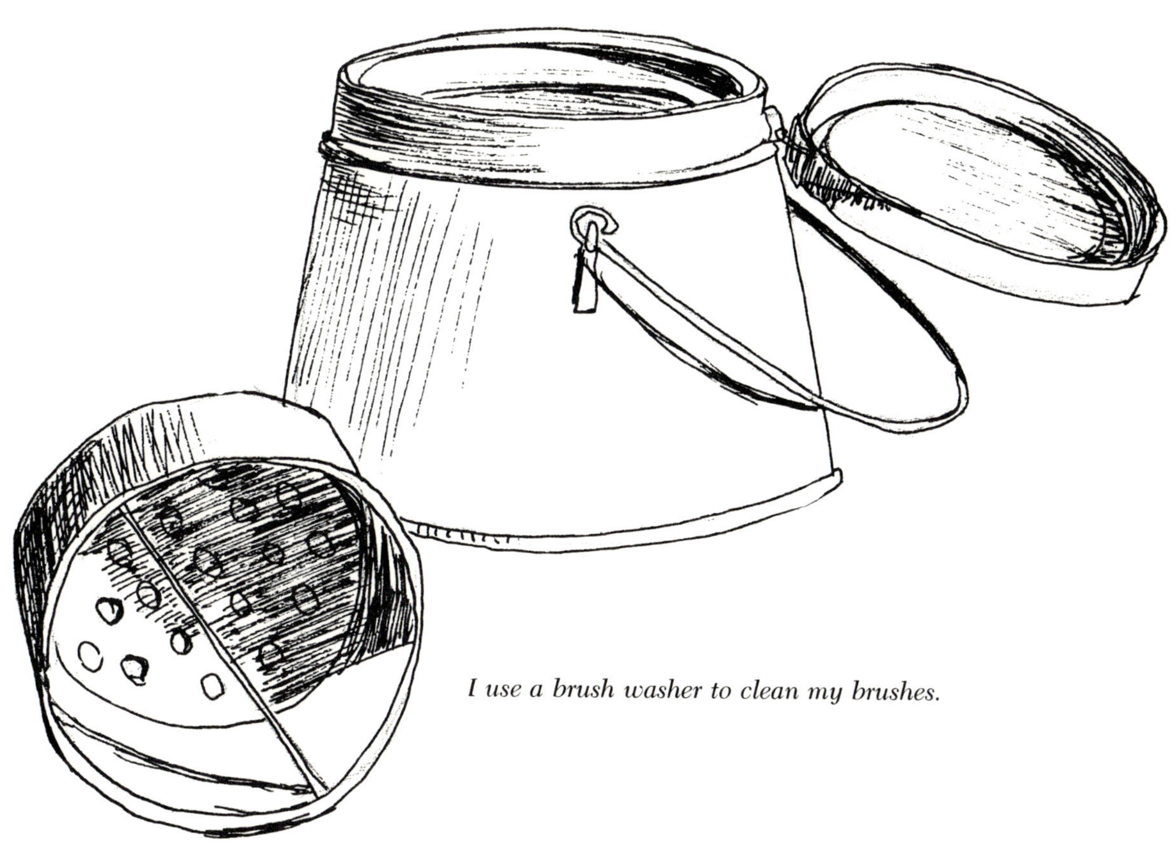

I use a brush washer to clean my brushes.

BRUSHES

The three types of oil brushes most commonly used are brights, filberts, and rounds (see below). Brights are good for short, choppy strokes where you want to lay down some paint and leave it alone. An example would be in painting a rock.

Some artists can use brights successfully for just about anything, but I can't. When it comes to painting soft edges of foam or clouds, or blending colors right on the canvas, I prefer the filbert brushes.

Filberts are thin and flat like brights, but they have longer, more pliable bristles and no sharp corners. Their rounded shoulders allow easy brushwork without leaving brushmarks where you don't want them. The round brushes achieve much the same result, but are best suited for painting in large areas.

The size of the brush should be determined by the size of the area you wish to cover. Obviously, a large brush should be used for large areas and small brushes for small areas. I recommend buying bristle brushes in Nos. 2, 4, 6, 8, 10, and 12.

In addition, I find two other kinds of brushes indispensible (see below). Sable are good to use when painting thin or tiny lines. They are sold in sizes ranging from No. 0000 to Nos. 1, 2, and 3. Then, for a soft edge in order to create the effect of distance or foam or whatever, I use a 2-inch or 1½-inch hog-bristle varnish brush. This brush isn't for painting; it's for hazing and should be used clean and dry. Just whip it back and forth across a sharp edge or line to soften it. Mine cost about 59 cents. I suggest you look for hog bristle rather than nylon, because nylon is usually too thick and too stiff.

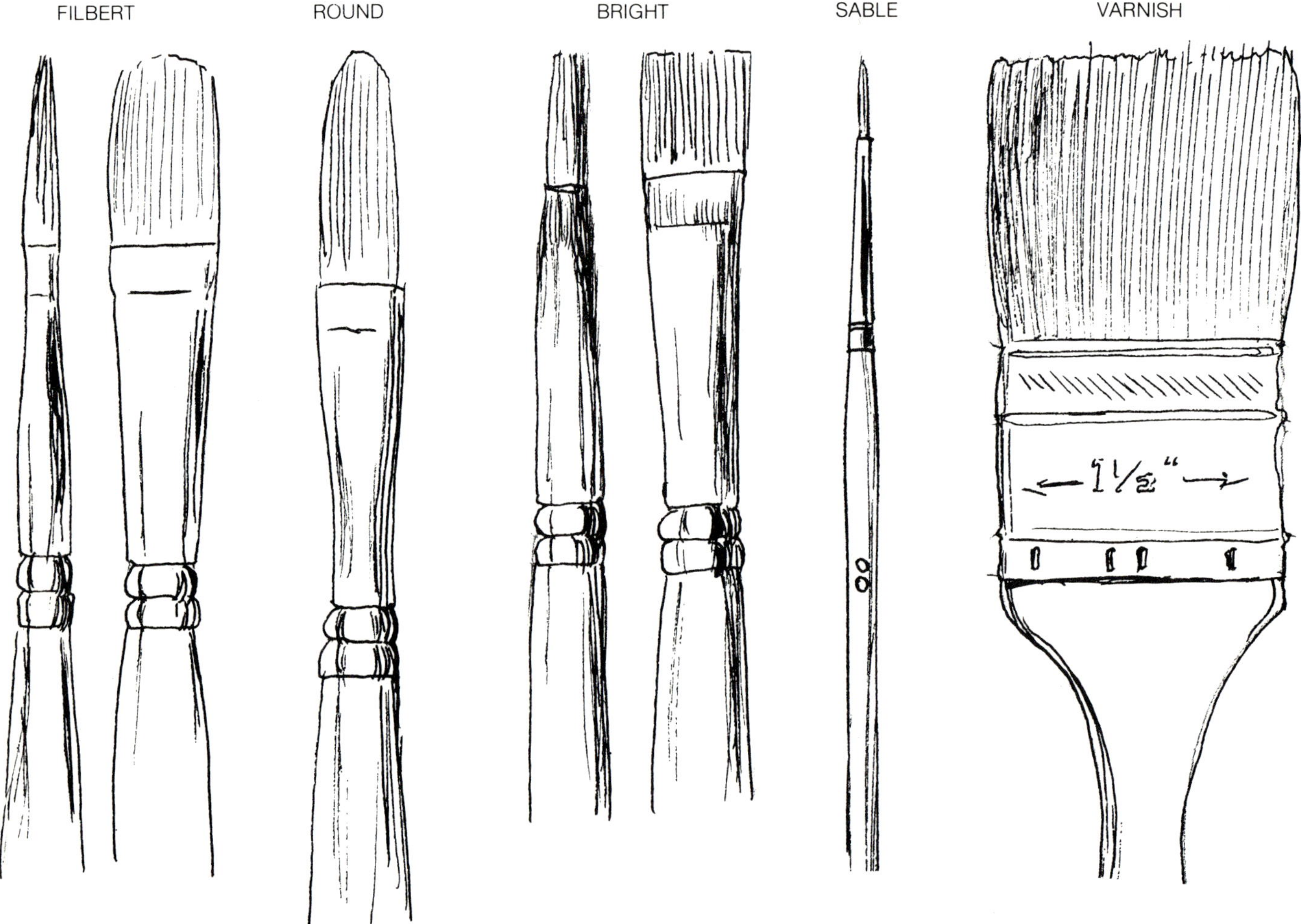

The oil brushes on the left are the most common ones on the market. I personally prefer the filberts. A small watercolor sable and a large varnish brush are two indispensible extras.

KNIVES

Some artists do remarkably well applying paint to canvas with nothing but painting knives. While I am a "brush man," I quite often use a painting knife for rocks. The knife gives a sharper edge to the rocks (or headlands) and can also create a more angular and textured effect.

Whether or not you paint with knives, you will at least need one to mix paint on your palette. Painting knives are better than ordinary palette knives for mixing because they can apply paint as well. I use the set pictured below, but you must experiment to find the ones best suited to your needs.

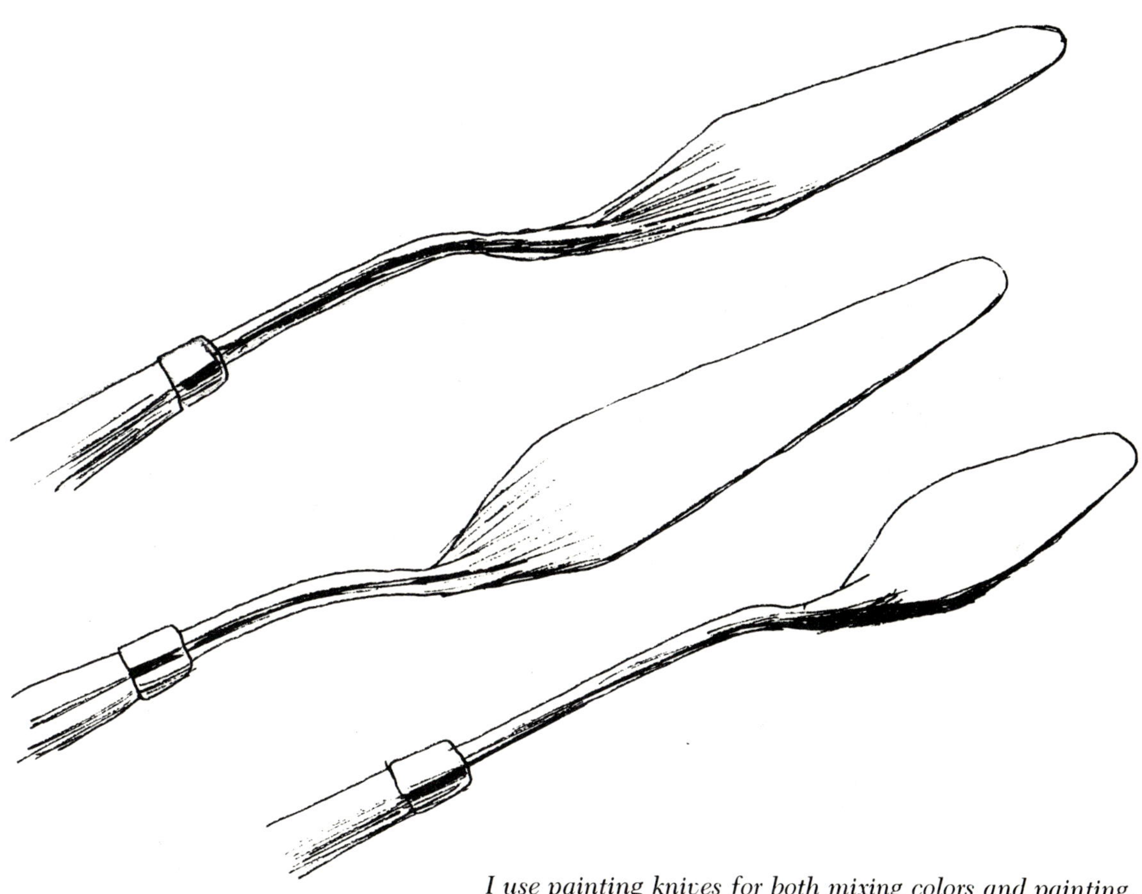

I use painting knives for both mixing colors and painting.

CANVAS OR BOARDS

I'm continually asked for advice regarding the merits of canvas as opposed to canvasboard or sized pressed wood, etc. My answer is simply, "There is no comparison." Each material is different and gives a different result.

Properly stretched canvas has a springy feeling that can't be duplicated with any other material. It also has a variety of textures, depending on the type you buy.

Hard boards, on the other hand, don't have the spring of canvas, but they're cheaper and can be sized in just about any color and textured at the same time. Canvas boards are also cheap and give the texture of canvas. However, they may also warp.

The way you use materials is another factor in their selection. Obviously, it's too expensive to experiment with mixing colors on a good linen canvas. On the other hand, many galleries and exhibits won't accept your work unless it's on canvas—many specify linen canvas. Again, you must decide for yourself. However, you may stretch your own canvas and save some money. If you do, I suggest you buy a tack gun and canvas pliers (below). It makes the job much easier.

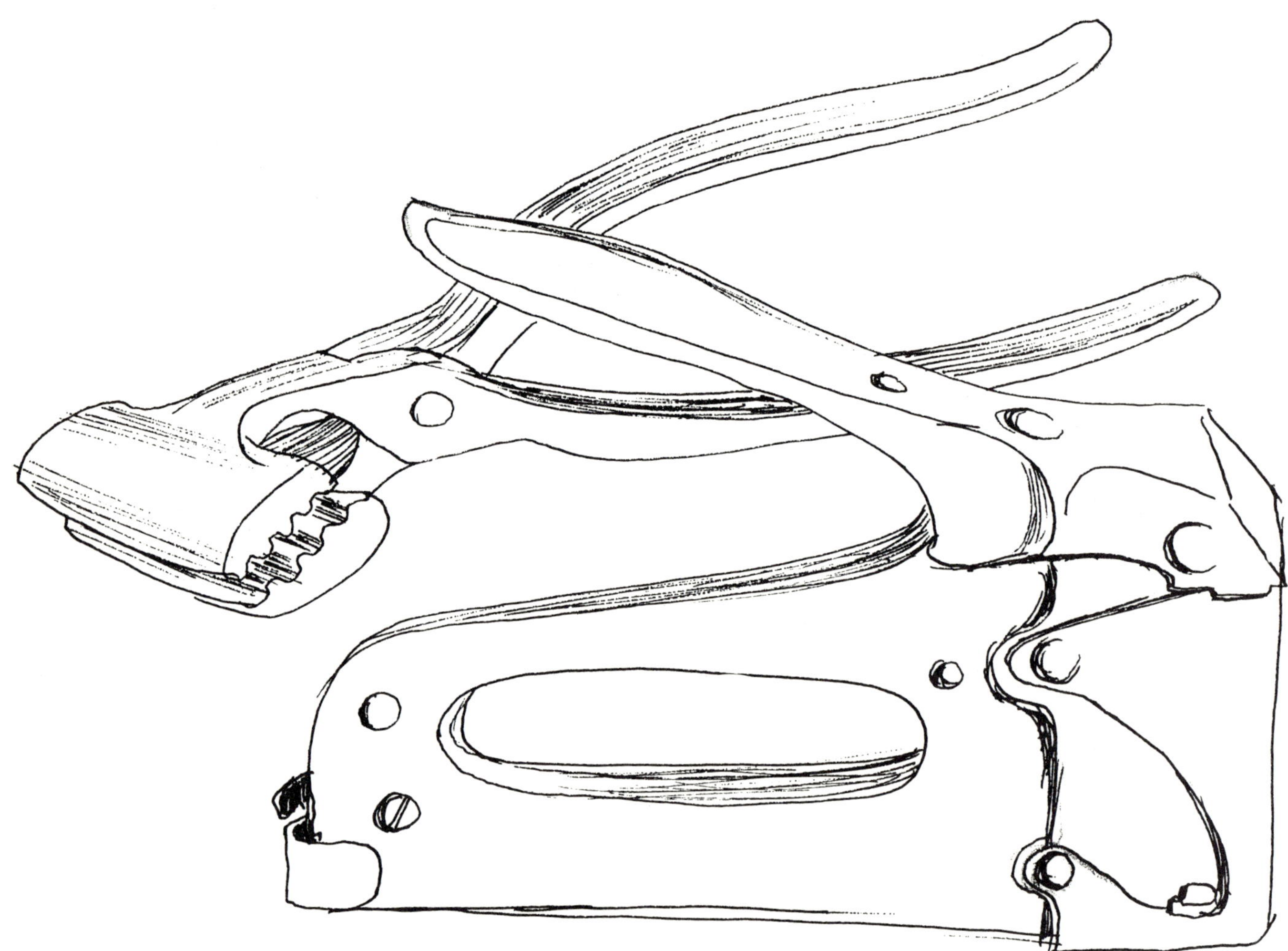

A sturdy tack gun and wide-grip canvas pliers are handy for stretching canvas.

LIGHTING

I have a large skylight over my easel as well as a floodlight for dark days or night painting. The skylight leaks and the floodlight is nothing special, but both do the job for which they were intended. That's all you can ask of any material or piece of equipment.

TRAVEL SETUP

When I paint on location, I sit on the ground or a rock and am more concerned with painting than personal comfort. The items pictured here fit into an old briefcase and are all that I need.

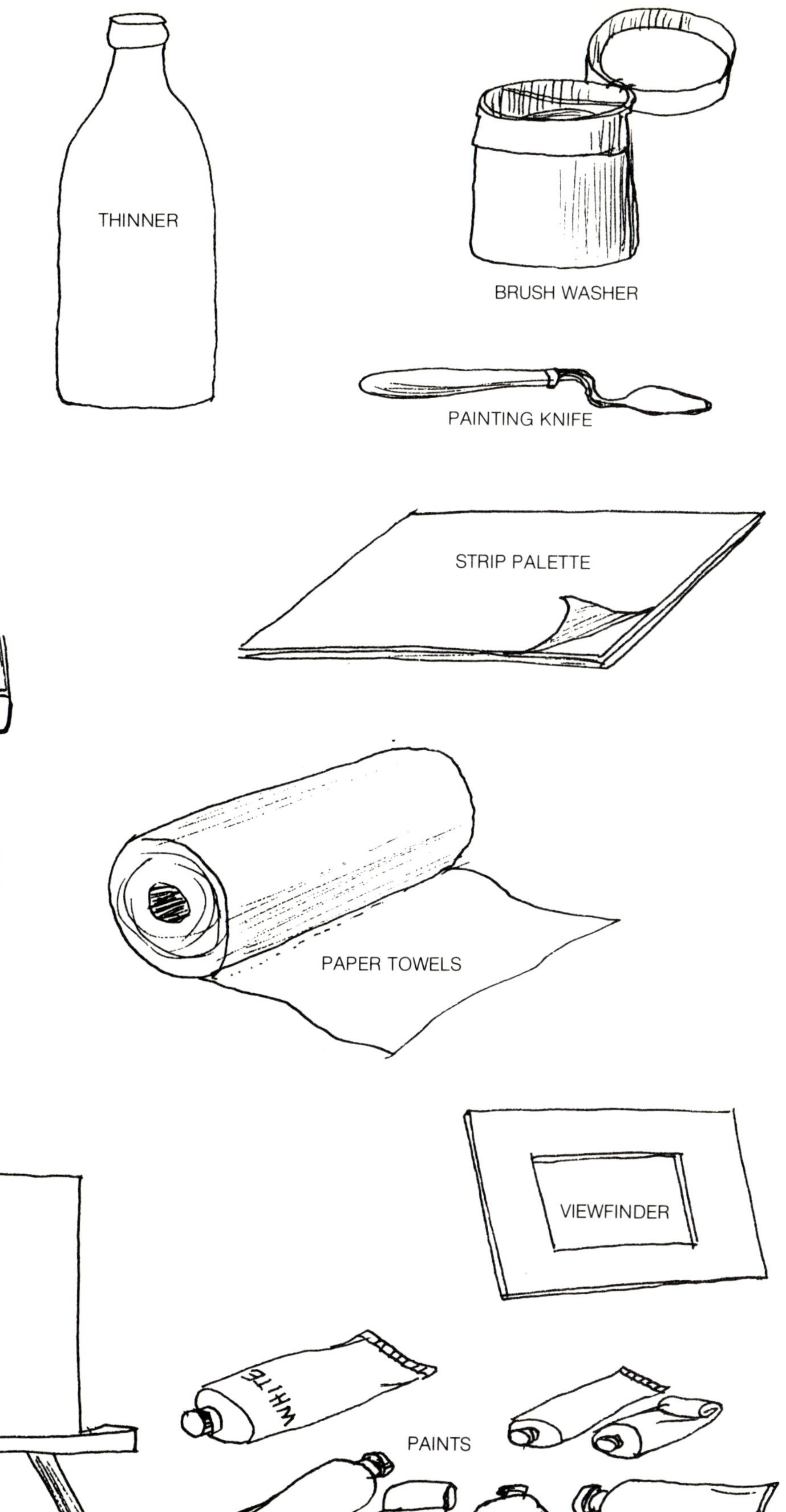

When I paint on location, I travel light. These items are all I need.

CHAPTER TWO

SKIES

Skies shouldn't present painting problems to marine painters, but they often do. For years I neglected a thorough study of skies because I spent all my time learning to paint the water. Finally, after taking a closer look, I found skies to be nearly as interesting as the sea.

Of course, there are many other types of clouds and skies, but this chapter will show the basic ones. If you learn to paint them with ease, then with just a bit of practice, the others will be yours when you need them. I still believe skies can easily become distracting in a seascape. But now I watch them carefully and try to make each one an interesting, one-of-a-kind type that fits my composition and even augments it.

As you'll notice throughout this book, my favorite lighting is back lighting. Whenever the sun is behind thin clouds, the clouds' edges turn silver or white, lending sparkle to what may be an otherwise uninteresting sky.

The nice thing about skies is that they, too, have movement and reflect light and shadow, just as the sea does. Looking at skies now makes me wonder how I could have ignored them for so long.

Actually, I didn't ignore them. I just kept them low key so as not to distract from the ocean in my paintings. There's still a need for this. There are times when the sea is so active that the only area of calm is in the sky (see Figure 1) and an active sky would destroy the balance and harmony of the painting. Either the lines of movement are not in keeping with the rest, or the painting is already active and needs no more.

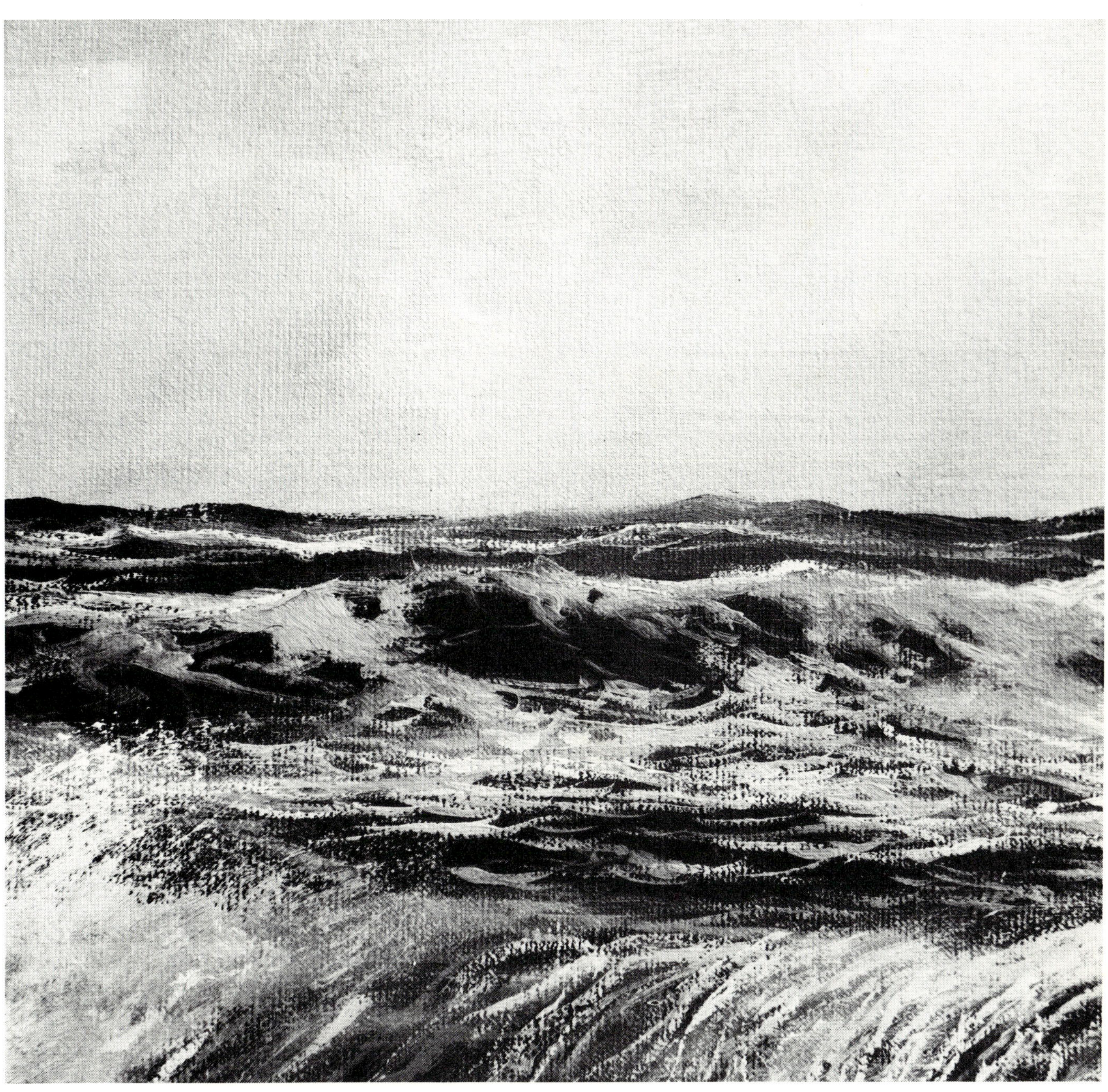

Figure 1. An uncluttered sky adds an area of calm to an active painting.

CUMULUS CLOUDS

Cumulus clouds aren't the most common clouds over the sea; but when they do appear, they add a lightness—a rising, uplifting quality that is so important to some paintings. I used to stay away from them for fear they'd distract from the sea, but I've since learned that they can be a real asset. Cumulus clouds keep the movement or rhythm going in some compositions (Figure 2), and allow the artist to balance out a painting with their moving lines and subtle shadings. In Figure 3 the sky enhances rather than distracts from the sea, backing it up with nearly the same arching curves. The brushstrokes have been hazed somewhat to allow the foreground more strength.

Painting cumulus clouds is not easy. They can easily get too interesting unless kept subtle (Figure 2). Remember that they really have definite form, and that form is best shown with side or back lighting. To see how to paint cumulus clouds in back lighting, refer to Demonstration 11.

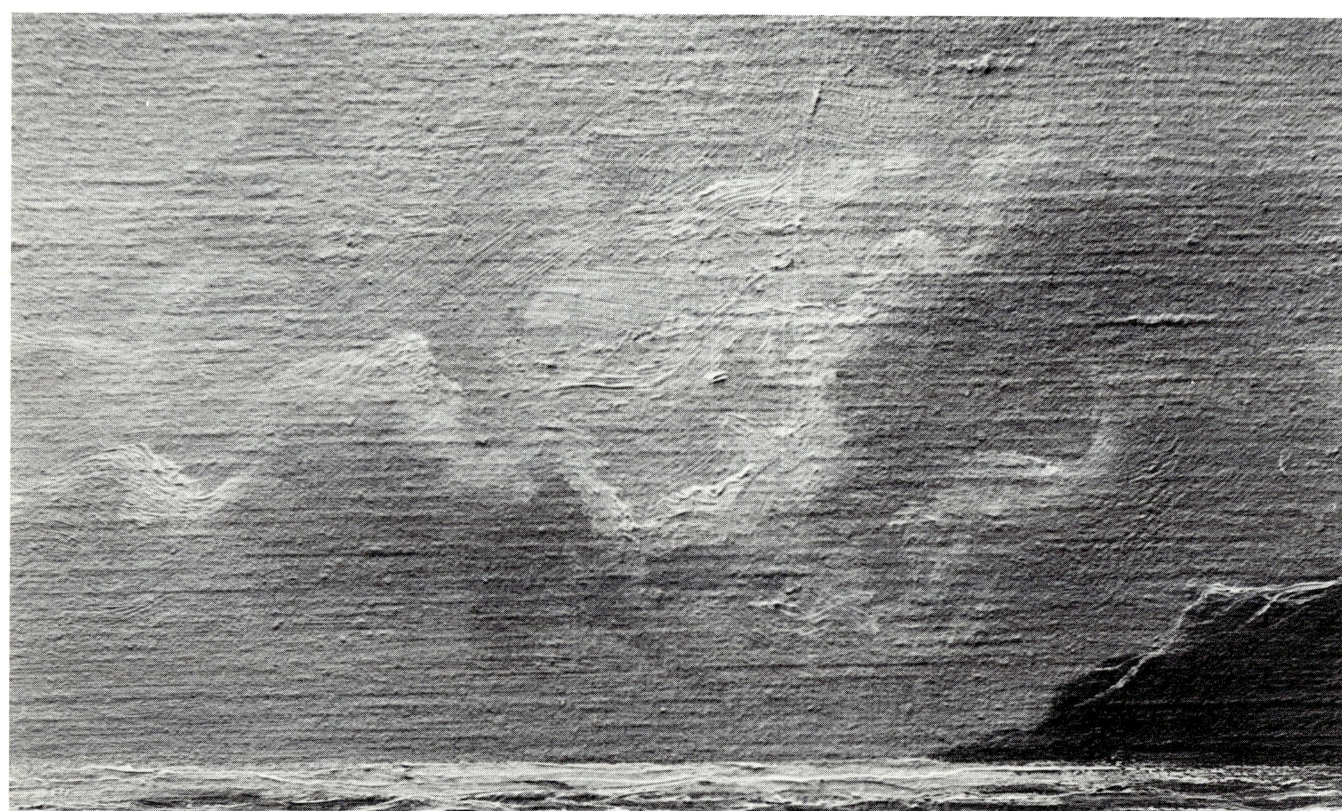

Figure 2. This detail shows the rhythm of movement between sea and sky.

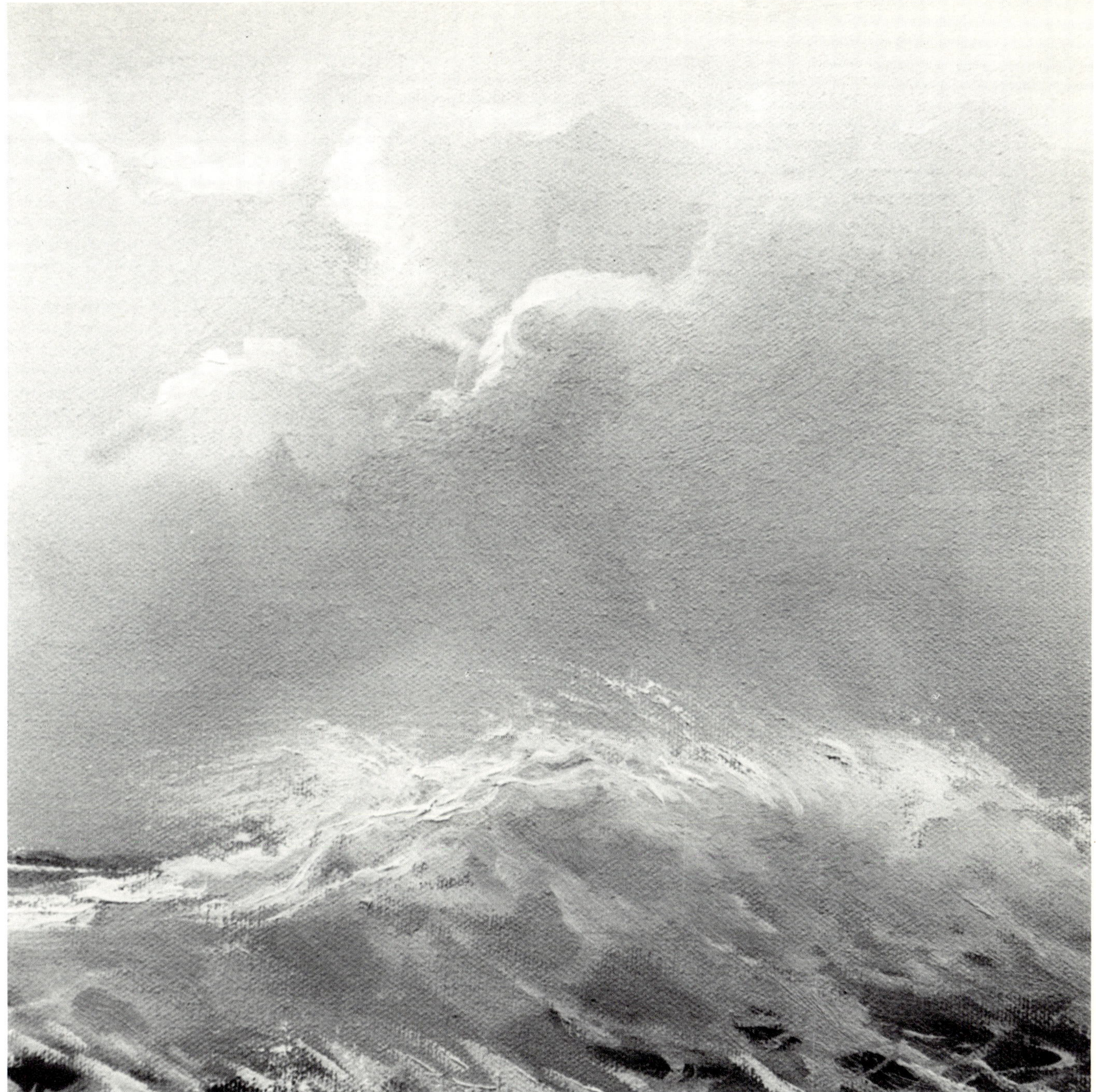

Figure 3. I played down the values so the sky doesn't distract from the sea.

STRATUS CLOUDS

These are the most common type of clouds found above the horizon line of the sea and are most often seen toward evening. They lend themselves to horizontal compositions where their generally horizontal lines match those of the sea (Figure 4). But play them down so they don't distract from the sea itself. Occasionally they sweep upward on an oblique angle from winds. This effect, too, lends itself to particular needs.

Whenever you paint clouds, first decide whether you want them to be horizontal (stratus), rising (cumulus), or falling (nimbus), or see if they're there simply to support your composition.

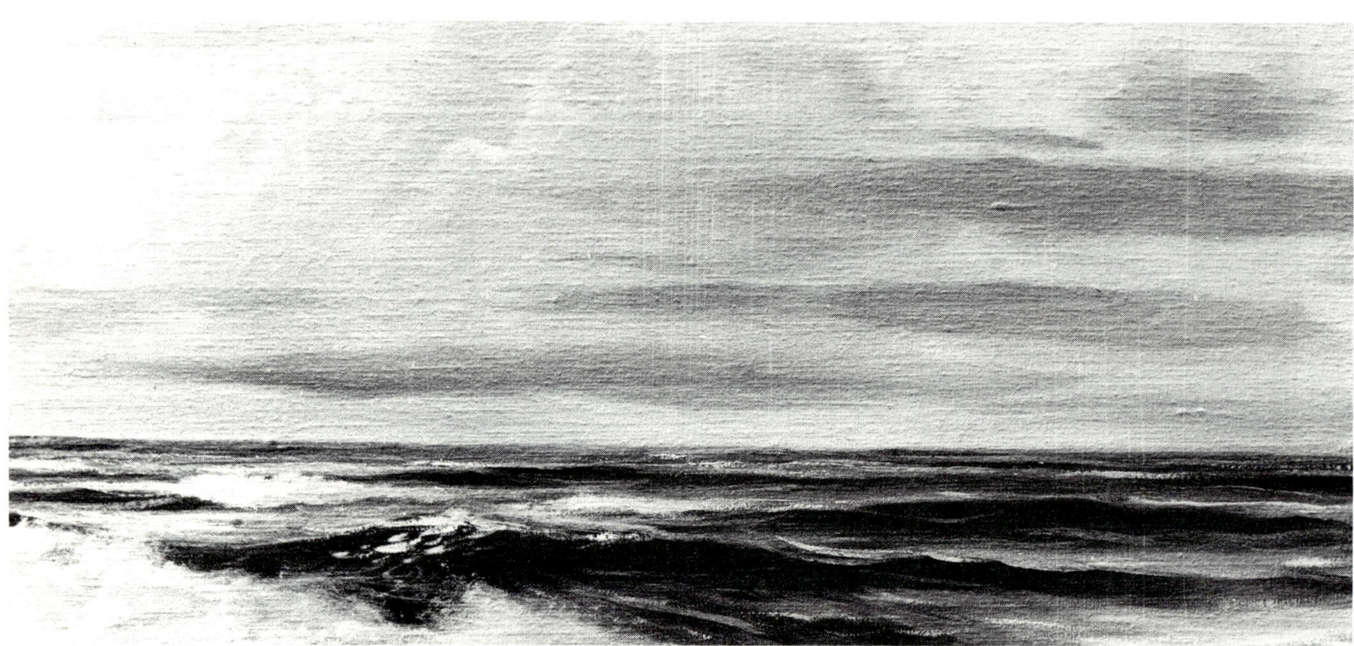

Figure 4. The horizontal lines of the sky repeat the rhythms of the sea.

RAIN SQUALLS

Rain squalls falling from nimbus clouds are best used as part of storm paintings. Of course, if they're painted in very lightly and in the distance, they may serve to announce a coming storm or the end of one. In any case, nimbus clouds are falling rather than rising clouds and should be matched to a sea of like mood; that is, one that is angry or dark or stormy (Figure 5).

Because they're often very dark, it's best to contrast them sharply in the foreground in order to attract attention. Don't be concerned about painting a "depressing" subject. Rain and dark skies can be stimulating as well.

I consider their use in seascapes so important that I show how to paint them step-by-step (Demonstration 1). Try painting them several times, and then incorporate them into a painting related to

storms. But keep your colors subdued and the detail and interest on the sea, or the sky itself may become the subject of your painting. Notice the variation of light and dark tones in the sky and how they harmonize with the values of the sea in Figure 6. Note also that the movement created by the sky is a repeat of the foreground wave, though the sky is softer and more distant.

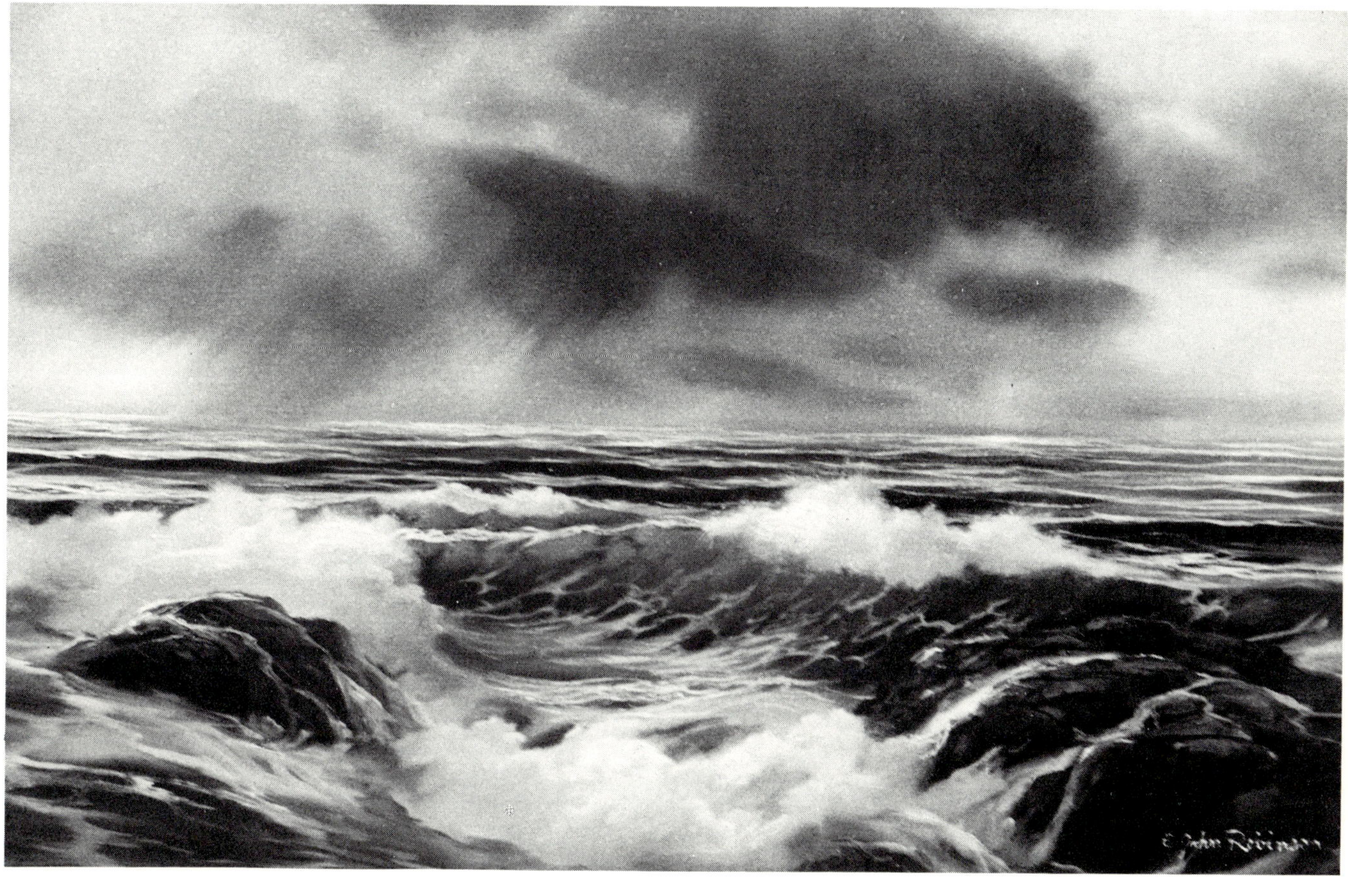

Figure 5. Rain squalls intensify the mood of a darkening sea.

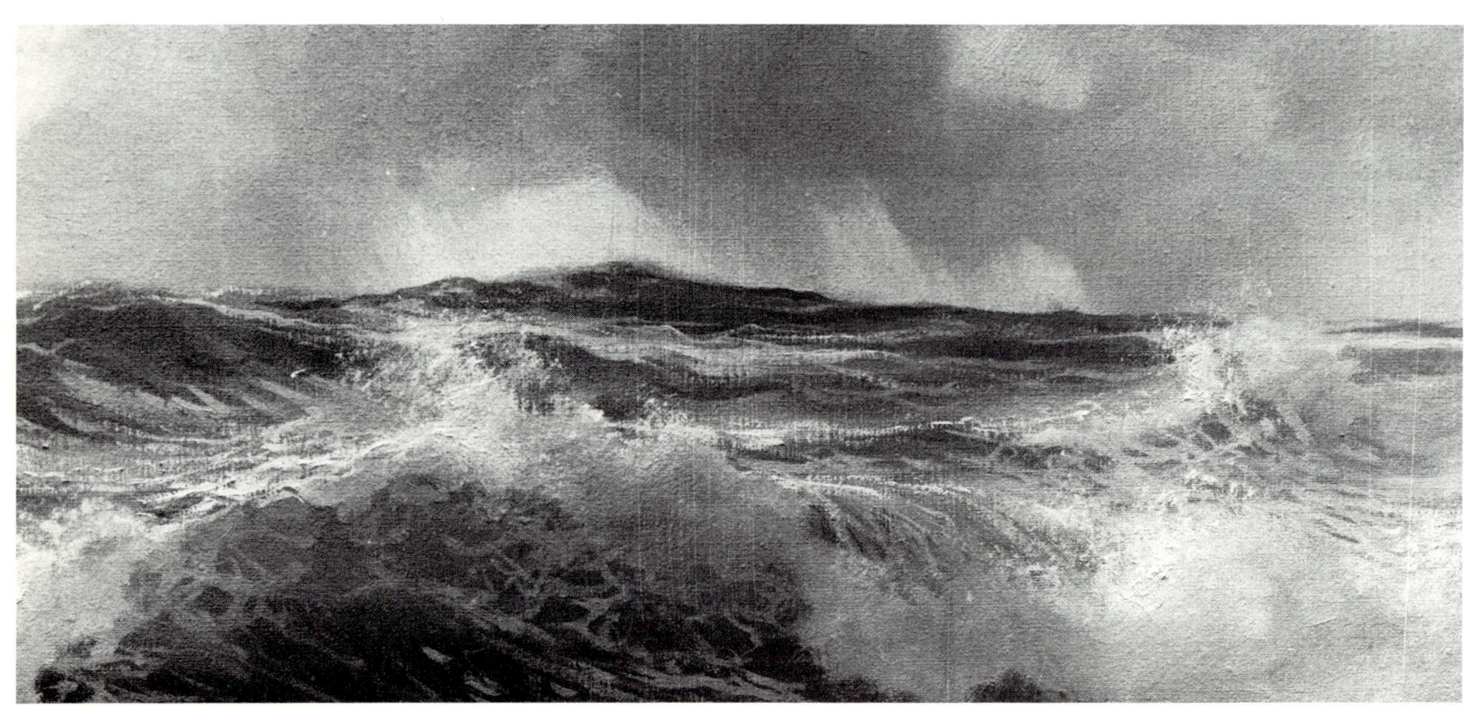

Figure 6. Here's another example of nimbus clouds during a rain squall.

DISTANT FOG BANKS

I've made use of distant fog banks to keep a painting low-key, but never gave them the attention I do today. Because of their importance in some paintings, I show how to paint them in Demonstration 2 at the end of this chapter.

Distant fog forms a transition between the light value of the sky against the dark of the sea (Figure 7). Here the fog bank is a middle value between the light sky and the darker sea, thus taking away the contrast that commands too much attention.

When the sun is above the fog bank, pay special attention to the glow that lightens the fog bank and the background sea. (See Chapter Three and Demonstration 15 for more information about glow.) In Figure 8, the brushstrokes of light appear at the top of a distant fog bank. The darker area has been softened with a dry brush, so no brushstrokes show. This makes a good background for the flying spray in the foreground. If the fog bank had not been hazed, the brushstrokes may have interfered with the interest and importance of the foam.

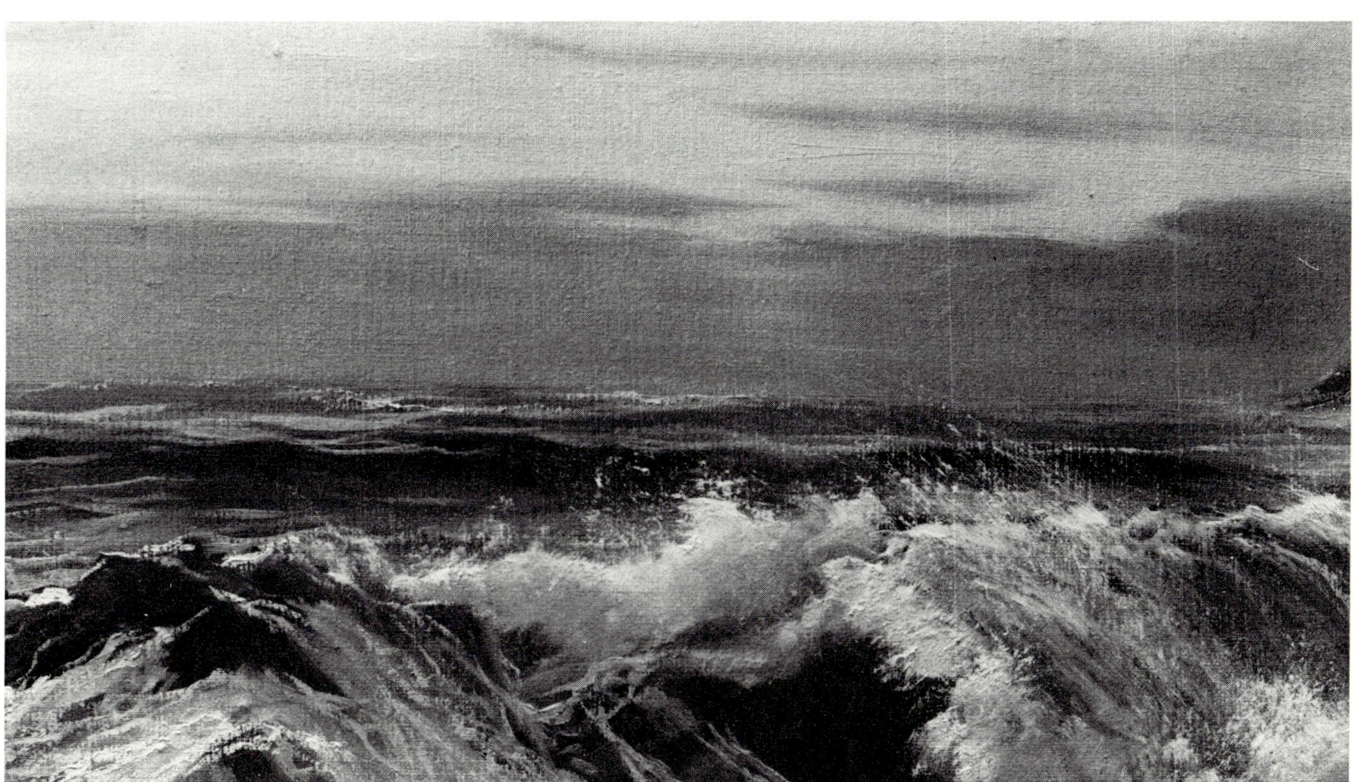

Figure 7. A fog bank softens the transition between sea and sky.

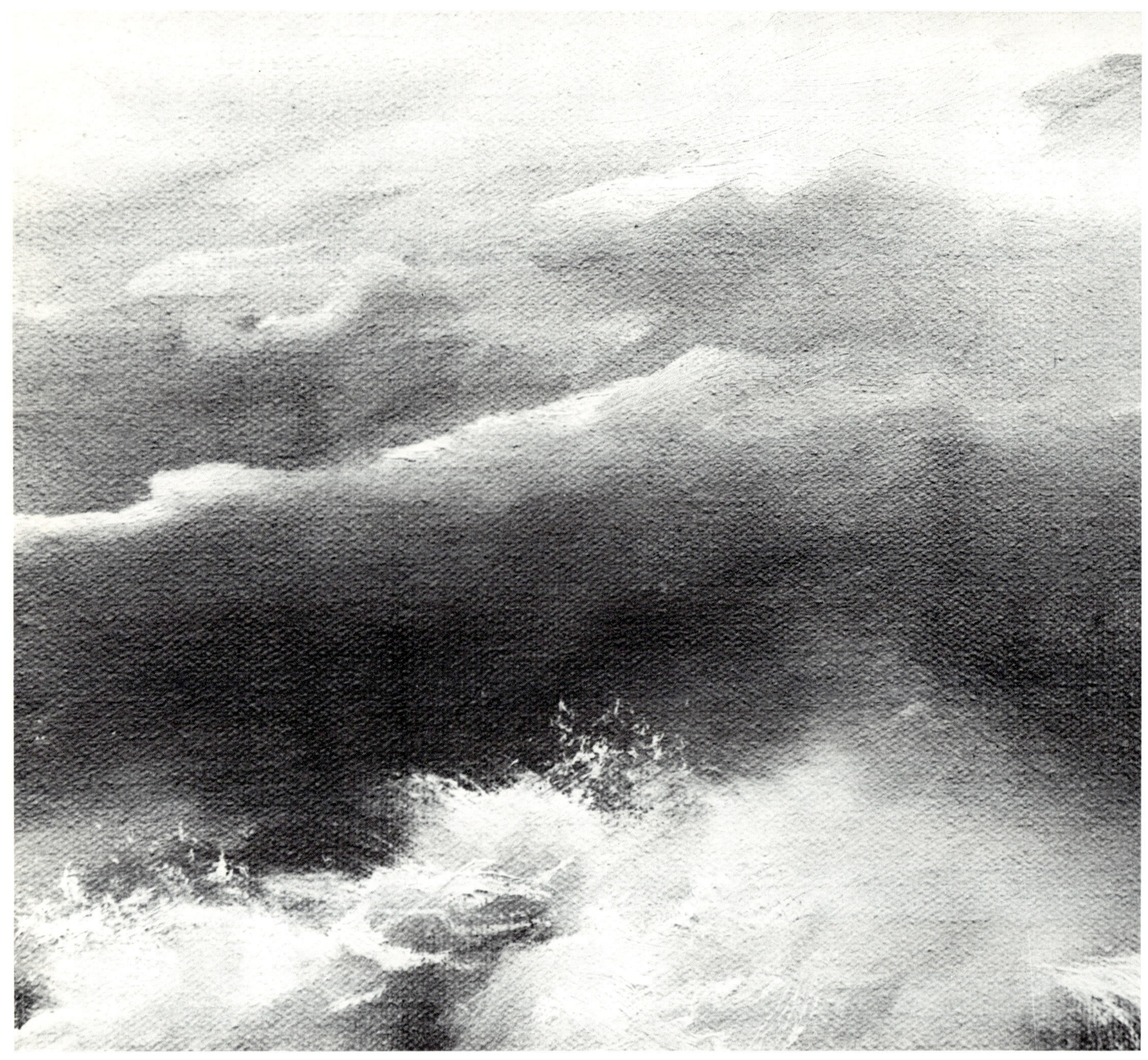

Figure 8. A distant fog bank provides a foil for foreground spray.

CLOSE FOG

Close fog is caused by heavy moisture in the air that moves in to shore. To observe it at close hand means you're standing in it and looking through it at the surf. The closer and thicker it is, the less you can see into the distance. The advantage of this is that you may put the fog wherever you wish it. In other words, you may show only as much of a scene as you choose.

For real softness and a hint of mystery, try moving fog in close to the middle or foreground, as I have in Figure 9. This keeps the interest of the painting up close and prevents the eye from moving to a horizon line or away from the subject. Another variation of close fog appears in Figure 10. Notice that the sky area is lightest in the upper right-hand corner and gradually darkens as it reaches the sea. This shows that some sunlight is showing through the fog and reflecting off the chops and swells.

The color of fog presents a problem too. Actually, fog has a grayish white appearance that may be either warm or cool, depending on the amount and direction of sunlight. I've found that a mixture of viridian and alizarin crimson into white is excellent for portraying the color of fog. I try to make it neutral at first, then either warm the color with more red or cool it with more green, according to the mood of the painting. Of course, the color of sunlight should also have an influence on the color of fog (for examples of this in full color, see Chapter Ten, Plates 9 and 10).

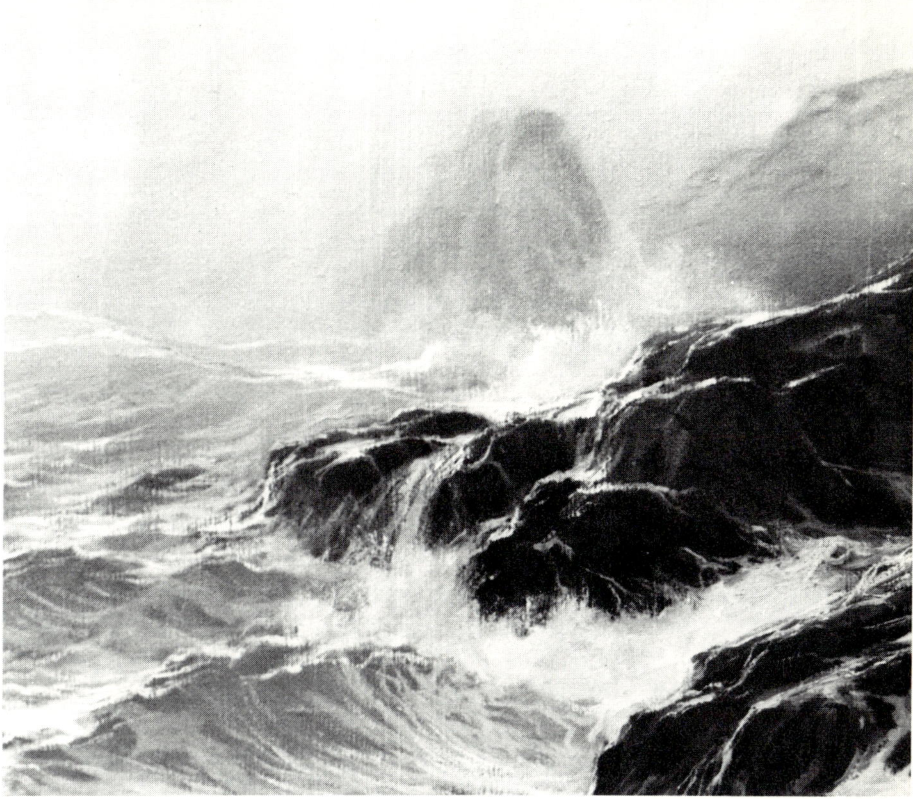

Figure 9. Close fog focuses the interest of a painting in the foreground.

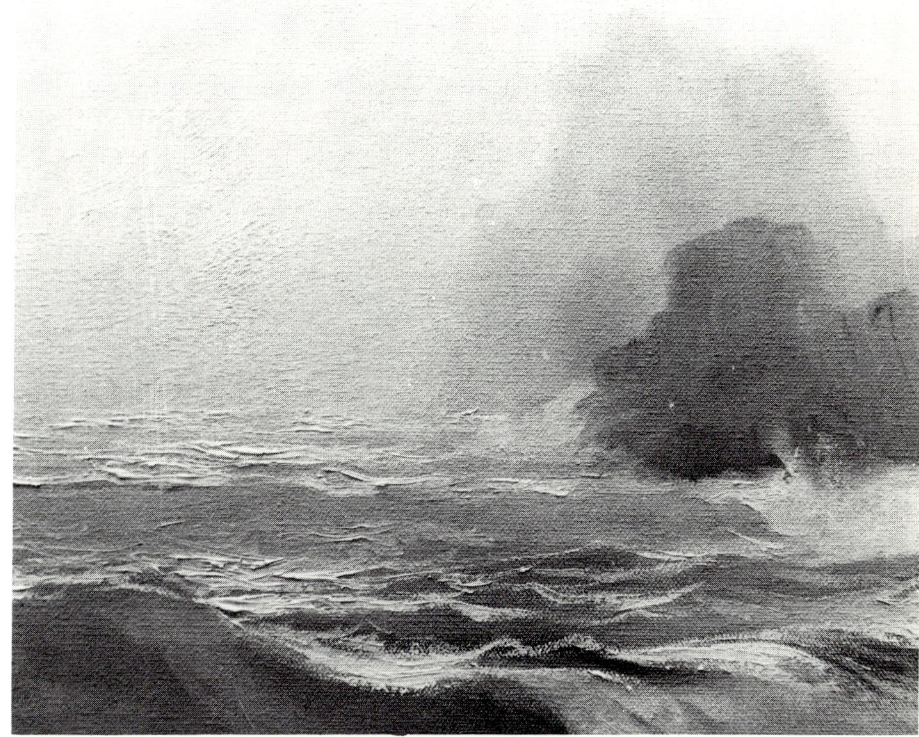

Figure 10. Close fog adds softness and mystery to a seascape.

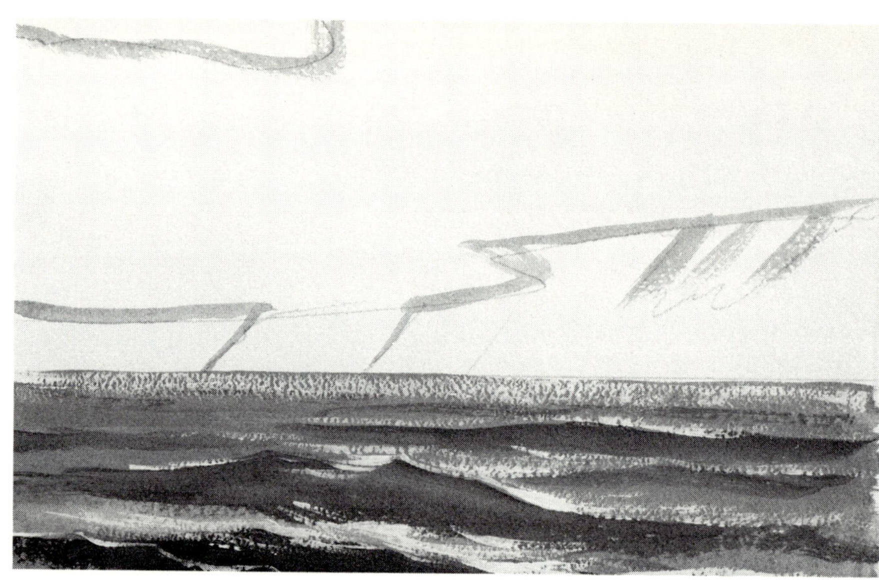

Step 1: Paint in a background sea with a few swells and highlights and draw in a good-sized cloud. Show where the rain would be falling and the angle you wish it to appear in the sky. (See Chapter Three for further study of background swells.)

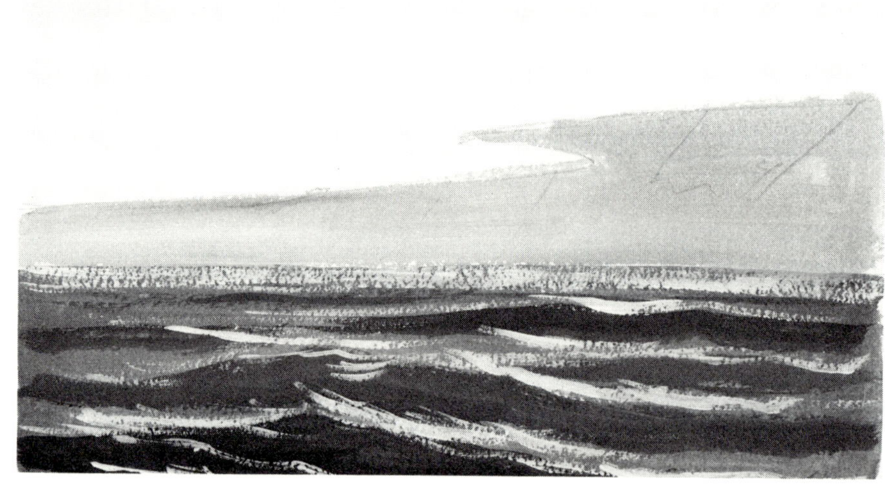

Step 2: Choose a light blue (ultramarine blue and white) or gray blue (ultramarine and white with a touch of burnt sienna) for the sky and paint in all but the cloud. Paint over the directional marks for the rain, but keep in mind where you want them. Notice that the upper portion of sky is lighter than the lower.

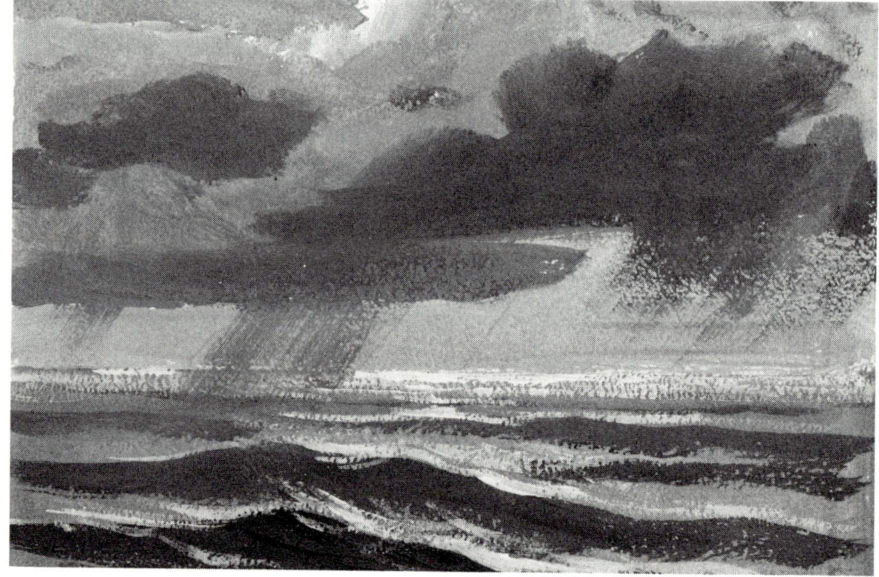

Step 3. Choose a gray-purple (ultramarine and white plus a touch of alizarin crimson) or gray-blue and begin by painting the lightest portion of the cloud. Paint this light value over the entire cloud. Next, darken this same mixture and work in another (closer) group of clouds. Allow some to streak down over the horizon line. Finally, paint in the darkest cloud. Try to make some clouds overlap others. Notice that one section of rain doesn't reach the ocean.

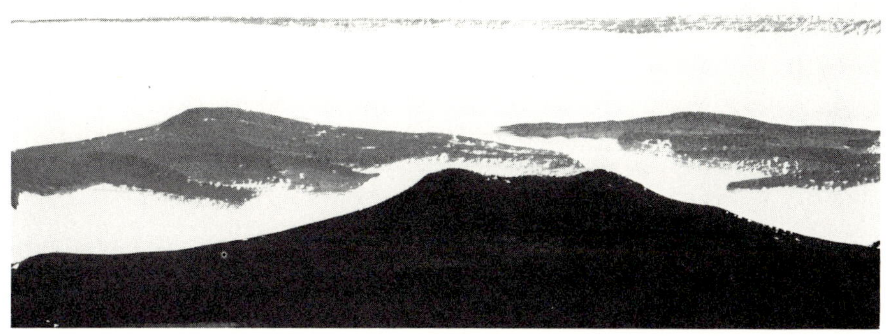

Step 1. Begin this study by painting in a dark swell in the foreground and a couple of lighter ones behind it. Next, draw in where a horizon line may be, even though you'll cover it up later. Use viridian or ultramarine and lighten with a gray. For gray, you may mix black and white or mix any combination of complements into white.

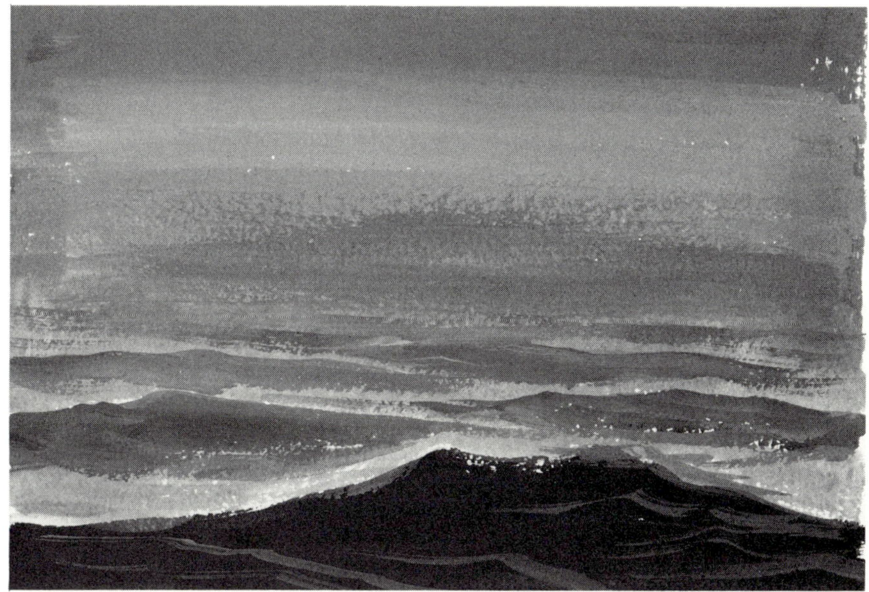

Step 2. Begin with a fairly dark gray in the upper portion of the sky and gradually lighten it with white as you move down. Paint right over the horizon line and up to the swells. Now with viridian or ultramarine blue, blend in a few secondary swells behind the first ones. Let them fade into the gray.

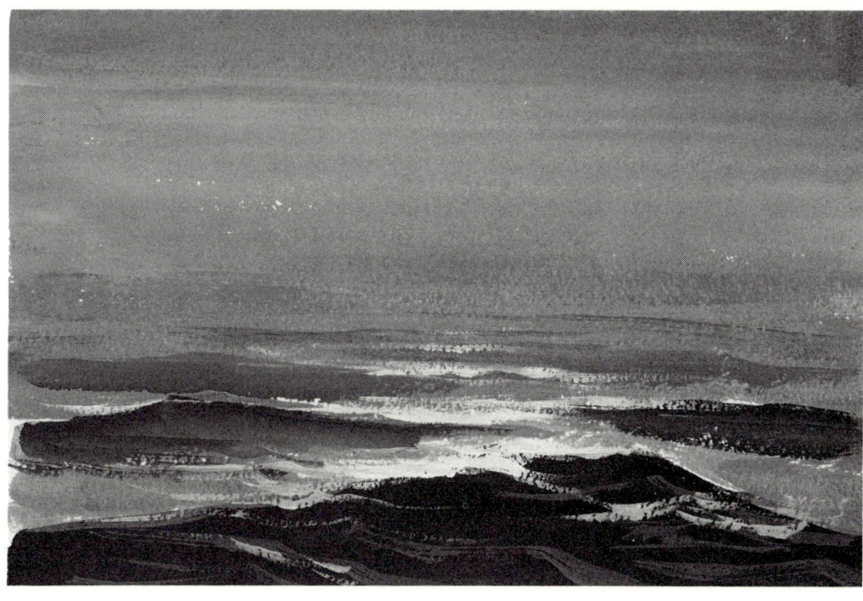

Step 3. You could just about leave the study as it appears in Step 2, but I prefer a touch of sunlight even in my foggiest paintings. For this purpose, mix a touch of cadmium yellow into white and paint a small area near the foreground. This too may fade into the gray background.

THE BACKGROUND SEA

Like the sky, the background sea is too often ignored or played down. The background sea sets the mood for the foreground and it also reflects the sky. Hence it not only provides a transition between sea and sky, but it also reflects the colors of the sky and relates its color to the foreground.

Resolve to pay more attention to the backgrounds in your paintings. Study the sea and all of its interests, not just the spectacular. Too often I've seen a painting flop, even though there was a beautiful wave or foam burst, because the artist had glossed over the background in order to pay more attention to the center of interest.

Sometimes a painting fails because of impatience. You paint a fantastic wave, and then you're in a hurry to finish the painting. Sometimes it's simply because you don't have a full understanding of what is needed. In either case, it can be solved by taking the time to study, to practice, and to feel a bit unsatisfied.

DISTANT SWELLS

Many students don't spend enough time on the background sea. And all too often I've seen students paint a background sea that neither reflected the colors of the sky nor related its color to the foreground.

If, for example, you have a green foreground wave and a blue background, the closest swells behind the wave should have some of the green in them. Likewise, the green wave should contain some of the background blue. Both should reflect the colors of the sky.

In Figure 11, the distant sea contains numerous swells that reflect the sky and sun. Also note the foam patterns forming on the face of the nearby swell as it picks up foam from the previous breaker. In Demonstration 4 I show how to paint distant swells. The demonstration is in black and white, but try to incorporate a transition of color when you practice it.

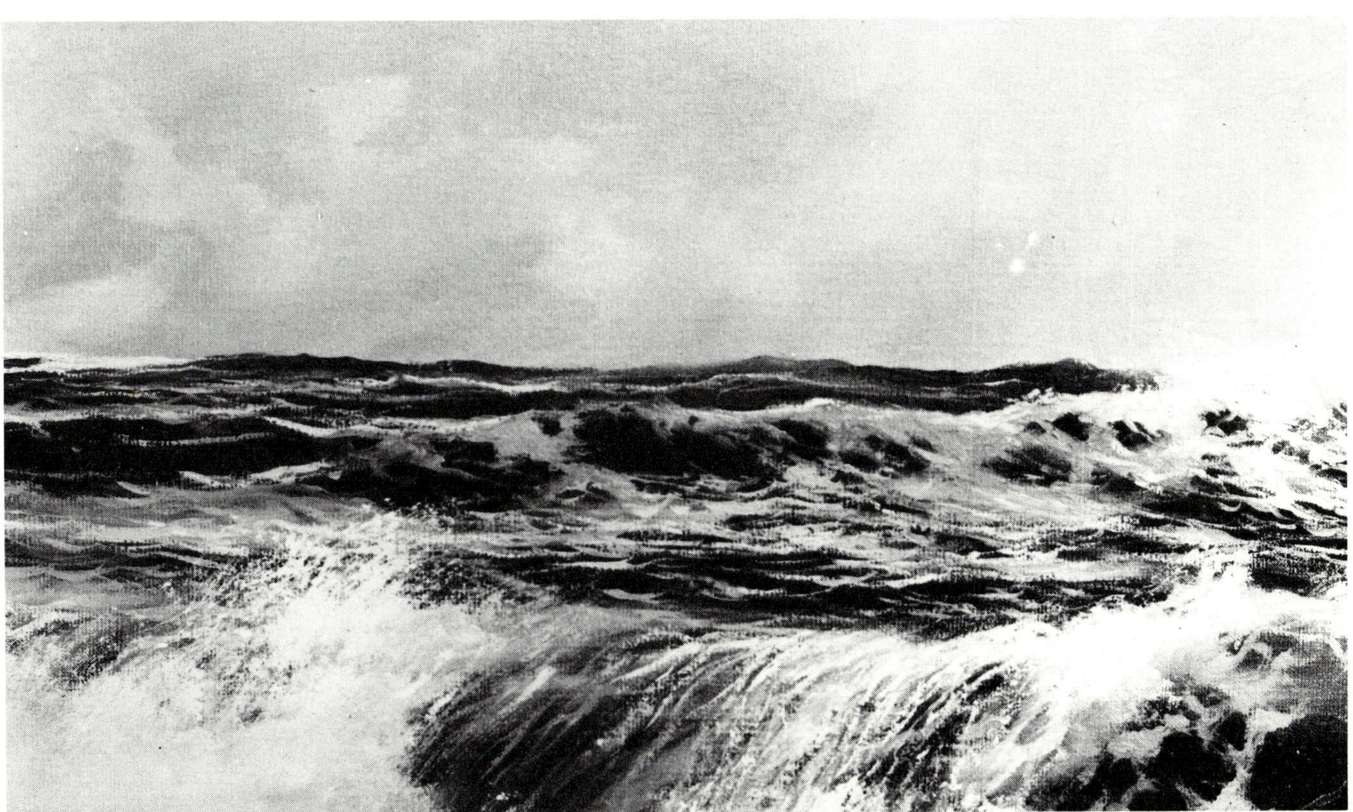

Figure 11. Distant swells reflect the sun and sky.

GROUND SWELLS

Ground swells are so named because they rise up from the ground; that is, the moving water is slowed down and forced upward by the rising ocean floor. Ground swells are billowing waves growing larger and preparing to break. They are not yet breakers, though they may become breakers under the right circumstances. Ground swells generally appear in the middle and foreground of the sea.

However, they may also be placed in the background or used as a center of interest as in Figure 12.

A heavy, solid body of water such as the ground swell is generally too thick to show any light coming through until it rises near to the breaking point. Don't give it as much translucent light as you would a breaker.

When using ground swells as the center of interest (as in Chapter Ten, Plates 13, 14, and 15), give them a personality by adding different characteristics. In Figure 13, for example, the face of the swell is choppy, and consists of minor swells. Translucent water, foam patterns, and bits of foam and light all add up to individuality for each wave. Avoid making all your waves look alike. (Demonstration 5 will show you how to paint ground swells.)

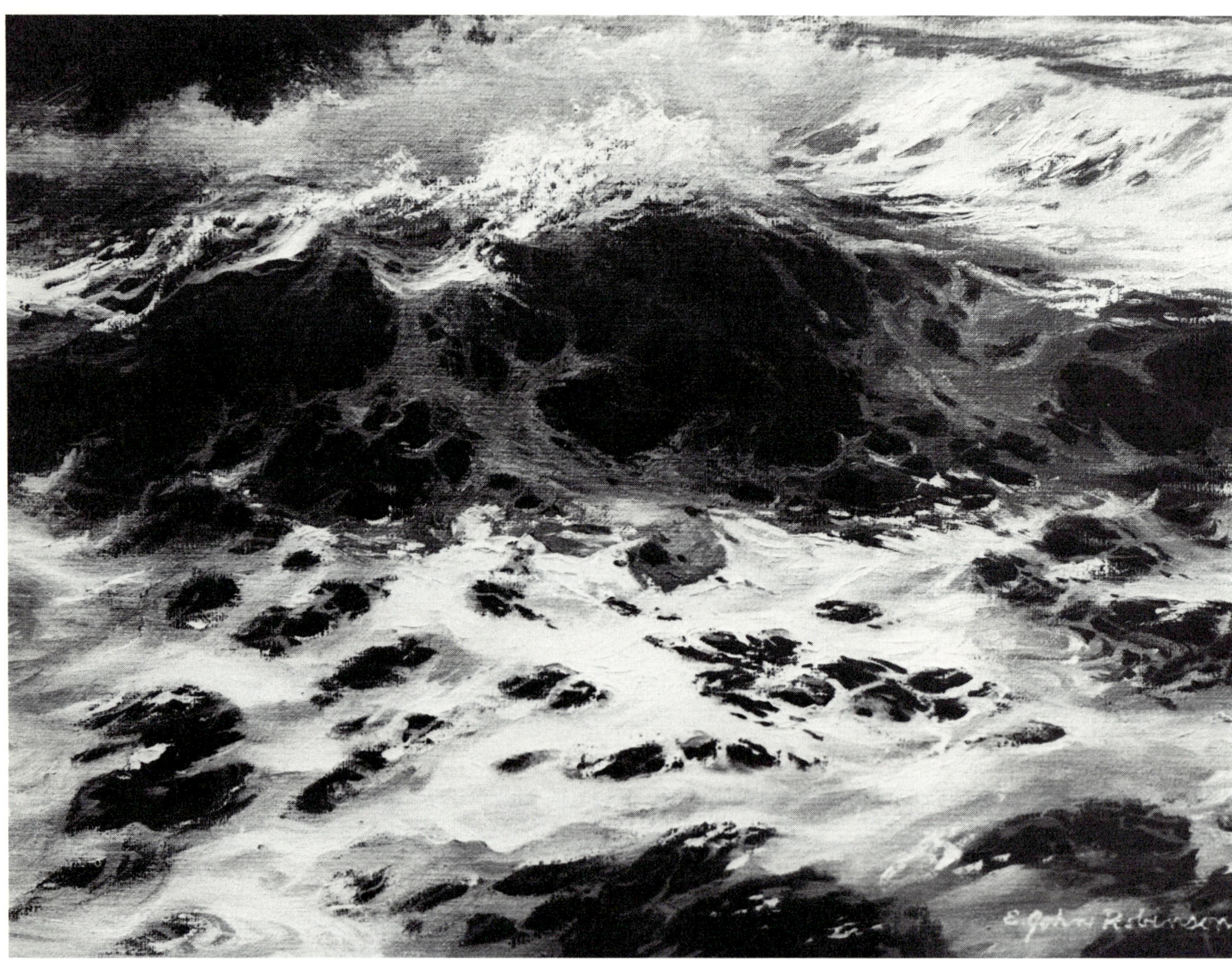

Figure 12. The ground swell twists up unevenly as it swings toward the viewer.

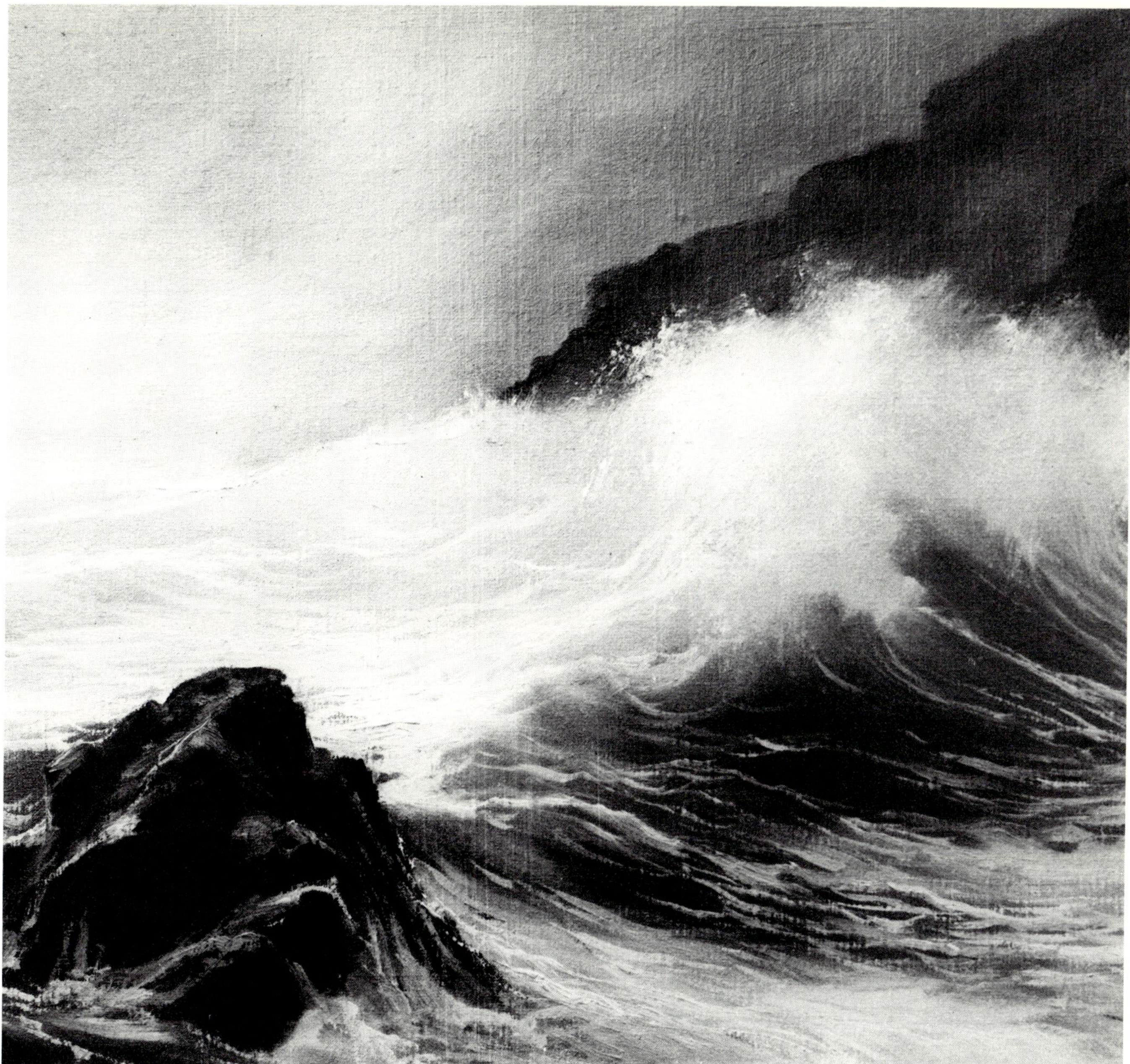

Figure 13. Turbulent ground swells are whipped by the wind.

WHITECAPS

I added whitecaps as a problem because I've too often seen them misused or at least misunderstood. A whitecap is neither a breaker nor a comber.

A breaker results when a swell rises too high above the ocean floor and falls forward. A comber is a wave trying to break, but it's moving at a level where the leading edge is falling but never breaking because the wave doesn't rise enough. Often the wave will dip and move right out from under the foam of the comber.

Whitecaps are the result of wind whipping the thin tops of swells into foam (Figure 14). The swells move right out from under the foam, thus keeping a constant movement noticeable in the background sea. They appear and disappear as the chops form and lose themselves or move out from under the foam (Figure 14). I recall one excited tourist who, upon viewing the surface of the sea, thought one day she'd seen hundreds of whales blowing. A stiff breeze not only whips the top edge of a whitecap into foam; it also blows it off in a puff of mist much like that of a spouting whale.

Again, I show how to paint whitecaps in Demonstration 6. Use your own imagination and experiment with the colors to use. Also, remember that whitecaps may be used to break up an uninteresting background. Also, as in Figure 15, they add to the effect of depth (perspective) by diminishing their size as they recede. But don't use too many or the background may distract from the center of interest.

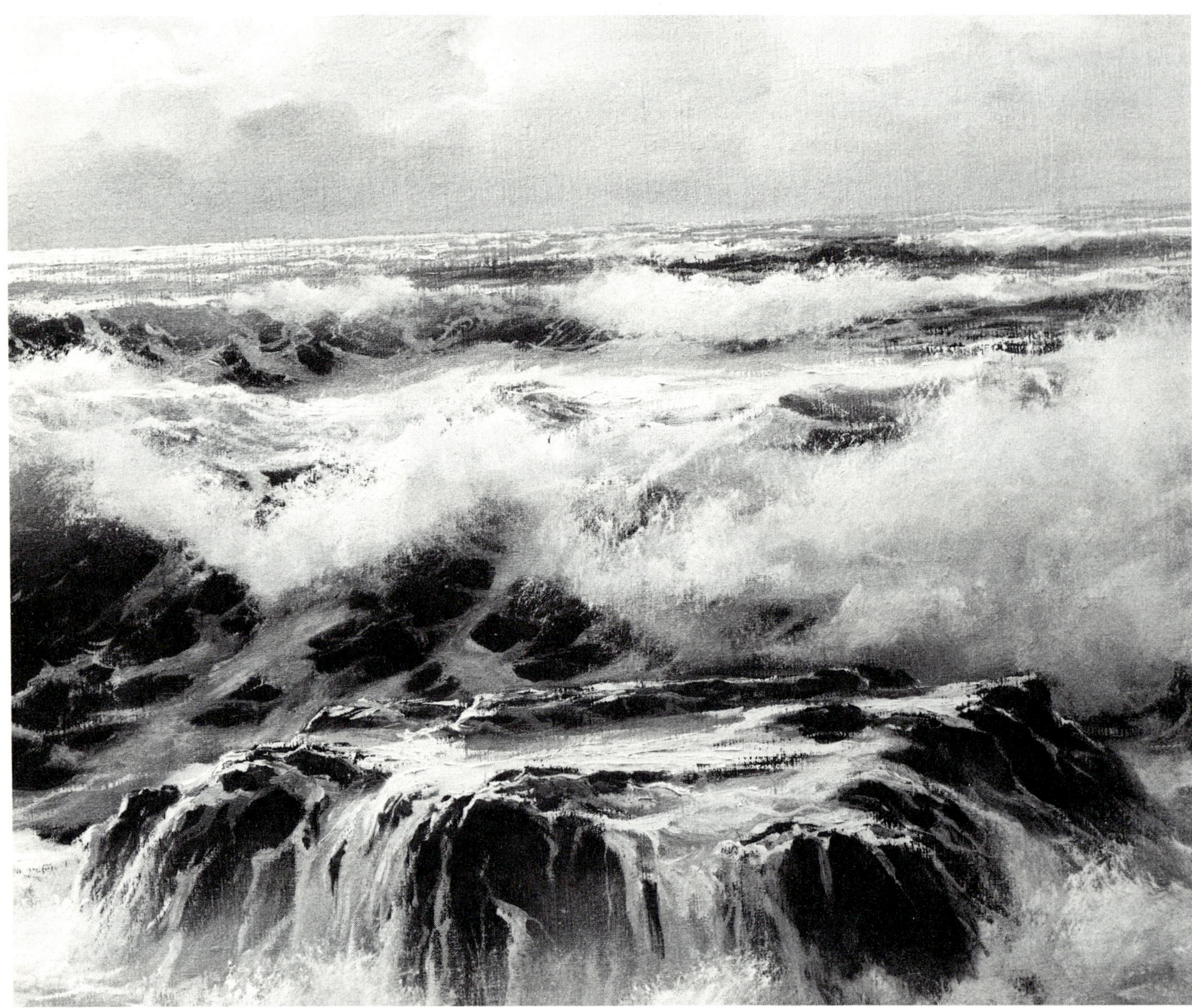

Figure 14. Whitecaps are wind-whipped foam on the thin leading edge of swells.

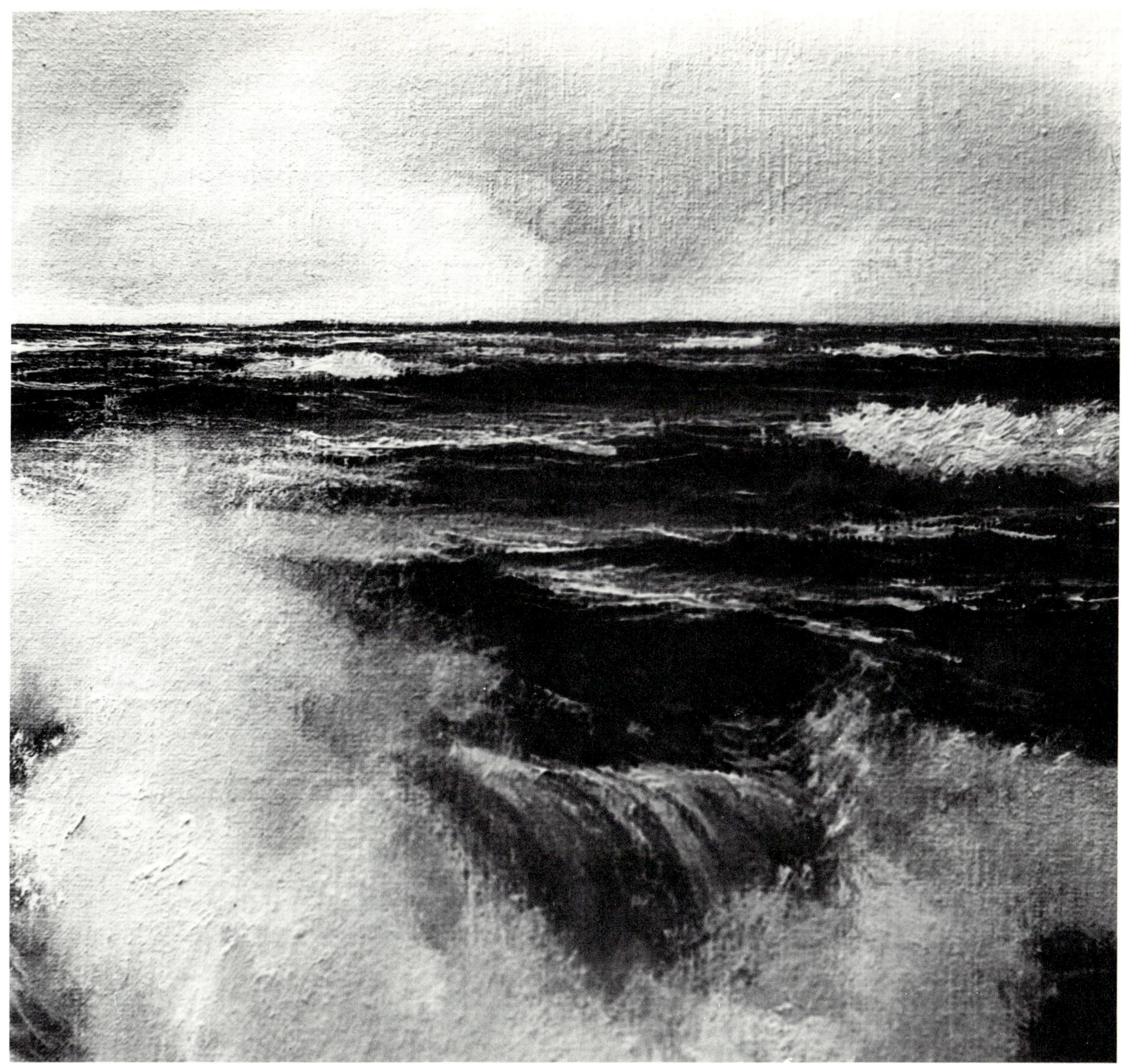

Figure 15. Whitecaps used sparingly help break up an otherwise too-dark sea.

BACKGROUND GLITTER

Background glitter should be used much as you'd use whitecaps—to break up an uninteresting or monotonous area. Again, too much glitter and the effect is lost. Also, it's easy for glitter to become so interesting that it distracts from the center of interest. So whenever you use glitter, keep it concentrated in small areas. If too much of the painting is sparkling with glitter, it becomes too busy or simply loses its effectiveness.

In the closeup in Figure 16, notice that brushstrokes of light tone are painted over a fairly dark sea. Some strokes were dragged lightly over the surface, leaving a broken line. Other strokes were laid down heavily, concentrating the light to indicate either a stronger reflection or a smoother surface. In working out the problem of glitter in Figure 16, notice that I paint glitter *after* I paint the center of interest.

The color of glitter depends on the atmosphere and color of sunlight. Generally, it's white with a touch of one of the yellows to warm it. Use a small brush and make a series of horizontal dabs. Don't dig in with the paint or it will mix with what's already there. Try to lay in these bits of paint one on top of the other. (See Demonstration 7 on painting background glitter.)

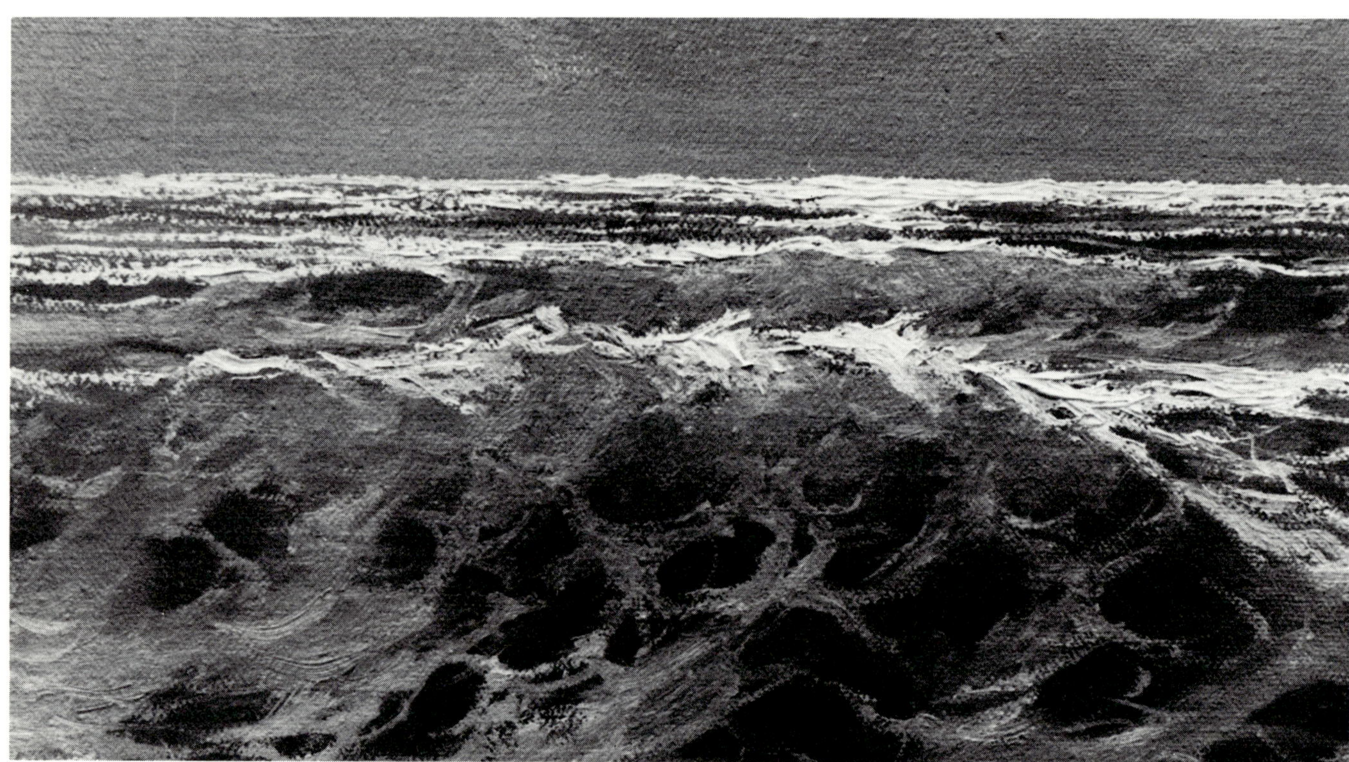

Figure 16. Sunlight glittering on distant sea is beautiful but not easy to paint.

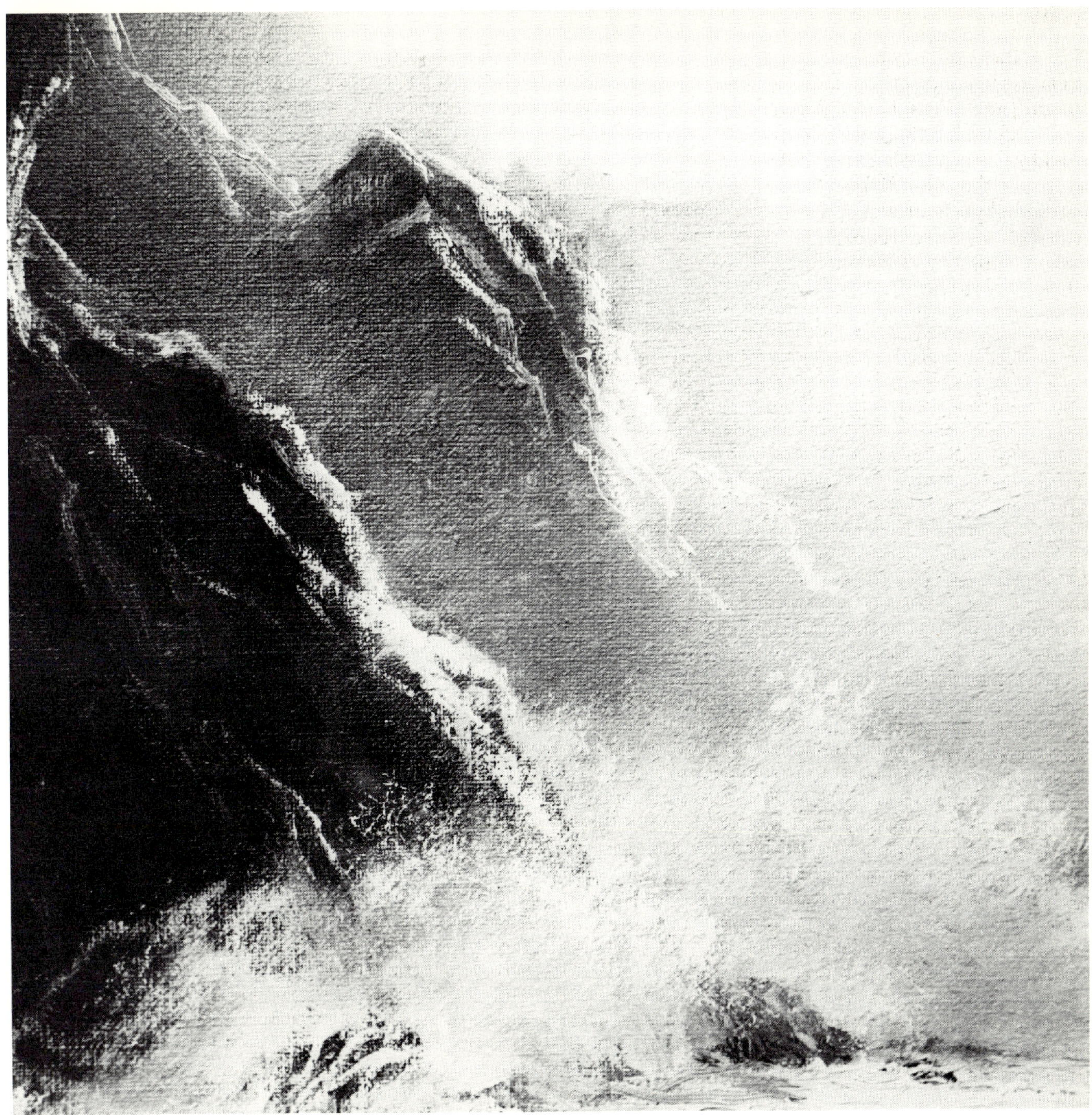

Figure 17. Glitter can also appear on the wet surface of rocks.

GLOW

Glow is the result of sunlight spreading from its source. You generally use it with back lighting or side lighting, if the sun is close enough. The atmosphere will help determine the color. Remember that sunlight is lightest and warmest at its source; it darkens and cools in color as it spreads away.

Use glow to warm a sky and background, to add interest, to give a reason for a light patch on the sea, or to break up the color of the sky. But however you use it, use it cautiously. Too much orange or red, and suddenly the painting becomes gaudy.

In Figure 18 the sunlight color was whipped into the area affected by the sunlight; then glitter effects were added over the top. The result is a fading of color and detail in the area of glow. The detail shot of Figure 19 shows another variation in the use of spreading light. Rather than being concentrated in a path (as in Figure 18), it spreads over the entire background sea. The sun is not visible in either figure, but there should be no question as to its location. (For a demonstration on painting glow, see Demonstration 12.)

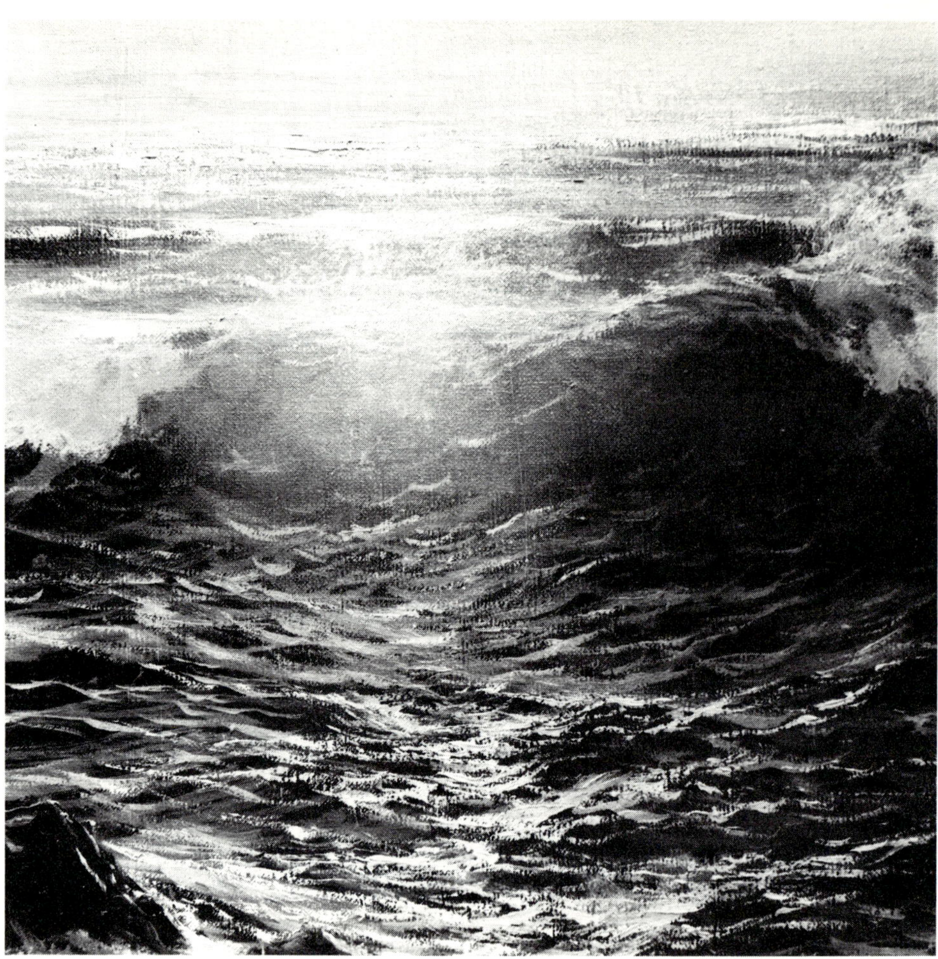

Figure 18. A concentrated path of glow obscures all color and detail.

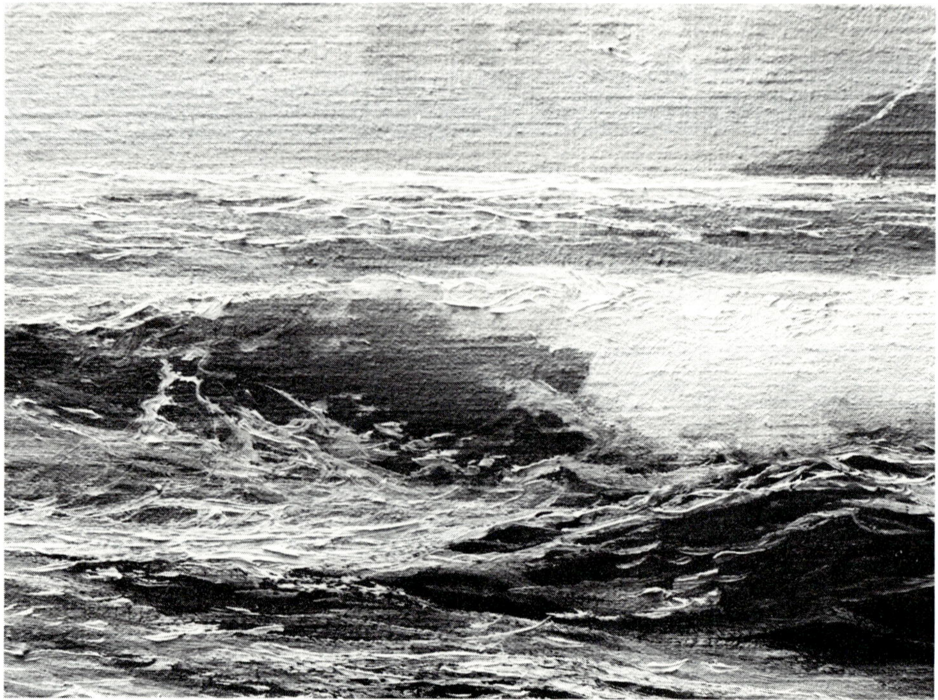

Figure 19. In this variation, glow spreads over the entire sea.

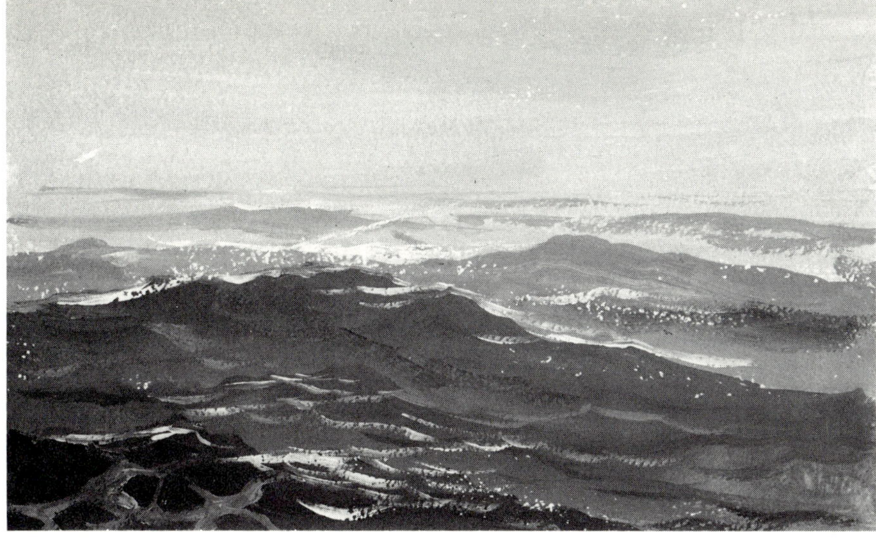

Method 1, Fog. If it's necessary to break the horizon line, the softening effect of fog is ideal. Notice here that the horizon line is nearly visible yet it is not in the least distracting.

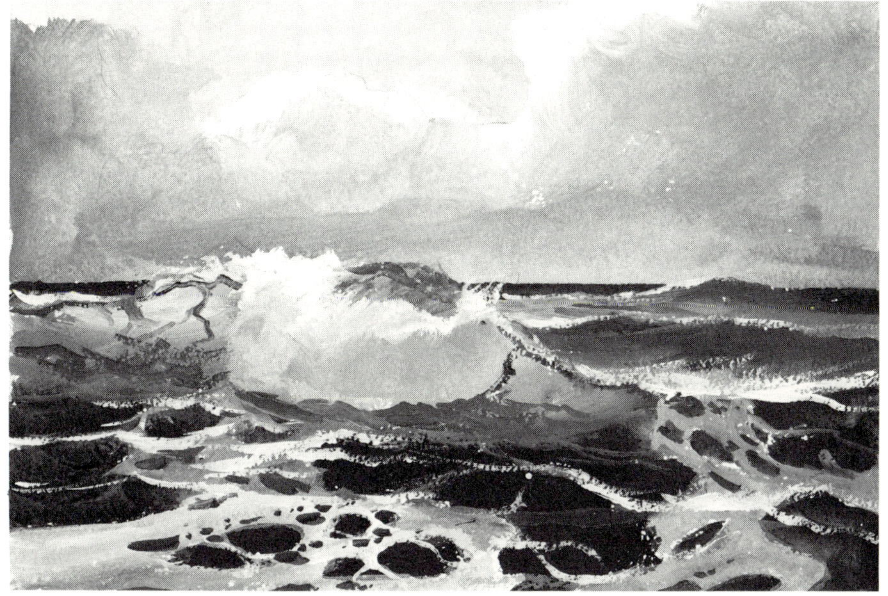

Method 2, Waves. This method allows for a strong, dark horizon line but prevents it from being a straight line across the painting. Notice that the main break is caused by a corner of the foreground wave; also, a less obvious break is created by a background swell.

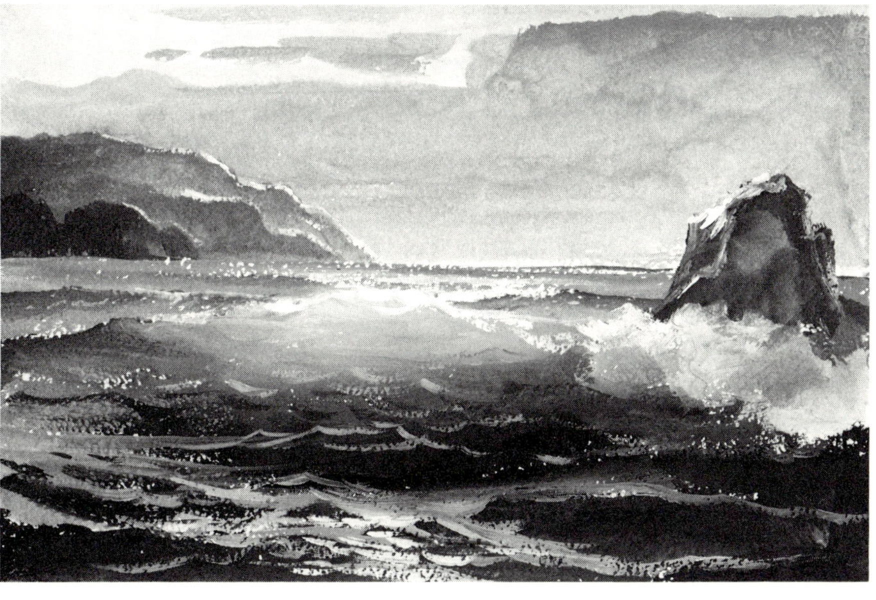

Method 3, Land and Rocks. The third means of breaking the monotony of the horizon line is with the placement of headlands and/ or rocks. When using this method, be sure to place them so that the remaining line is not divided equally.

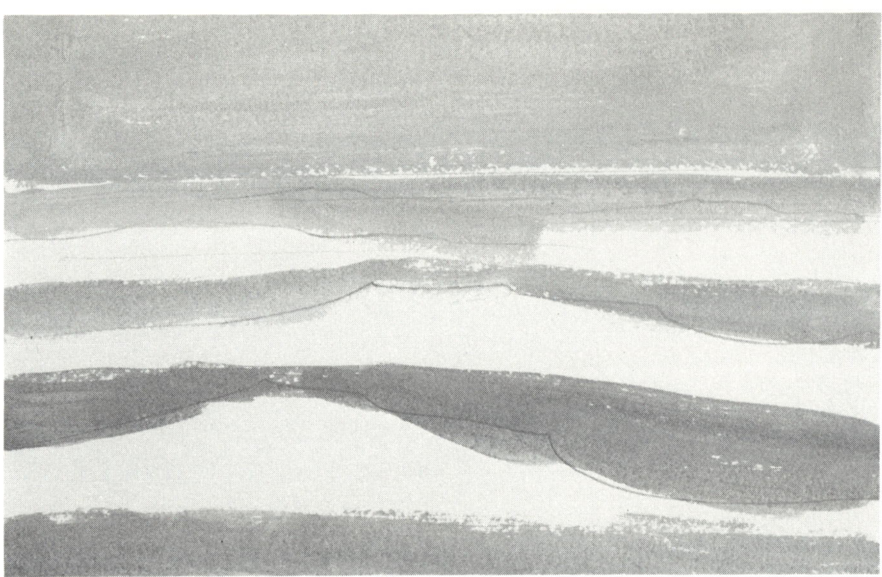

Step 1. Just for another approach, paint in the sky with a medium to pale blue or blue gray and continue down to the trough area between swells. Remember, the trough or horizontal areas reflect the sky.

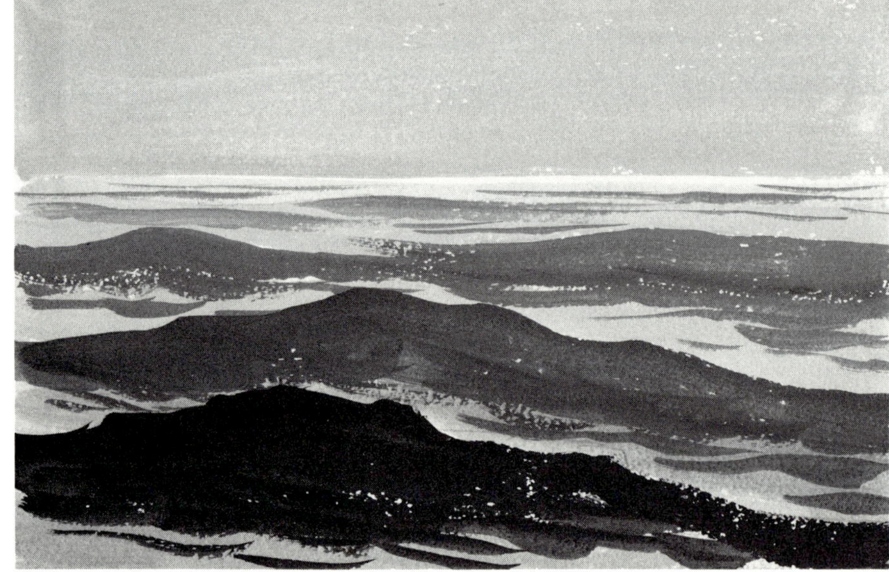

Step 2. Next, paint in the swells starting in the near foreground with a dark blue-green (ultramarine and viridian), fading the color with some of the sky color as the swells recede. This could be done in reverse; i.e., you could start in the background and work forward, making the waves darker as you go.

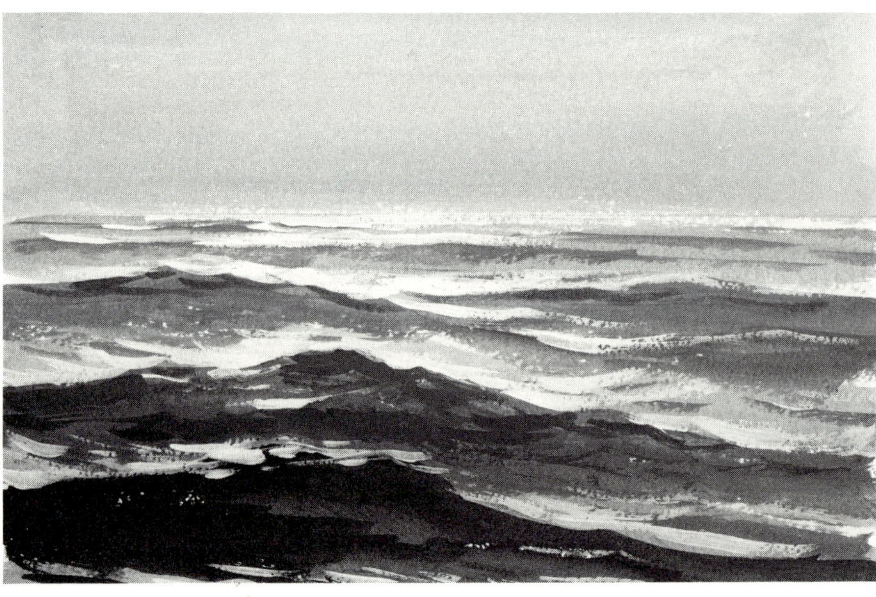

Step 3. The final step clarifies the outline of the swells and adds the interest of sunlight. In all but front lighting, sunlight may be used in this way. Back lighting makes the strongest outline. As before, use a mixture of cadmium yellow pale and white for the sunlight color.

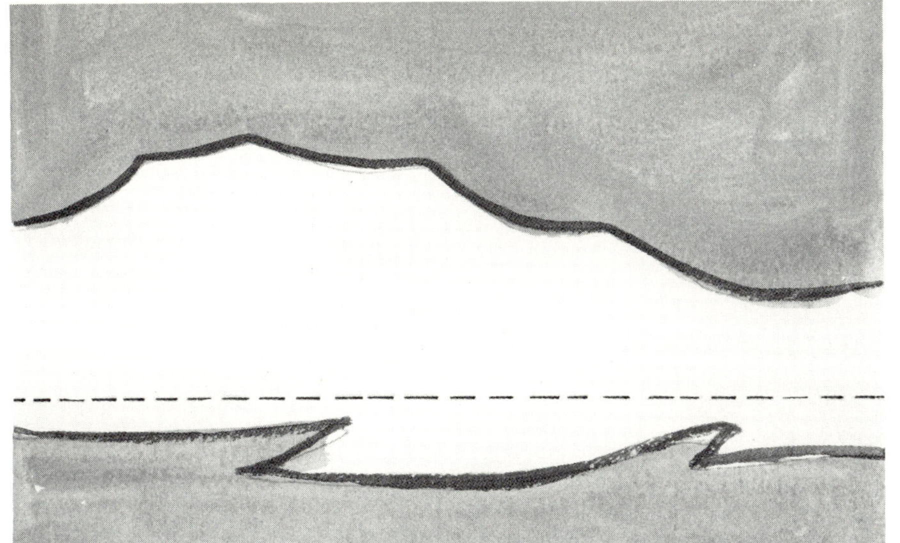

Step 1. A ground swell is like a distant swell; but because it's closer, more detail is visible. Start by making just an outline. (The dotted line shows that even though the top edge and lower lines are irregular, the whole wave is based upon a horizontal line.) Next, paint in the background as you did for distant swells, using a light gray. Repeat the gray below the wave.

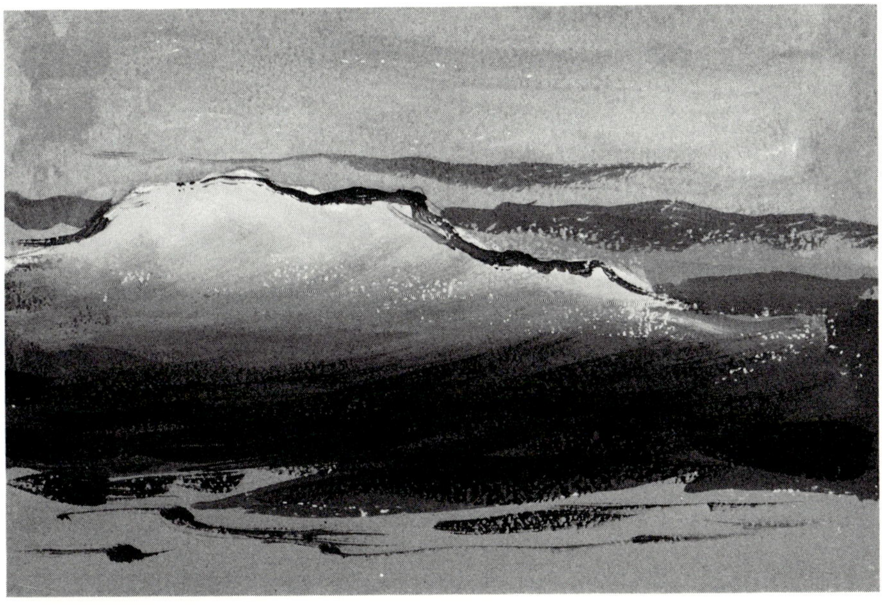

Step 2. Again as in Demonstration 4, add the background swells. For the major swell, mix nearly equal parts of viridian and ultramarine blue and paint in the lower portion of the swell. As you paint upward, add more and more of the gray of the sky to lighten it. Finally, at the top inch or so, blend in a pale yellow-white. Be sure there are no distinct lines separating this gradual blend of color and value.

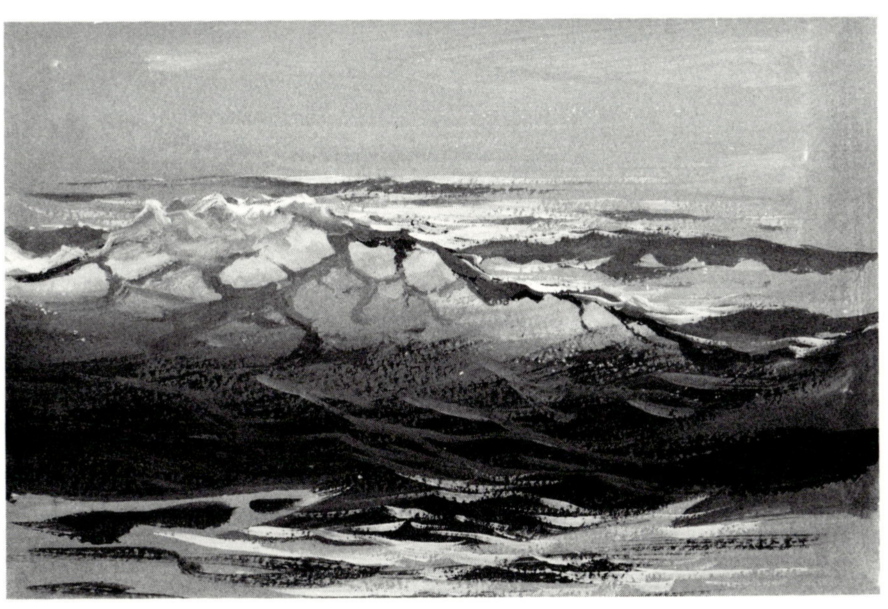

Step 3. Practice this step several times, if necessary. Using the wave color from near the base, add silhouette patterns in the translucent area of the wave. Next, reflect the sky on secondary chops at the base of the wave. Finally, with a mixture of cadmium yellow pale and white, add sun reflections in the background and foreground.

DEMONSTRATION 6: WHITECAPS

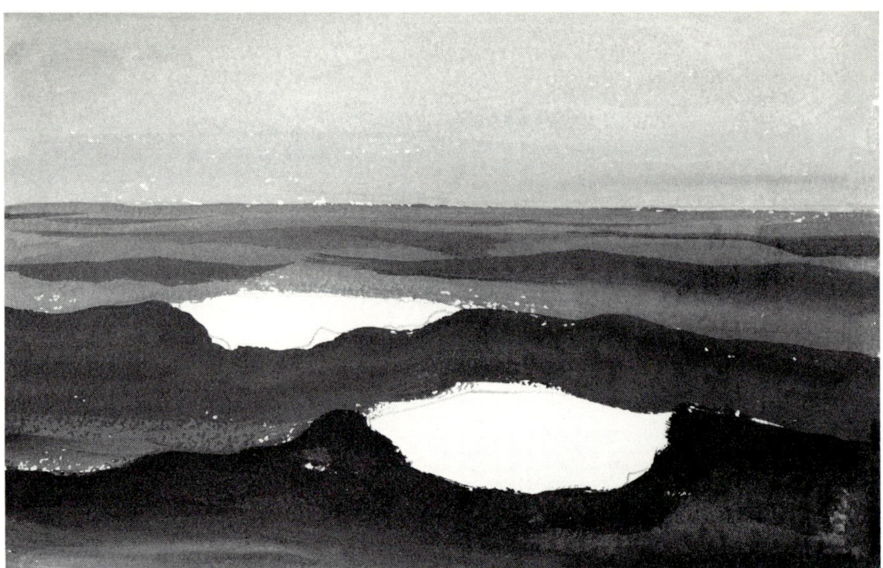

Step 1. Painting background swells will help in painting whitecaps, and painting whitecaps will eventually help in painting a breaker. Start this lesson by working in a sky and background and a couple of major swells. Choose your own colors this time, but remember to keep the darker and purer colors, in the foreground, lightening them with the sky color as you work to the background. Leave the area of foam unpainted.

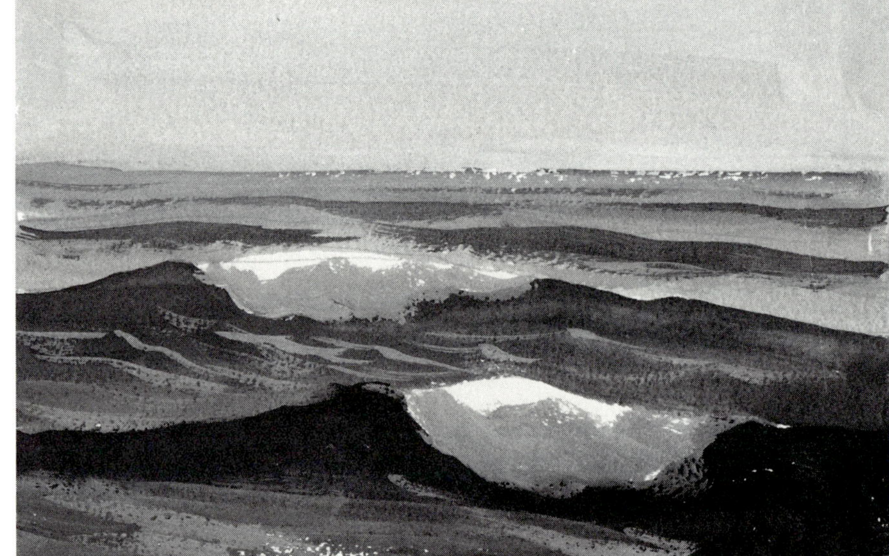

Step 2. Reflect the lightness of the sky between the swells and on the lower portion of the major swells. Notice that the reflections are used to indicate minor chops. Work in the shadow area of the foam, but leave the light area still unpainted.

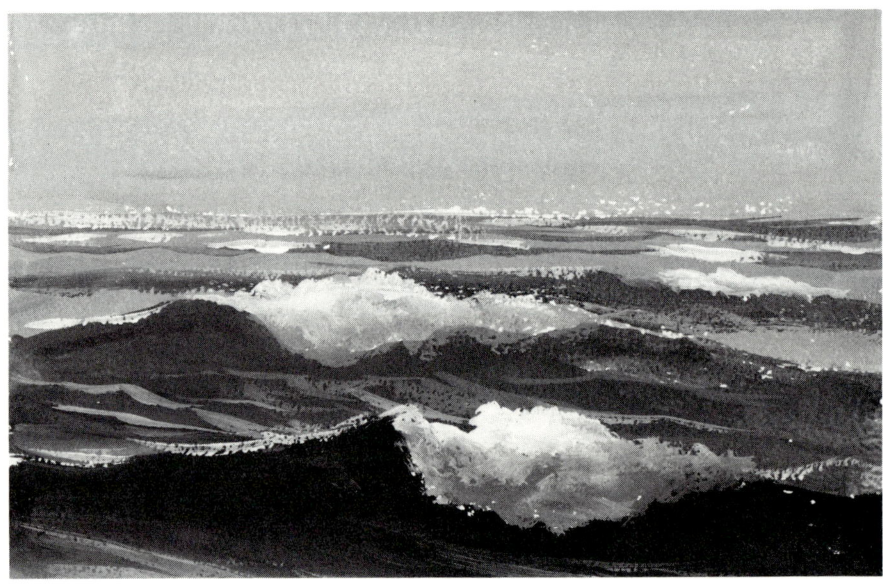

Step 3. The reason for leaving the foam area unpainted was to prevent the foam from blending with the other colors. Foam is white or near-transparent material. There are times when you may want the background color to blend in, but not when the foam is thick. Soften the top edges of the foam and, for practice, add a bit of glitter in the background.

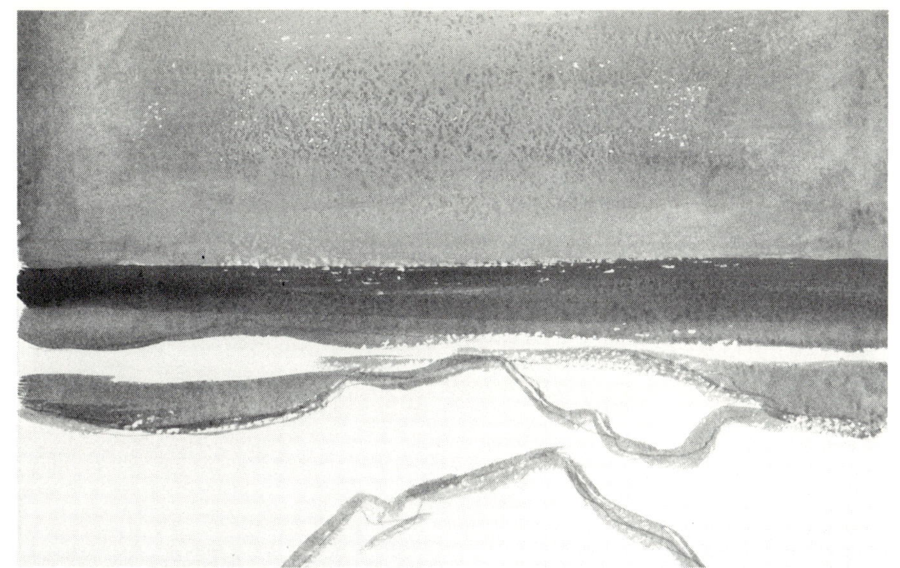

Step 1. Glitter shows best against a dark background. For a change of pace, use a deep yellow sky (cadmium yellow deep) that gradually becomes darker on each side. Darken the yellow with purple (alizarin and ultramarine). Paint in the background sea with a darker version of the sky and indicate where you want swells, a wave, and a foreground rock.

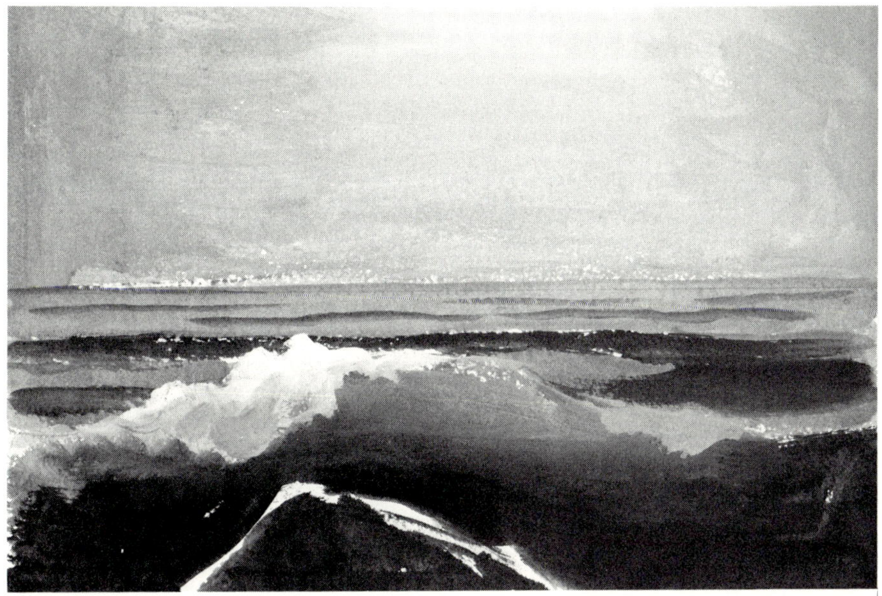

Step 2. Using your mixture of yellow and purple, paint in darker versions of background swells. Darken the major swell with viridian. Paint in the rock with the same mixture. The foam should be shadowed with purple or ultramarine blue mixed into white. The light portion should be done with yellow-white.

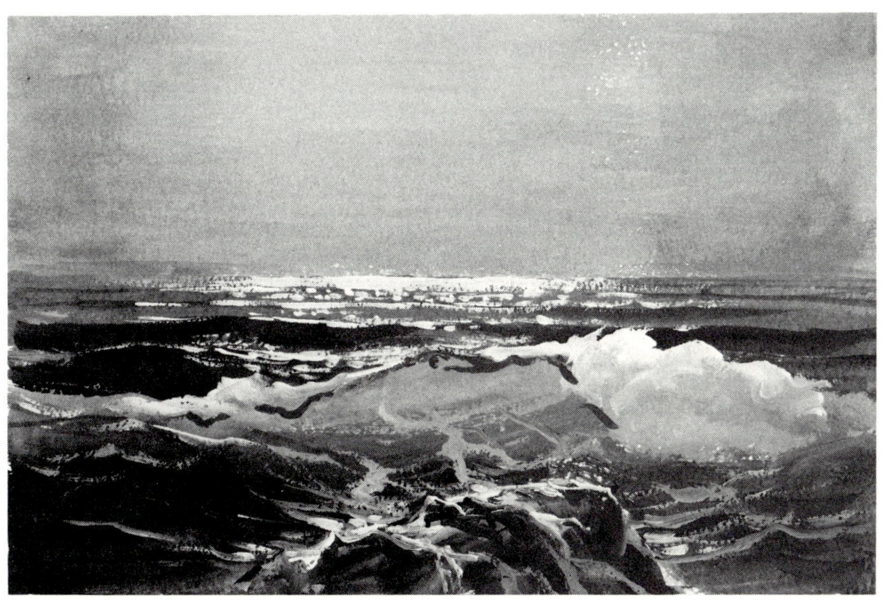

Step 3. Finally, add the glitter with the yellow-white mixture. Use this sparingly! Overuse of glitter destroys its impact. Because this demonstration makes use of back lighting, the glitter helps to outline the contours of the swells and rock.

CHAPTER FOUR

THE MAJOR WAVE

The major wave, the breaker with all of its interest, is truly the most important item to learn in painting seascapes. More often than not, it's the major wave that commands the attention in a painting. The major wave is also a complex subject with many facets. If a student is having problems, it is most likely with some portion of the major wave.

You should have a basic knowledge of the anatomy of a wave before attempting to paint one. For that, I refer you to my basic book, *Marine Painting in Oil.* However, in this chapter I'll review and explain each important part of the major wave, including the foam created by the wave. (This doesn't include foam patterns on the surface, which will be found in Chapter Seven.)

If you want individuality in your work, concentrate on making each painting different, but with your own style or approach. One way will be found in how you handle your center of interest or in the kind of individuality you give to the major waves. If you must choose one chapter to study more than all others, please choose this one, and practice the lessons faithfully. Then go on to create your own variations.

In each section I show two ways of handling the same problem. The main idea is to learn a technique, then learn to build on it. Never remain satisfied.

THE BREAKER

The true breaker has a wide base, an irregular leading edge, and a section (or sections) of falling water that creates foam. Think of the breaker as a sort of waterfall. Notice in Figure 20 the effect of water falling from the leading edge, hitting the trough, and rebounding as foam. *The face of the wave is concave to the viewer, but the falling water is convex.* This seems to be one of the tough facts to get across to most students, so please study this carefully.

Every breaker you paint should be different. If you tend to copy a particular wave over and over again, you may not fully understand the anatomy of a wave. In that case, make an effort to gain more knowledge and understanding. Figure 20 contains an example of a breaker that has never been painted before and should never be painted again. By way of comparison, the breaker in Figure 21 has a thicker leading edge, a foamier roll, a harsher breaker foam, and a lesser area of translucent water. Again, every wave is unique. Besides, isn't it more fun to work out something different each time?

The step-by-step lesson on painting the breaker (Demonstration 8) should give you a basic knowledge of painting a wave, but to master it fully, you must practice it many times and from several different angles. You may also find the next demonstration on painting breaker foam (Demonstration 9) useful. However, you may discover, that the answer to one problem may lie in the material in a future section. So read on.

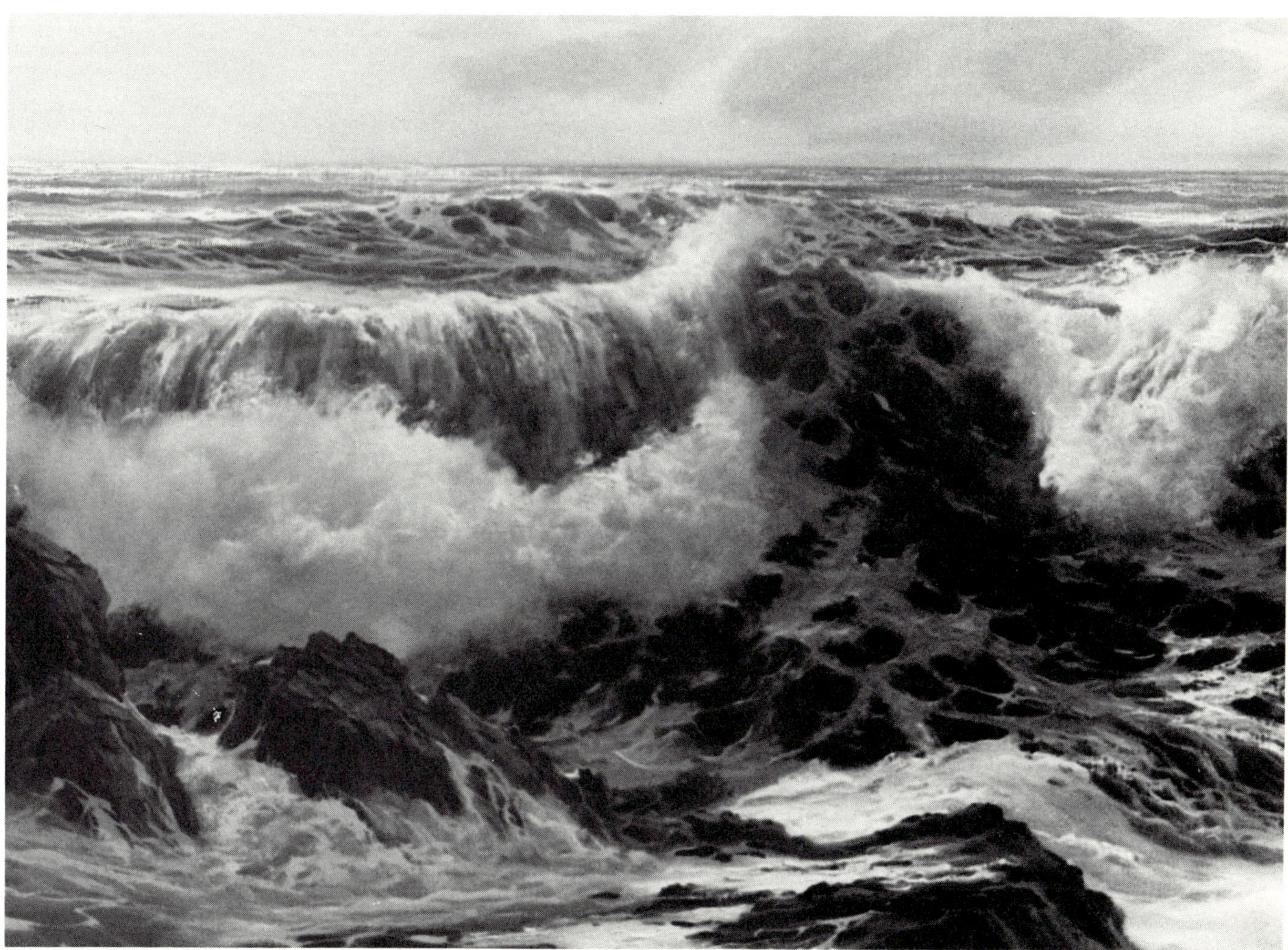

Figure 20. Think of the breaker as a sort of waterfall.

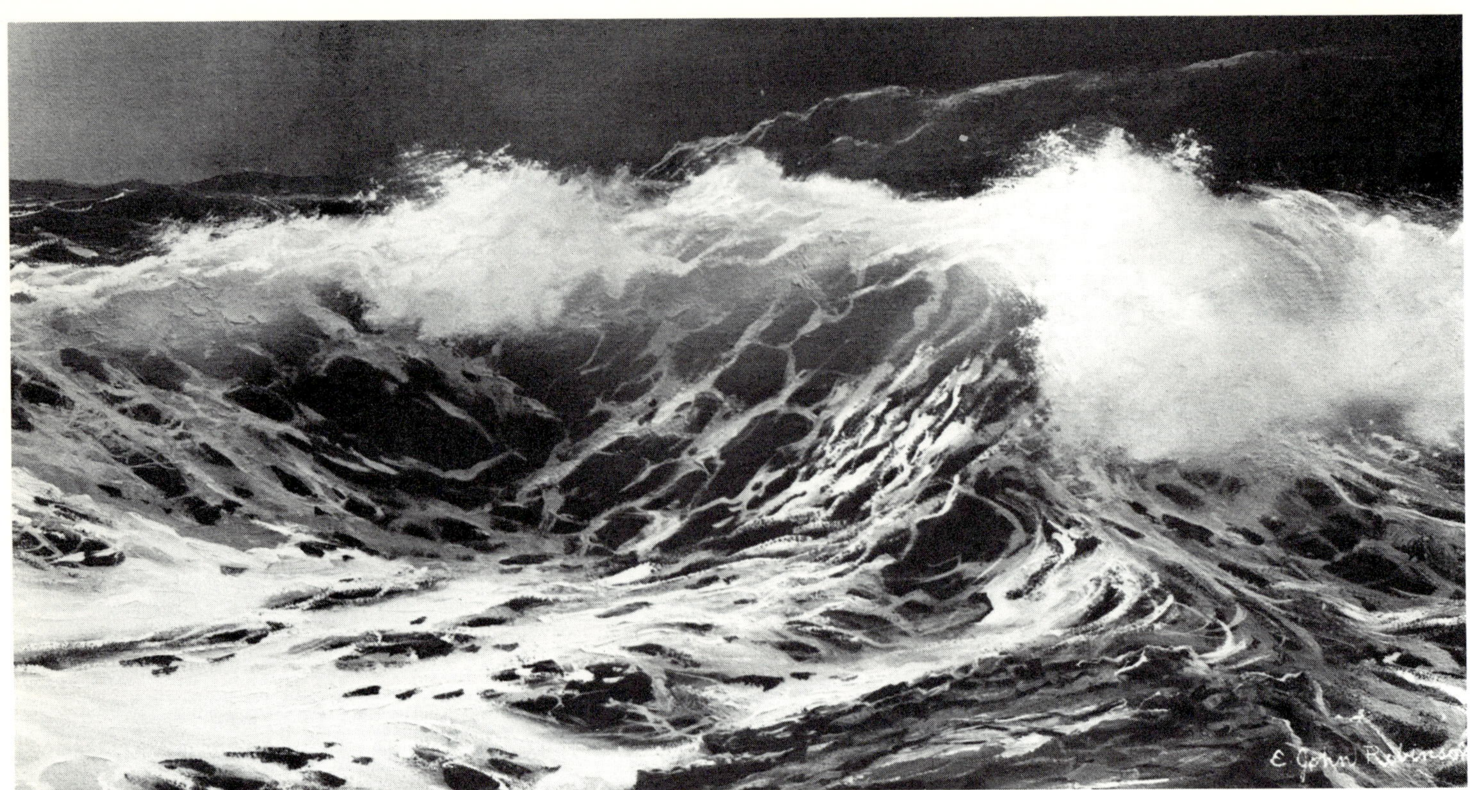

Figure 21. Remember, every wave is unique.

THE LEADING EDGE

The leading (or top) edge of a wave is irregular. The edge, far from being a straight line, curves, dips, and falls forward completely where it breaks. Sometimes the leading edge is like a series of edges, one on top of the other, each spilling over in a different manner. In Figure 22 I've painted the edge as it becomes a roll in the breaker. In Figure 23 the leading edge is very soft, but the foam and shape of the wave are apparent just the same.

Edges tell more about a subject than any other part. Because edges are seen by the viewer first, before the rest of the area, they must be exact, or at least informative. As an example, a rough, sharp-edged rock would not be perceived as such unless the edges were painted in sharp, angular strokes. On the other hand, the moving, irregular edges of a wave cannot be sharp and angular but must be rising and falling with a smooth leading line. Learn to study edges before anything else!

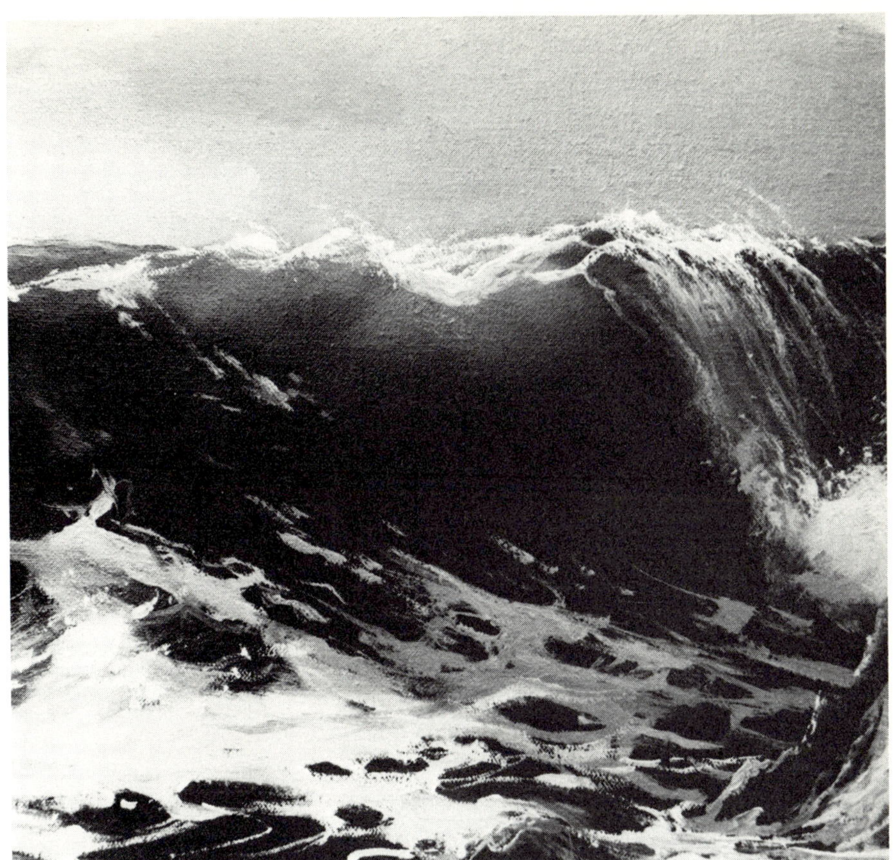

Figure 22. Here the leading edge is becoming a roll.

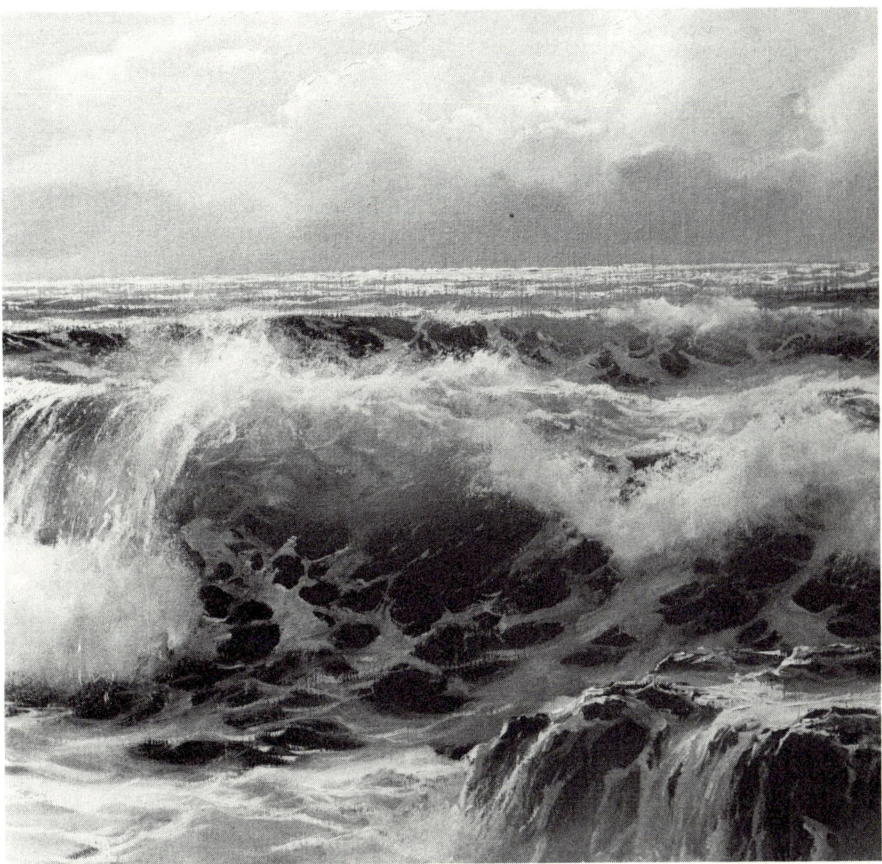

Figure 23. The leading edge is lost in soft whipped foam and dancing sunlight.

THE ROLL

The leading edge sets the mood—or at least the character—of the roll. As the leading edge falls forward the water is transparent, but as it mixes with air it becomes foamy. Flecks of foam already on the edge peel over and are spread in the direction of the fall. Then, when the water hits the trough, it sprays back up as foam. So the roll may be described as a falling body of water that picks up air and lightens in color as it falls into the trough (Figure 24).

The roll presents a *convex* or outward-rounded shape of water to the viewer. I emphasize this because too many beginners' paintings show breaking foam and falling water on the *concave* face of the wave. This simply can't happen; painting it so is due to a lack of understanding on the part of the student.

Sunlight, or rather the direction of the light, plays a big part in varying the effects of the sea. The roll in Figure 23 looks different from that in Figure 24. Sunlight is glittering over the surface, and the water is less transparent because of so much foam within. This is a typical effect of back lighting and an active surf.

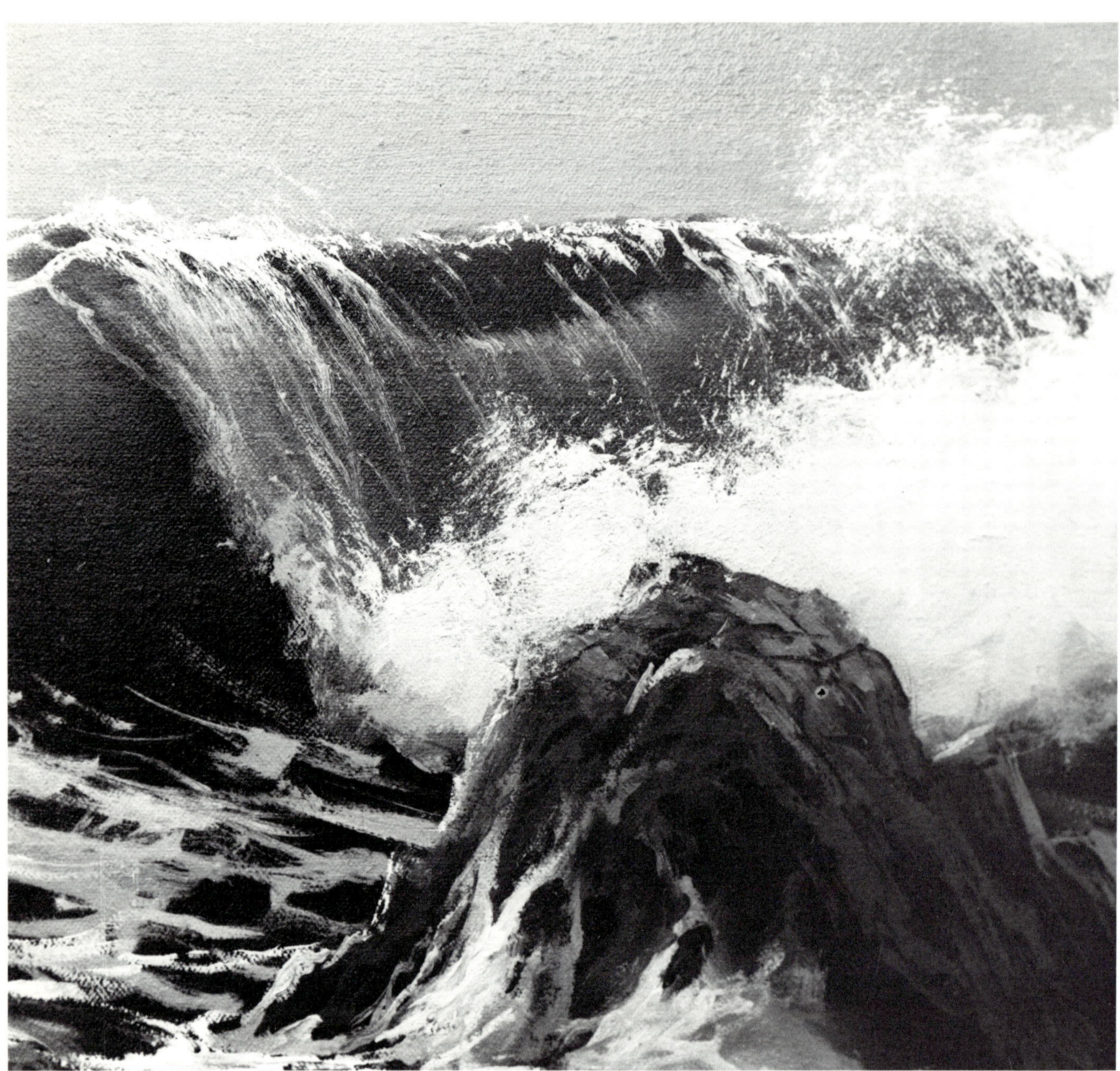

Figure 24. The roll is a convex falling body of water.

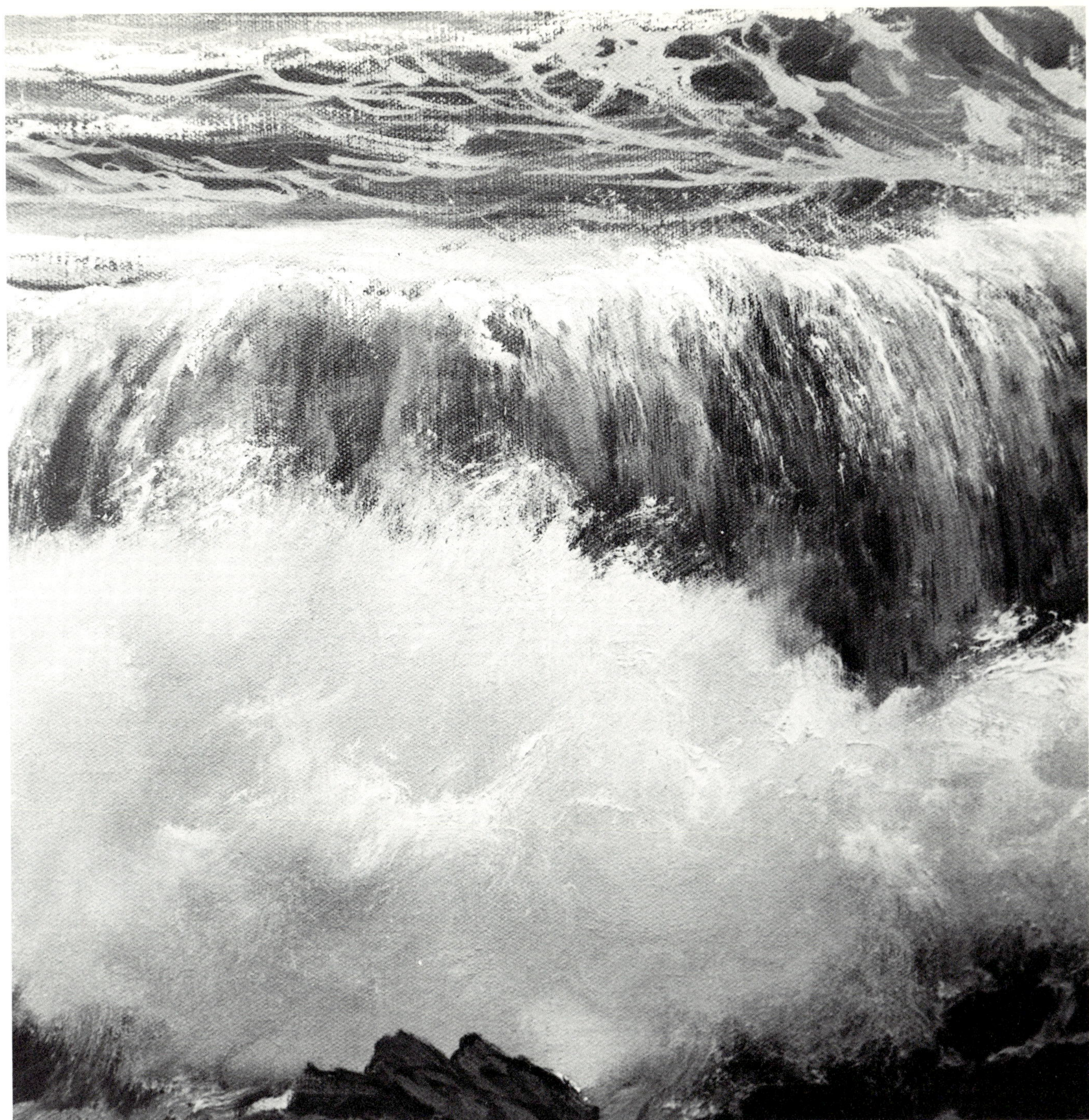

Figure 25. Lighting and an active sea can vary the appearance of a roll.

BREAKER FOAM

By the time the water reaches the trough, it's well aerated. When actually strikes the trough, it bounces into the air, creating foam. After the foam sprays back up, more and more water falls, creating more and more foam, which becomes boiling and turbulent. However, the foam resulting from a breaker has little or no direction; it simply tumbles about in front of the roll (Figure 26).

The interior section of foam is a jumble of moving forces. Light, shadow, and reflected light are important here. The light areas should be white with a touch of sunlight color. The shadow should be the compliment of the sunlight color mixed into white.

Don't try to show the direction of breaker foam with brushstrokes. Try to depict it instead with light and dark shadings and very few

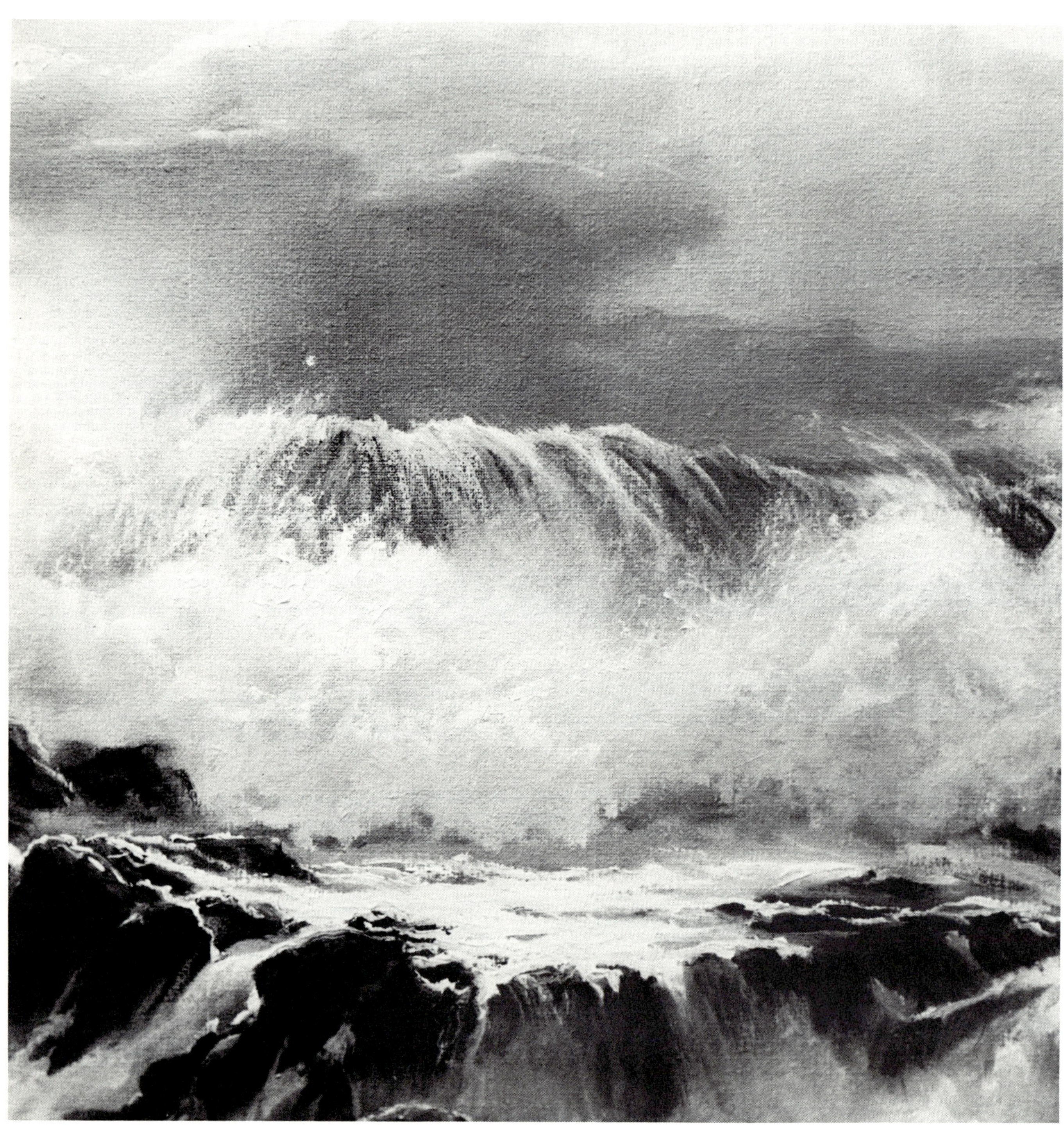

Figure 26. Breaker foam has little or no direction.

visible brushstrokes. In Figure 27 the upper portion of foam varies from misty softness to rather harsh flecks. Also notice the irregular dark shadow beneath the foam. Sometimes it's the combination of effects such as these that lends personality to a painting. Try varying each effect with different combinations.

In order to paint breaker foam realistically, pay special attention to edges. At the base, the foam overlays a shadowed, irregular line. At the top and outer edges, the foam edges range from ghostly mistiness through harsh sharpness. The main point is that while foam edges change, they're mostly soft.

Follow Demonstration 9 carefully, then do several studies on your own, paying close attention to the edges. Whenever feasible, use a soft, dry varnish brush to fade some of the foam edges. But don't overdo it, or the foam edges will all be too soft.

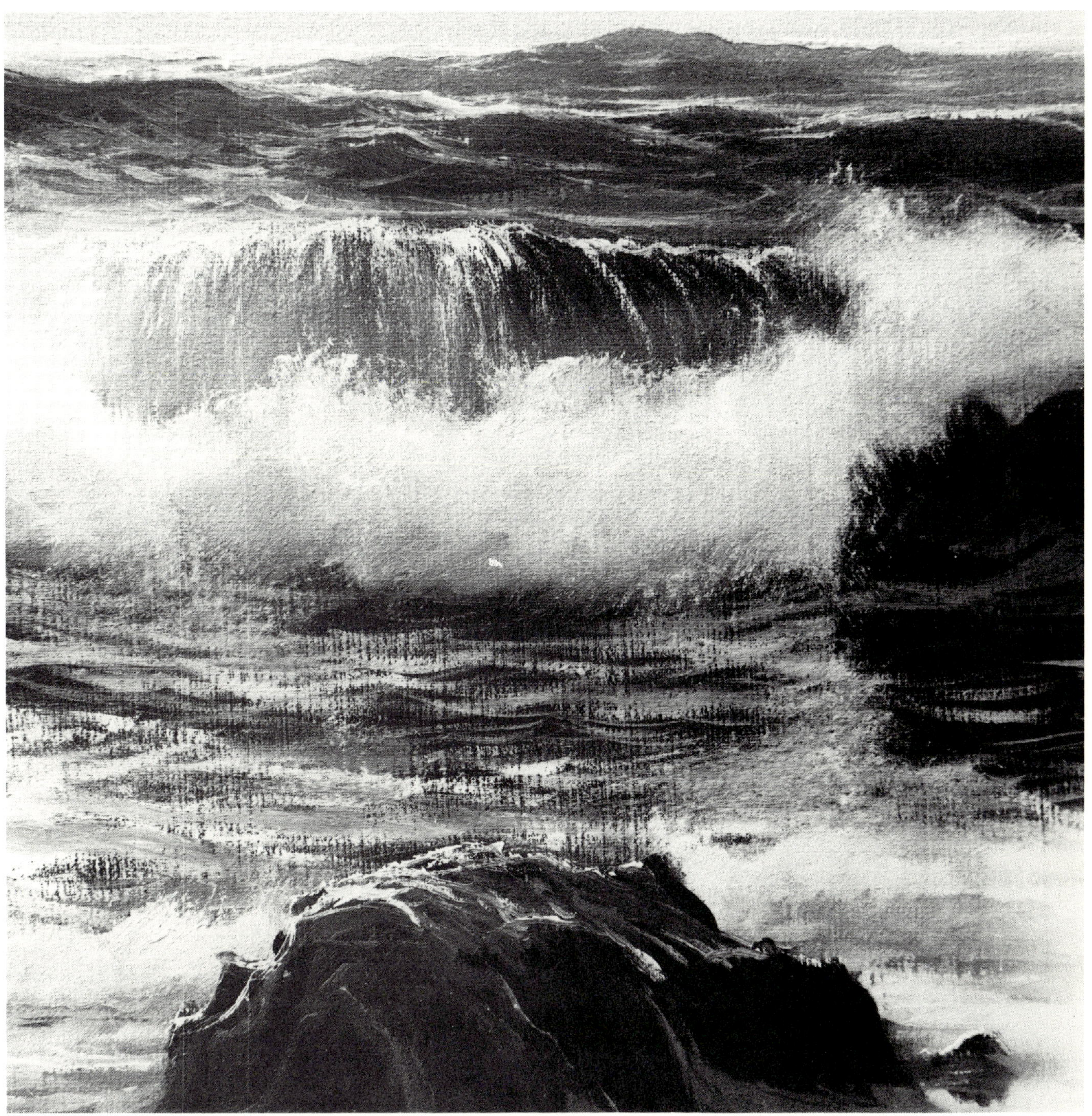

Figure 27. Foam can vary from misty softness to harsh flecks.

THE FOAM BURST

You may recall that breaker foam is a result of water falling from the top of a wave and therefore has little or no direction. The foam burst acts much like breaker foam, but it does, however, have a direction. It's usually traveling upward and is the result of water striking something else.

Most often the foam burst is caused by water striking rocks, but sometimes it's simply a result of water striking water, as it hits a backwash or cross current. When this happens, the foam burst may spread like a fan or travel in all directions at once.

The spread of water is the color of the water at the base of where it meets the rock. Like breaker foam, the farther it moves from the point of impact, the more it is aerated and, hence, the lighter it becomes. Once it leaves the area of water, foam is white; but remember that white is influenced by sunlight color and shadow.

Painting the foam burst (see Demonstration 10) is similar to painting breaker foam. The edges are about the same. The difference lies in how they're created and in what direction they're moving. Avoid a mechanical, stiff look by varying the edges. Make the interior portion a jumble of strokes rather than long, upward strokes that look more like long, upward strokes than they do foam. The direction will be obvious by the shape of the foam burst and the spread of water. Observe in Figure 28 that the foam is painted much the same as breaker foam but is more vertically shaped. In Figure 29 I combined misty foam with a foam burst, thus letting the rock fade into the foam.

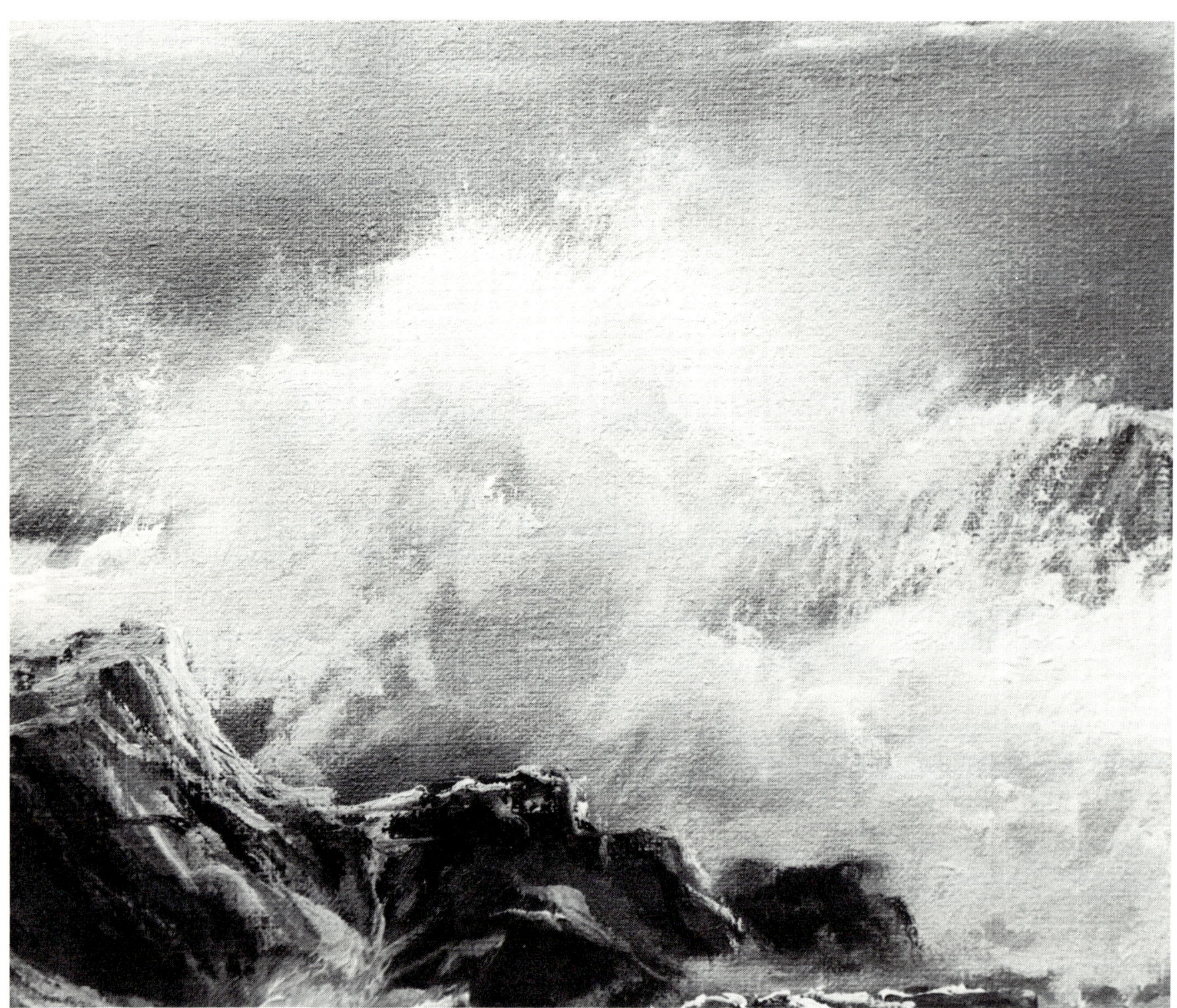

Figure 28. Paint the foam burst like breaker foam, but more vertically.

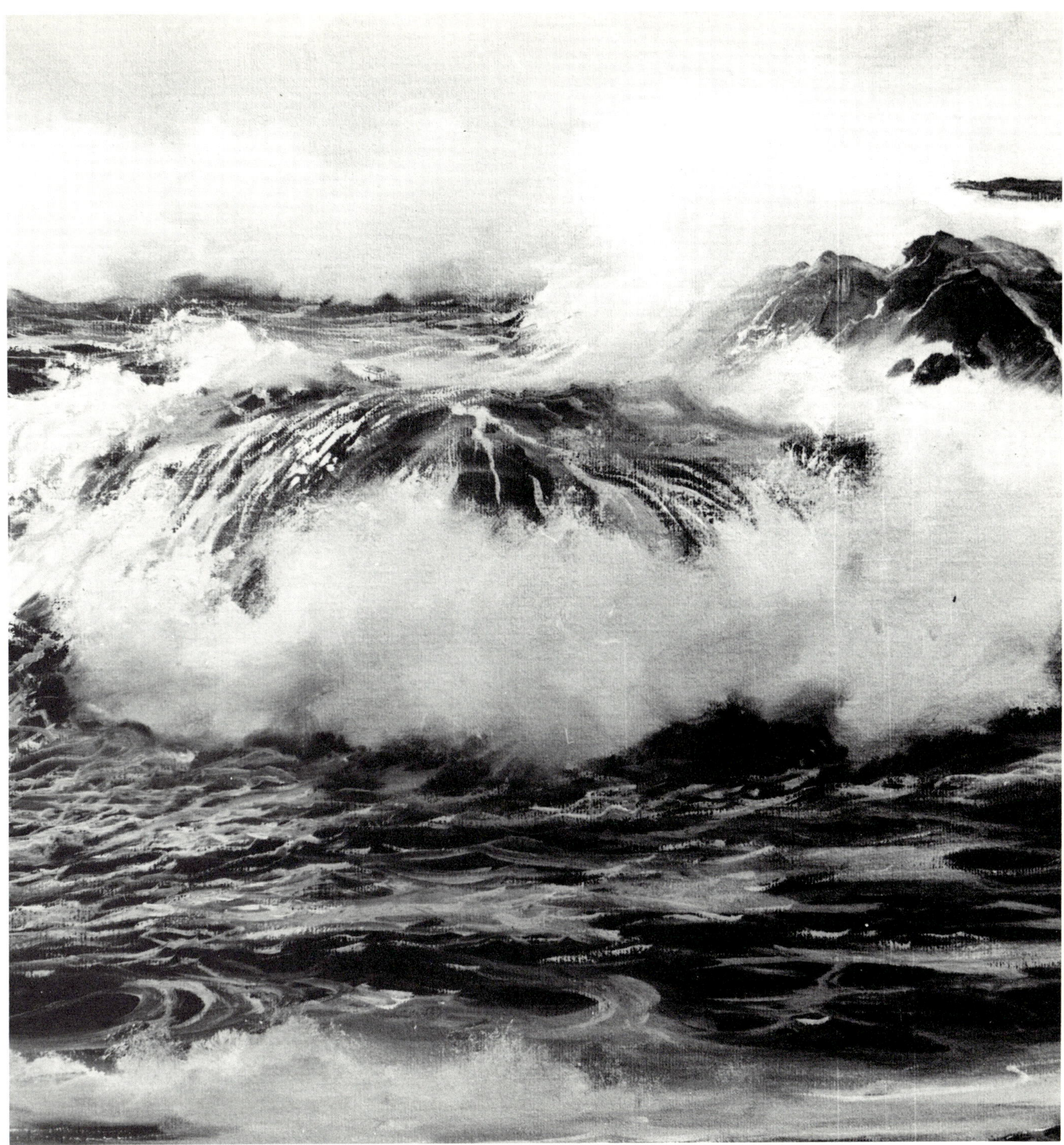

Figure 29. Contrast the misty foam burst with the thicker breaker foam.

Another important part of painting a wave is the use of foam mist. This is neither the thick foam of the breaker nor the foam burst. It's the hazy film of water particles left in the wake of foam burst or heavy activity in the surf (Figure 30). Foam mist causes the lightness at the base of the background rocks.

Mist carries the color of the foam but has no edges like foam bursts or breaker foam. The best way to paint mist is to work the color of the foam (light or shadow) into the rock or whatever object is behind the foam, then blend it with a hazing brush. In other words, lighten the background by blending into it the color you've chosen to use as foam. Be careful to blend the edges out completely, or you'll be painting a thin foam burst.

The closeup in Figure 31 shows how I brushed the foam into the background rock. To do this, the paint of the rock must be scraped down—if it's not nearly dry—or the foam will become mud instead of mist.

Sometimes when the wind comes from on-shore, the foam from a breaking wave is whipped back over the roll and sprays beyond the wave. These sprays are often called "horsetails," and can be used to add interest in some paintings. They're painted just the same way as mist, except that you allow some direction to show in the brushstrokes.

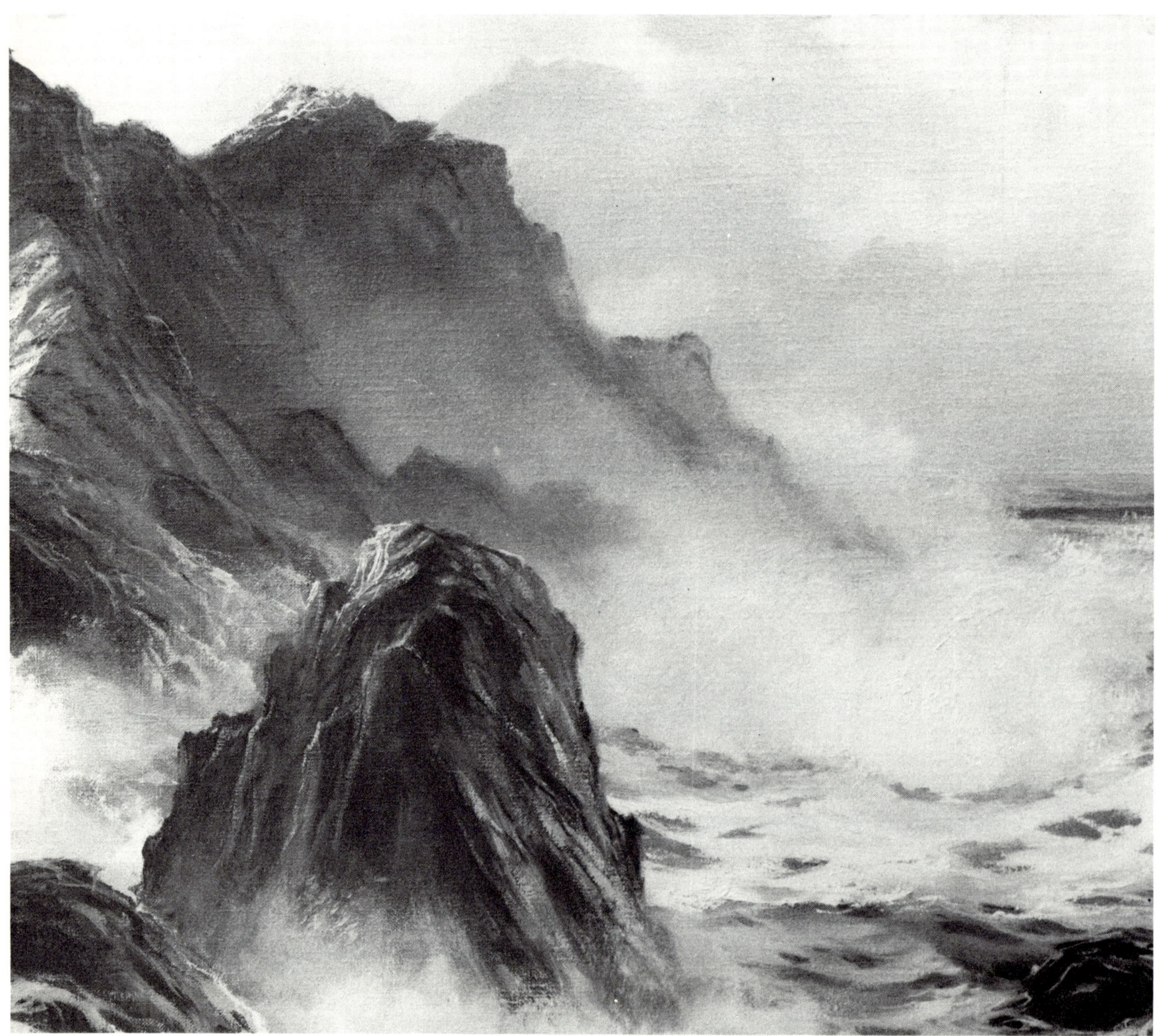

Figure 30. Foam mist is a hazy film of water particles.

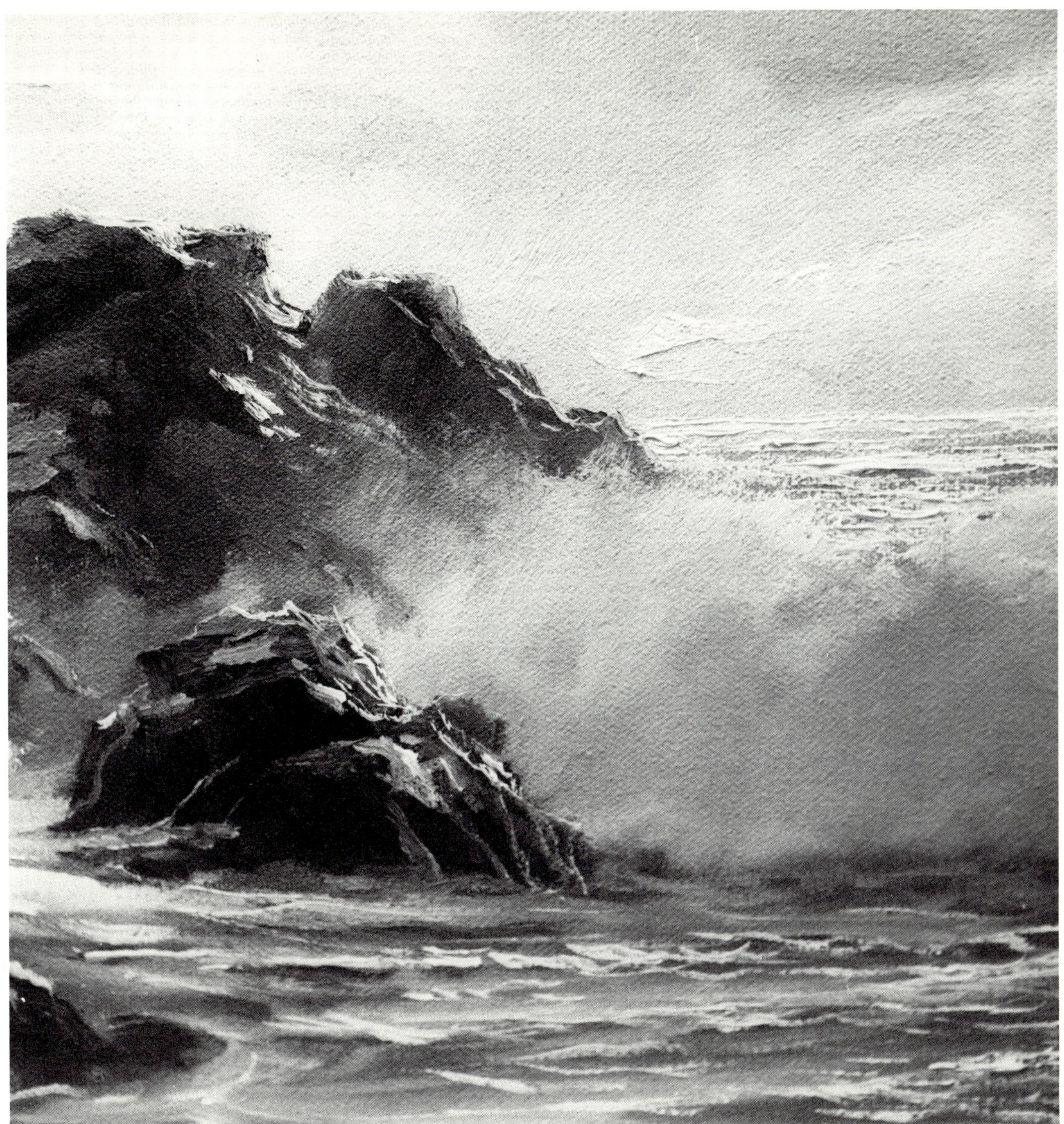

Figure 31. Lightness at the base of background rocks is due to foam mist.

VEILING

For a new way to add interest to a major wave, try what I call "veiling." It has much the same look as folds of soft material. The movement is downward, but in a lazy folding motion, one layer over another. Veiling may be defined as thin, filmy strings of foam that are in the process of falling. When they appear between areas of breaker foam, as in Figure 32, they're the result of a multiple leading edge on a wave, where thin sections fall ahead of others. On the face of a wave such as in Figure 33, the strings of foam are still the result of thin edges falling away, but this time falling on an angle along the face of the wave.

Paint them with soft, moving edges and allow them to pass through areas of sunlight and shadow to add more interest and more character to your waves.

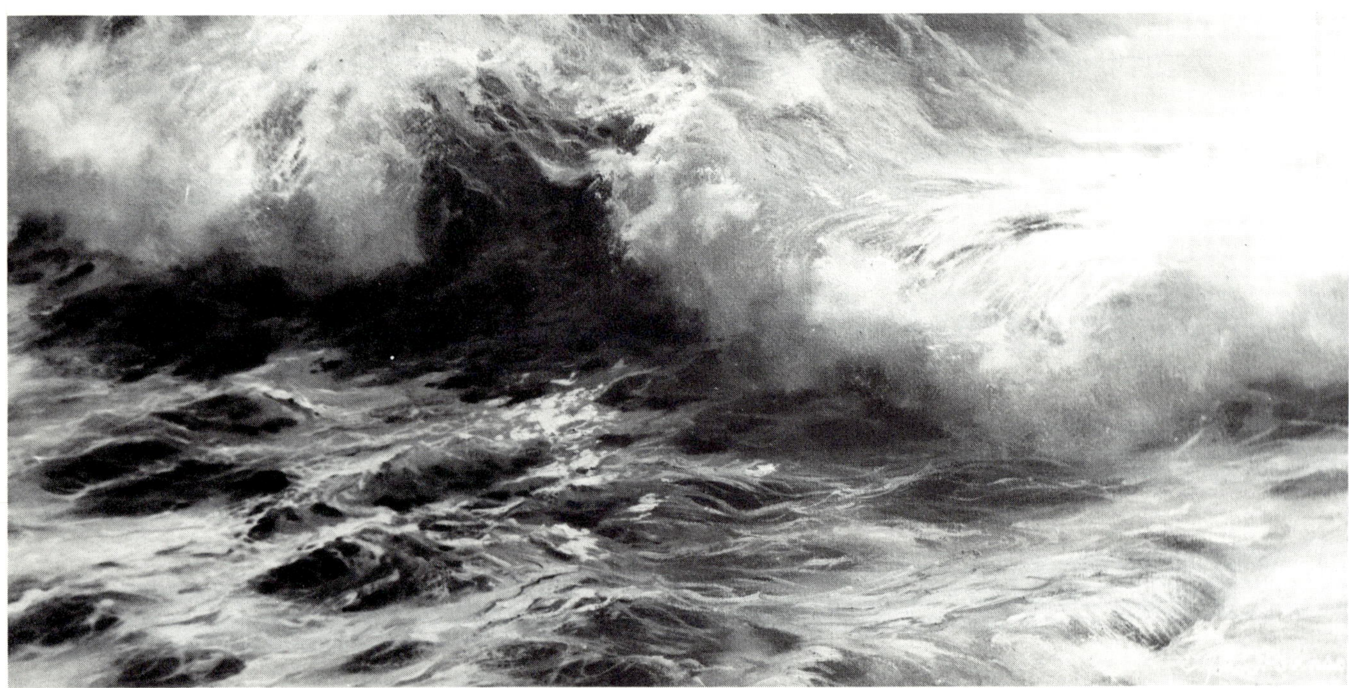

Figure 32. Veiling occurs here between two areas of breaker foam.

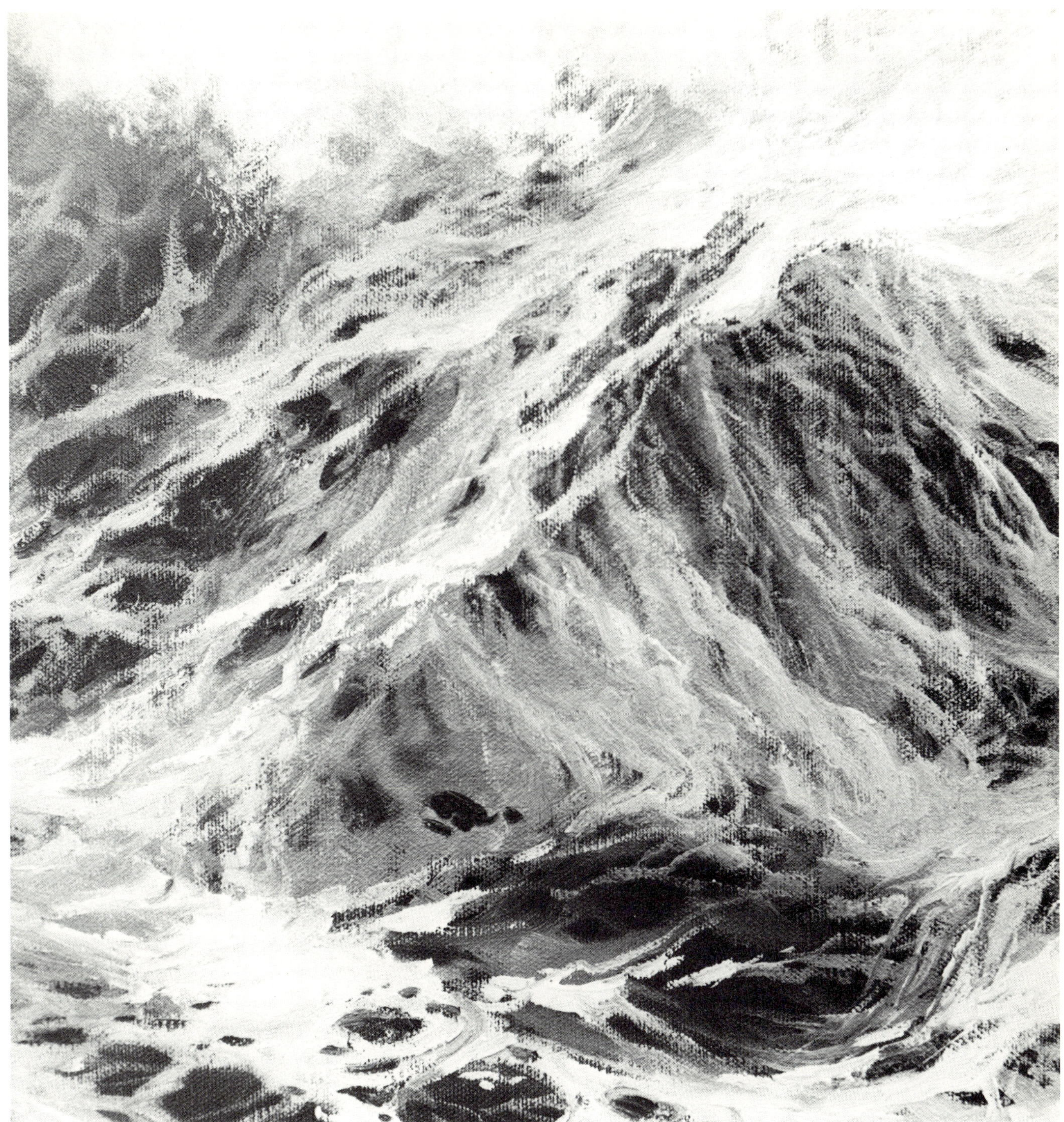

Figure 33. Veiling appears on the face of a wave.

TRANSLUCENT WATER

All right! I made a mistake in *Marine Painting in Oil.* Water that allows light to pass through is translucent. Water you can see through is transparent. I used "transparent" for both incidents in my last book. A wave crest with back lighting will become lighter as light passes through it. It's translucent, it's not transparent if you can't see through it (Figure 34).

Water is most translucent when the sunlight comes from behind, as in Figure 35, where the sun is rather high in the sky. Even though the water is somewhat translucent, it is less so than in Figure 34. The translucent effect is also enhanced if silhouettes of foam patterns are visible. Use the effect sparingly because any translucent water will command attention, and your painting may become too busy, with too many areas of interest.

Painting instructions on translucent waves can be found in Demonstration 13 in the color section. Keep in mind that the color of sunlight determines what color to use to lighten the wave. Don't use pure white to lighten water; white is opaque. Translucent water is lighter because light (sunlight) is passing through. Choose the color you wish for sunlight (such as pale cadmium yellow) and lighten the color you've chosen for the wave with that. Be sure to lighten it gradually. A line between the darker and translucent portions of water is not natural. You can blend any such line by whipping a brush back and forth between the two values.

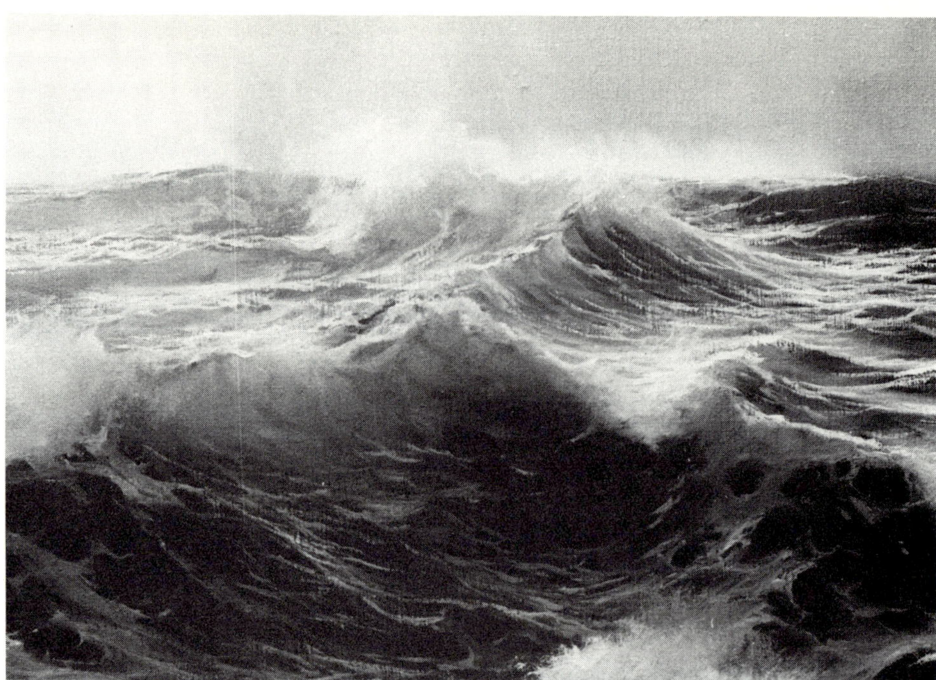

Figure 34. Light comes through the wave, creating a translucent effect.

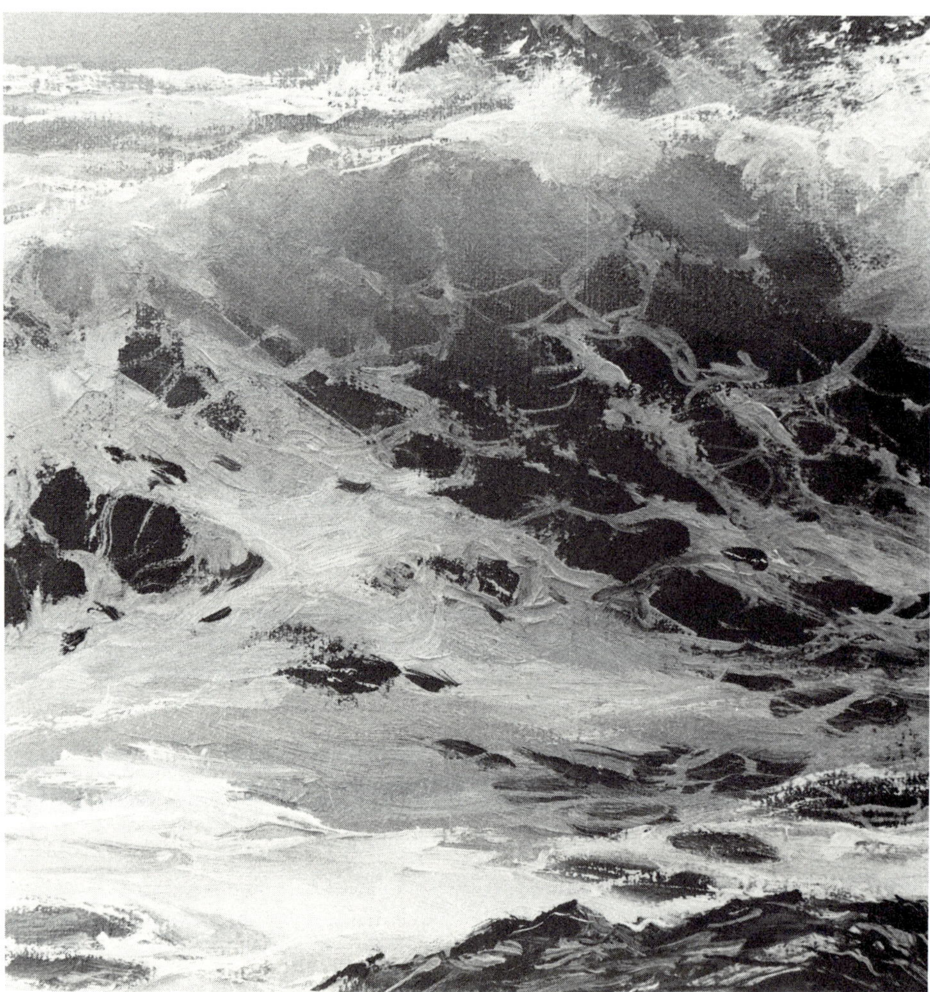

Figure 35. The sun, high in the sky, makes this water less translucent.

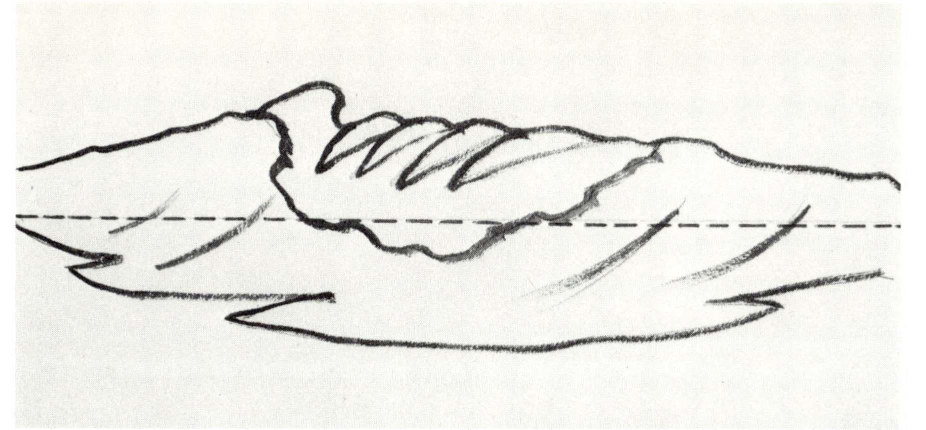

Step 1. The basic breaker is a variation of the ground swell. The ground swell becomes a breaker when the leading edge peels over and rebounds as foam. To start, draw an outline similar to this one. I've once again added a base line to help you understand the horizontal placement of the wave.

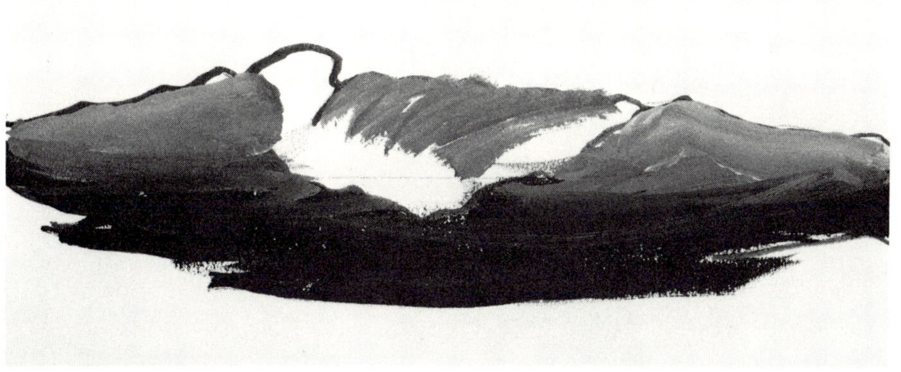

Step 2. Mix a blue-green (ultramarine and viridian) and start painting the base of the wave. As you work up into the thinner portion of the wave, add more and more cadmium yellow pale to lighten the mixture. Don't use white. For the roll section, just about the middle section of the wave, use your blue-green mixture. Leave the foam area unpainted.

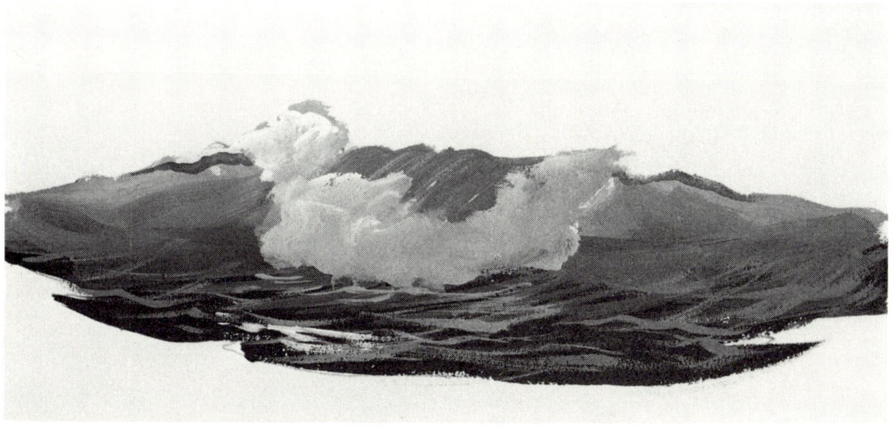

Step 3. Now paint in the foam, using a bit of ultramarine blue mixed into white for the shadow area and cadmium yellow pale mixed into white for the sunlight area. Reflect the foam below using the same colors as the foam itself.

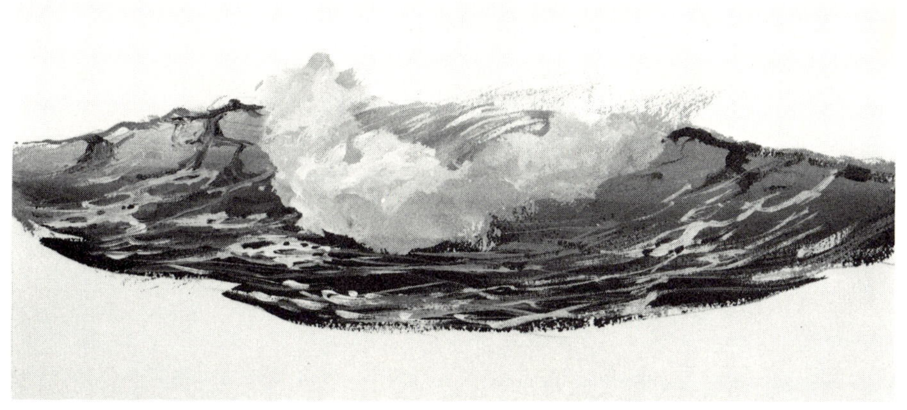

Step 4. Finally, work in silhouette patterns into the translucent areas, foam patterns into the foreground, and highlights onto the upper portion of the roll as well as into the major foam. (Also see Demonstration 13 in the color section for information on painting a translucent wave.)

DEMONSTRATION 9:
BREAKER FOAM

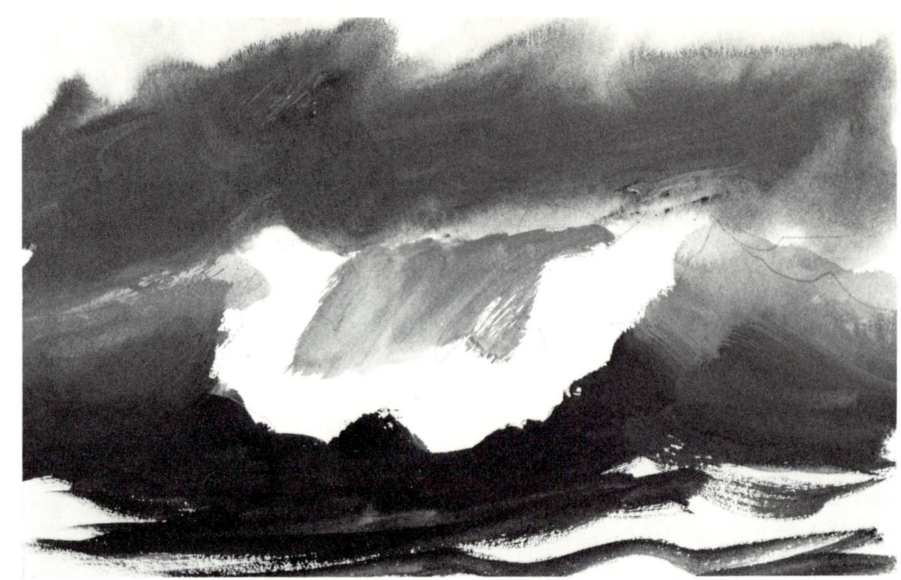

Step 1. If you ran into trouble with the last lesson, perhaps it was because of problems with foam. Choose whatever colors you wish and work in a background, leaving an area for foam unpainted. This is very important, because foam generally shouldn't be blended with another color—at least not until you're ready for it.

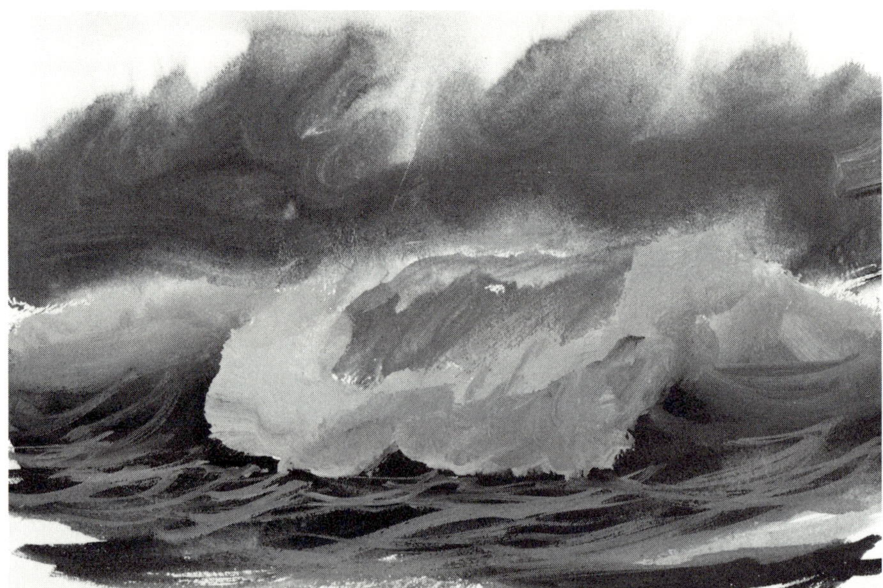

Step 2. Mix up a shadowed white—a white with a bit of blue or blue-purple (ultramarine and/or alizarin) to darken it—and paint in the entire foam area. Keep the edges soft and uneven.

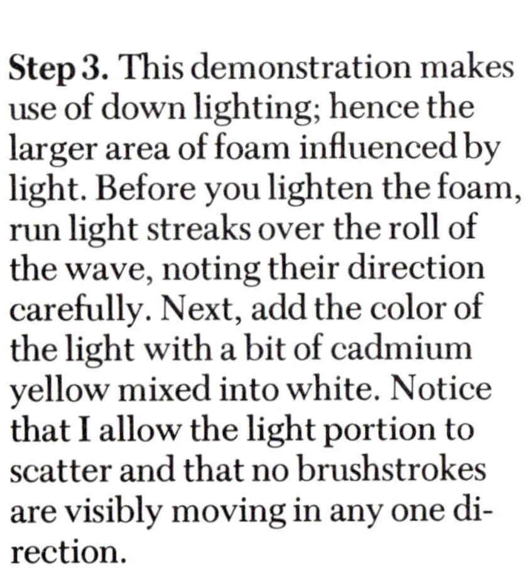

Step 3. This demonstration makes use of down lighting; hence the larger area of foam influenced by light. Before you lighten the foam, run light streaks over the roll of the wave, noting their direction carefully. Next, add the color of the light with a bit of cadmium yellow mixed into white. Notice that I allow the light portion to scatter and that no brushstrokes are visibly moving in any one direction.

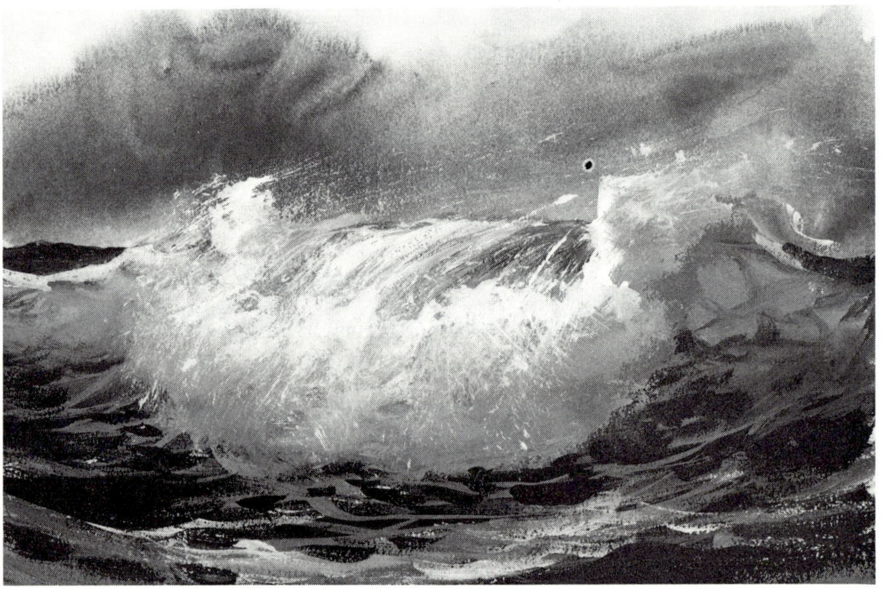

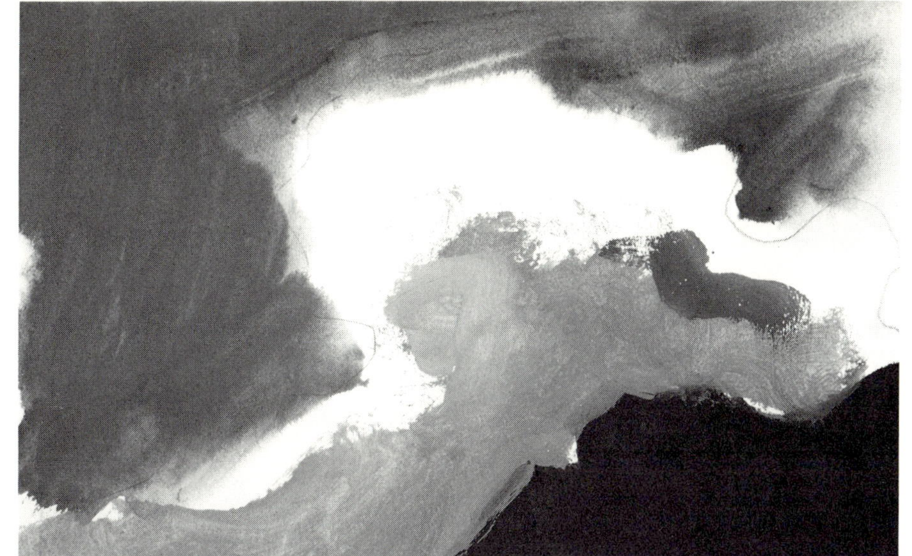

Step 1. Painting a foam burst is very different from painting breaker foam. To start, paint in a dark area for a rock. Next, paint in a color for translucent water. (The same mixture you used for painting the translucent wave would be fine.) Leave the area for the foam unpainted, but paint in the sky behind it. You're now ready to add the foam, which will be in front of the sky and the water, but behind or over the rock.

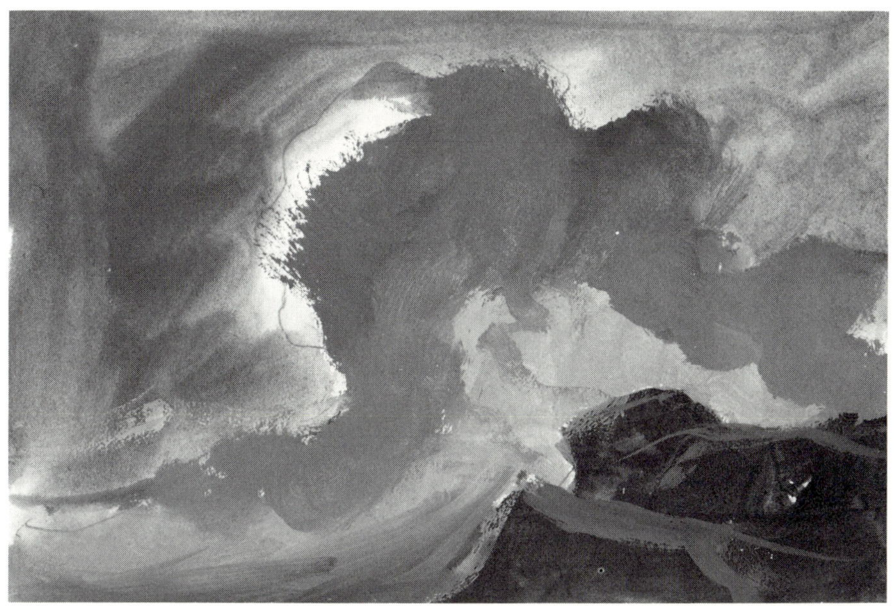

Step 2. Your first job is to mix a dark blue-purple shadow for the foam—it may even be darker than the translucent water—from a combination of white, ultramarine blue, and alizarin crimson. Brush it into the foam quickly, and don't belabor it with any extra effort at this time. Also reflect this shadow color on the upper portion of the rock.

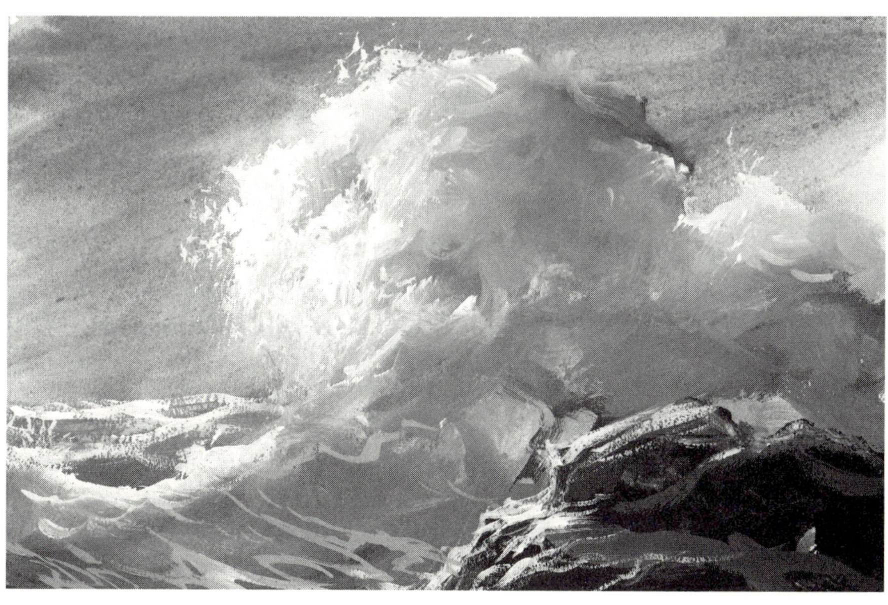

Step 3. Using a pale yellow-white mixture, paint in the light portion of the foam. Notice the use of a scatter effect rather than directional brushstrokes. Also reflect this same sunlight on the rock, wave, and background sea, if you put one in. Notice the echo of light on the right side of the foam burst. It now has form, with light on the left, shadow, and, finally, reflected light on the right.

COLOR DEMONSTRATIONS

People who have seen the ocean are often quite certain they know its true color and may be very critical of your painting if it doesn't match their image. But the color of the sea actually varies from one location to the next because of the amount and color of seaweed, sand, rocks, and marine life. Add to that weather changes and the position and color of the sunlight, and the sea could be almost any color—almost, but not quite.

There are no hard and fast rules. You must study your own locale and choose the colors or mixtures of colors that best represent what you see: the color of the rocks and water, the color and position of the sun, and then the color and amount of atmosphere to reflect on the sea.

There is more. You must decide if you want a warm or cool painting (color temperature). You may emphasize either the warm side of the color wheel by using more yellow, orange, red, or purple in your painting, or the cool side, by leaning toward the blues, greens, or some yellows such as lemon or chartreuse.

If the center of interest in a painting is weak or lacking, color can emphasize it by striking a new, strong note. A dull painting may come alive with the sparkle of sunlight or the warmth (or coolness) of cast shadows. Remember: sunlight, shadow, atmosphere, and reflected light—all of these are made up of color. And all of these colors influence the sea, which, in turn, is also a color.

Learn to think in terms of color. Look at each object and try to think how you would mix that color—or better still, test out your colors on a quick sketch.

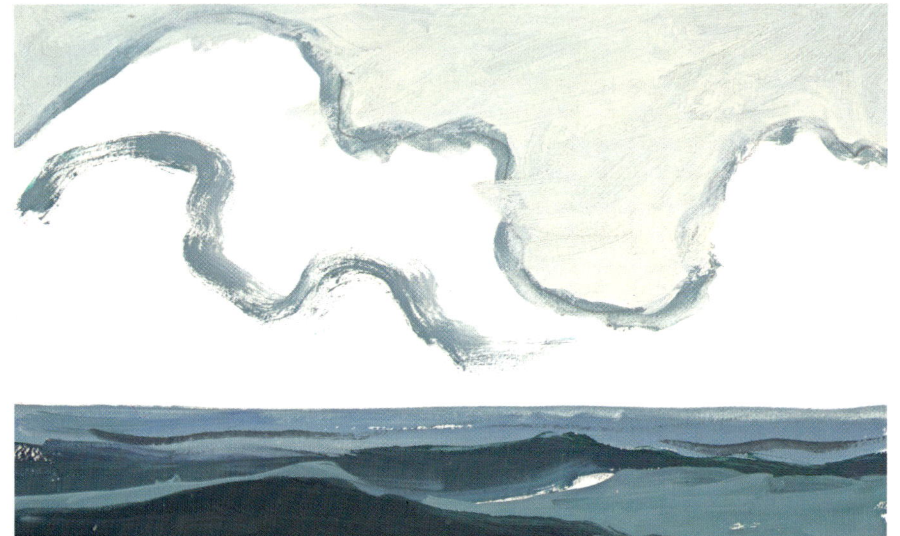

Step 1. Draw a low horizon line and fill the upper area with large, rounded clouds. In the sky behind the clouds, paint in a pale blue of ultramarine and white with a bit of cadmium yellow medium and white in the central portion. For the sea, using ultramarine blue and viridian, paint in dark blue-green swells against a lighter blue-green background. Leave the cloud area unpainted.

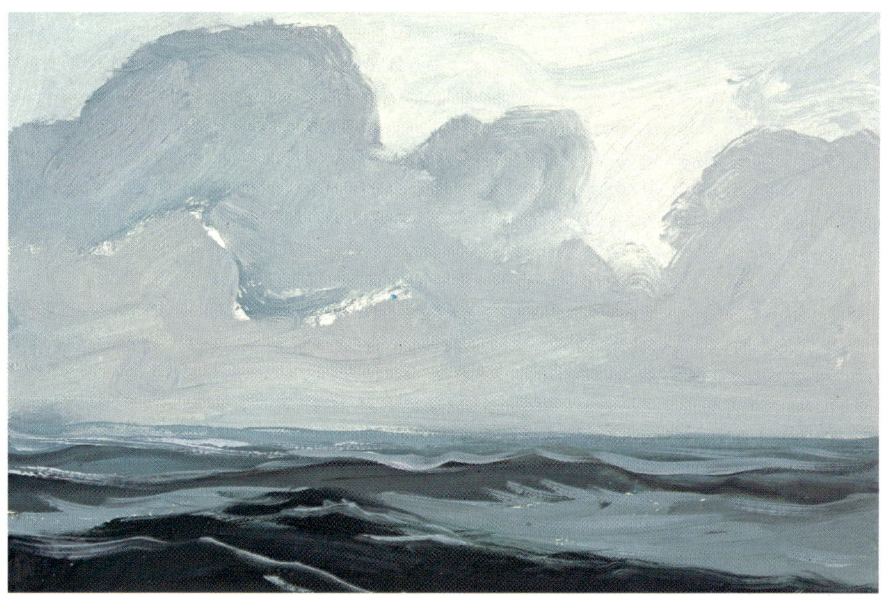

Step 2. Mix ultramarine and alizarin into white for the clouds, but make it darker than the sky and lighter than the sea. Use the same color mix to indicate reflections upon the sea. Allow the reflected color to strike between swells and to indicate minor chops on the face of larger swells.

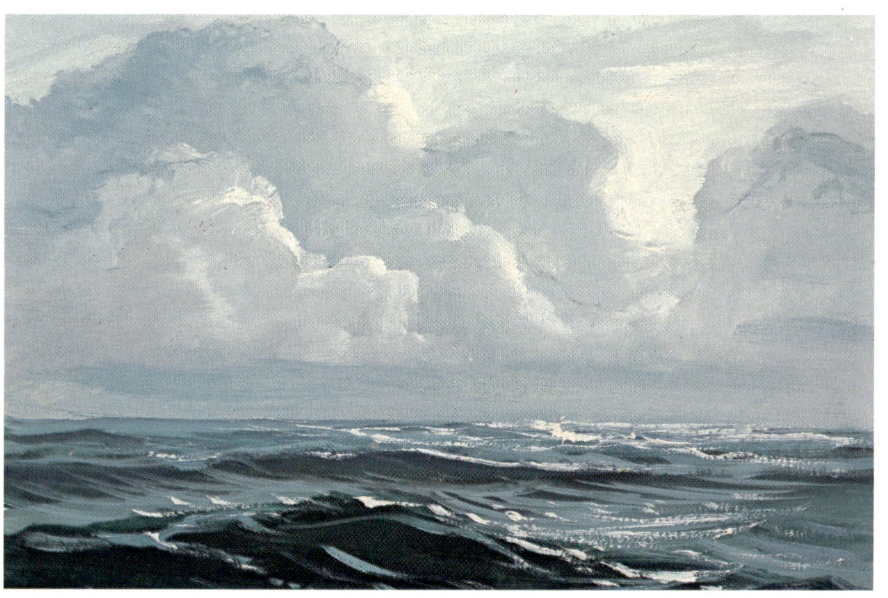

Step 3. Mix cadmium yellow pale into white for the sunlight. Assume the sun is behind the clouds and reflects outward. Notice how the sunlight touches major and minor billows in the clouds and sparkles on the ocean. Cumulus clouds should be rising, billowing, fluffy clouds with light, shadow, and reflected light.

**DEMONSTRATION 12:
GLOW**

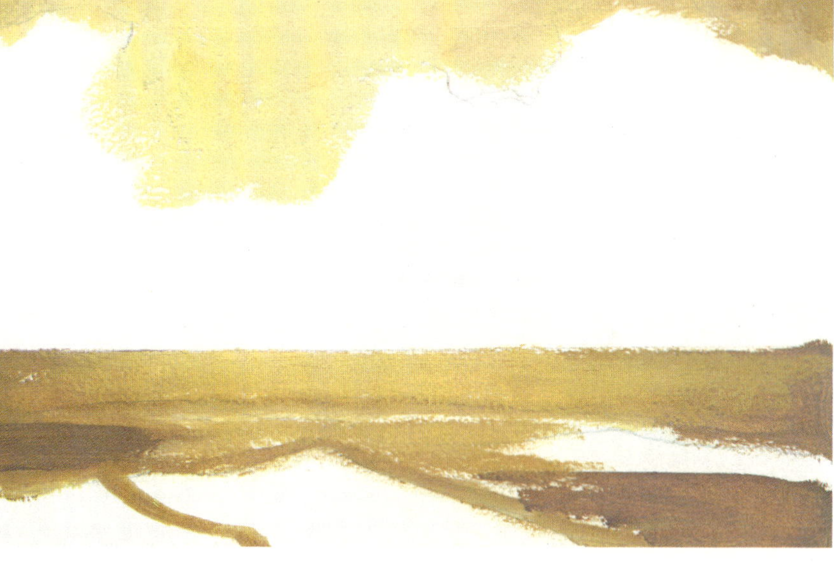

Step 1. Once again, start with a low horizon line. Draw in a distant fog bank and, in the foreground, major and minor swells. Use cadmium yellow medium in the sky and background sea. Add a bit of white to the lighter portion, but darken the yellow with burnt sienna as it moves out on either side. Leave the cloud bank and foreground swells unpainted at this time.

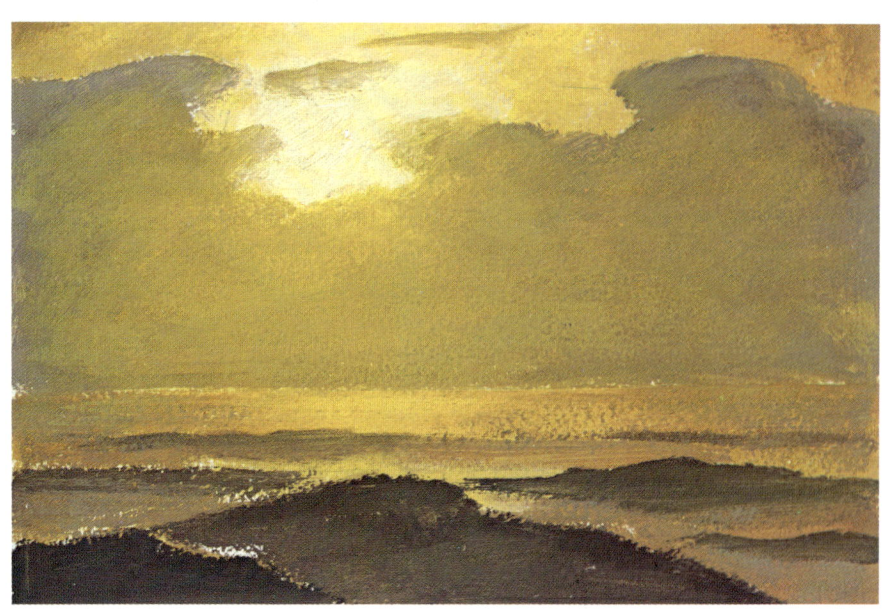

Step 2. The color of the clouds comes from the cadmium yellow medium used in Step 1, but with the addition of purple (alizarin crimson and ultramarine blue) for the darkening effect. The central cloud area has more yellow than purple, but the mixture changes to more purple on the extreme sides of the light area. The same mixture is used for the foreground swells.

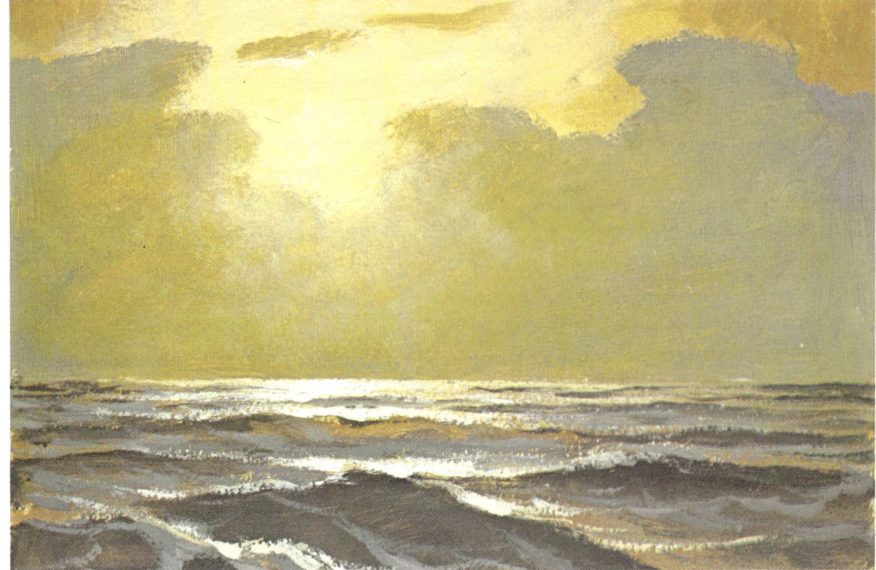

Step 3. The final step requires cadmium yellow medium mixed with white. Lighten the area of the sun and let it wash over the background sea and the troughs of the foreground. In addition, use a bit of purple-white on the shadow side of the swells.

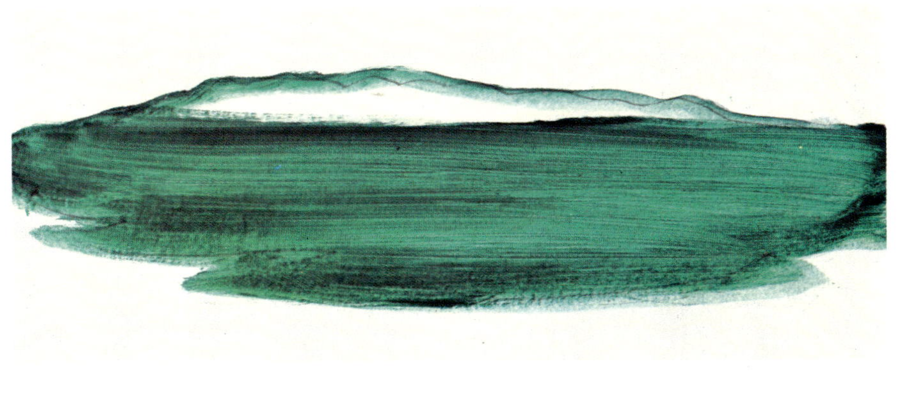

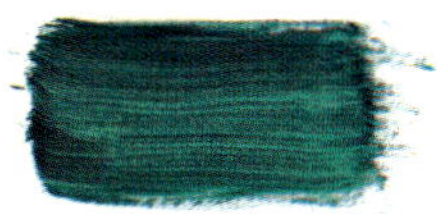

Step 1. As the color patch indicates, use only viridian in this beginning step. Paint in a wave with horizontal strokes, but leave the upper portion unpainted.

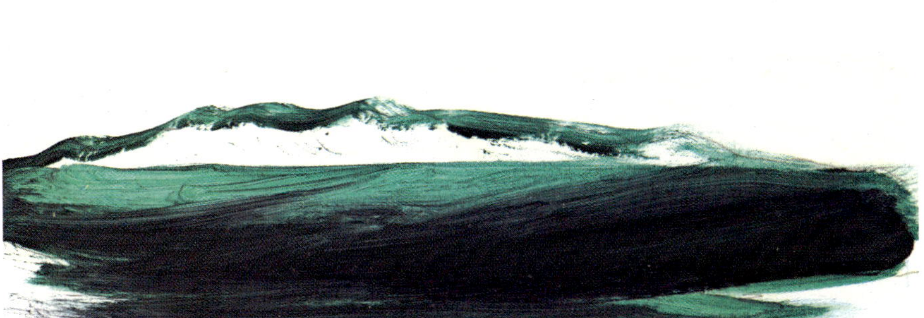

Step 2. Next, darken the viridian with purple (alizarin and ultramarine) as shown in the color patch. Notice that the darkened area is at the base but doesn't extend through all of the viridian. The upper portion still remains an untouched viridian.

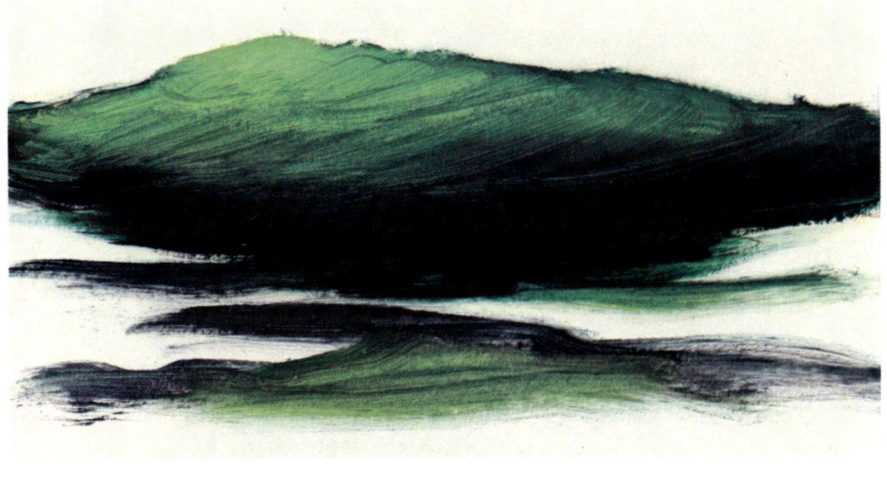

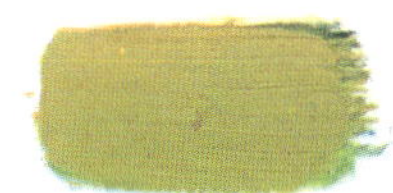

Step 3. The color patch shows the addition of lemon yellow or pale yellow. Use it to lighten the viridian at the top of the wave. For practice, add a few minor swells at the base of the wave.

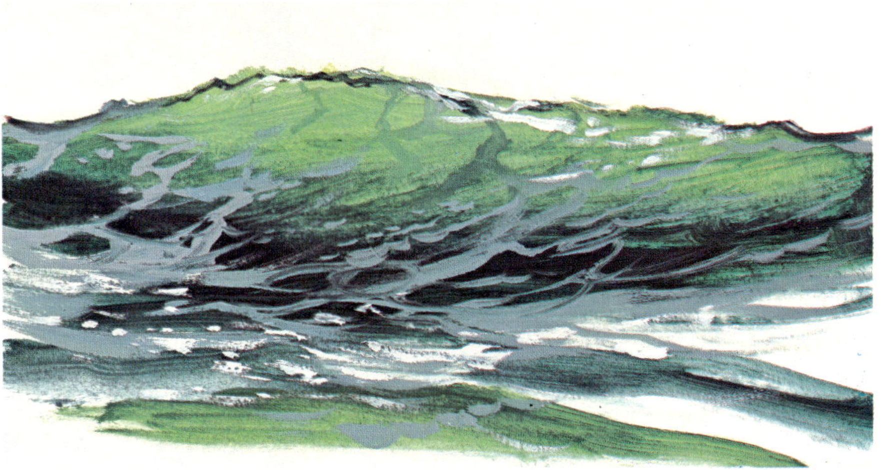

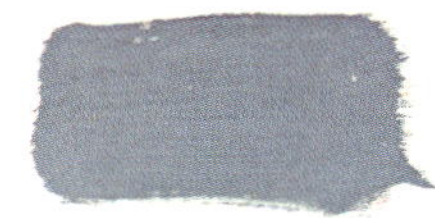

Step 4. This is the first use of white in the demonstration; and it's only for foam patterns, not for the color of the water. As the patch shows, mix a gray (alizarin/viridian) or a blue purple (alizarin/ultramarine) into white to paint in patterns. Use a bit of pure white to reflect sunlight on the wave and foreground.

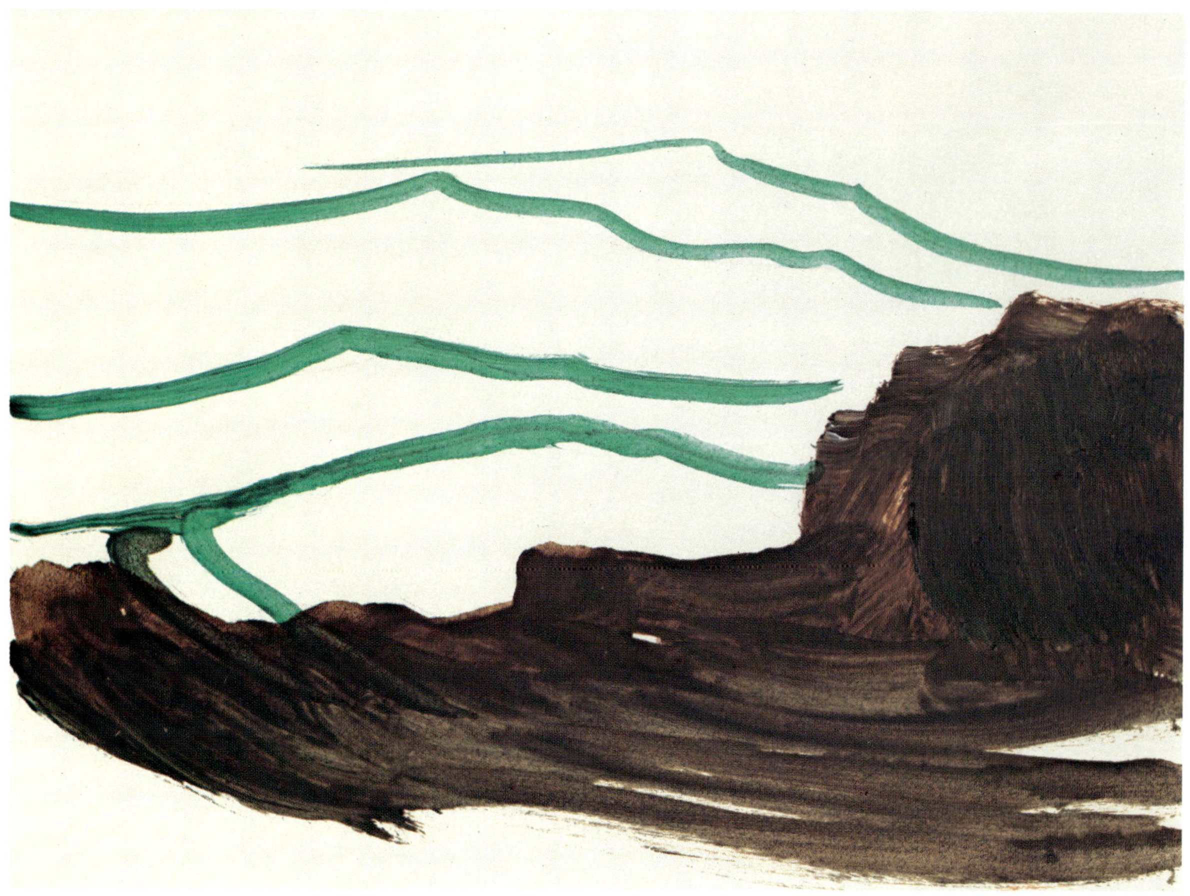

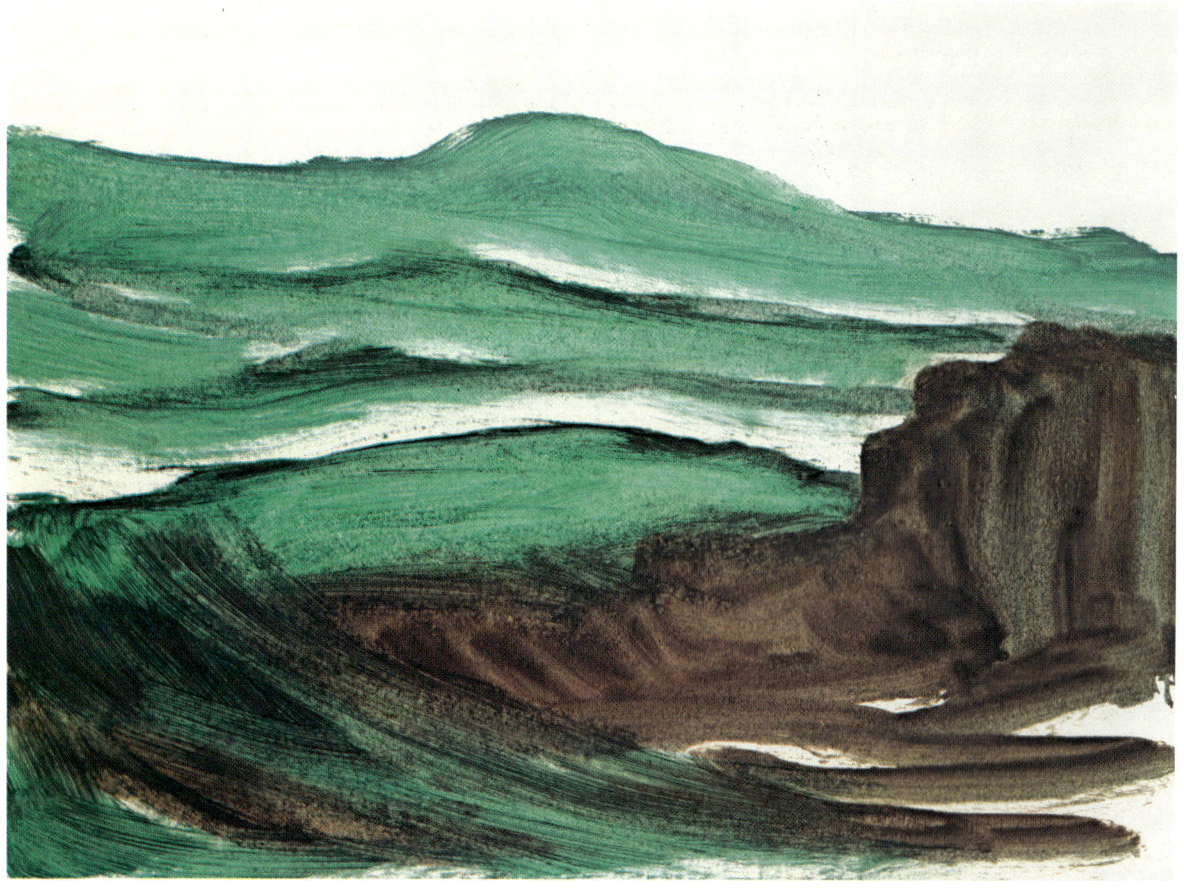

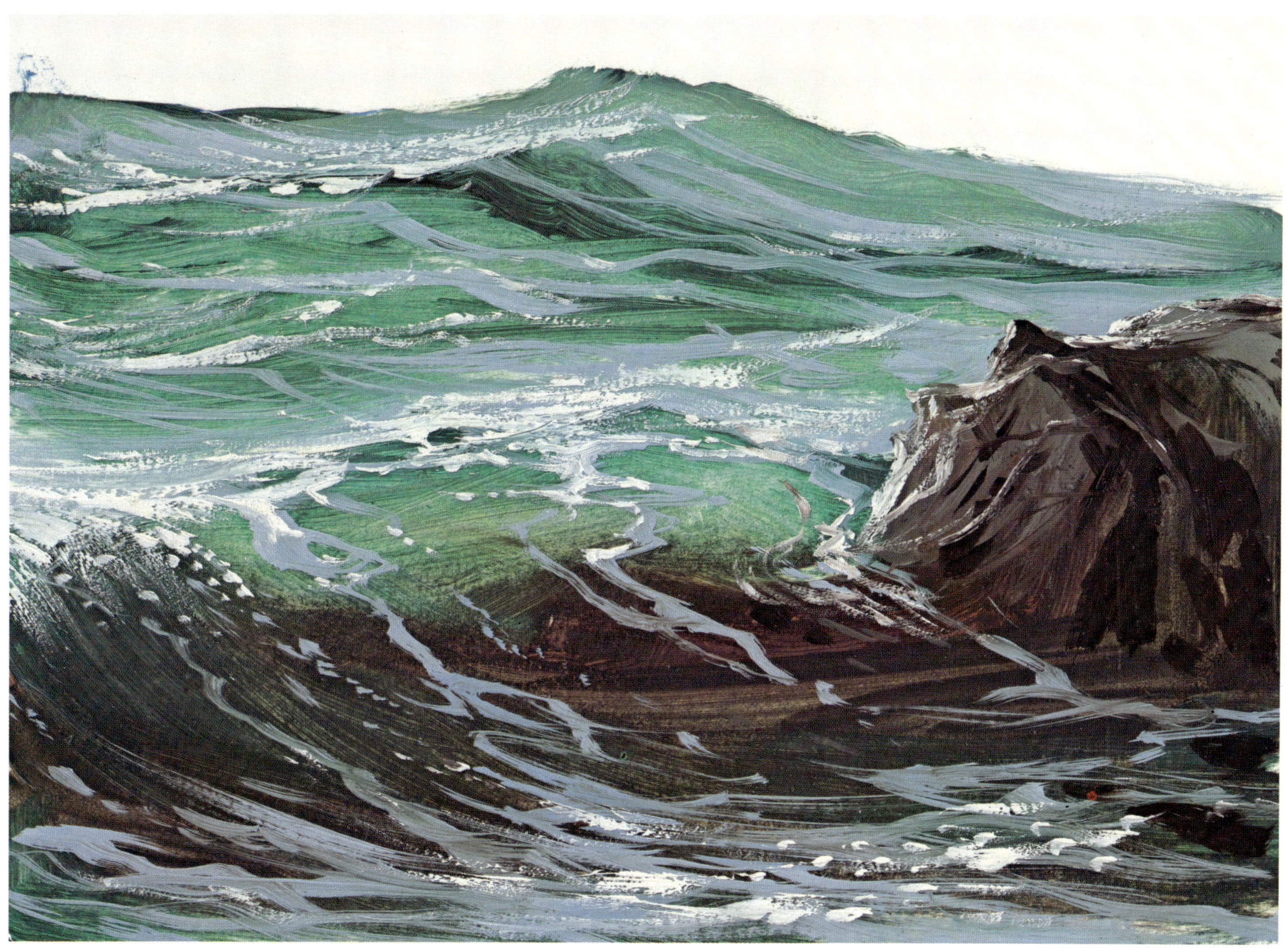

Step 1. (Top left) Here the prime concern is to paint a rock above and below water. First indicate the background water with viridian. Then mix burnt sienna with viridian for a basic rock color. Paint the rock color in thinly, as it will be necessary to go over it with another color.

Step 2. (Left) Use viridian for this step. Sweep in the major swells and allow the lower portion to move right over the left-hand rocks. Keep the central and right-hand rocks clear.

Step 3. (Above) Reflect a pale ultramarine blue from the sky and paint in foam patterns that cross over the water and the submerged rocks at the same time. Use these patterns elsewhere and then add a few spots of glitter from sunlight.

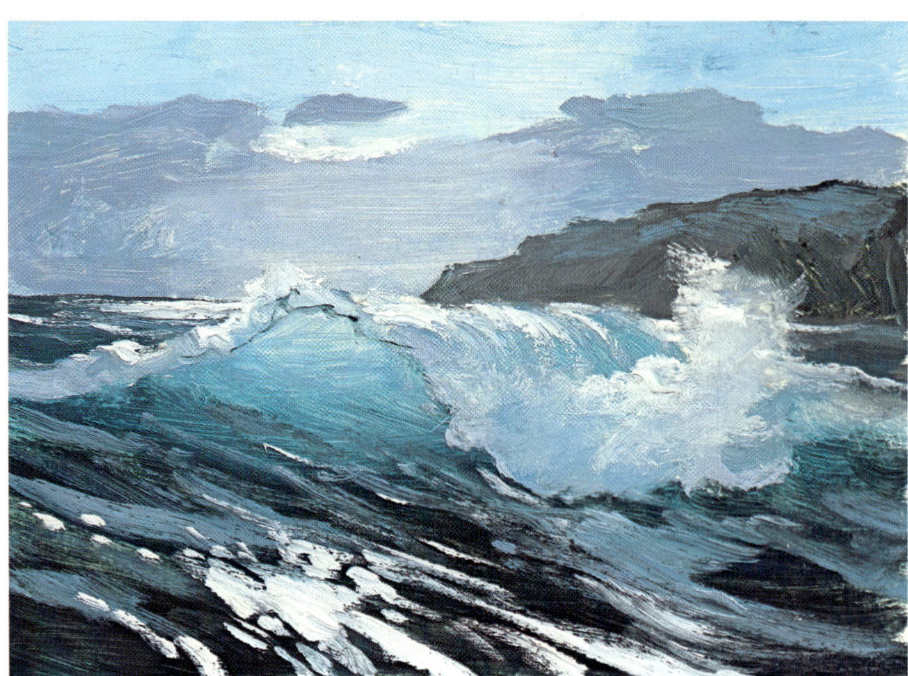

Example 1. Using pure white for
sunlight and manganese blue for
the water and sky, this sketch has a
cold, almost arctic feel about it.
The cloud bank, too, is cold, as it is
a purple made from manganese
blue and alizarin crimson mixed
with white. This is not my favorite
sunlight, but I include it to contrast it with the others.

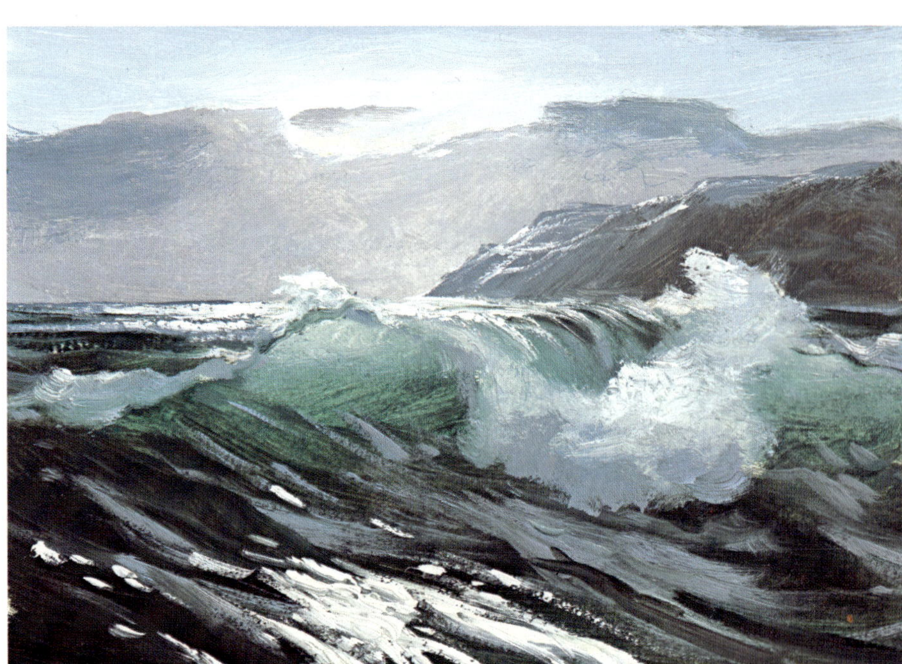

Example 2. This sketch is only
slightly warmer in feeling than
Example 1. The sunlight here has
a touch of yellow. The background lavenders help to warm up
the mood, but the viridian of the
foreground is still very cold.

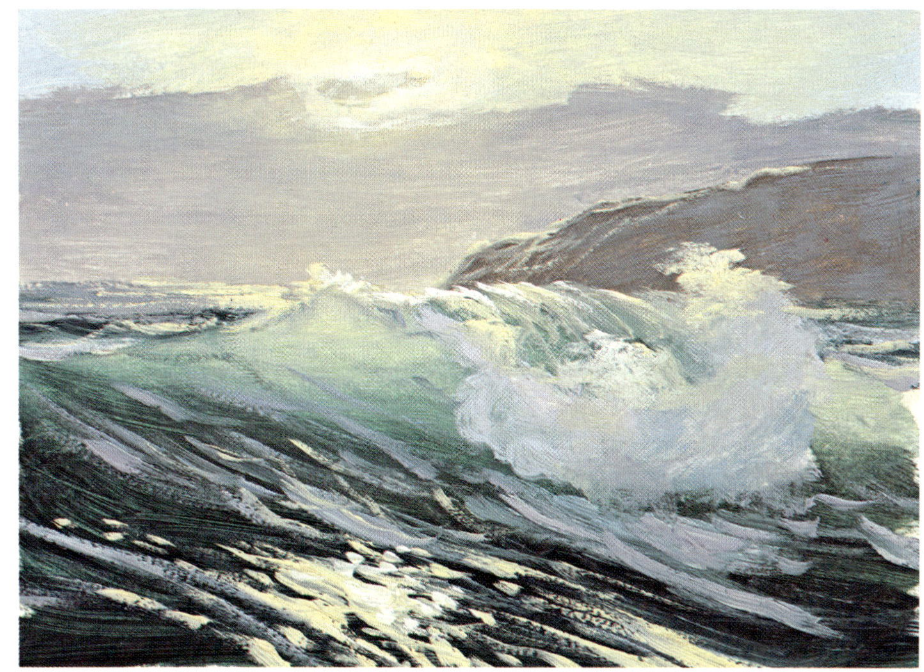

Example 3. To show the warming effect of sunlight, this sketch is made of the same colors as Example 2. The only difference is the amount of sunlight and an increase in the use of cadmium yellow. Notice that the sunlight spreads over a wide area of the sky and reflects its warmth on the otherwise cold foreground.

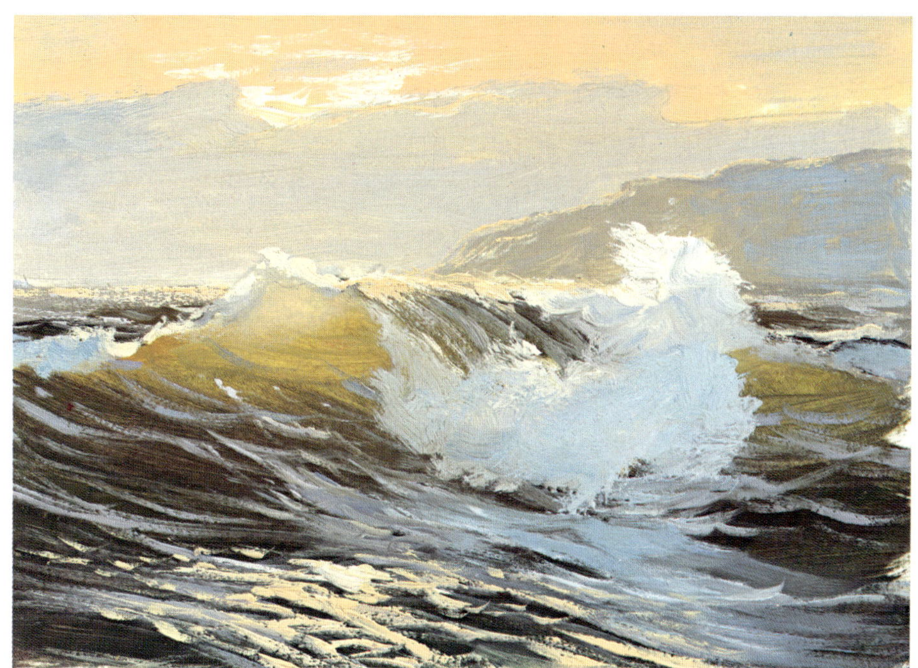

Example 4. To really warm up your painting, switch to an orange or a cadmium yellow deep for sunlight. Compare this with the first three examples. Notice that in each case the sunlight influences all of the colors in the painting according to its strength and how much is used.

CHAPTER FIVE

THE TRANSPARENT SURFACE

In this chapter I use the word "transparent" to indicate water you can see through, or clear water. By the description "transparent surface" I mean the clear water found in the foreground, not the clear water of a wave. The transparent surface is most evident when one looks down on water from a cliff.

In the foreground, when there are few disturbances, it is not unusual to see through the surface to rocks, sand, and the weeds below. Sometimes you can see much deeper than other times, depending on how clear the water is and how much activity is present. Activity adds air to the water and makes it opaque, and heavy activity stirs up sand and mud from the bottom.

While the best views of transparent surface water are gained from a cliff or high point, other good examples occur as water pours over rocks or spills beneath them. Chapter Eight will take up the subject of rocks and spills in greater detail, but the transparent effect of water over and below rocks will be studied now.

To paint transparent water, start with the farthest level and paint it in thinly. You needn't add a thinner to the paint; you may also whip it with a dry varnish brush. This not only reduces its thickness, but it also knocks off lumps and ridges that may later mix where you don't want them. Proceed through each level of depth in the same manner.

CLEAR WATER OVER ROCKS

All water over rocks is not transparent; it may also be foamy or white. But when it is transparent, the most obvious sign is that the color of the rock shows through.

Try to think in terms of layers of viewing planes or levels of depth. Start first with the rock surface as one plane. Next, because rushing and slightly foamy water covers but does not hide the rock, it creates another plane. Finally, a third plane of trickles or glints of sunlight on the surface intensifies the illusion of depth (Demonstration 14).

In Figure 36, I show the transparent effect with only a hint of foamy water below the surface. This is a good example of creating secondary interest in the foreground, which usually is difficult to make interesting. The detail in Figure 37 varies slightly in color and texture. This is what makes each subject fun: adding a personality, or at least individuality, so that you're not dependent on copying what you've done before.

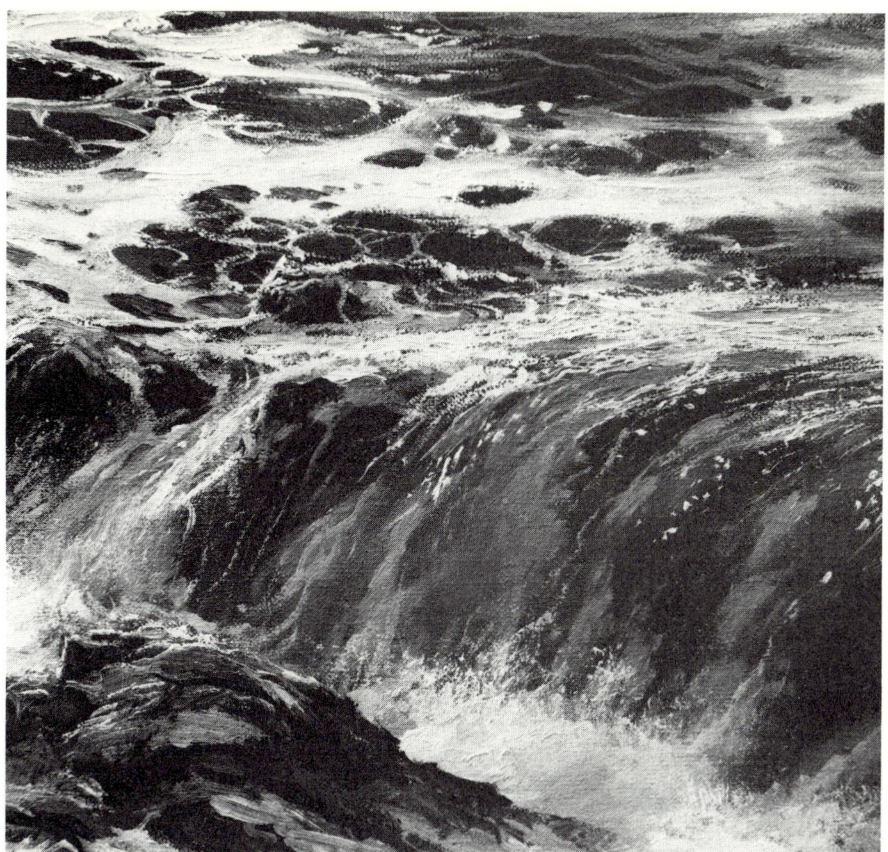

Figure 36. Sunlight glinting off the water intensifies the illusion of depth.

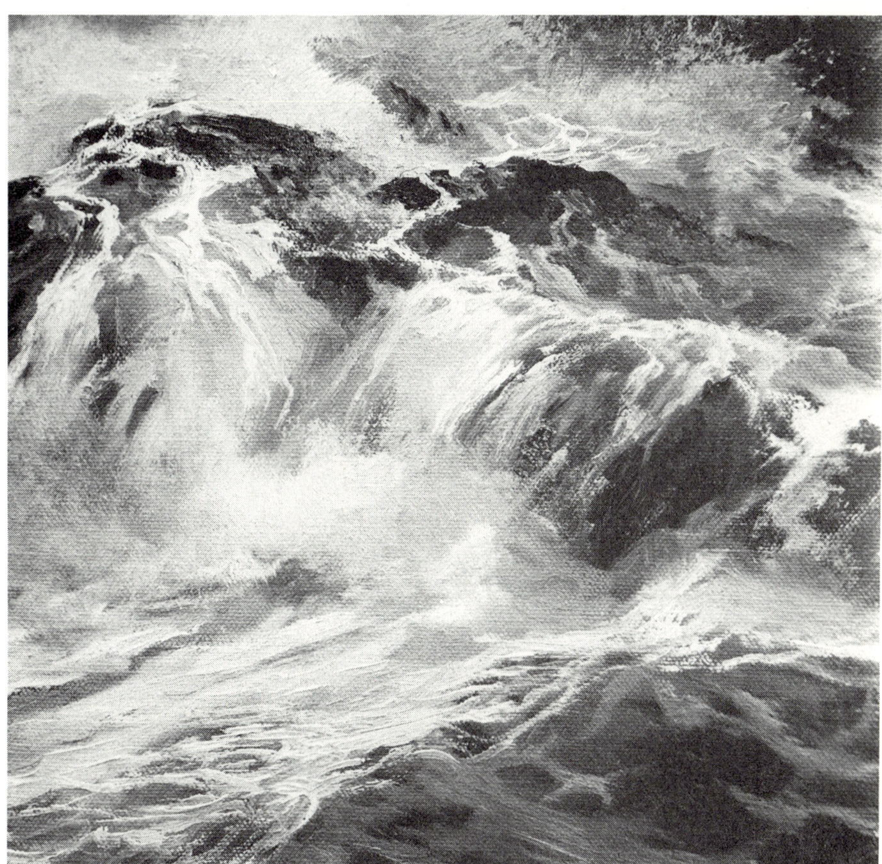

Figure 37. Compare this slightly different treatment with the one in Figure 36.

WATER BELOW ROCKS

Have you ever watched water from a faucet pouring into a tub or bucket? You must have noticed that the falling water didn't stop at the surface, but continued on some way below. Much the same thing occurs when water spills over rocks.

When water falls and strikes the rock, some of it rebounds as foam or splatter; but some continues on its downward motion below the water's surface. The movement forces air into the water, which lightens its color. In Figure 38 the falling water has continued below the surface and its action obscures the color of the rock. The patterns on the surface of the water show it as a flat plane above the plane of the underwater rock.

The area of water seen just below the rock discussed here should not be confused with areas of water that reflect the rock, which occur under other circumstances.

Notice in Figure 39 that sharpness of detail is found only on or above the surface. Underwater detail is blurred.

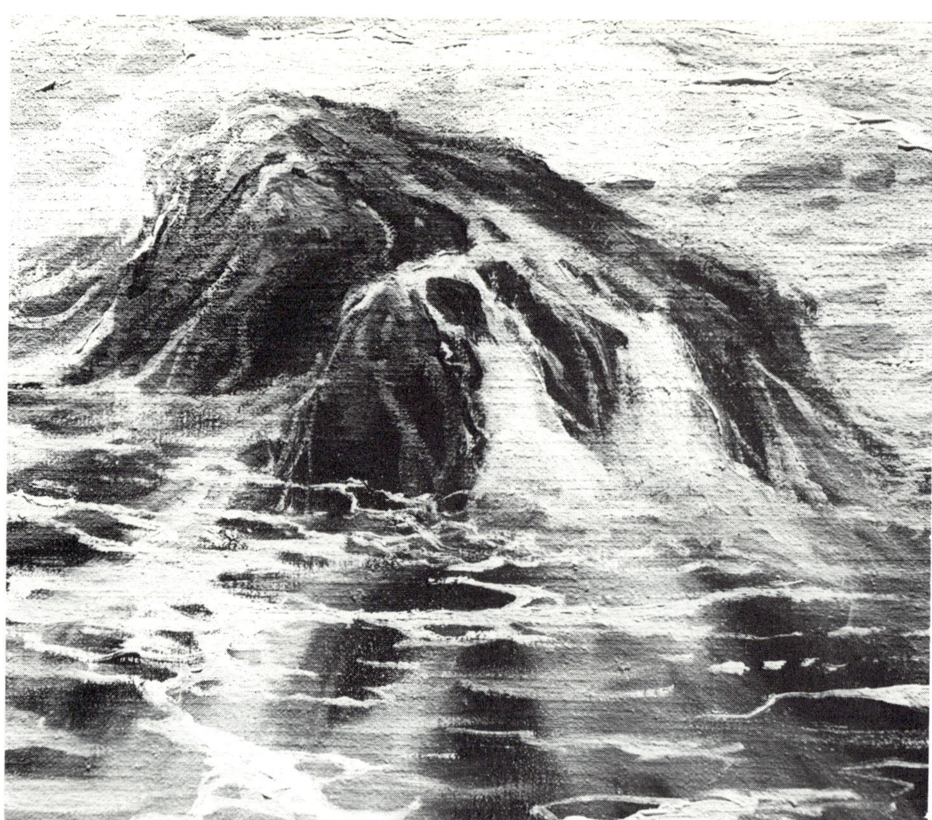

Figure 38. Water falling from a rock continues its movement underwater.

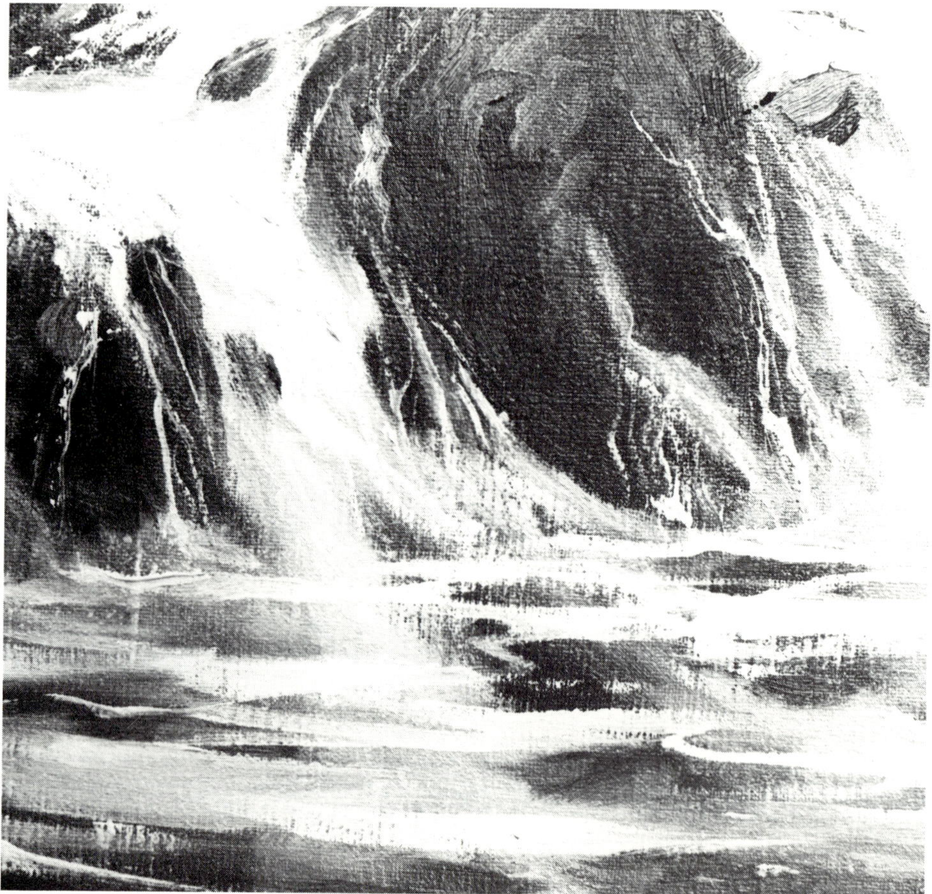

Figure 39. This extreme closeup shows how blurred underwater detail can become.

FALLING WATER

The water in Figure 40 is also falling over a rock or rock ledge. But in this case, it acts very much like the roll of a breaker; as the water falls, it mixes with air and becomes foamy in appearance. Leaving a portion transparent adds to the interest of the subject. The falling water is aerated on the left, but at least two planes of foamy water are visible. On the right, the dark rock is partially covered with clear water and partially with foamy water so that you get the feeling of two or three levels of depth.

When painting these planes or levels of depth, try to run the lines or brushstrokes in a slightly different direction for each level. In that way, there's less confusion and more chance of distinguishing one plane from another.

In Figure 41, the effect of falling water is used to strengthen the painting and lead to the main interest, the major wave. Without this foreground pattern and activity, the painting would be less interesting and more like others we've seen.

Try the step-by-step lessons on painting clear water below rocks (Demonstration 16), over sand (Demonstration 17), and in tide pools (Demonstration 18). Each one will give you something different and unusual to add to your paintings. You will find a demonstration of how to paint clear water over rocks in Demonstration 14.

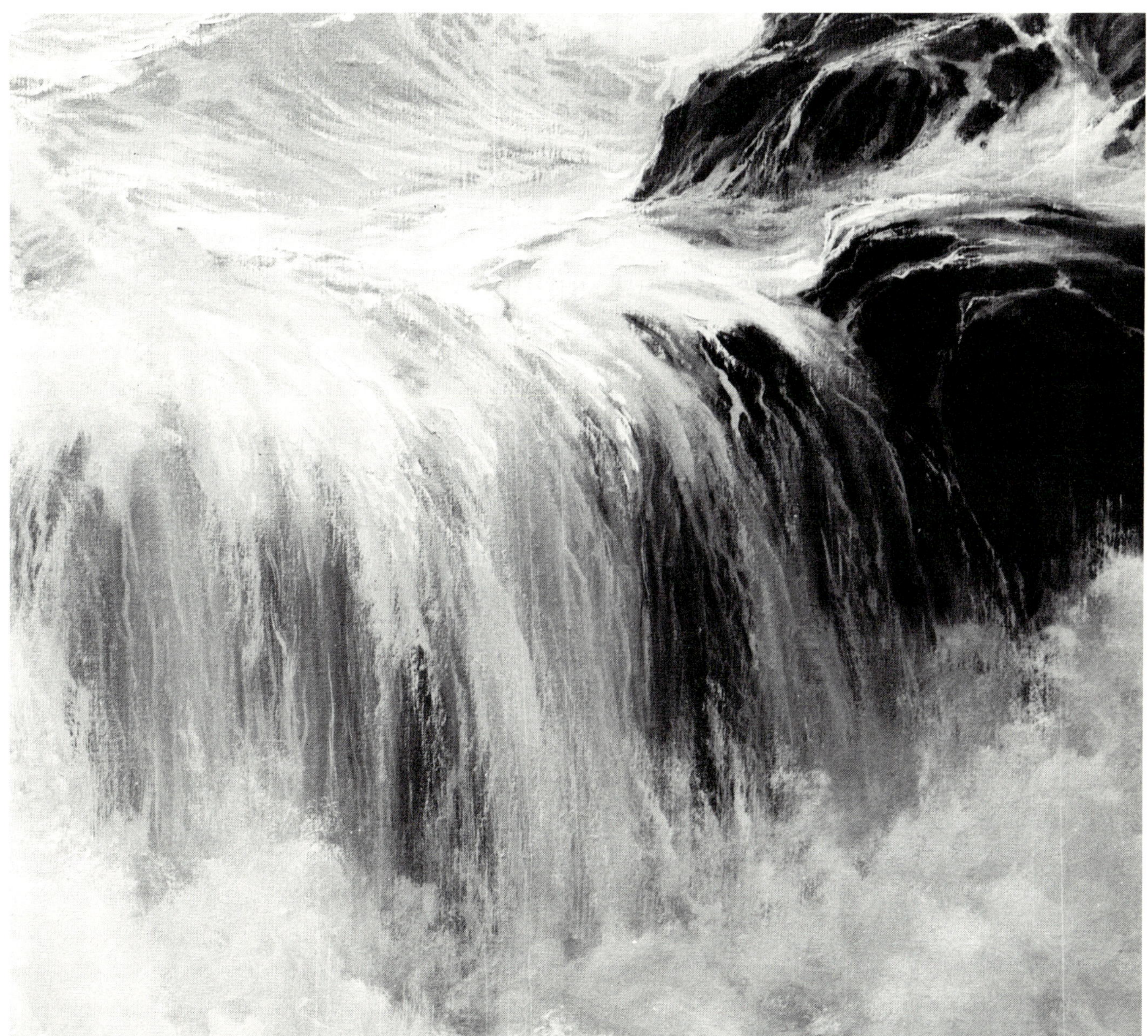

Figure 40. Here water falling over rocks acts more like a roll.

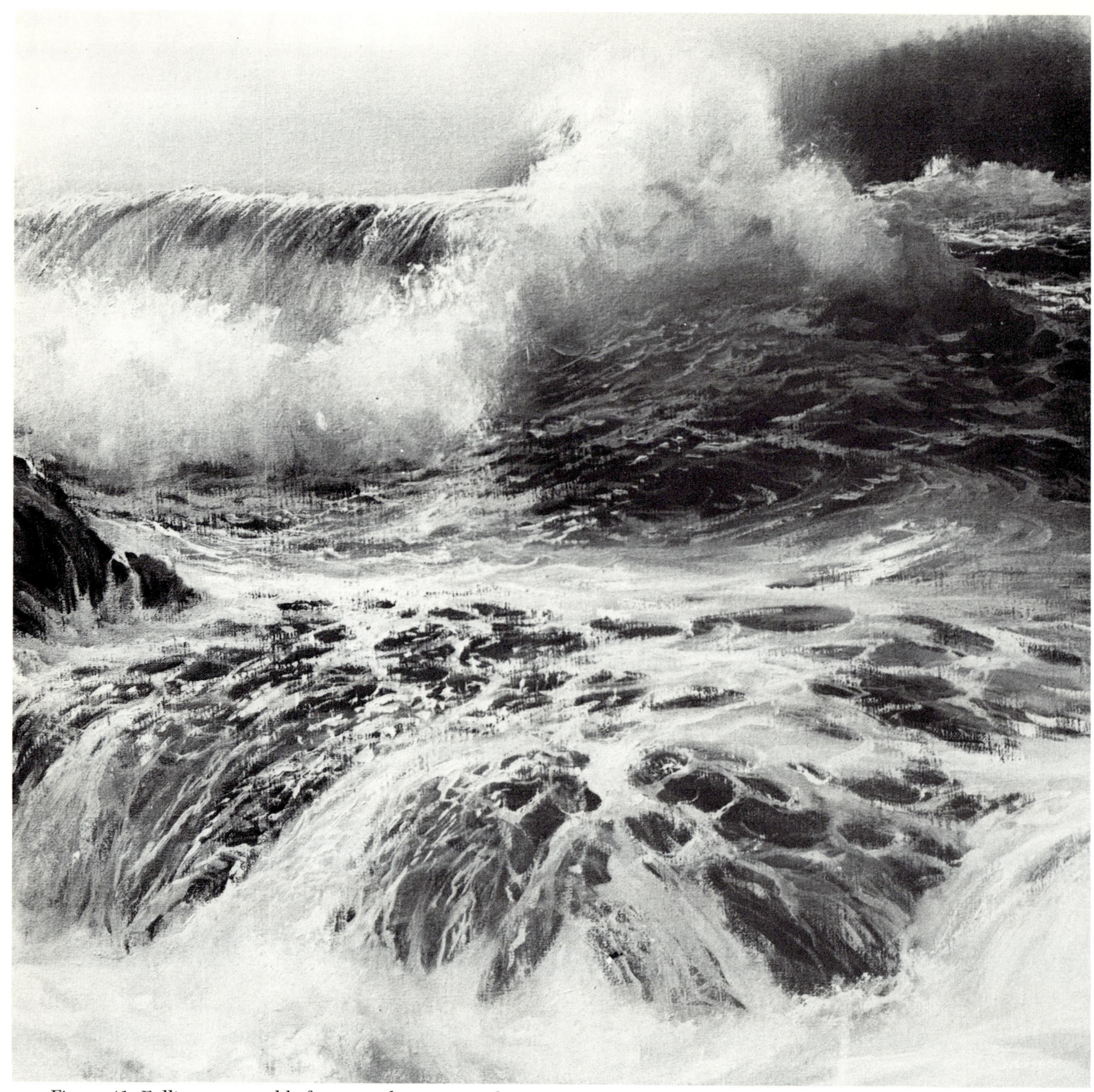

Figure 41. Falling water adds foreground interest to this painting of a major wave.

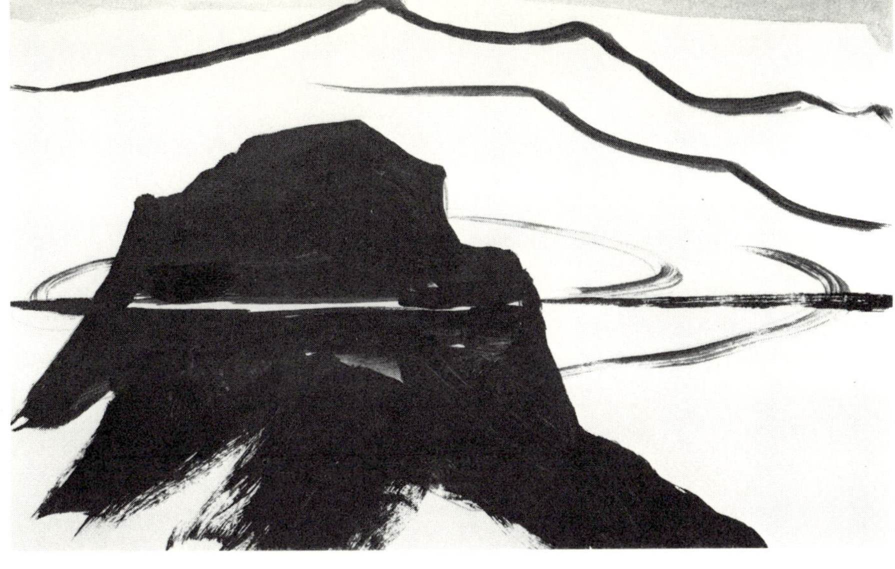

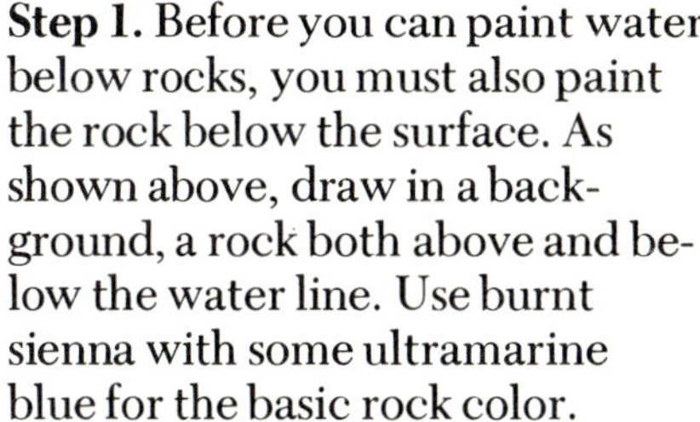

Step 1. Before you can paint water below rocks, you must also paint the rock below the surface. As shown above, draw in a background, a rock both above and below the water line. Use burnt sienna with some ultramarine blue for the basic rock color.

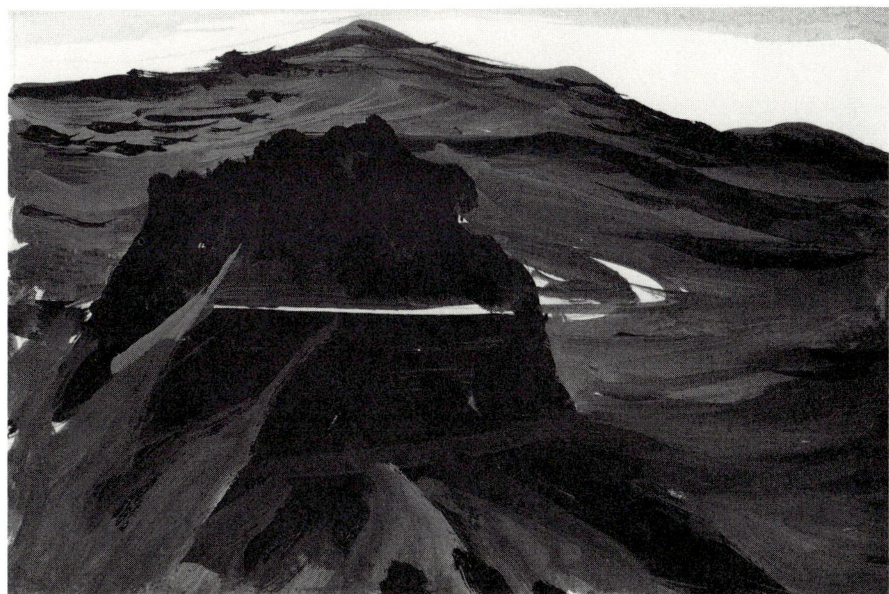

Step 2. Work in the color of water in the background and foreground. Start in the back with a dark blue and make it gradually greener (by using less blue in the blue-green mixture) as it reaches the foreground. Mix a pale blue-green (ultramarine/viridian) into white and paint it in where water would be pouring over the rock, even though the area is below the water line. Work a sky into the picture, and reflect it on the wave.

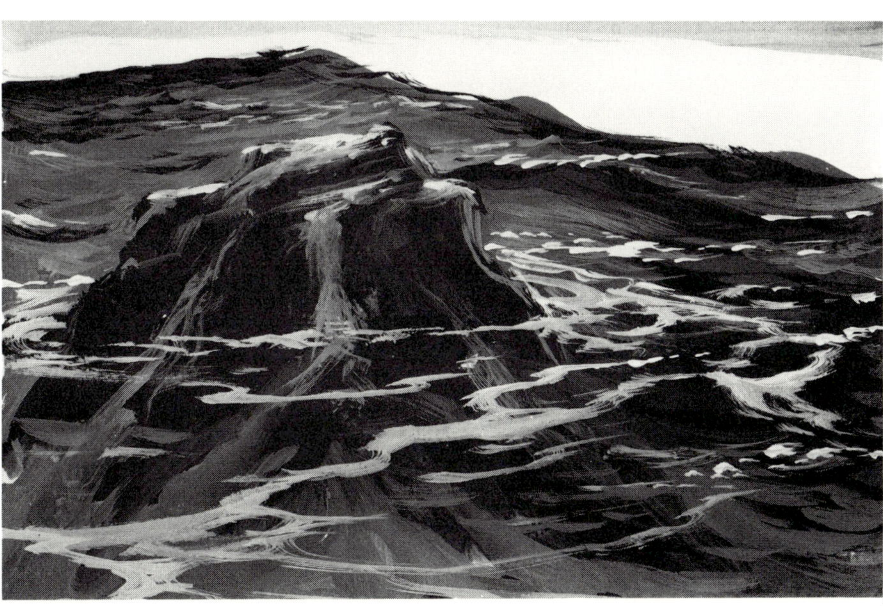

Step 3. This is the tricky part. Show the spills of water on the upper portion of rock and make them connect with those painted below the rock. Now, working in a different direction, paint in strokes of sky color. Then, using one mixture for light and one for shadowed foam (see Demonstrations 9 and 10 for color suggestions), paint in foam patterns to indicate the surface of the water. This lesson shows how to establish depth of water with two or more layers. The top layer, of course, is shown with a combination of sky and foam patterns.

DEMONSTRATION 17:
WATER OVER SAND

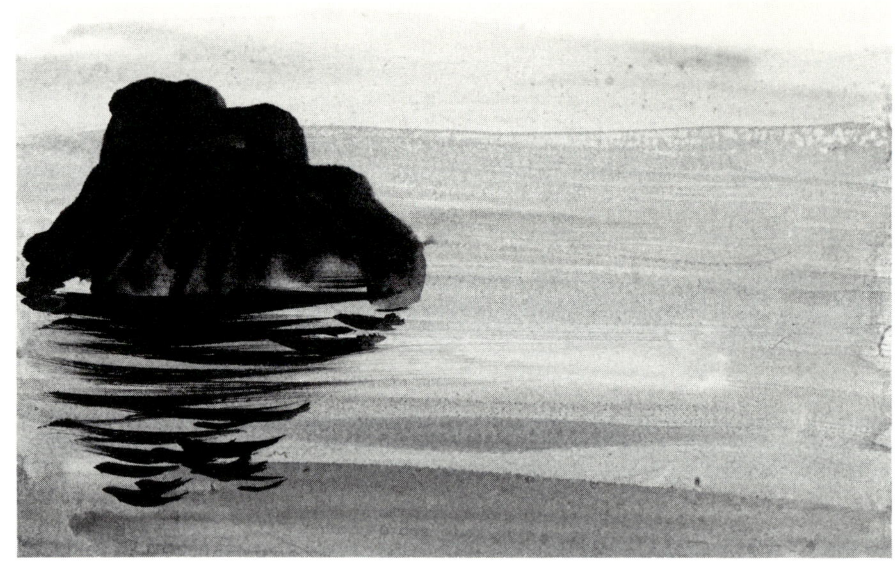

Step 1. When sand is wet but not flooded with foam, its true color shows through. Rocks and other objects reflect beautifully in it, and it also reflects the sky. Start with a simple composition of a rock, sky, and sand. Choose any color you wish for the rock and sky, but paint the sand with a mixture of burnt sienna and yellow ochre into white. Reflect the color of the rock in it after the sand color has been laid down.

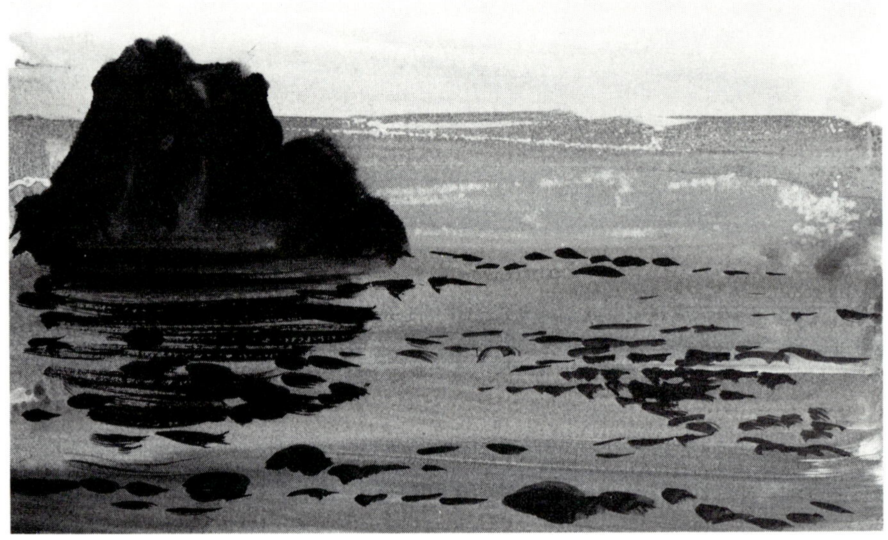

Step 2. For variety, add a few small rocks and pebbles to your composition, using the same color as the first rock, and place them in groups. Adding paint to paint can be messy unless you follow this advice: The underpaint should be thin, and the paint to be added should be thick. Lay down the new paint in one clean stroke, if possible.

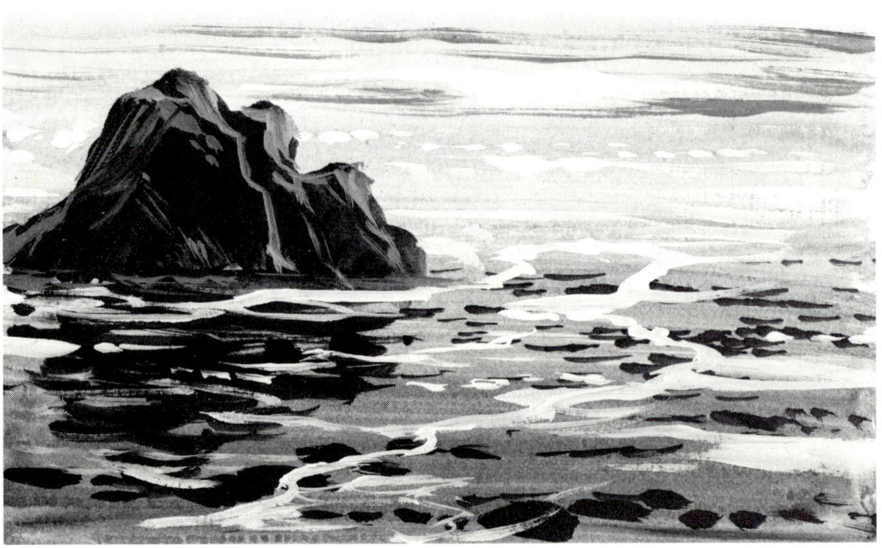

Step 3. This is similar to painting water below rocks; you're establishing more than one level. Here you add to the sand a few strokes of color from the sky, but the major distinction will come when you add foam patterns or ripples that reflect light.

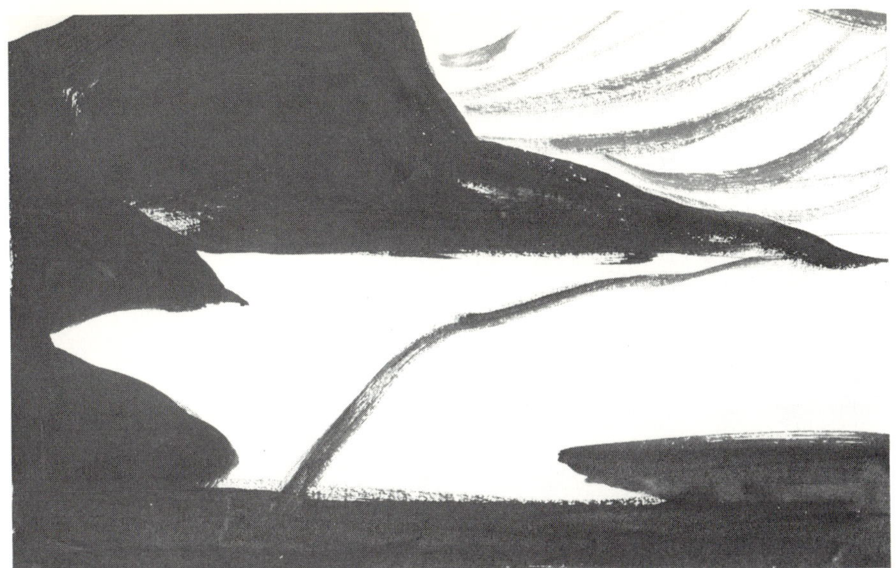

Step 1. Another form of transparent water is found in tide pools. These are usually so interesting that they might as well be the center of interest. However, there are times when you may want them in the foreground; so practice this method for painting them. Start with any background, but put in a large rock and some foreground rocks. Indicate where your rocks will reflect.

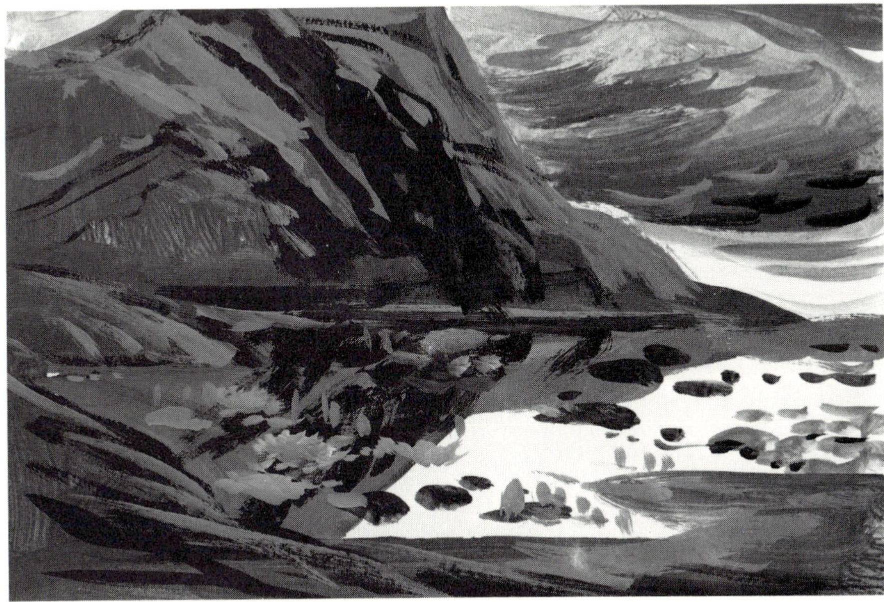

Step 2. Reflect the rocks and the sky, even though no sky shows, and add the reflected colors of the sky. Also add a few pebbles and anything else one might find in a tide pool.

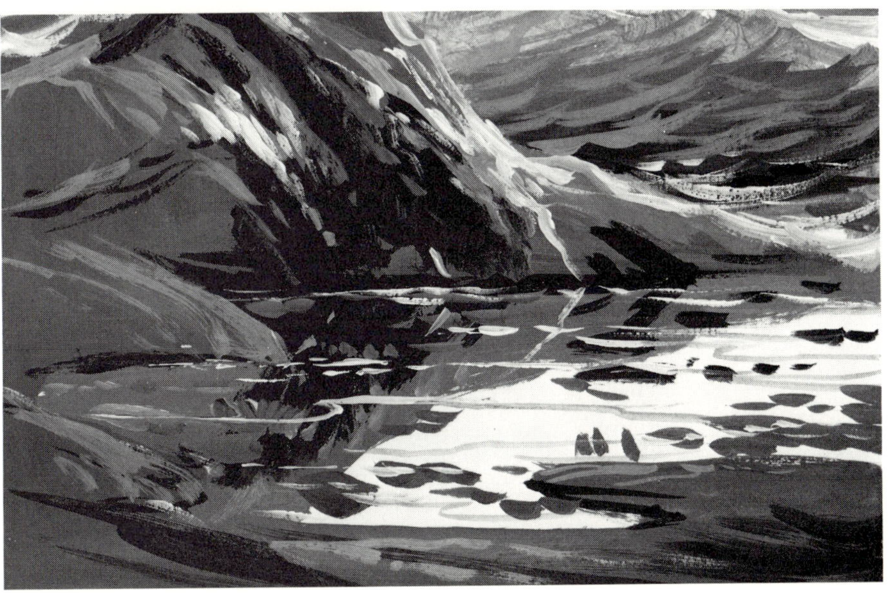

Step 3. For the final step, add sunlight reflections and a few ripples and glints on the water of the pool. There shouldn't be too much activity disturbing the quiet of the pool.

CHAPTER SIX

THE REFLECTING SURFACE

Water is a natural reflector of light. At its quietest, it acts like a mirror. As it becomes rippled with swells, the mirror image is lost, but it still reflects color and the objects above and around it. It's not until the surface is totally covered with choppy foam that the reflected image is lost. Even then, some reflection of color will remain.

Your paintings will achieve more realism if you have a basic understanding of surface reflection. First, keep in mind that the flat surface or troughs between waves always reflects the sky. Only the vertical face of the wave doesn't fully reflect the sky (the reflection usually appears only near the top edge).

Second, sunlight is always reflected from the surface of the sea. If the angle is correct, it may even be reflected from a vertical wave. Third, objects may or may not reflect from the water's surface, depending on their distance and the activity of the sea.

With sky color (atmosphere) and sunlight always reflecting from the sea—and rocks and other objects sometimes reflecting, the next consideration is *how* they reflect.

Practice the step-by-step lessons at the end of this chapter on reflecting the sun, rocks, and foam in the water. As you paint, keep in mind the idea of a mirror, but with a wrinkled surface. Think of the mirror as having the ability to reflect not only what is above, but also what is below. When you understand this, you'll understand the reflecting properties of the sea.

REFLECTING THE SKY
IN SMOOTH WATER

As I mentioned earlier the sky is always reflected from the surface of the sea. The exceptions are on the vertical face of a wave or body of foam, and on heavy surface foam, where very little of the sky's reflection is seen. There's really nothing mysterious or difficult involved here, so I'm surprised that more students don't practice this.

Smooth water allows more of the sky color to reflect than rough water. Other than denoting the outline of some swells or small chops, the sky's reflection almost always remains in the troughs between swells. It doesn't reflect off the vertical faces of waves or rocks enough to warrant attention.

To reflect the sky, first determine the color of the sea and paint it in. Next, choose the sky color and paint it in. Finally, draw the contours of background swells, using the same mixture as the sky. In the middle and foregrounds, blend the sky color into the water's color in the troughs between the swells (Figure 42).

Figure 43 shows another example of using the sky to reflect in smooth water. Here the viewer is looking down, seeing more of the trough. The reflections of the sky actually create the contours of the waves and indicate their direction at the same time.

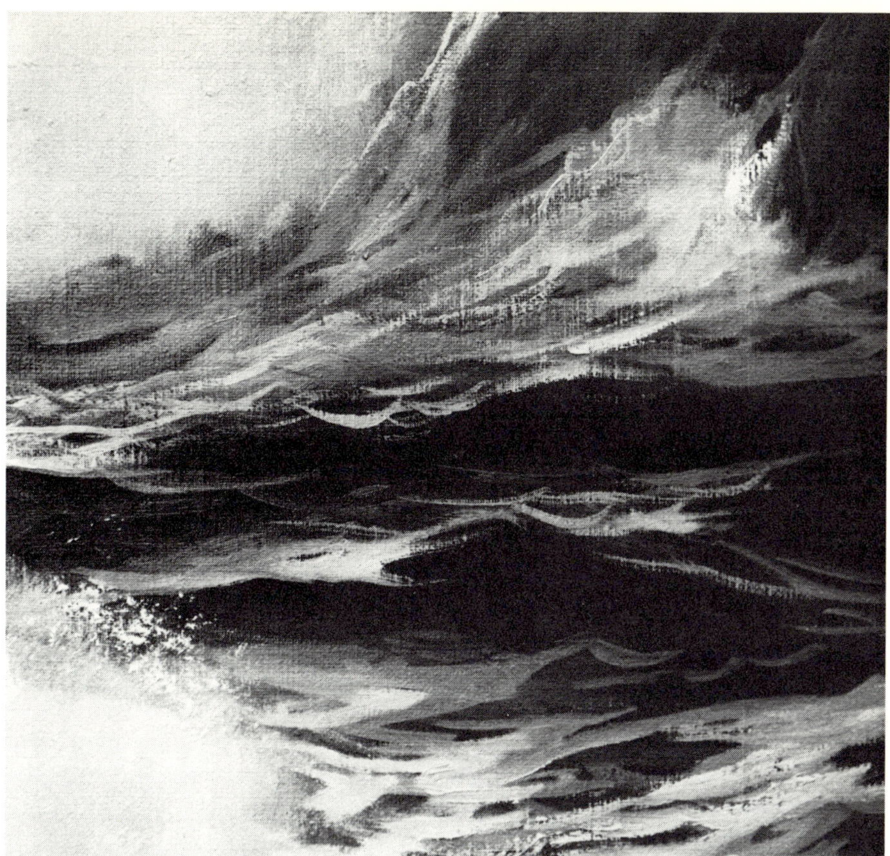

Figure 42. The color of the sky is reflected in the troughs between swells.

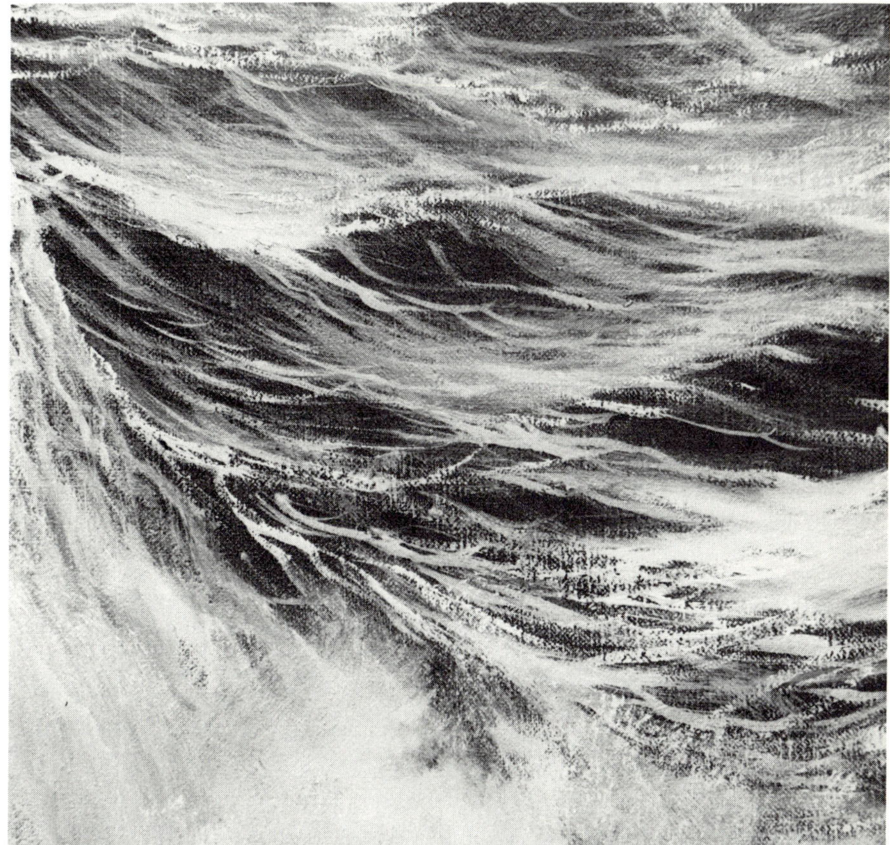

Figure 43. Sky light draws the contours of the wave and indicates their direction.

Choppy water, unless covered with foam, still reflects the value and color of the sky. In the detail (Figure 44) the sky reflections can be seen as the middle-toned strokes that show up in the dark areas. The very light reflections are sunlight. Combining sky, sunlight, and other objects along with light and shadowed foam trails can be confusing.

Figure 45 shows a portion of a larger composition in which the background is brilliant light in fog. Therefore, the sky is very light and backlights this choppy water. It's nearly as light as the reflection of the sun; but in fog, sunlight and sky are nearly one.

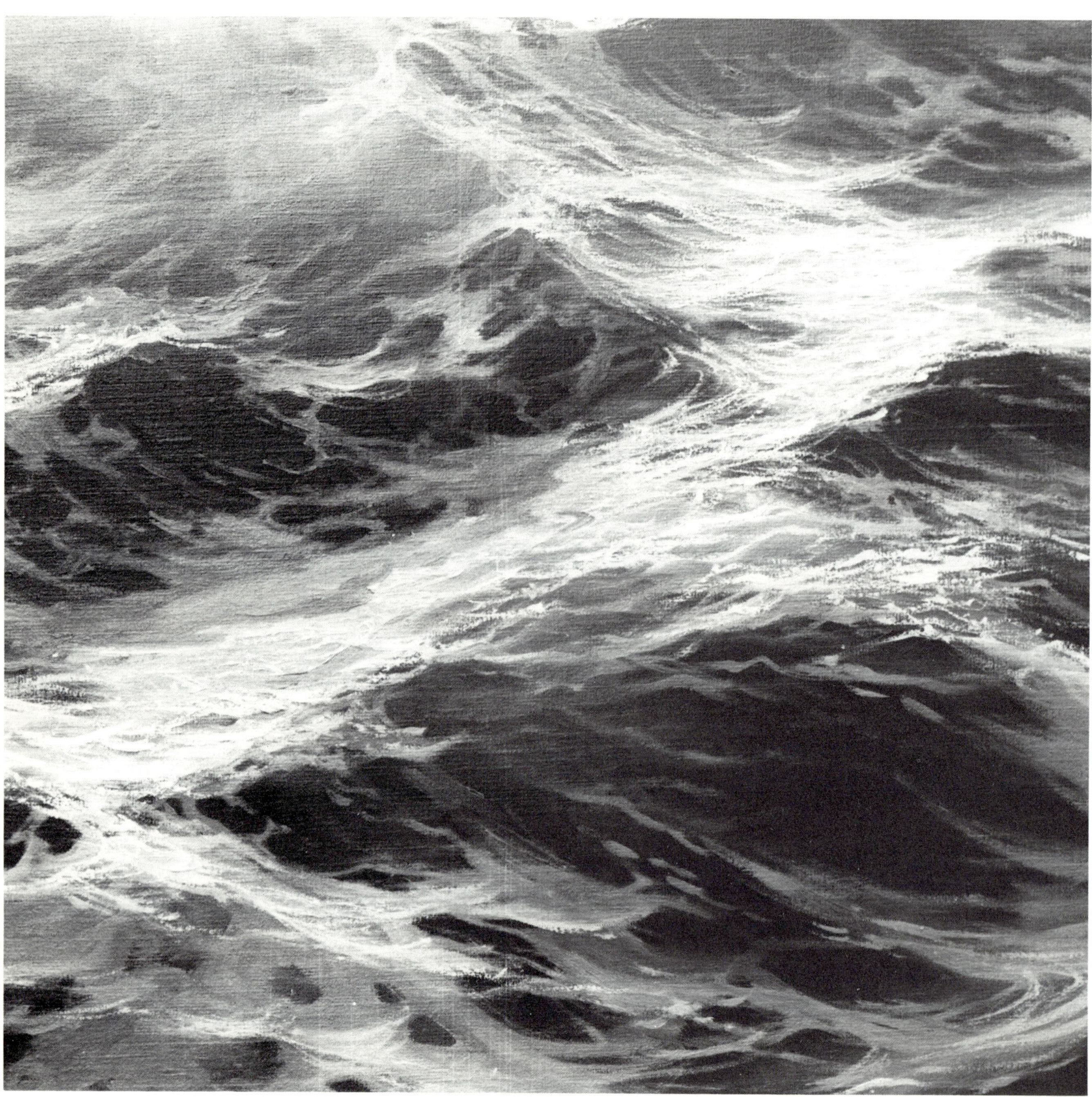

Figure 44. Both sky light (in the darker areas) and sunlight contour waves here.

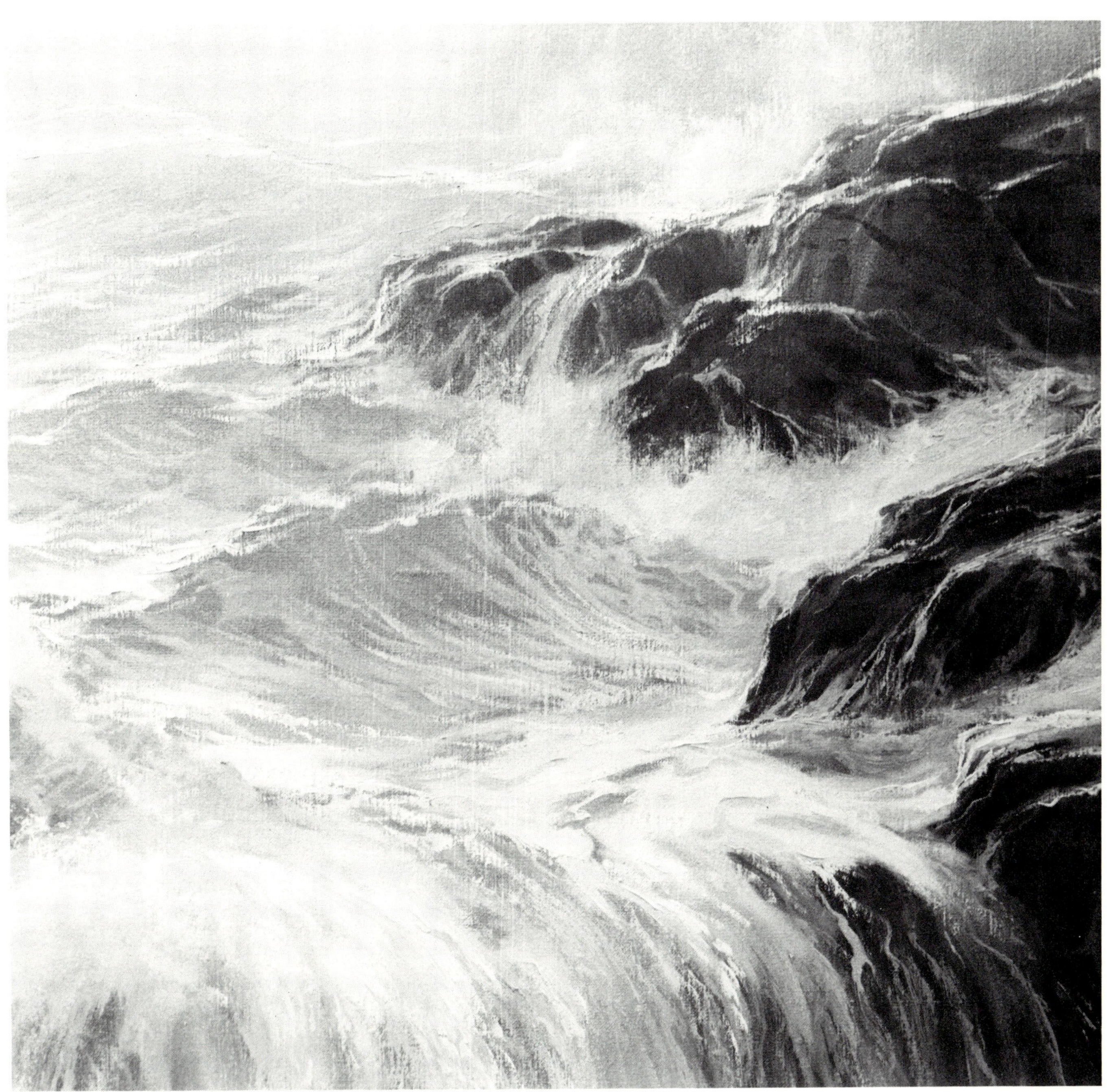

Figure 45. A brilliant light shining through fog back lights this choppy water.

By "the sun" I mean the physical body of the sun rather than general sunlight, which will be discussed in Chapter Nine. The ball of sun itself sometimes reflects an image to the viewer's eyes when the angle of the sun to the sea is equal to the angle from which you view it.

The sharp, bright reflection of the sun in the foreground can help a center of interest, be an echo of light needed for balance, or it can simply add interest to your painting. Reflecting the sun itself is also a tricky but useful device for breaking the monotony of too many foam patterns.

Be careful to keep the image natural. For example, an impossible image would be reflected sun in the foreground with the real sun in the background behind a cloud.

As in Figure 46, it's most effective when confined to a small area. Notice that the dark holes in the foam are all around the area reflecting the sun and that the foam itself continues right through the reflecting area. In Figure 47 the sun, glaring off a spot of smooth water, is reflected in the holes of mass foam patterns. Its primary effect here is to diminish detail, even blur it, in the area of reflecting light. For a lesson on how to paint the sun's reflections on water, see Demonstration 19.

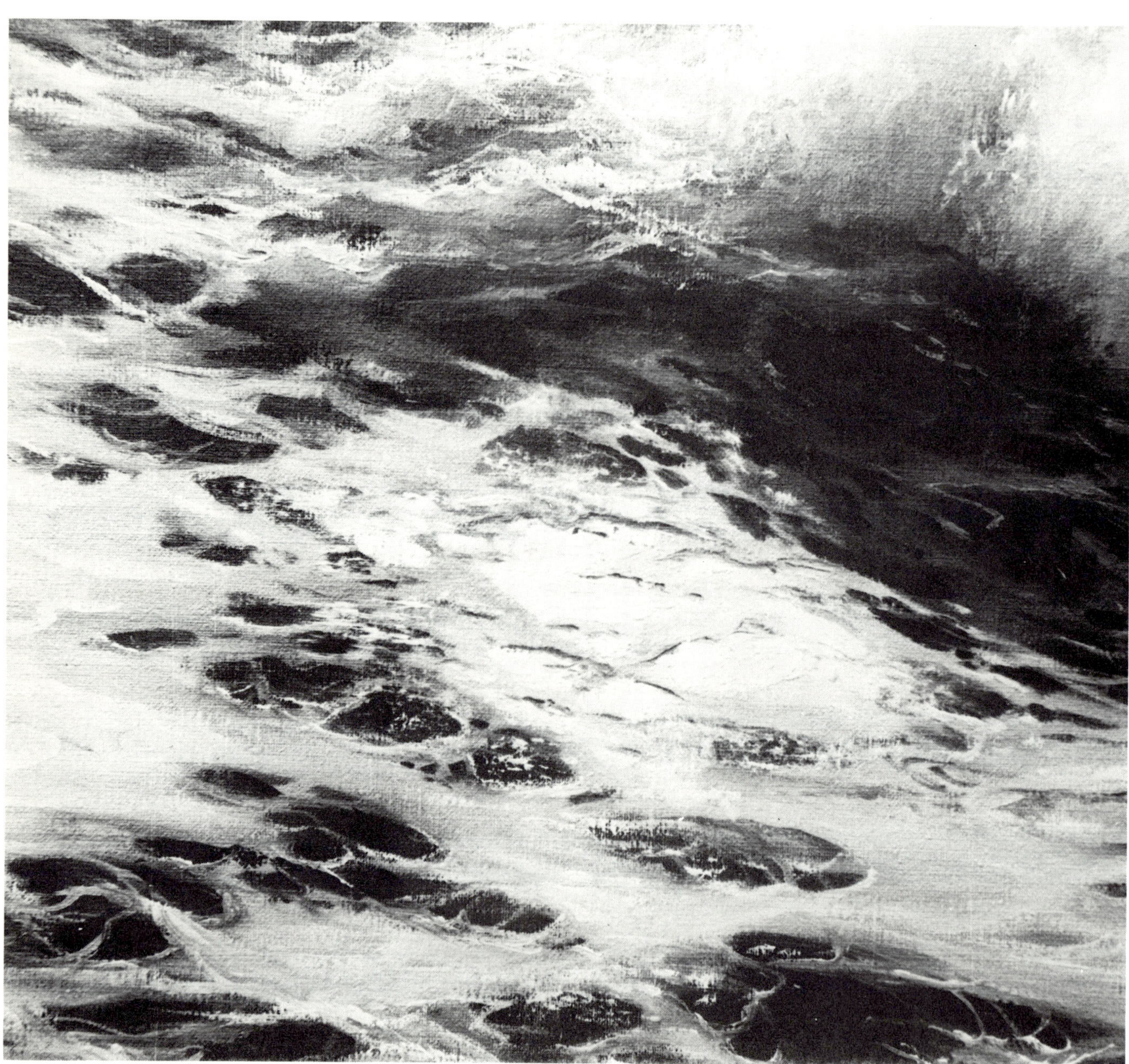

Figure 46. Try reflecting the sun as a device to break up too many foam patterns.

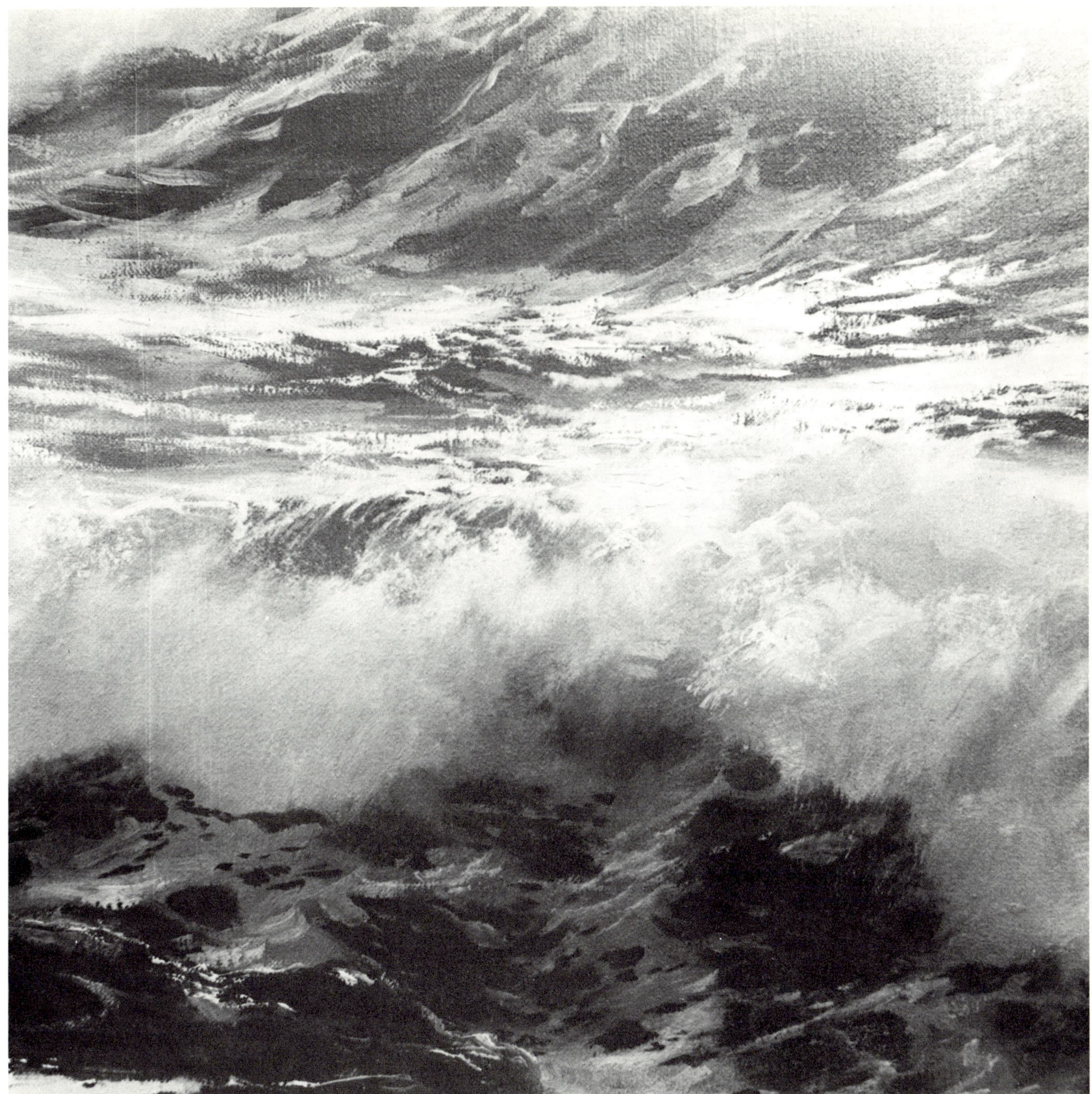

Figure 47. The sun obscures detail wherever it strikes.

REFLECTING ROCKS
IN SMOOTH WATER

If the water lies absolutely still, a rock may reflect a mirror image. The problem most students have with reflections is getting the mirror image to look right. The mirror image occurs only on very smooth water, which is rather unusual in the surf.

In Figure 48, I show a closeup of a rock that is partially mirrored. The image is broken by ridges of sand and reflection of the sky. If the water were choppy, the image would be nearly lost, as it is in Demonstration 20 at the end of this chapter. Figure 49 shows another variation on reflecting a rock. The water is smooth because it's on the beach. Even so, there are ripples and pebbles, etc., to break up the image. Notice the reflected sunlight and sky on the chops behind the rock.

When reflecting rocks or bluffs in choppy water, keep the reflecting color in the same general area as you would a mirror image, but allow it to actually reflect only in the troughs between chops.

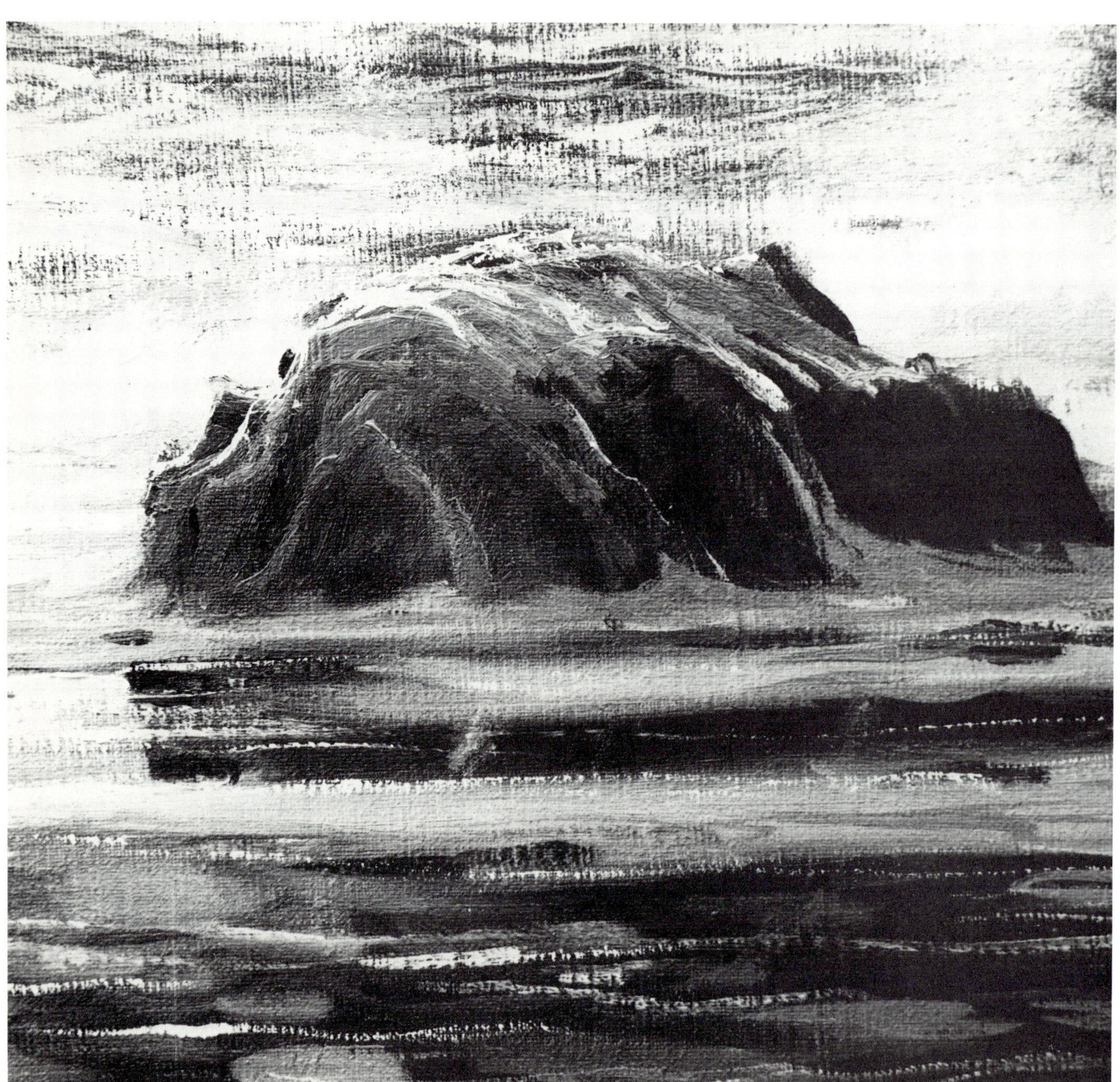

Figure 48. I prefer to hint at reflections rather than exploit them.

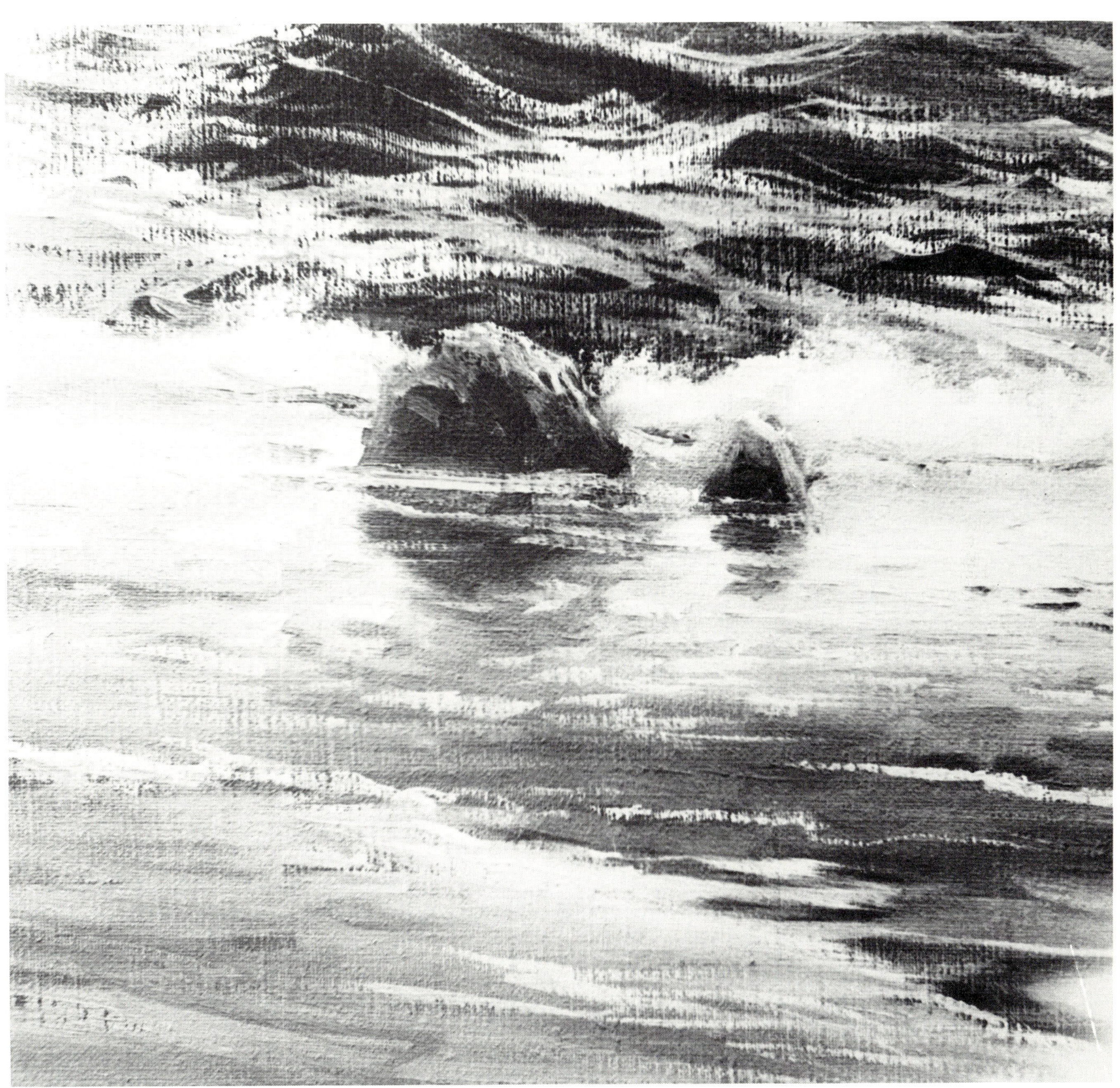

Figure 49. A rock is reflected in the smooth wet sand of a beach.

REFLECTING FOAM
IN SMOOTH WATER

Many students forget that the white foam of breakers and foam bursts reflect on the surface below them. If the surface is relatively smooth, as in Figure 50, quite a bit of foam is reflected below. Again, I'm not referring to mirror image reflections. Smooth water in the surf is just water that has little or no foam on it and a minimum of chops. In this case, the wave foam reflects directly below to the surface and actually points up the minor chops.

In Figure 51 the water is rippled with tiny chops. Although the foam reflects less, the sea is still smooth enough to reflect the white foam of the breaker. In both figures, please note that the light-reflecting strokes are used to show the extent of the water's activity. In other words, let the reflections on the foam draw the contours of the water in the foreground.

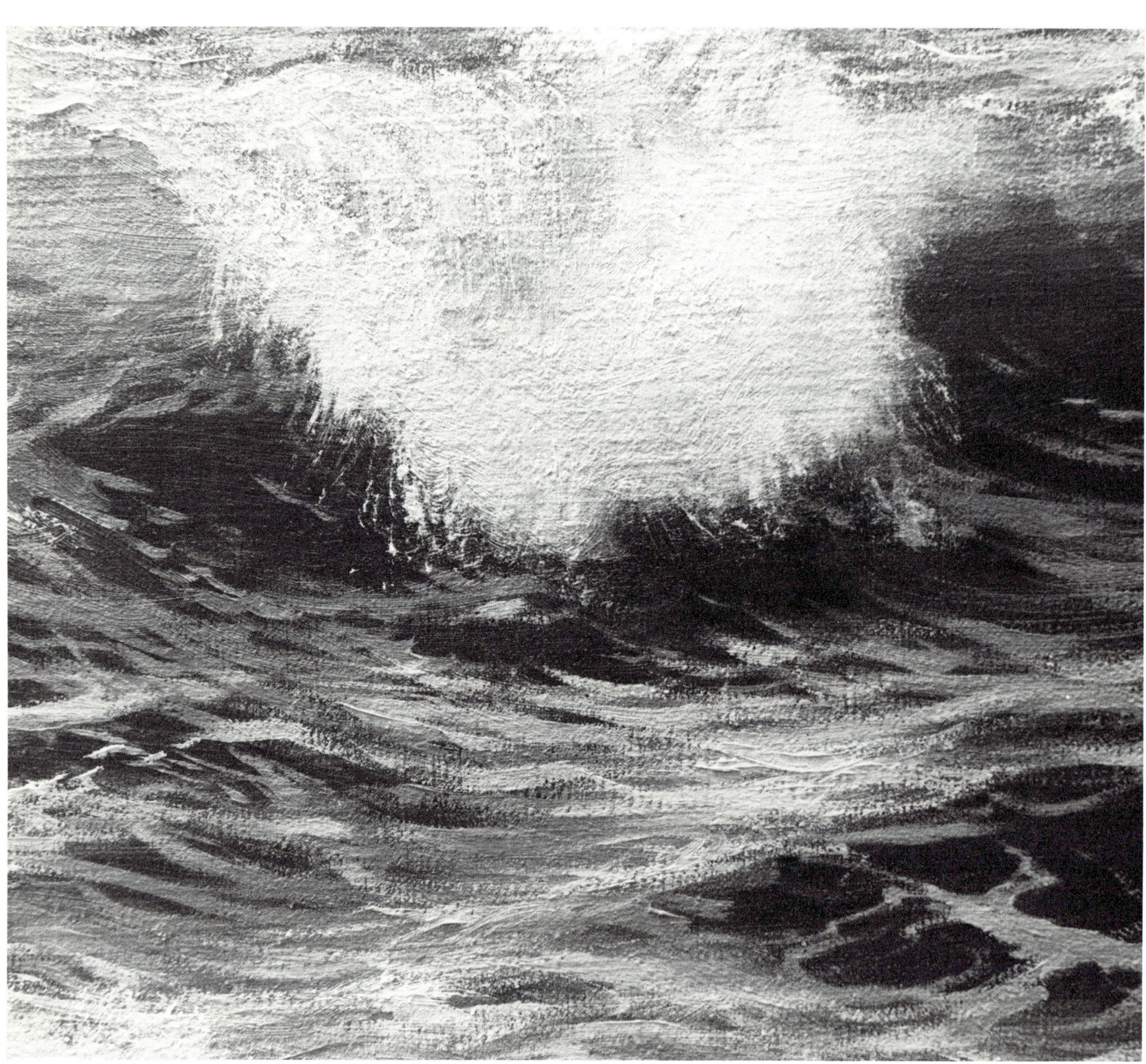

Figure 50. The smoother the water's surface, the more foam reflecting below.

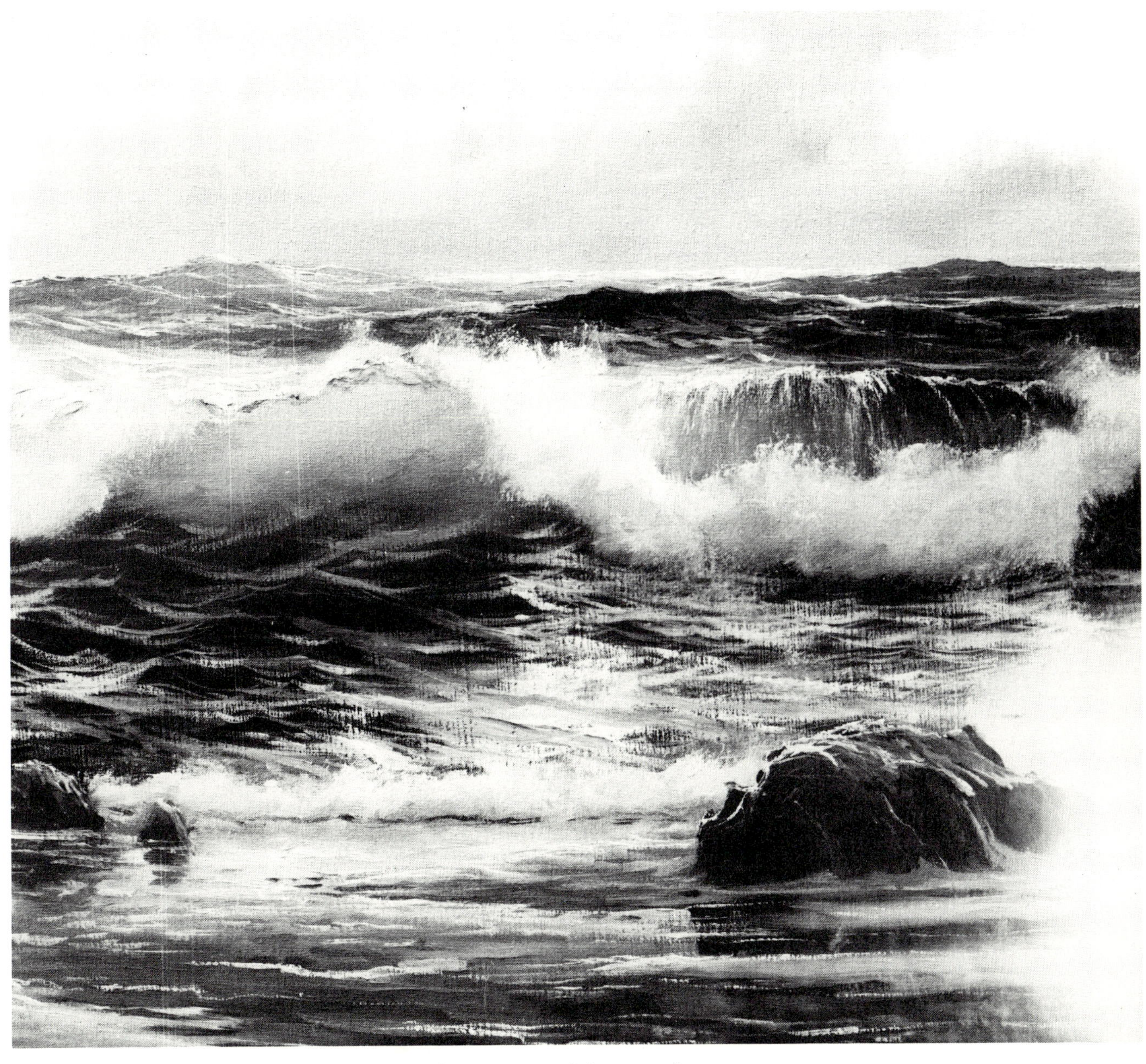

Figure 51. Notice how the reflections follow the contours of the tiny chops.

REFLECTING FOAM
IN CHOPPY WATER

Figure 52 shows the use of reflecting foam in water that is somewhat more choppy than in Figures 50 and 51. If the surface were to become much choppier than this, it would either become foamy or simply cease to reflect accurately.

Sometimes the only way to show contours or changes in direction in a shadowed area is to lighten the surface with reflections. In Figure 53, the foam provides a way. Notice that it reflects in only a few strokes, but those few reflections completely change the basic shape and foam of the wave. (See also Demonstration 21 for how to paint reflecting foam.)

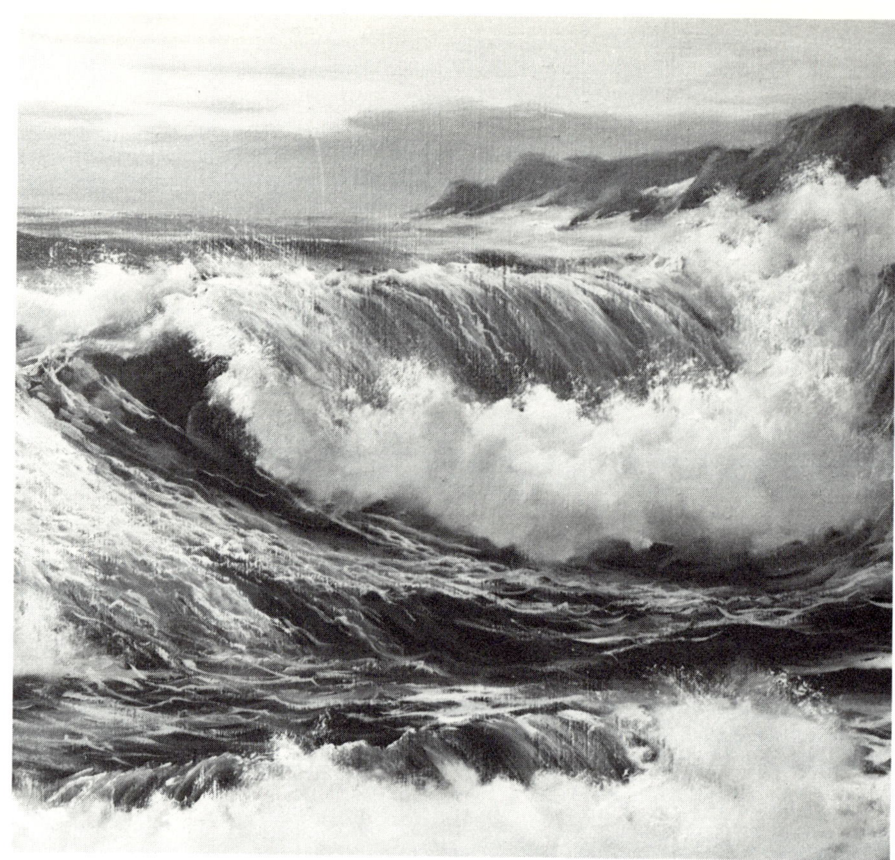

Figure 52. This is about as choppy as water can get and still reflect.

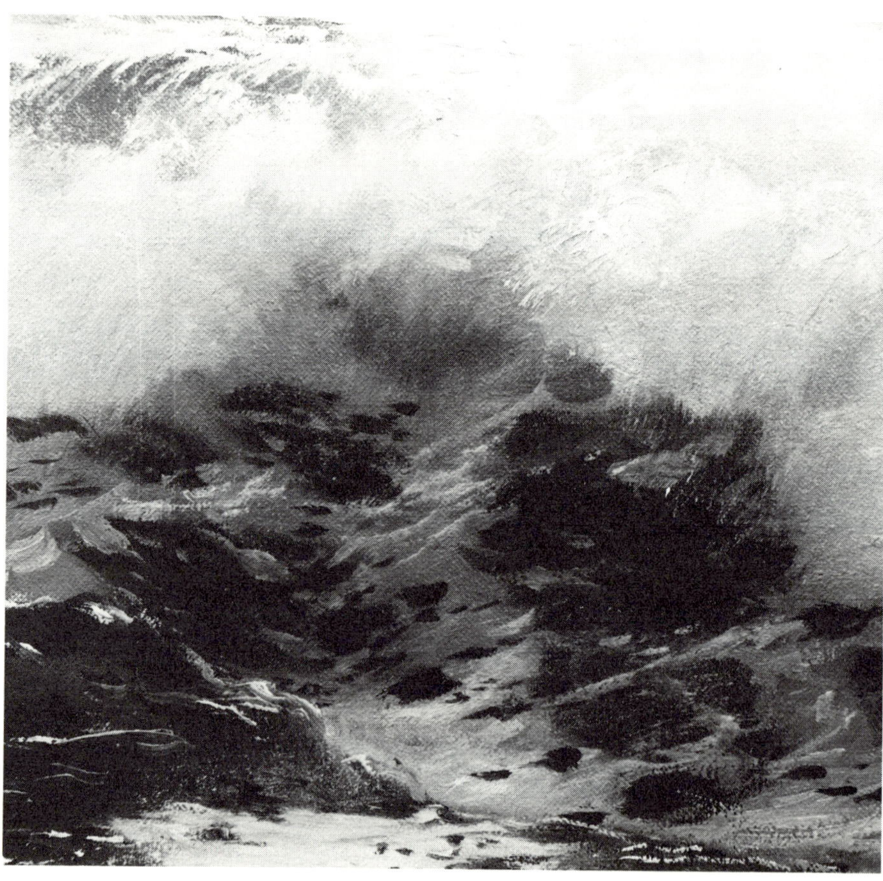

Figure 53. Foam provides an excuse for lightening a shadowed area.

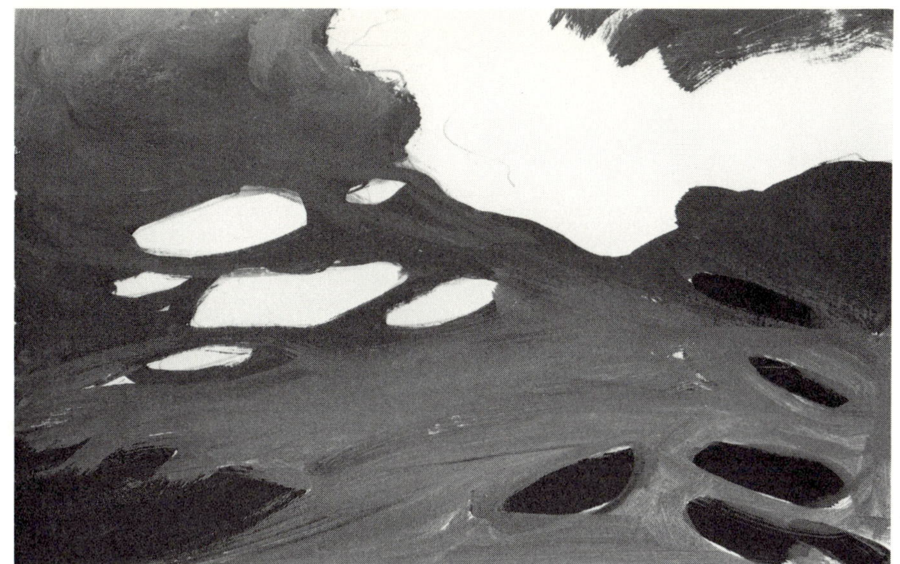

Step 1. Sometimes the sun hits a small area of smooth water at just the right angle and reflects back to our eyes. Draw a wave that will be covered with mass foam (see Chapter Seven) and group together holes where water shows through. Let some holes reflect the sun (use white with a touch of cadmium yellow) and paint in the rest as shadowed foam or reflected sky color and mass foam patterns.

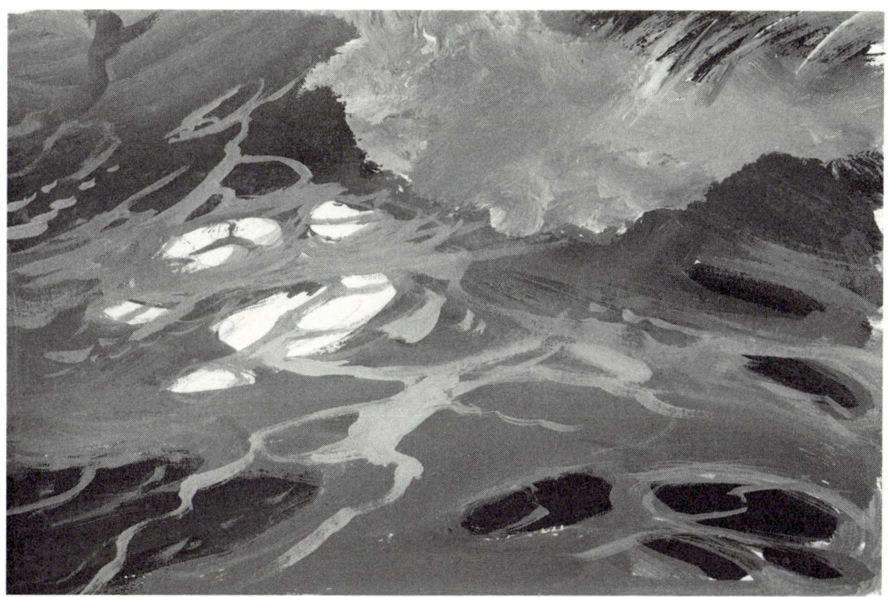

Step 2. Paint in the wave foam as you have before. Now add linear patterns of foam over the mass foam. Allow some to pass over the area reflecting the sun. (The foam patterns would not reflect the light.)

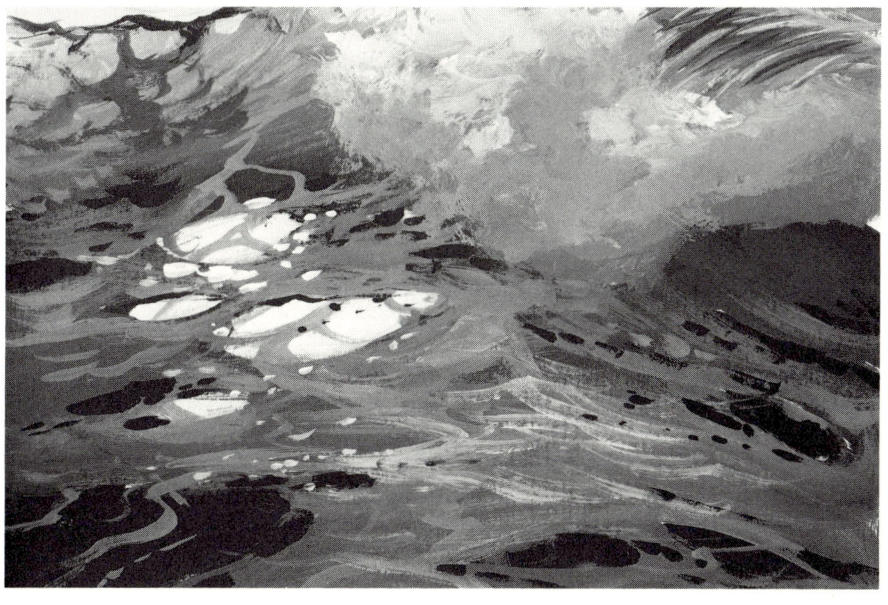

Step 3. Finally, here's more practice of previous lessons. Add highlights to the wave foam and reflect the foam in the foreground, working some silhouette patterns into the wave. Finally, add a few small spots of pure sunlight color near major holes of light in the water.

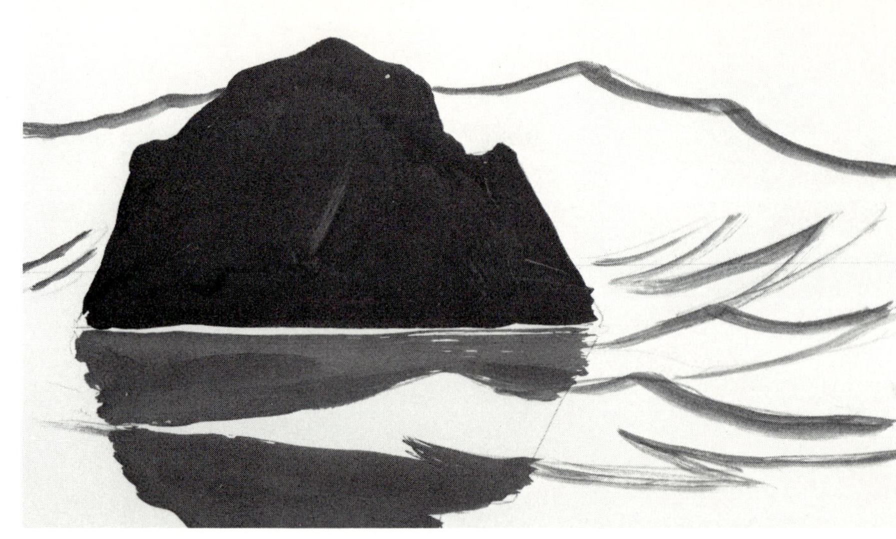

Step 1. Any reflection is a mirror image; but in the sea, the reflection will most often be very distorted, or at least interrupted. Start by drawing in a background and foreground of swells. Paint in a basic rock and let it reflect in the water. Notice that the reflection is slightly lighter than the rock, and that it hasn't been reflected where a minor swell will appear.

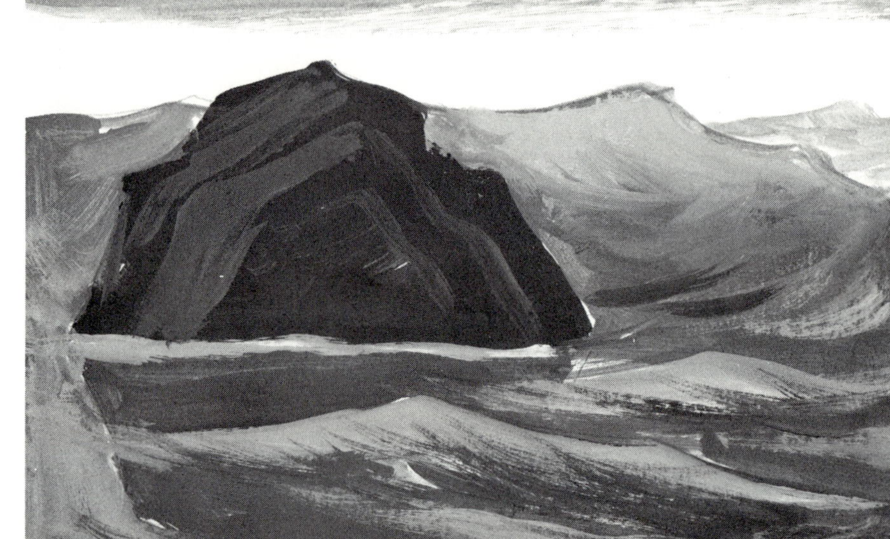

Step 2. Work in your basic color scheme for water and sky. Reflect the sky on the rocks and foreground. Notice that the swell in the area of the rock's reflection has a dark base and gradually lightens toward the top, just like a major swell that's thin at the top. and is therefore lighter.

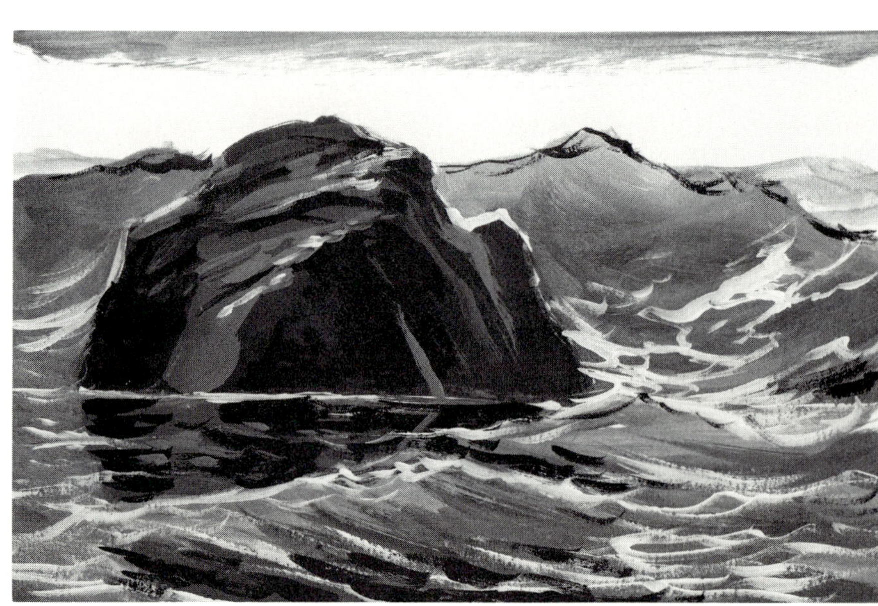

Step 3. Increase some of the darkness in the reflected area. Work in reflected lights to show contours on the rock, and paint in foam patterns or light ripples. Either one will show contours. This rock would ordinarily reflect its full image in smooth water, but the image has been broken by a swell and distorted by reflected sky and sunlight where the water is rippled.

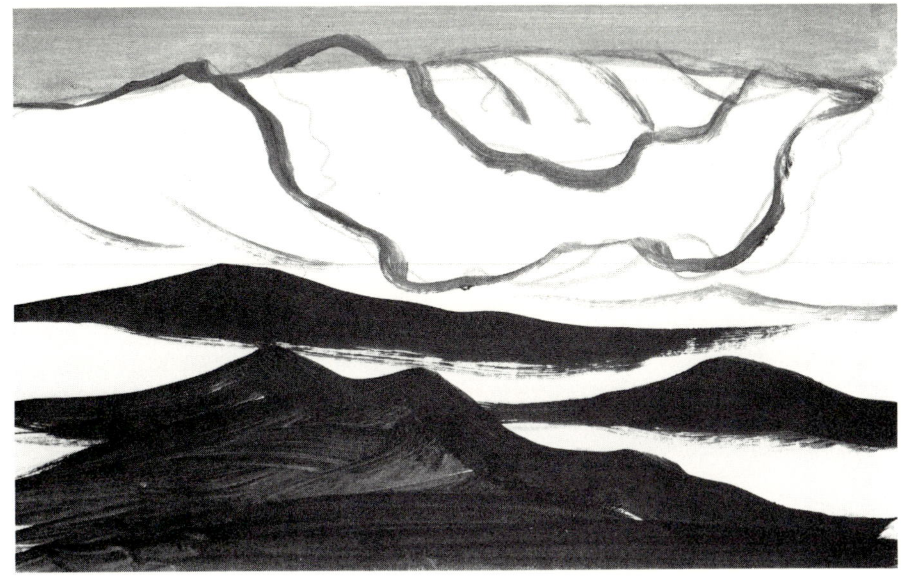

Step 1. Begin by drawing a breaker. Paint in the sky of your choice and a choppy foreground. Reflecting white foam will eventually show the contours of the foreground chops as well as the color of direct sunlight.

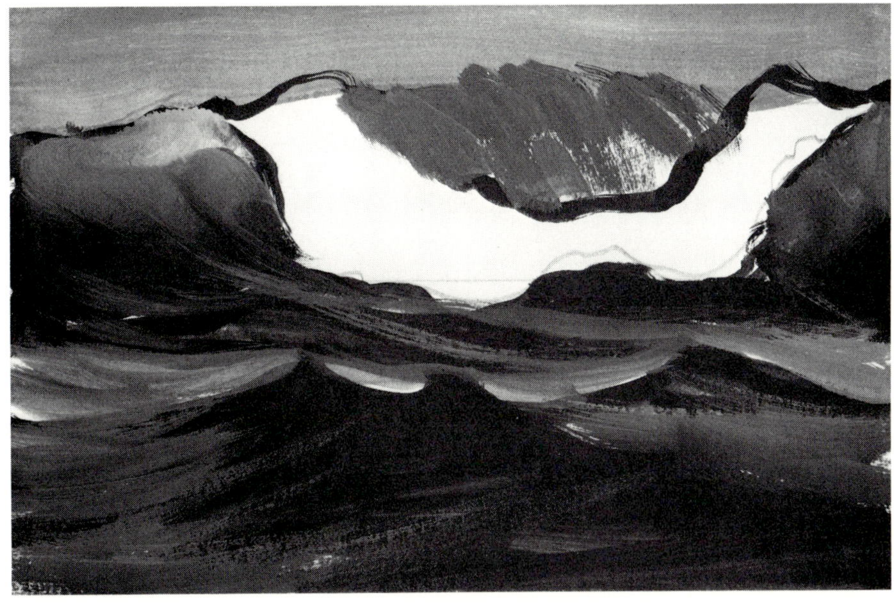

Step 2. Paint in the water. Here's a good place to practice painting the translucent water of the wave. Also, reflect the sky. Make sure the sky reflections show the dips and valleys and general contours of the foreground.

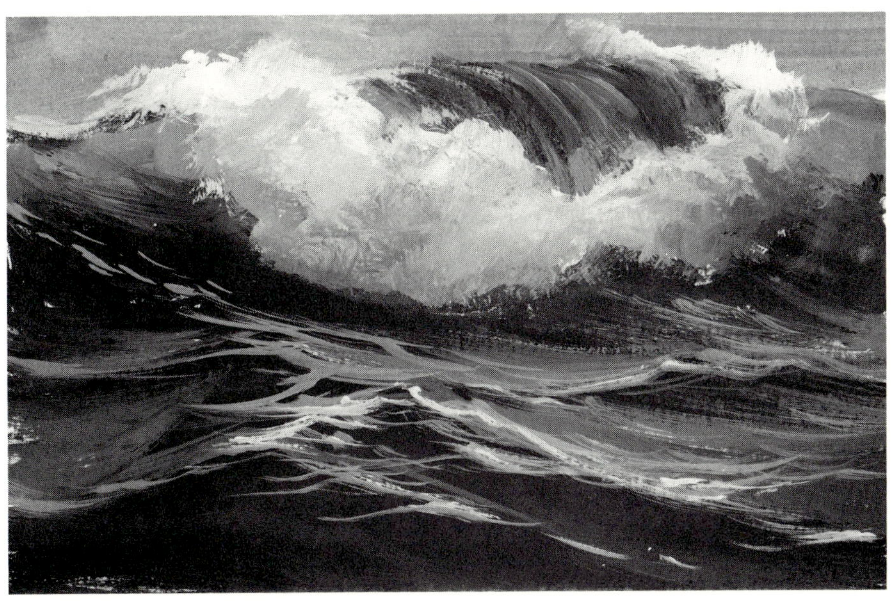

Step 3. Again you can practice what has been tried before. First paint the breaker foam, as in Demonstration 9, making sure that its edges range from soft to harsh, and light to shadow. Finally, reflect the foam color onto the foreground. Use a small brush and, in sweeping the reflected foam, follow the contours of the surface already established. Add a few more minor chops.

CHAPTER SEVEN

THE FOAMY SURFACE

I've stated before that foam is water and air mixed. In the case of breaker foam and foam bursts, the foam is in the process of mixing. In surface foam, the mixture is longer lasting and, because of the constant action, holds together as a body.

You'll need to continue thinking of the surface as a mirror, but now you must picture the mirror partially covered with a thin layer of foam.

The step-by-step lessons that follow at the end of this chapter will give you further help in painting foam. Practice them and try to achieve some mastery before applying them to a painting.

LINEAR PATTERNS

Linear foam patterns are a problem to all sea painters, beginners or old-timers. Keep in mind that they look best when allowed to vary in size, connect and break, run through light and shadow, and show the contours of the surface over which they lie. If that seems like a big order, it shows the importance of using linear patterns correctly.

The lines that the foam breaks up into are ideal for showing the contours of the rising and falling surface (Figure 54). Know your source of light and learn to use sunlight and shadow (which will be discussed in Chapter Nine). Under the strong lighting effects of sunlight and shadow, the linear foam patterns show form.

In Figure 55 the main pattern of line is the path of sunlight, but it's supported by shadowed linear foam patterns that add interest as well as break up an otherwise large, blank area of the composition.

Notice that the holes in the foam are neither perfectly rounded nor all the same size. However, when they lie flat they're more elliptical than the rounded form they take on when they're more nearly vertical. A step-by-step lesson on painting linear patterns follows at the end of this chapter (Demonstration 22).

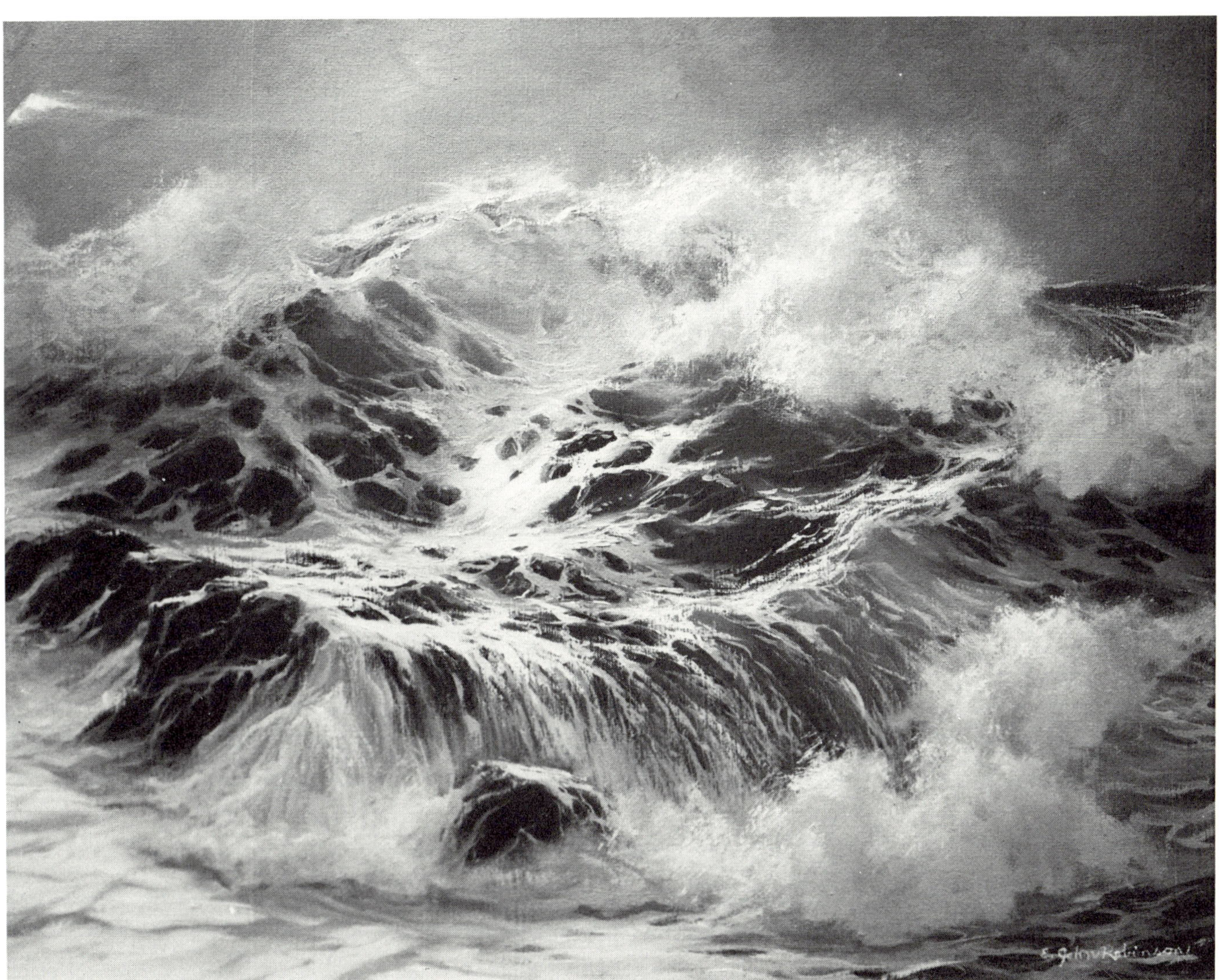

Figure 54. Lines of foam contour the rising and falling surface of the sea.

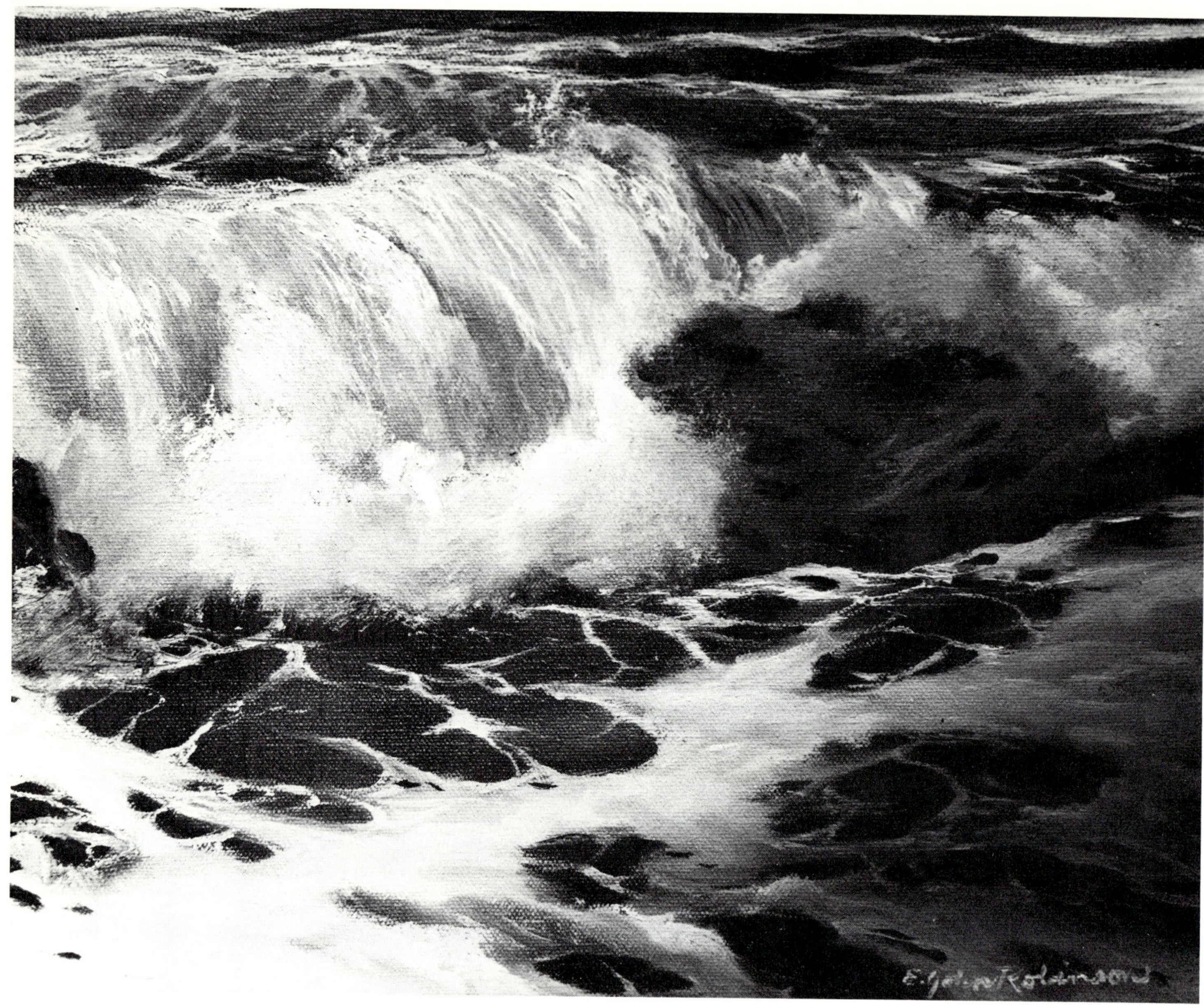

Figure 55. The main pattern of lines here is the path of sunlight.

MASS PATTERNS

Cover the entire surface with foam and watch a few holes appear. Surface foam is a substance, but it's always in the process of shrinking. The holes that appear allow the color of water to show through, so an immediate contrast appears. Be sure that the holes are of varying size, but group them to form a shape or line. If they're randomly scattered, a busyness is created which may not be desirable (see Demonstration 23).

When the whole surface is covered with foam and only a few holes show the water, I call it mass foam. When painting these, vary the size of the holes but group them together for a definite direction or area of value. In Figure 56, a patch of holes leads to a wave.

The foam in Figure 57 would have to be called mass foam because it covers a large area and is not in a linear direction. Line patterns are formed in the major holes in the foam. Combining the two adds more interest.

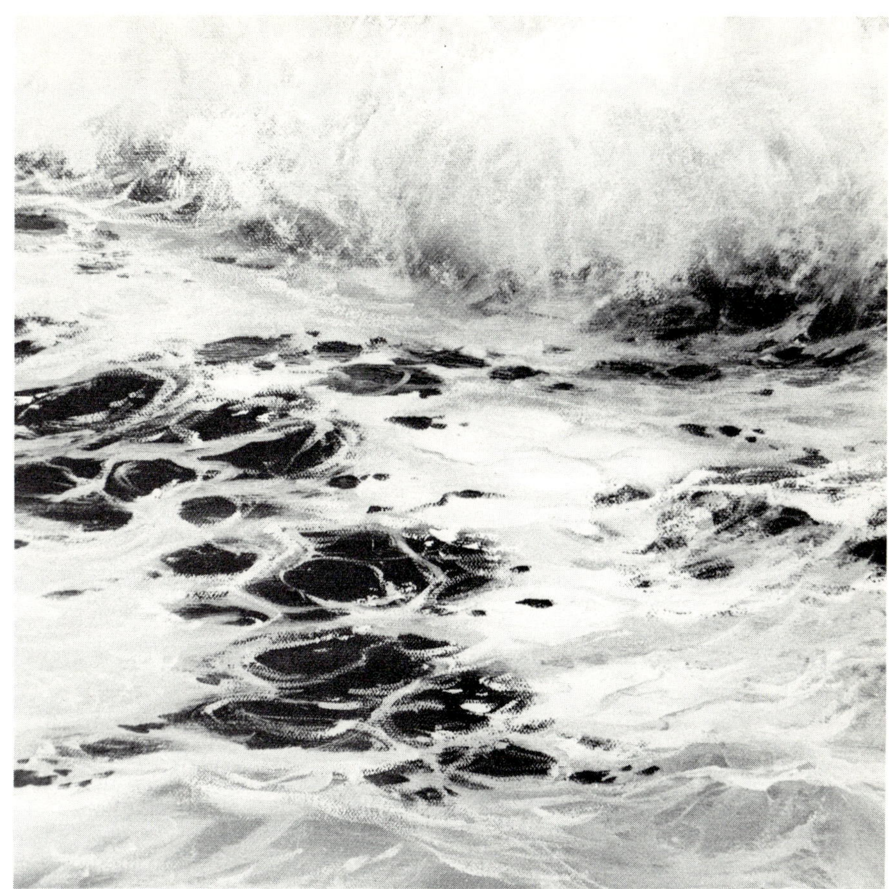

Figure 56. This is a closeup of a patch of holes that lead to a wave.

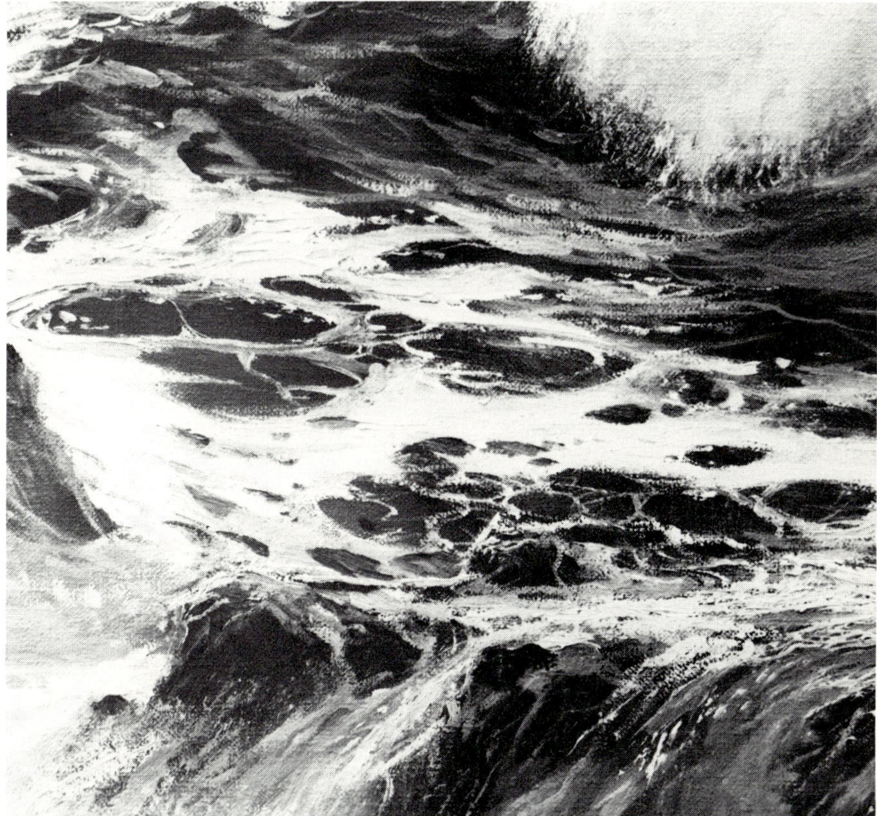

Figure 57. Mass foam covers a large area and is always shrinking.

PATTERNS IN SMOOTH
AND CHOPPY WATER

Use patterns in smooth and choppy water to add more variety and interest to your painting. Control the patterns with light and shadow and the direction of line.

Most linear foam patterns appear in choppy water and are in the form of ripples. Some, however, are in a momentary spot of smooth water and remain as the usual linear, circular patterns. Please note that the "circles" are not true circles but rather are rounded patterns.

Figure 58 shows the whiteness of foam in smooth and choppy water. Here again the contours are controlled by the use of light and shadow on the foam. This is an example of neither perfectly linear nor mass patterns, but of a more natural combination of the two. (See Figure 59 for an example of linear foam.)

The painting of both linear and mass patterns is taught step-by-step at the end of this chapter. I venture to say that you'll spend more time on them than you may think. Patterns—especially linear patterns—take a lot of practice.

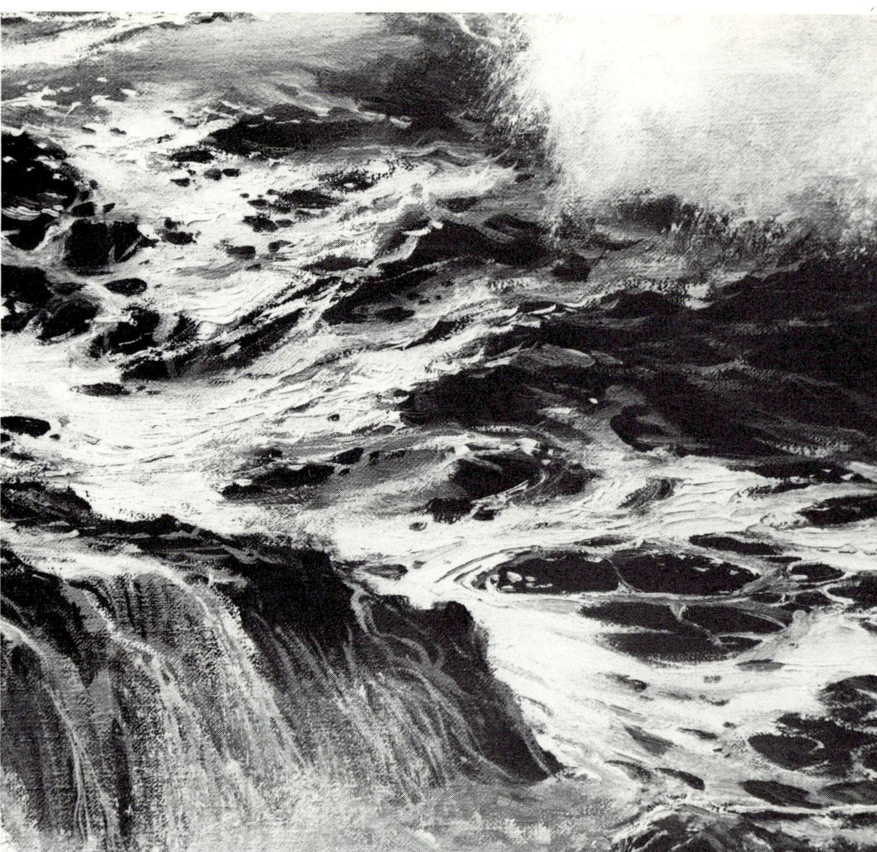

Figure 58. Both linear and mass patterns are combined here.

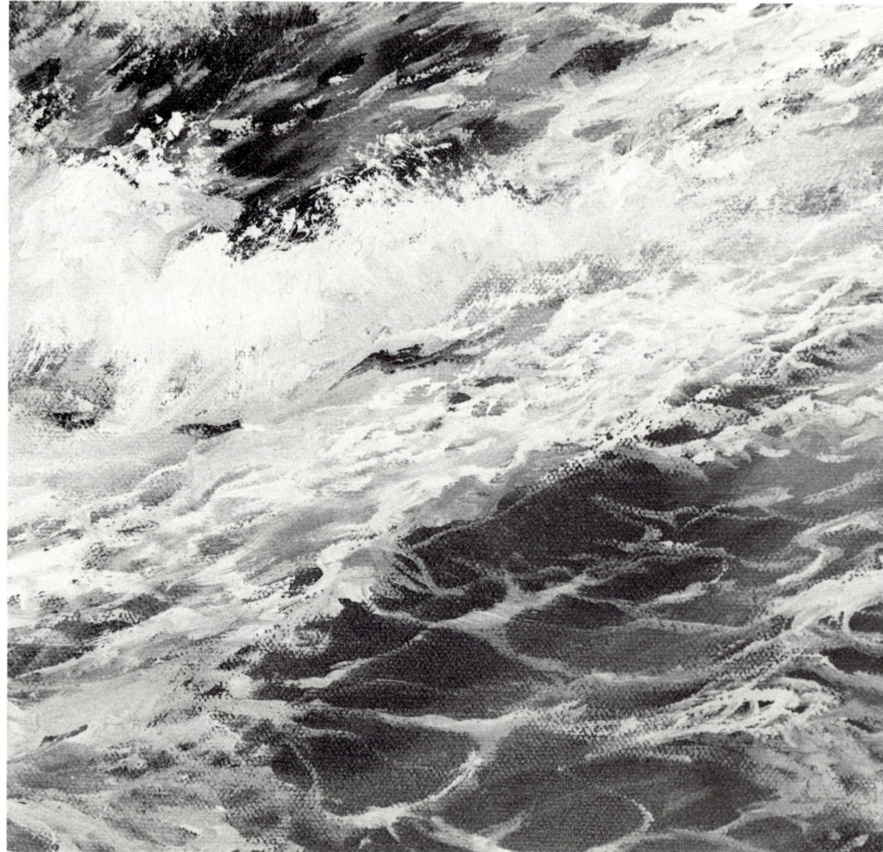

Figure 59. This closeup shows the brushwork I use in painting linear foam.

THE WHIPPED CREAM EFFECT

There are rare times when water is hammered unceasingly against rocks, and the surface is turned to solid foam with hardly a spot of water showing through. I call this the whipped cream effect (Figure 60). If you try painting this unusual effect, keep in mind a slightly wrinkled blanket—one with curved folds (see Demonstration 24).

By now, I'm sure you'll expect me to again mention the contours created by the light and shadow of the foam. Yes, it's so important that I'll continue to repeat it. With the whipped cream effect, light and shadow are even more important for showing contours because you don't have the benefit of strong sky reflections.

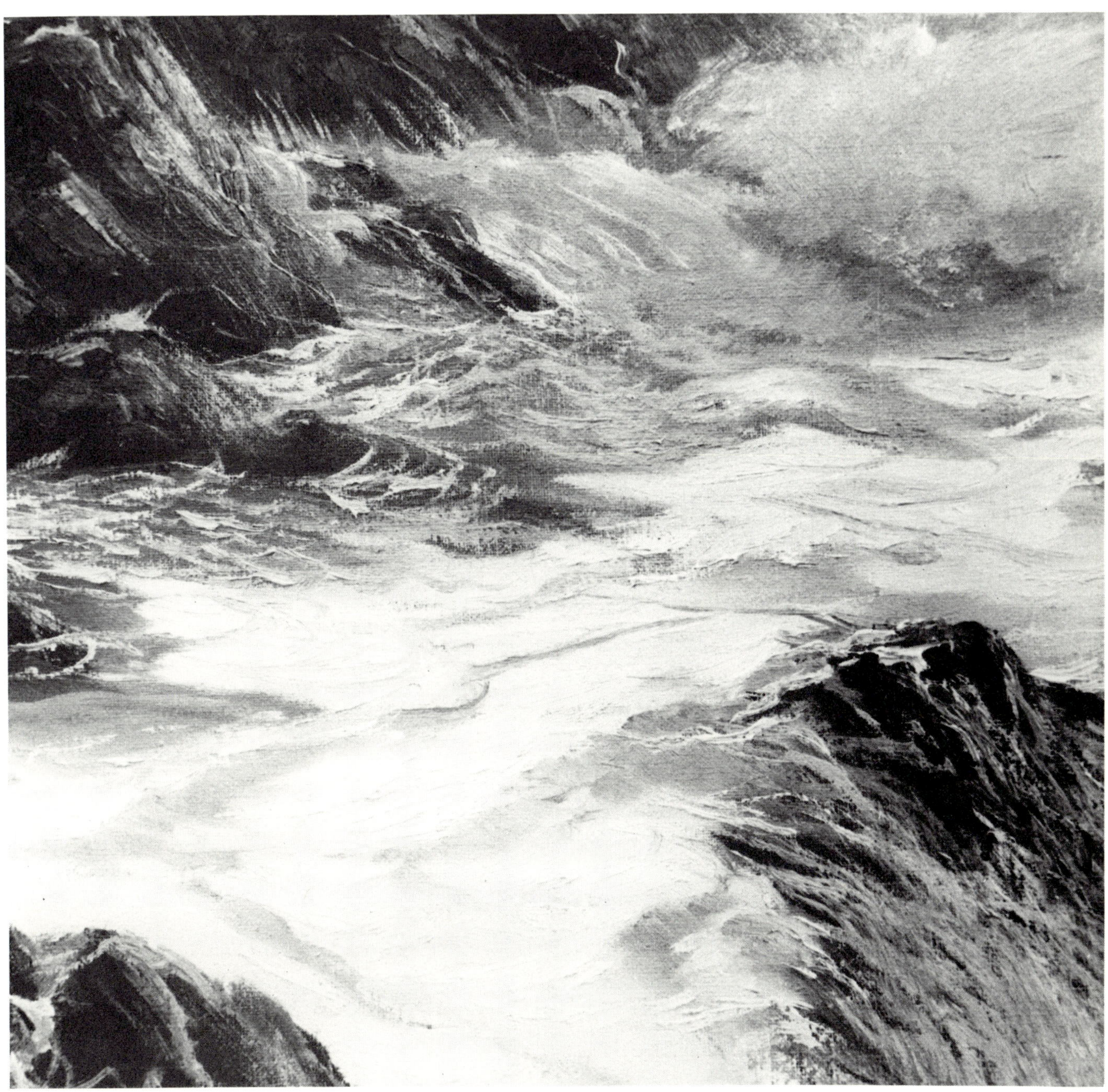

Figure 60. When the water turns to solid foam, we have the whipped cream effect.

THE LAYERED EFFECT

I'm introducing new names to seascape painting, but it's necessary because I don't believe anyone has ever taught certain effects I've observed.

The layered effect (Figure 61) could also be called the brocade look. It usually occurs in falling water, and is just what the name suggests. The layers of foam—which consist of long strings of foam crisscrossing each other—are created by agitated water from different directions, or by foam following on foam. Pay special attention to the overlapping of each line. They can't all move in the same direction. Each layer must change direction slightly in order to crisscross the other (Figure 62).

When painting the layered effect (Demonstration 25) keep in mind the information in Chapter Five on levels of depth, and apply it also to foam. To paint this effect, start with the shadowed or slightly dark foam patterns at the lowest level of depth and work upward. The second layer of patterns should be a bit lighter and should crisscross the lower layer, or at least have a slightly different direction. The third or fourth layer—or however far you go— should be the lightest and sharpest. The lower layers may be softened with the hazing brush, but the top layer should be crisp.

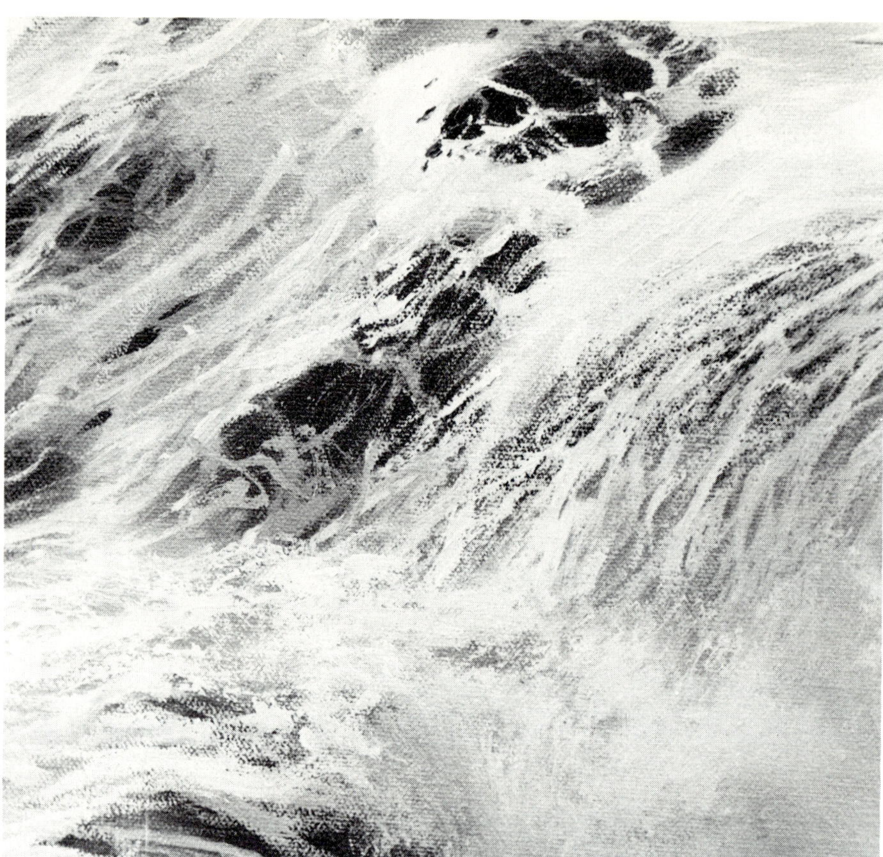

Figure 61. The layered or brocade effect usually occurs in falling water.

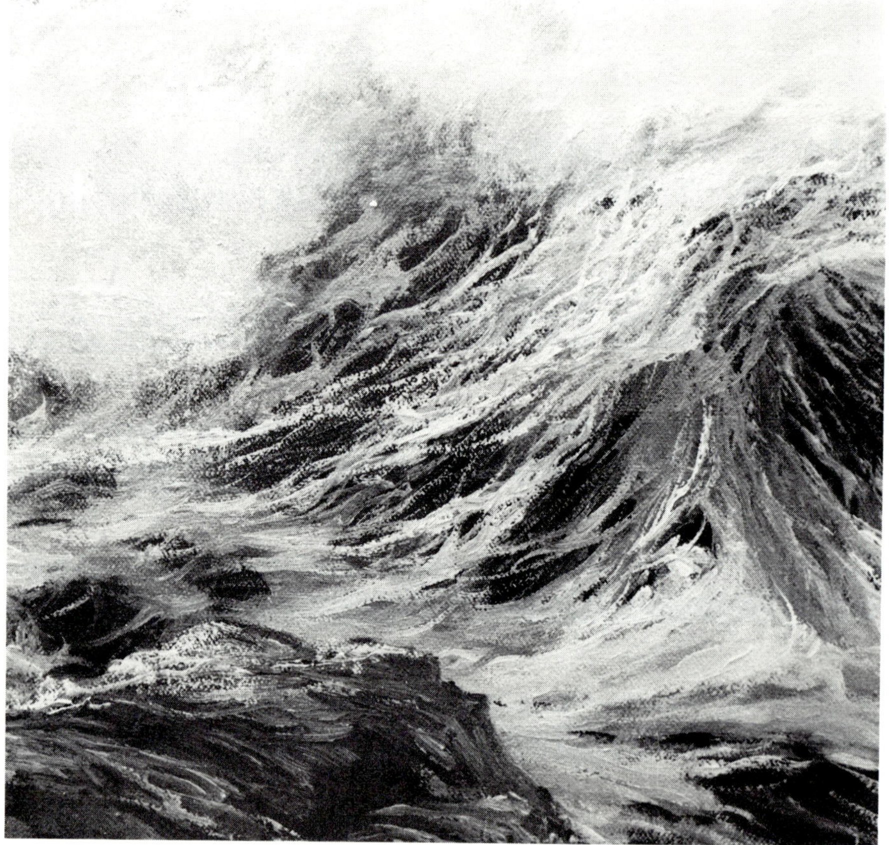

Figure 62. This is another example of the crisscrossed layered effect.

COMBINING EFFECTS

When you combine several effects of foam you add variety and interest to a painting. In Figure 63 I've used a mass foam, linear foam, misty foam, the layered effects, and a touch of the whipped cream effect. Together they create a very foamy picture!

Figure 64 provides another example of the use of foam patterns. Here again there are a variety of effects, without which the foreground would have been uninteresting. In fact, the foreground is really the center of interest in this painting.

Figure 65 shows a painting that is almost all mass foam patterns, including the vertical sides of the wave. Notice how the dark holes lead to the wave.

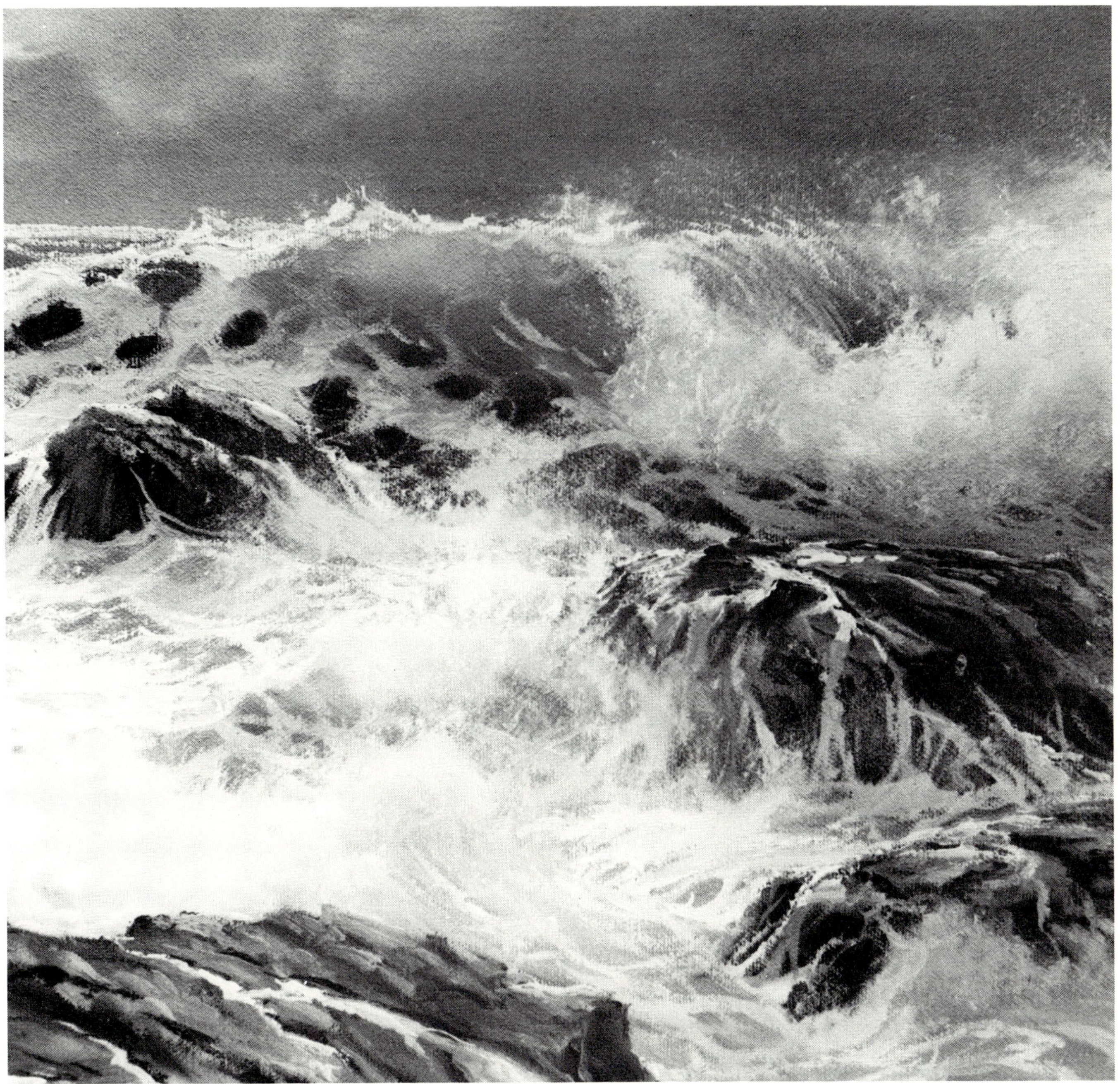

Figure 63: Try to spot the different effects of foam I used here.

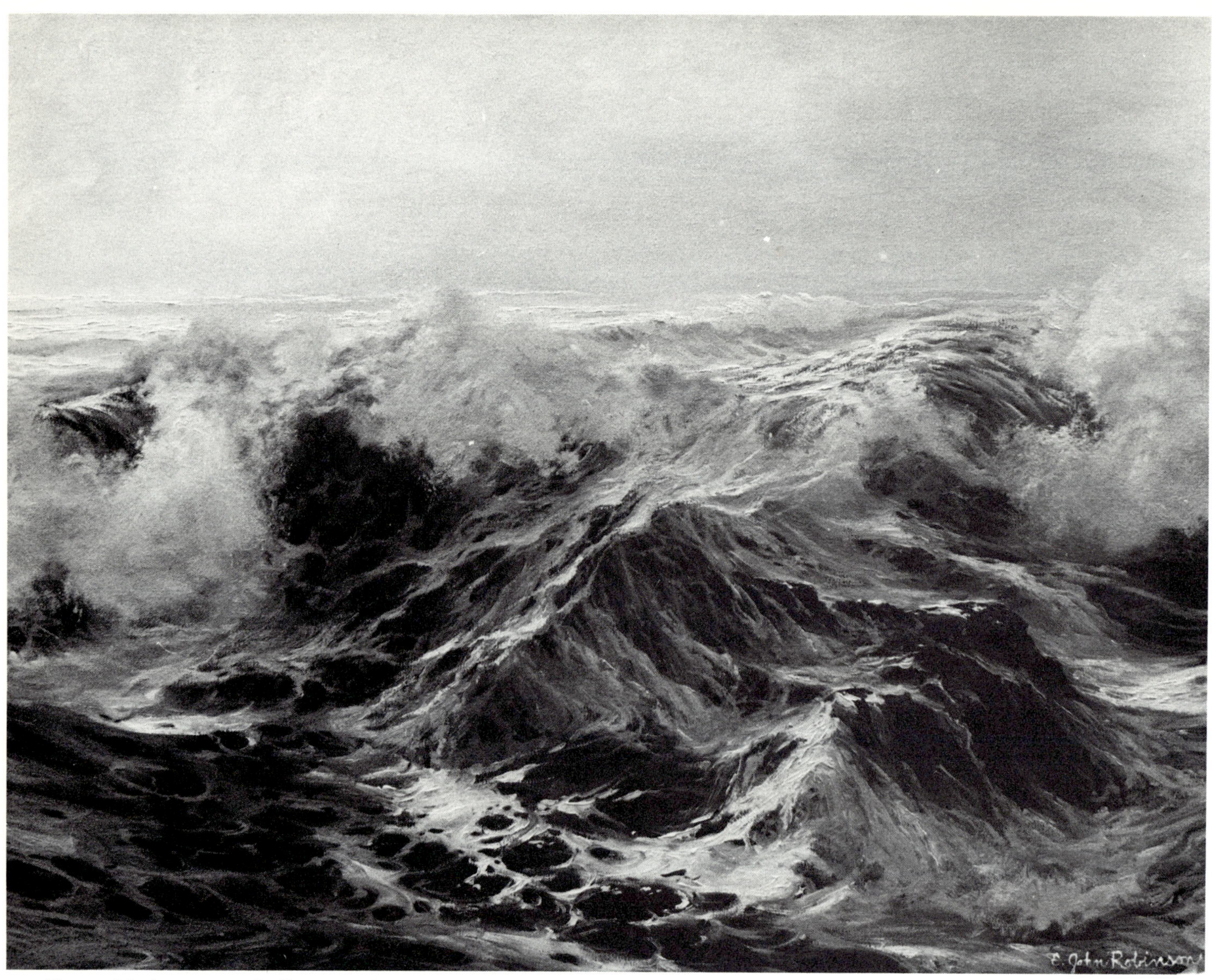

Figure 64. A variety of effects combine to make the foreground interesting.

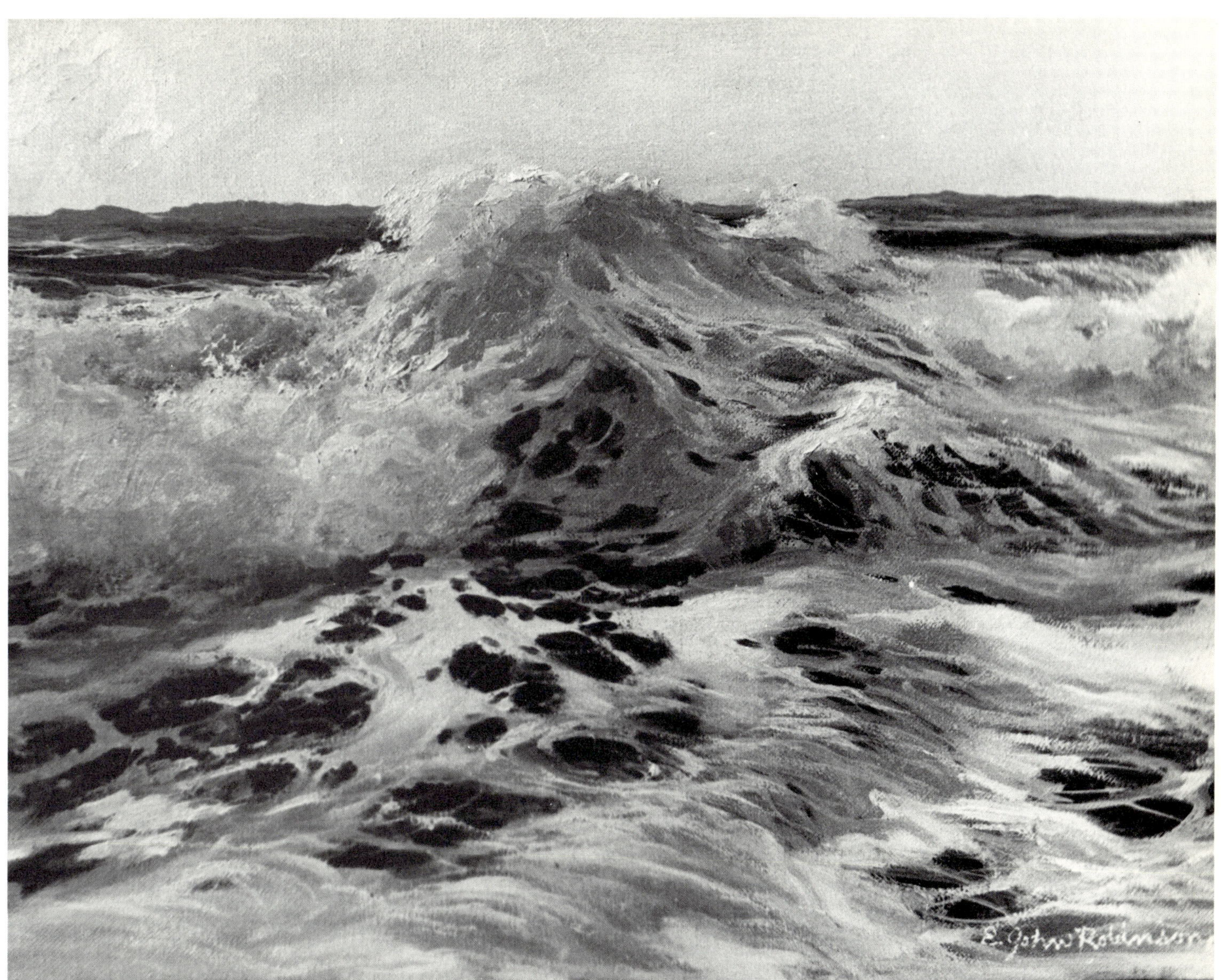

Figure 65. This painting is almost all mass foam patterns.

DEMONSTRATION 22: LINEAR PATTERNS

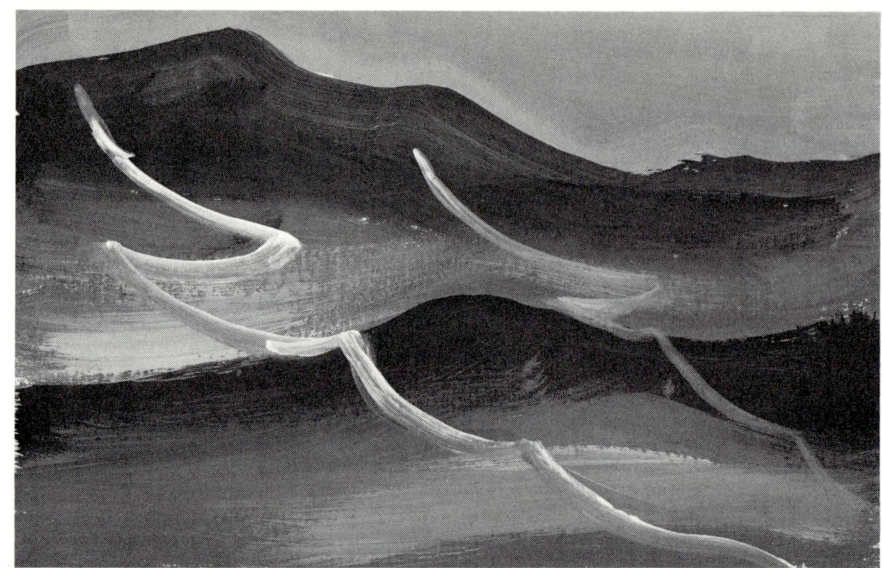

Step 1. To paint linear patterns correctly, you must have a direction. Starting with a background of heavy swells, draw a couple of lines to indicate the direction to be taken with the patterns. Notice that even though the lines move in only one direction, they may meander as well as show the contour of the swells.

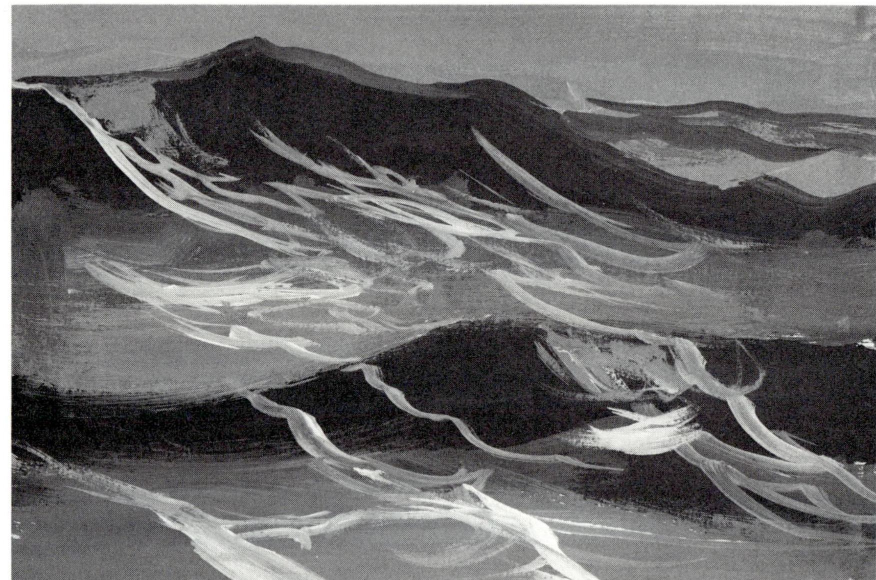

Step 2. Now begin to add a few more lines that still have the same basic direction, being careful not to scatter the lines. Also, begin to connect some lines to others.

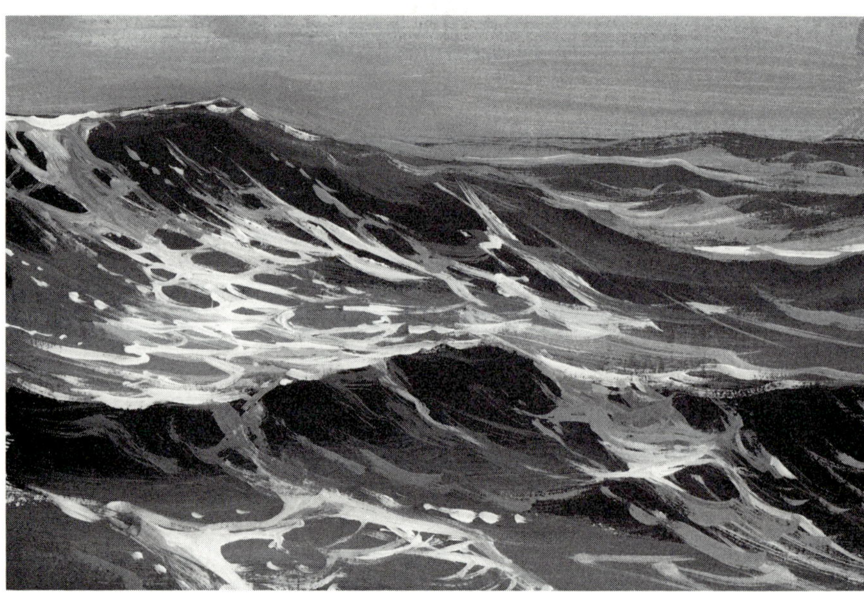

Step 3. The final step needn't go as far as this example. Please notice, however, that although the final result still maintains the original direction of the lines they're now connected as patterns in light and shadow.

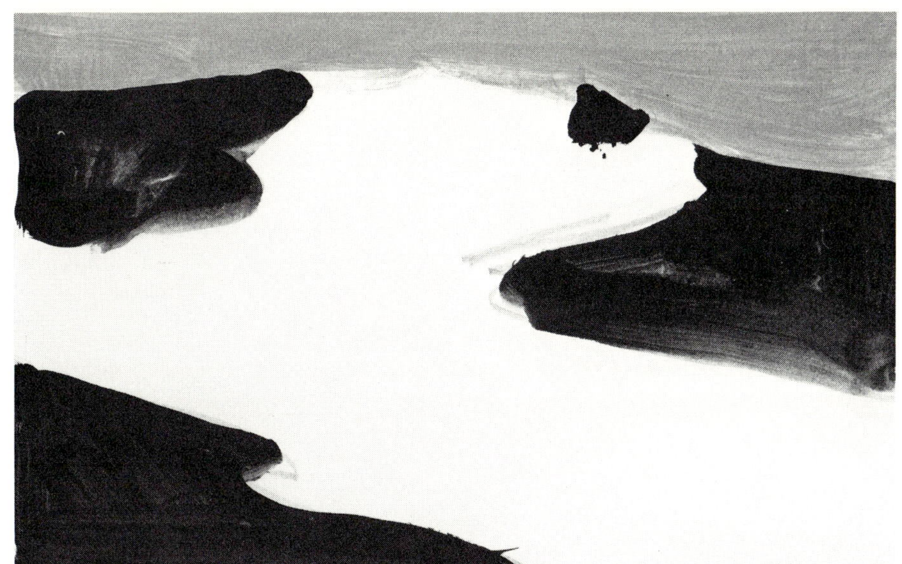

Step 1. Begin your study of mass patterns by painting in a background of a major swell. Leave the area of foam unpainted at this point, but give it a sweep or direction.

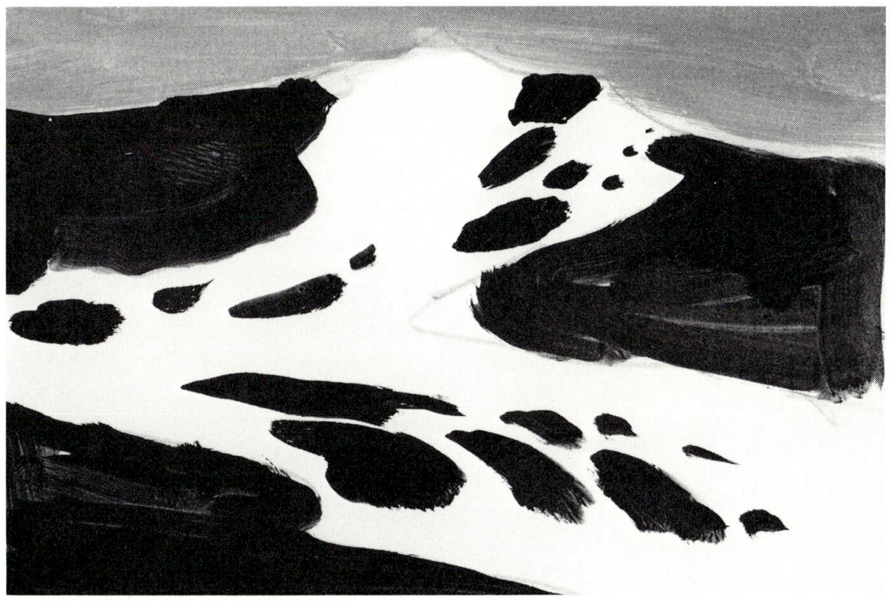

Step 2. Fill in the major holes in the foam. At this point, the foam area is still unpainted. Notice that the holes are arranged to enhance the direction of movement and are kept in groups instead of being scattered. The color of the holes will be the same as the water.

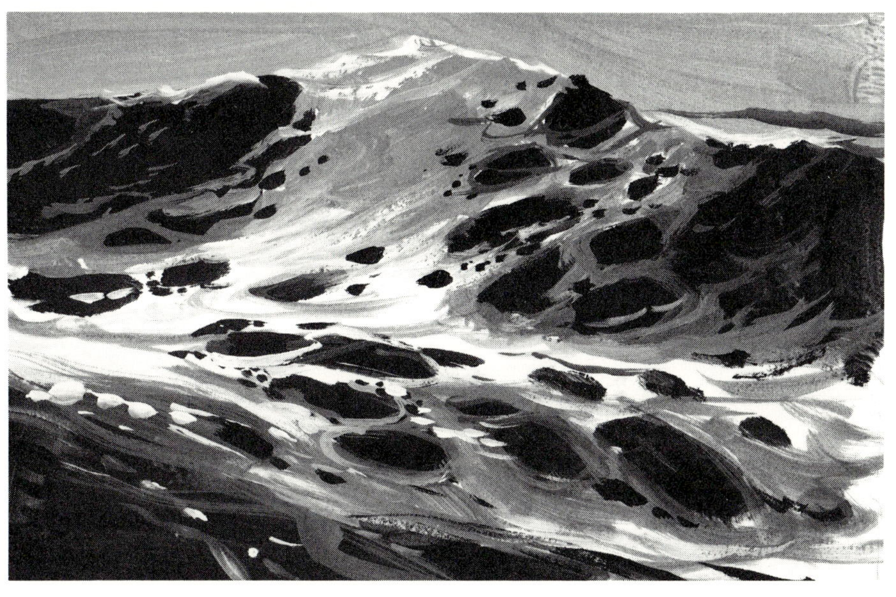

Step 3. Finally, paint in the foam around the major holes. Allow it to move from shadow into light and back to shadow again. Add a few minor linear patterns to the edges of the mass foam to keep it from being too contained. Finally, add a few small holes in the foam. Use the same color you used for the water.

DEMONSTRATION 24:
THE WHIPPED CREAM EFFECT

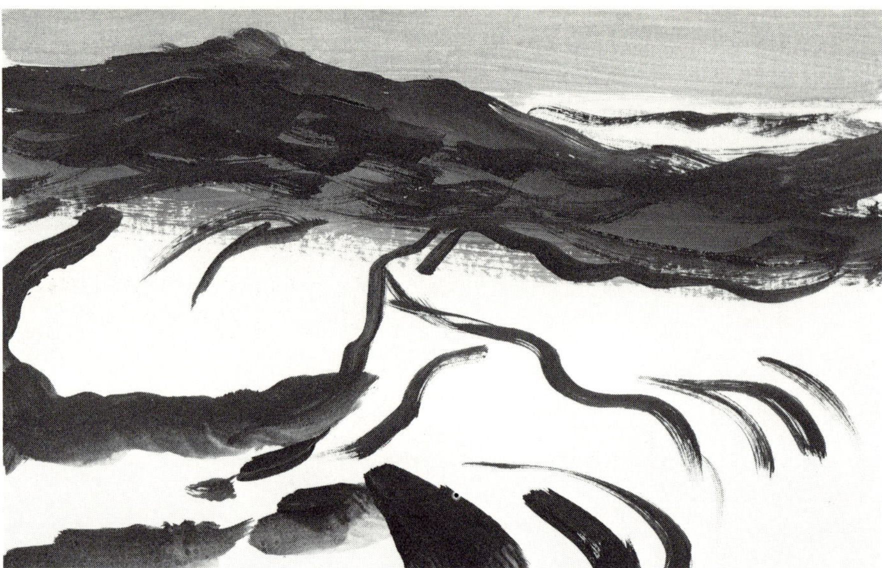

Step 1. By "whipped cream" I mean a fluffy, folded type of foam that appears during heavy foreground water action. To begin, paint in a background that threatens to create some action! Next, draw in a breaker and indicate shadow lines or lines of folds.

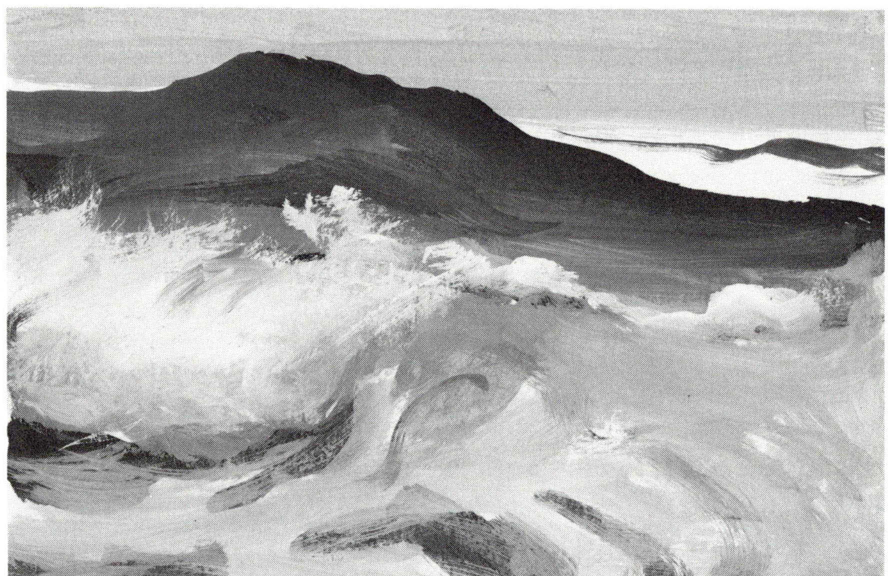

Step 2. Paint in the breaker foam as you learned in Demonstration 9. Paint in the entire wave face and foreground in light and shadowed foam. Don't cover all the shadow lines.

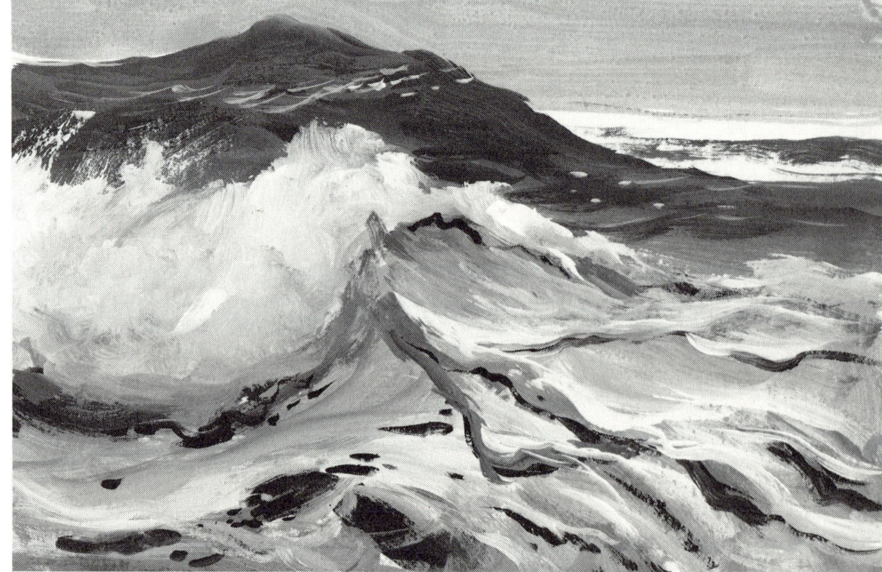

Step 3. This is where a study of folded drapery would help you to understand the way breaker foam works. Treat the foam as you would the drapery: highlight each fold, then underscore the shadow side with a still deeper shadow. Let the folds meander, and avoid making them all the same size. Finally, add a few holes in the foam, and add interest to the background sea.

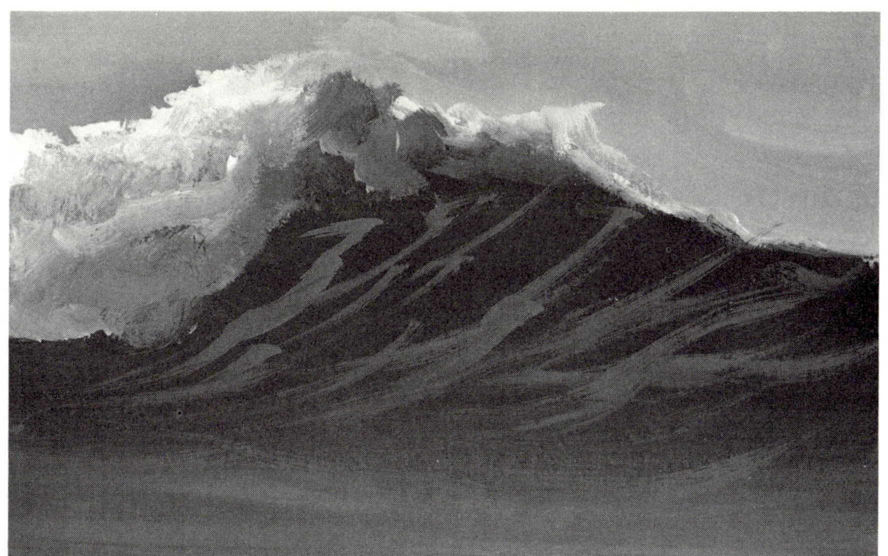

Step 1. This could be called a "brocade" look as well. Begin with a wave background and paint in some deeply shadowed foam lines. Keep them moving in the direction indicated by the wave.

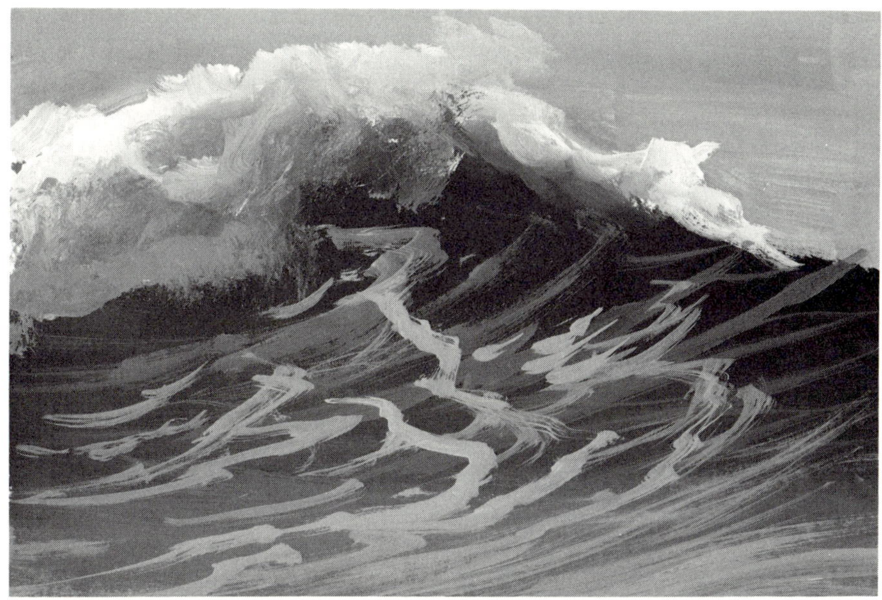

Step 2. Mix a lighter version of foam by adding more white. Paint in some lateral moving patterns that cross right over the first ones. Don't put in so many that you lose the direction of the first set.

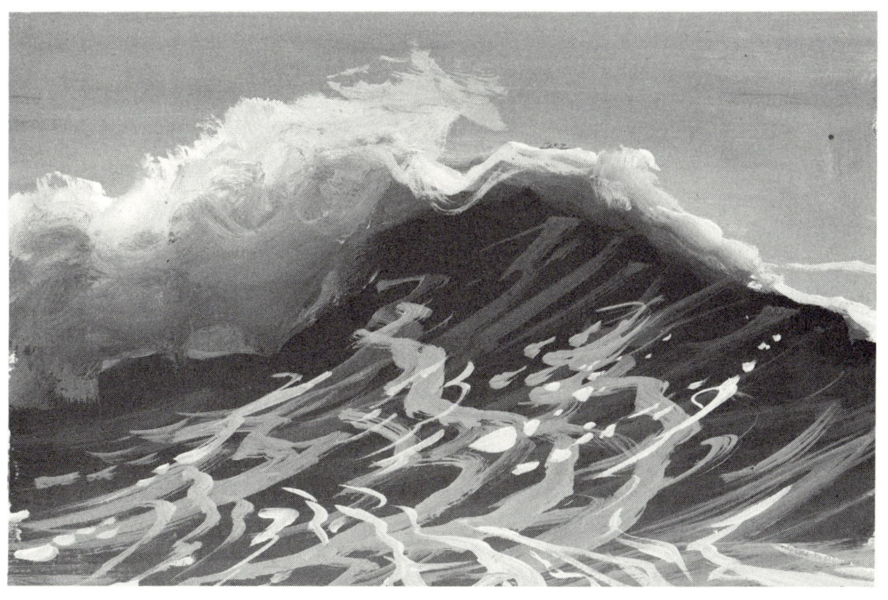

Step 3. Now, with the lightest version of the foam patterns, go over the area a third time. No matter where you place them, they should cross over previous patterns. A fourth or even fifth layer could be added, but do so only when you have the feel for this. The end result will be a thickened mass of foam in separate layers.

CHAPTER EIGHT

ROCKS AND FALLING WATER

I can't separate rocks from falling water, because they're constantly in combination in nature. Rocks are always in the process of erosion, and the sea is merciless. Great waves pound the rocks, rush over them, and work on cracks and fissures until they eventually crumble. It's a struggle between water and earth, and a fascinating subject to paint.

You should initially be aware of the shapes of rocks in your own locale. There will be differences from one area to another, but rocks are generally either angular or rounded. Also observe variations in their color, texture, and physical make-up.

Remember that the rocks you paint in the sea will not become a part of your seascape unless (1) they give the impression of being submerged, (2) they're either partially covered with water, (3) they're in some stage of draining water, or unless (4) they're at least wet enough to reflect the sky.

As I often advise students, pick up some small rocks at the beach that best resemble the large ones. Take them home, put a light on them, and paint them from different angles. Study the effects of light and shadow on them and experiment with water running off them. (Also turn to my demonstration on painting a rock, Demonstration 26.) Your ability to paint will be no stronger than your determination to learn.

ANGULAR ROCKS

Rocks vary in size, color, and shape according to locale. These rough, angular rocks may or may not be in your area; but they do show the erosion caused by years of the action of the surf. The angular, hard-edged rocks in Figure 66 create a sharp contrast to the softer, more liquid feeling of the sea and foam.

As I mentioned before, outside edges are more important than interior planes. An angular rock must have sharp, chiseled edges to convey the feeling of harshness. For a sharper edge, many artists use a painting knife instead of a brush.

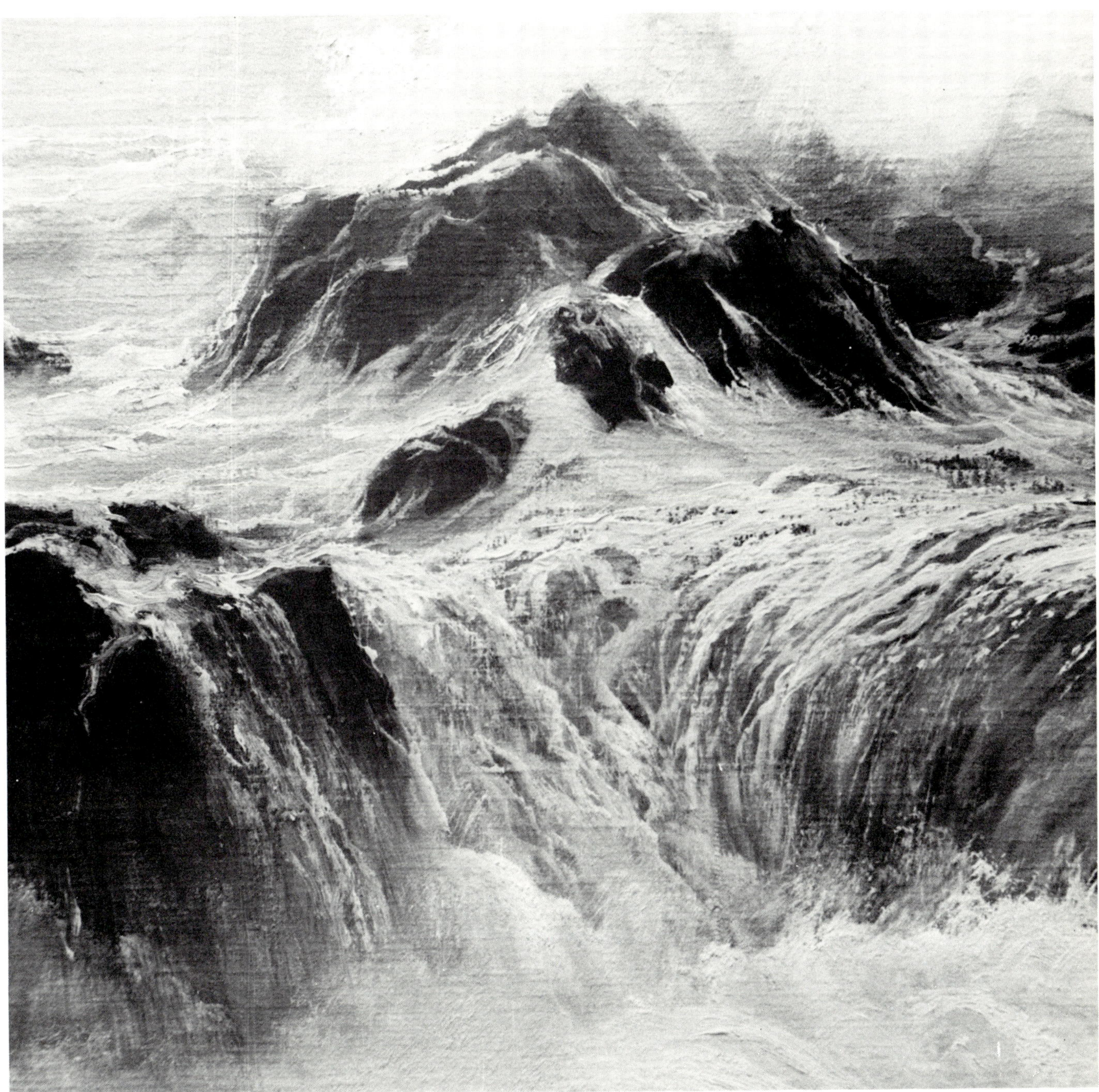

Figure 66. Angular rocks stand out in sharp relief from soft edges of foam.

ROUNDED ROCKS

There are many rounded rock shapes to be painted, but most of them don't appeal to me because they don't give the contrast to the sea that angular rocks do. Therefore, rounded rocks must attract extra attention, either through a contrast of values, extra texturing, or more detail.

In Figure 67 I painted the rock very dark against light foam. This way, even though the rock is neither sharp nor angular, it still stands in harsh contrast to the soft foam behind it. On this rock, notice also the light, shadow, and reflected light that help give it form. The trickles of water at the base also help to accentuate its shape.

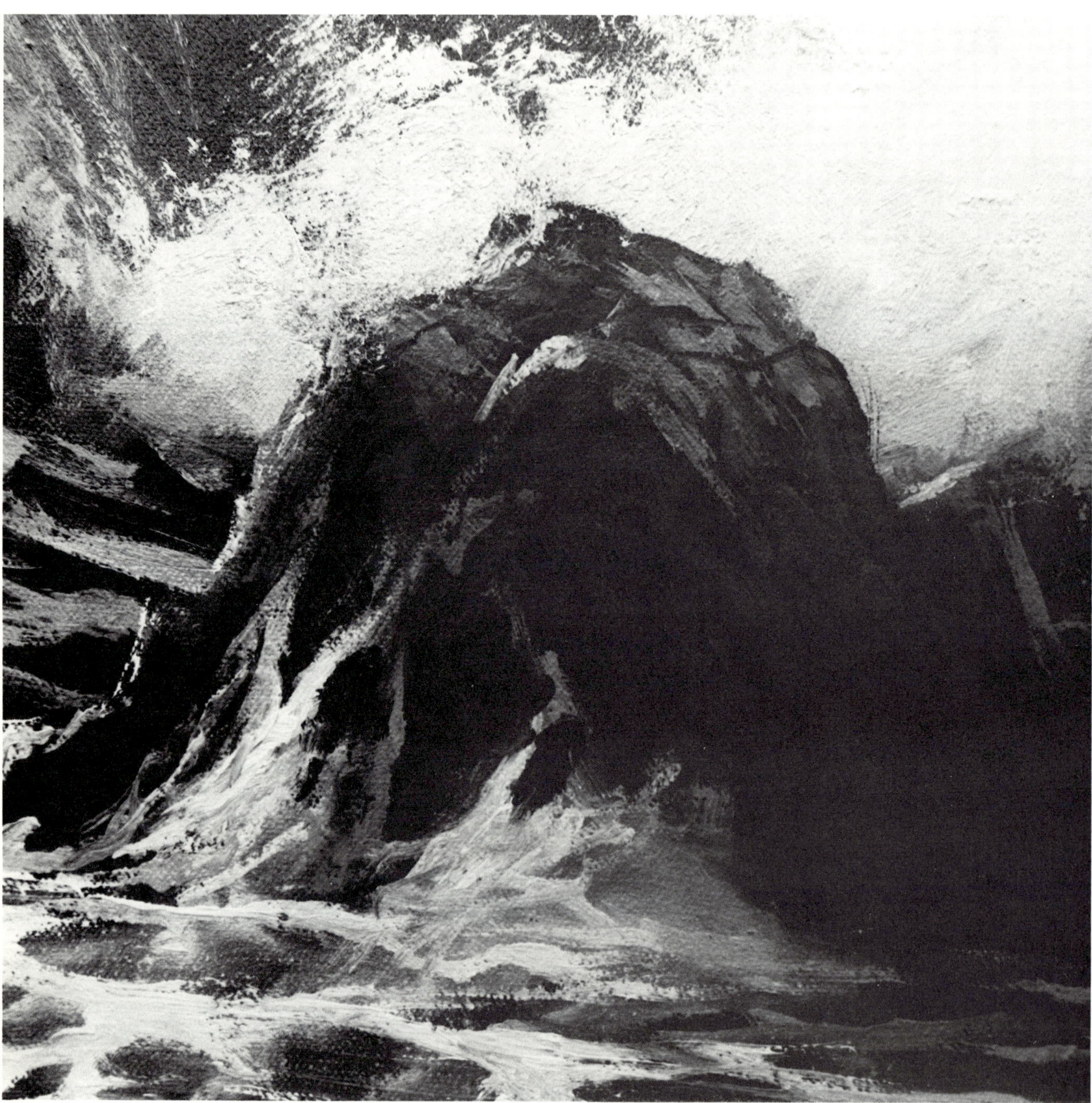

Figure 67. Look for a way to contrast rounded rocks with their surroundings.

TEXTURING ROCKS

Rocks also vary in texture according to their locale. Unless a rock is boulder smooth, there are cracks and fissures over the surface, so some texture is apparent almost anywhere.

Texturing rocks is important. First, it breaks up large areas of uninteresting planes. Then, it adds interest where you choose to attract attention. Finally, it provides a method of balancing a composition so one area isn't too dominant. Texturing rocks gives you the opportunity to reflect the sky or foam bursts when the rock is wet and is a natural means for placing runoffs just where you want them.

In Figure 68 I show a closeup of three methods of texturing a rock: (1) the sky reflects a patchwork of blue on its wet surface, (2) the planes of the rock are broken up by light and shadowed trickles, and (3) the rock itself has small cracks and a few lumps. Use a combination of these methods for variety.

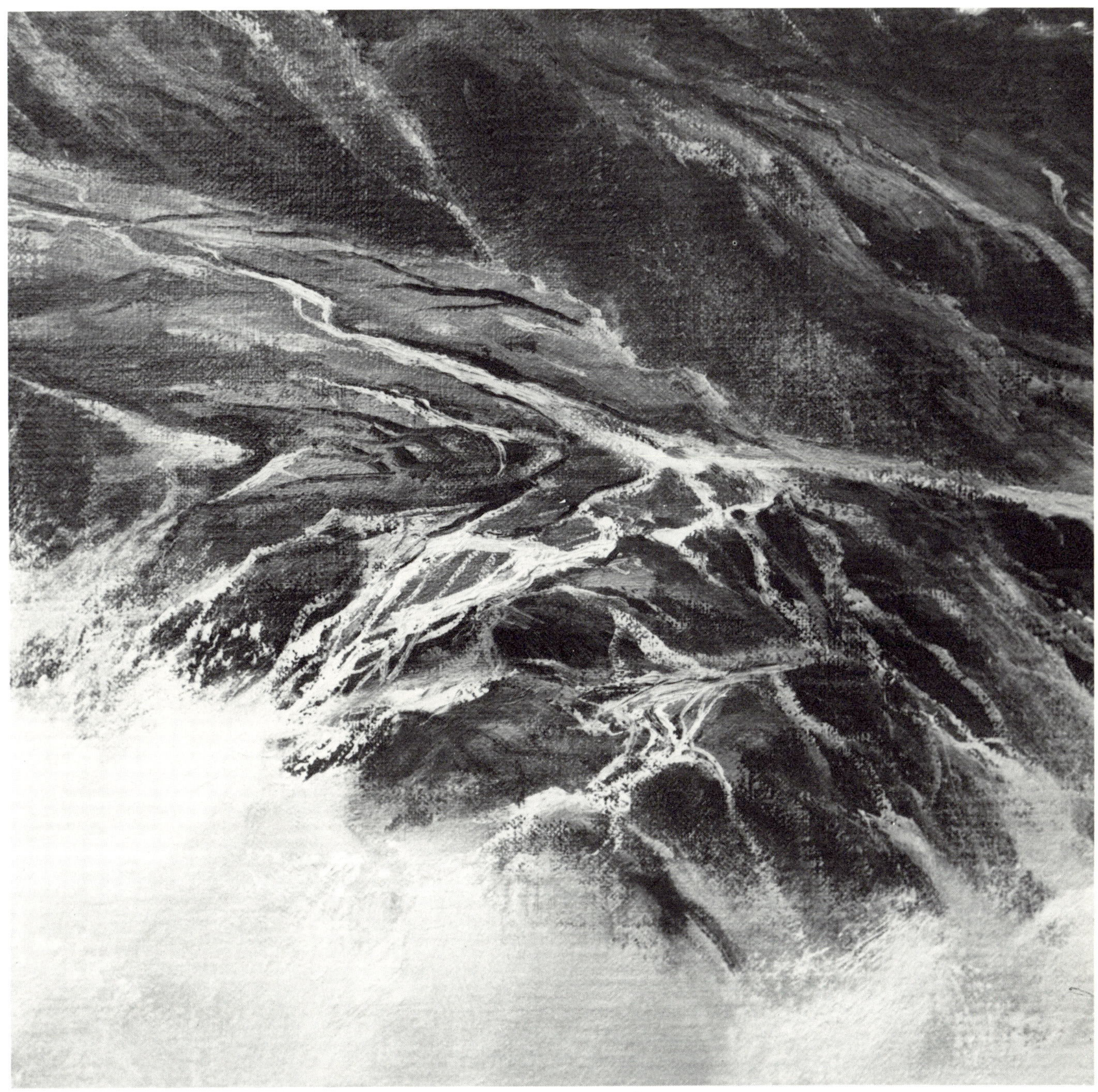

Figure 68. Cracks, sky reflections, and trickles texture the rock's surface.

WATER AGAINST ROCKS

I consider the placement of rocks in water to be a major problem with many students. Too often the rock appears to float on the surf rather than assume the solid, well-footed position it should have. Usually a "floating" rock effect is due to the improper use of water at the base. Some water flows around the rock, some slaps up against it, and some pours from the rock to the surface, rebounding as foam.

In Figure 69 I show a combination of all these effects. Some areas of the water are softened to mist or spray, while elsewhere water is crisp-edged and prominent. Try to use a variety of means to show water hitting against a rock. Of course, a calm surf wouldn't be splashing as it does here; but most action takes place around rocks, regardless.

Instead of portraying water lapping against the edge of the rocks, Figure 70 shows the effect of boiling foam and mistiness. Notice how sections of the rock fade into the mist, but its soft edges are contrasted with harsher lines.

The secret to painting rocks in water is to allow some of the rock color to show through when water either pours from or sweeps up the sides of the rock. Also, show some rock color below the surface when the water is clear (see Demonstration 27.)

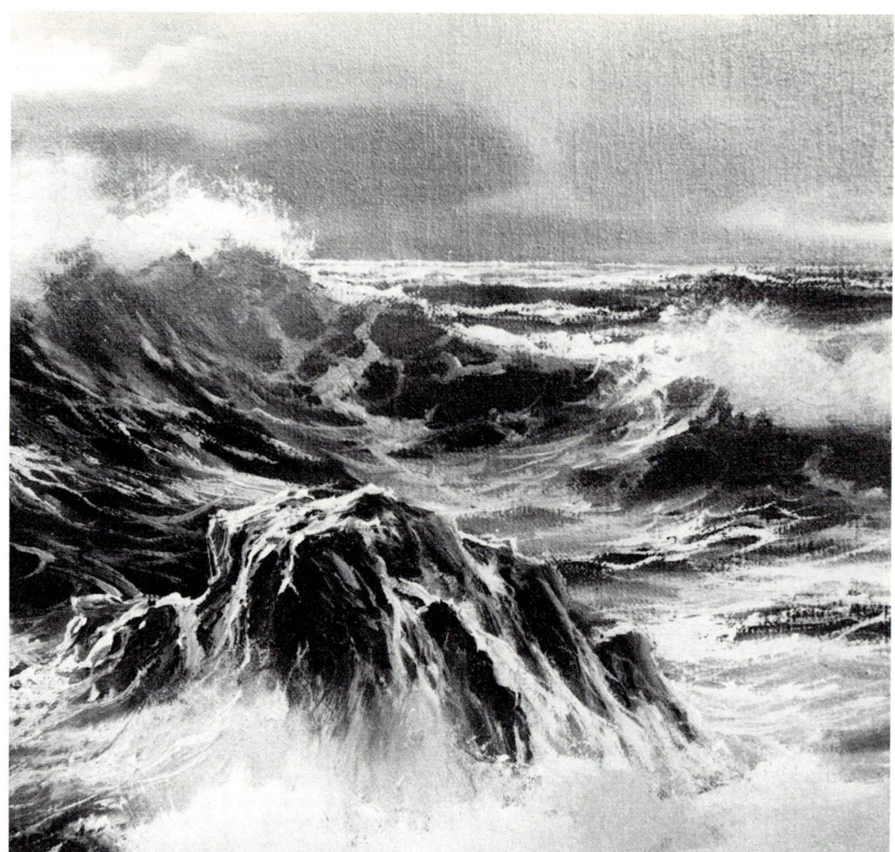

Figure 69. Several effects combine to show water hitting against a rock.

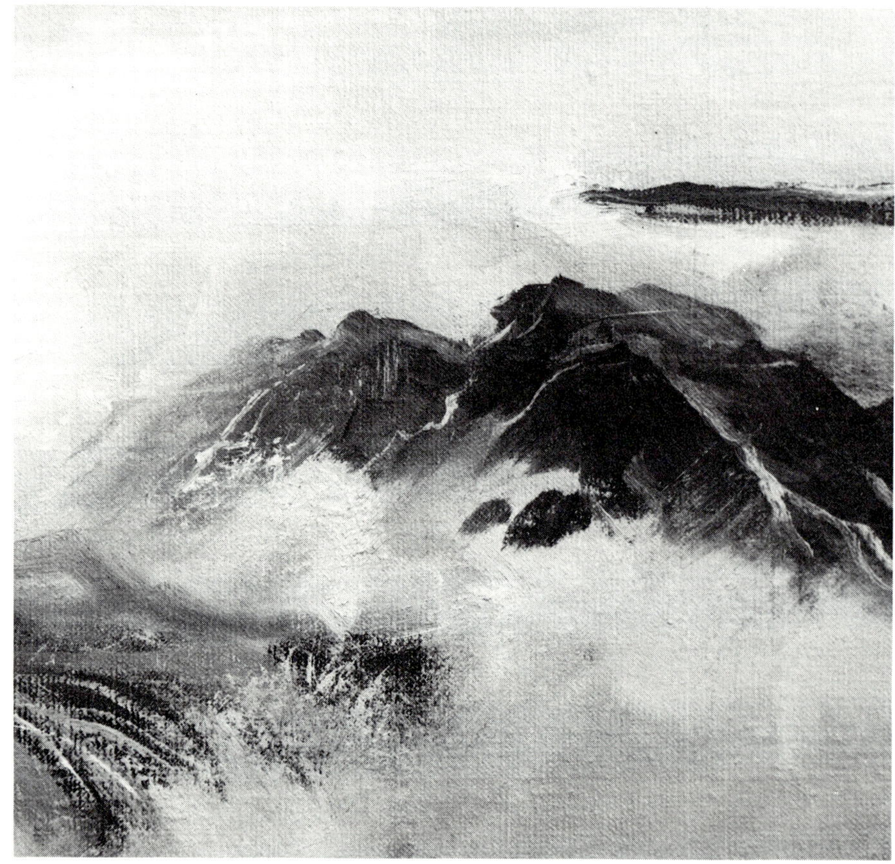

Figure 70. Bubbling foam and mistiness soften some of this rock's edges.

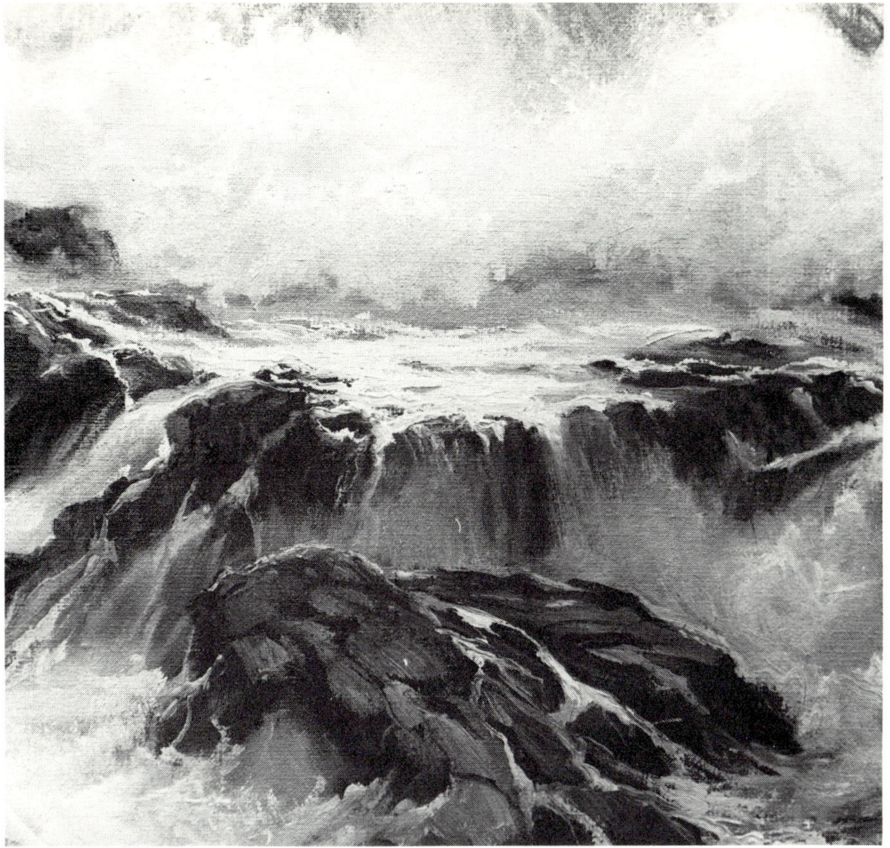

Figure 71. This tabletop rock barely shows through the foamy overflow.

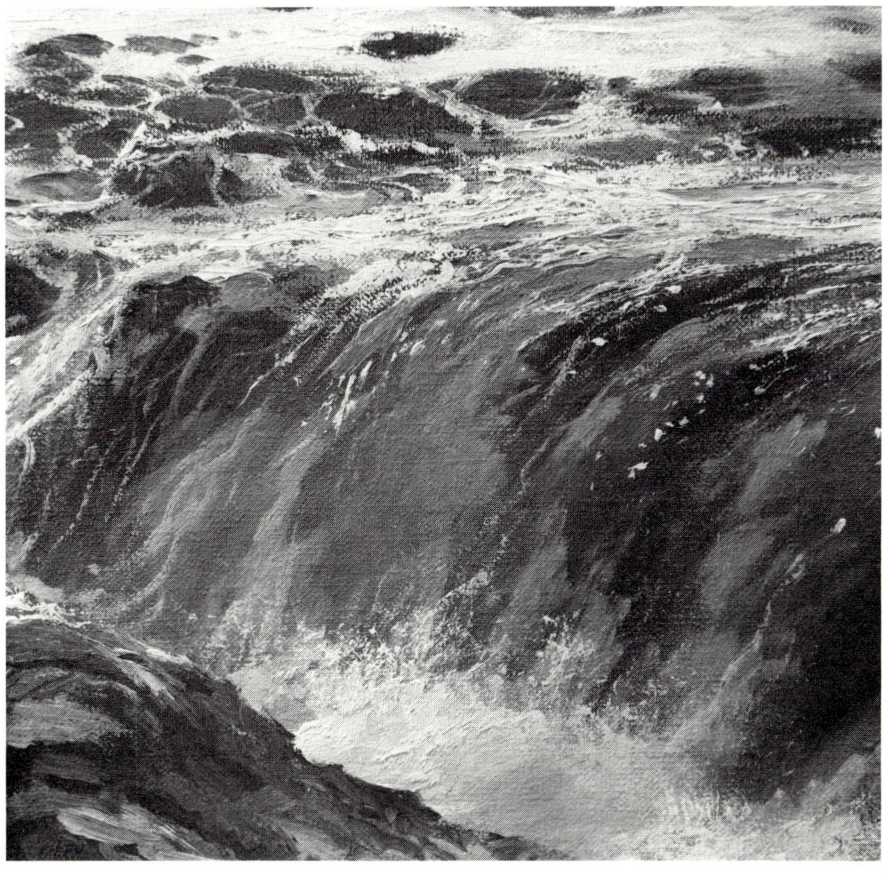

Figure 72. When the water is nearly clear, the shape of the rock is apparent.

OVERFLOWING WATER

I touched on the subject of overflowing water in Chapter 5 when discussing transparent water. Even though transparent overflow is interesting and occurs often, foamy overflow is most common.

Remember that the water overflowing a rock is the result of a wave having just broken over it. You're showing the first moments following the collapse of the wave. When water completely covers a rock, at first the rock may be hidden. But after a short time, it has drained enough so while only a few lumps are visible, the shape of the rock is apparent. Notice that light and shadow play a big role in portraying this in Figure 71.

In painting foamy overflowing water, some rock color will show through, but not as much as with transparent water (See Demonstration 28). In Figure 71 I show a tabletop rock covered with foamy water. Little rock color shows through on top, but some does show on the sides. Even there, the water is too foamy for much rock color to show.

All overflowing water needn't be gushing and foamy. In Figure 72, the water is nearly clear and the shape of the rock is visible even though it's completely covered by water.

Just following an overflow are the moments of major spills. Water gushes from rocks in paths of least resistance. Usually it's between lumps and bumps and is best visible shortly after the overflow effect. There's not as much water then, but still plenty. At this time, the higher points of the rock are above water, but the major crevices are overflowing heavily. Major spills are often heavy enough to keep you from seeing the color of the rocks beneath them.

Figure 73 is an extension of the left-hand side of Figure 71. The left side of this rock area is higher and doesn't have as much water remaining as does the right.

Figure 74 provides an example of major spills that still remain in the overflow stage. On the left, the water spills over the edge of a rock, and even though you can't see the rock, its shape is there. On the right, where the rock is very rough and uneven, spills are mixed and uneven as well.

To paint overflowing water spilling over rocks, I suggest you paint the rock first but leave the portions of foamy water unpainted. This is so you don't pick up rock color where you want clear or foamy water. Try the step-by-step lessons that follow, and add one or two variations of your own.

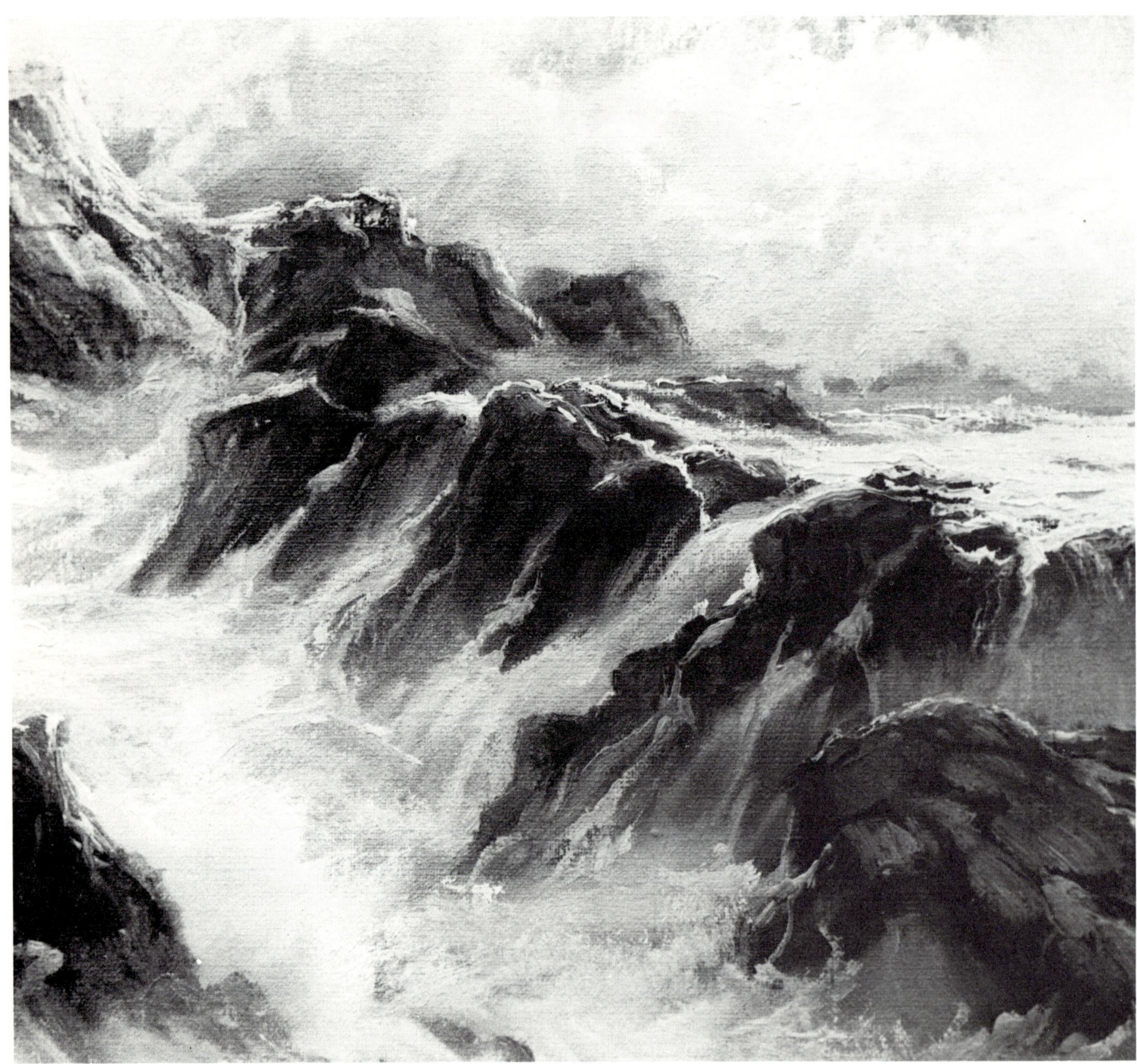

Figure 73. An overflow often combines with the next stage, major spills.

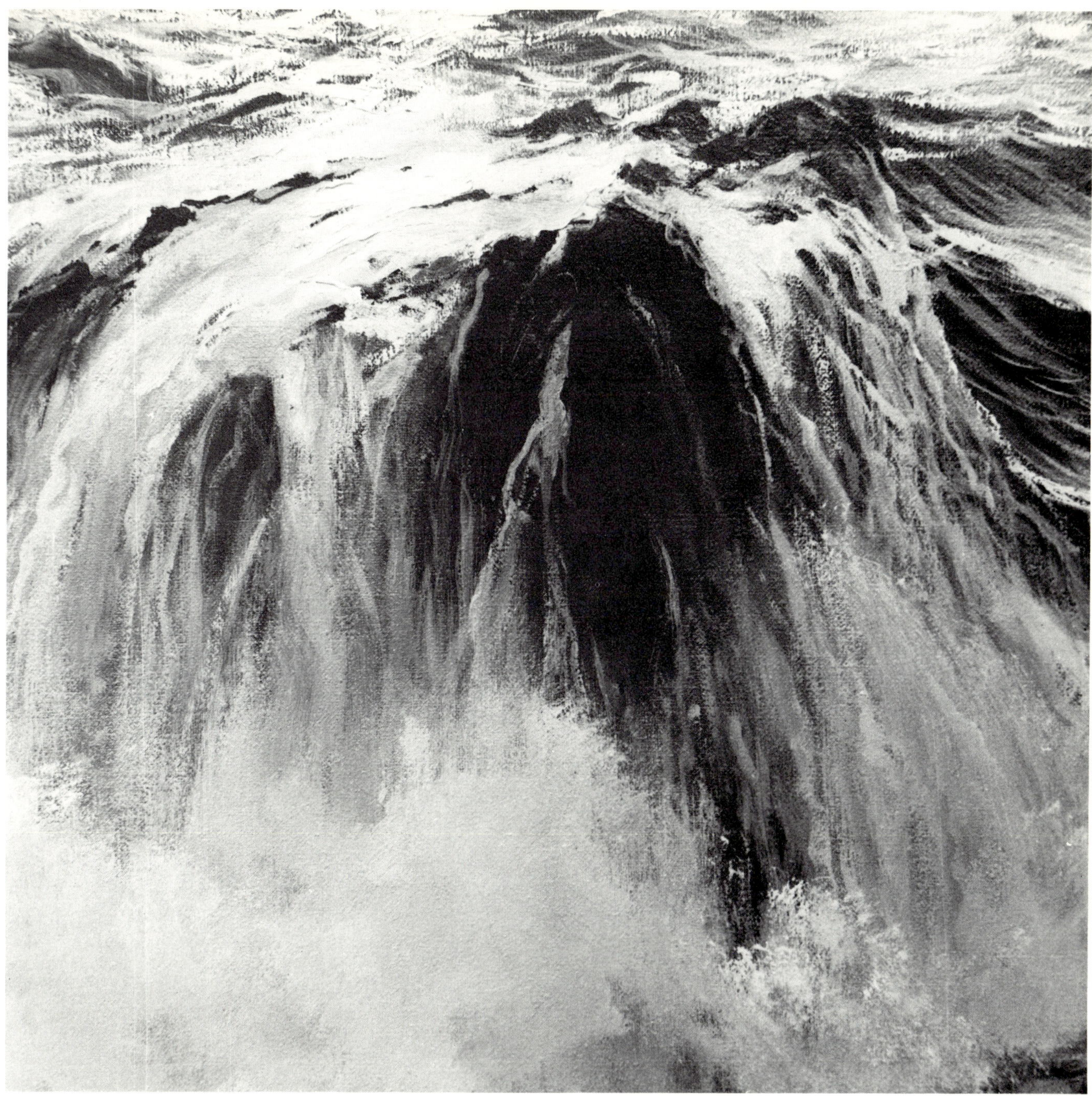

Figure 74. The remaining water varies in form with the rock's surface.

TRICKLES

Trickles are the last remnants of falling water after the wave has broken. First the rock has been overflowing with water, then there's been a spilling in the major cracks and between rocks. Now only trickles are left.

Trickles don't have to follow major cracks. They may appear nearly anywhere. Trickles follow the paths of least resistance, but show up in the tiniest of cracks as well as larger ones. They're perfect to use for showing the cracks and contours of the rock.

In Figure 75, I show them covering a lot of rock, but in Figure 76 very little water is left to run off. The remaining trickles help define the rock's shape and also help in texturing it. You must decide on the number of trickles you wish to show and work them into your composition.

When painting trickles, the rock must be completed first. Paint in all of the rock, including the light and shadowed planes, texturing, and reflected colors. Then paint in the trickles with a tiny brush loaded with paint. Don't press on the brush unless you wish to pick up rock color. Let the weight of the brush be the only pressure in order to achieve thin, broken lines.

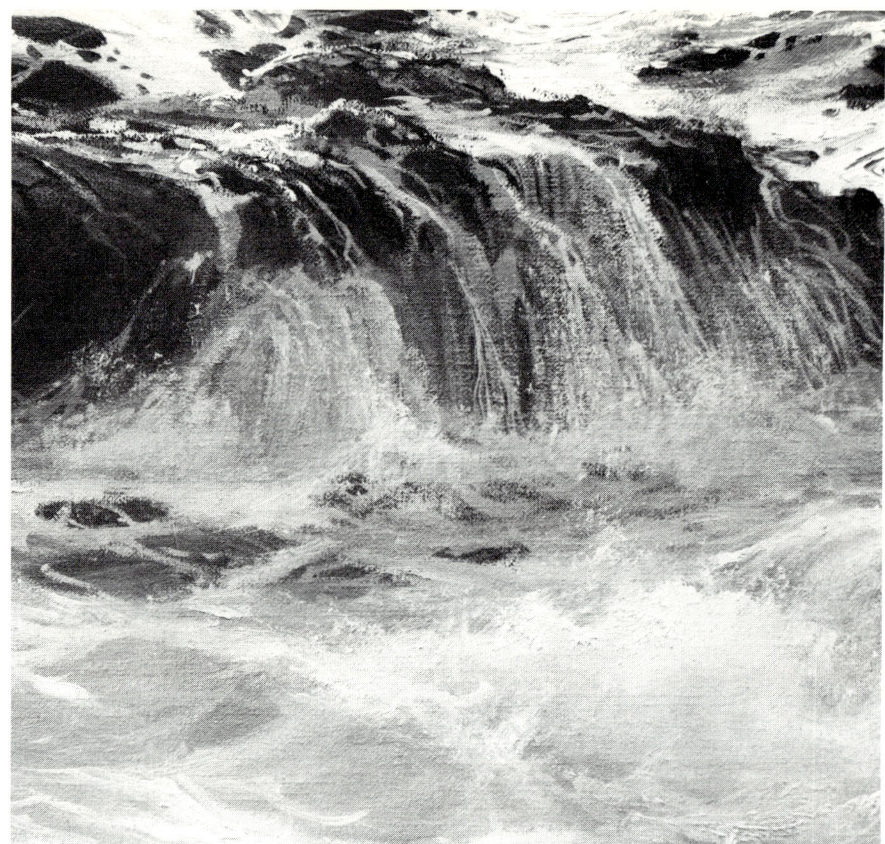

Figure 75. Trickles may cover much of the rock.

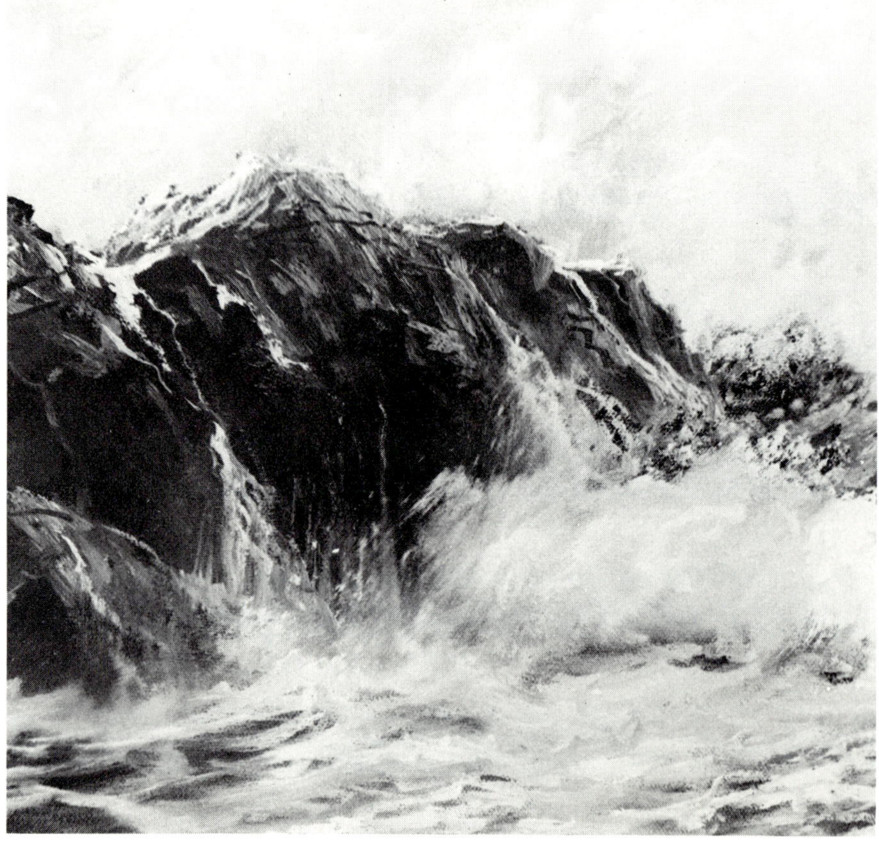

Figure 76. Very little water is left to drain off this angular rock.

Figure 77 is a good example of a
combination of effects. Notice
that the major spills are flanked by
trickles. The rock is sharp-edged
at the top but fades into mistiness
at the bottom. All of the runoff is
played up through light and
shadow, softness and hardness,
and rounded and angular shapes.
Demonstration 29 shows you how
to combine spills and trickles in a
painting.

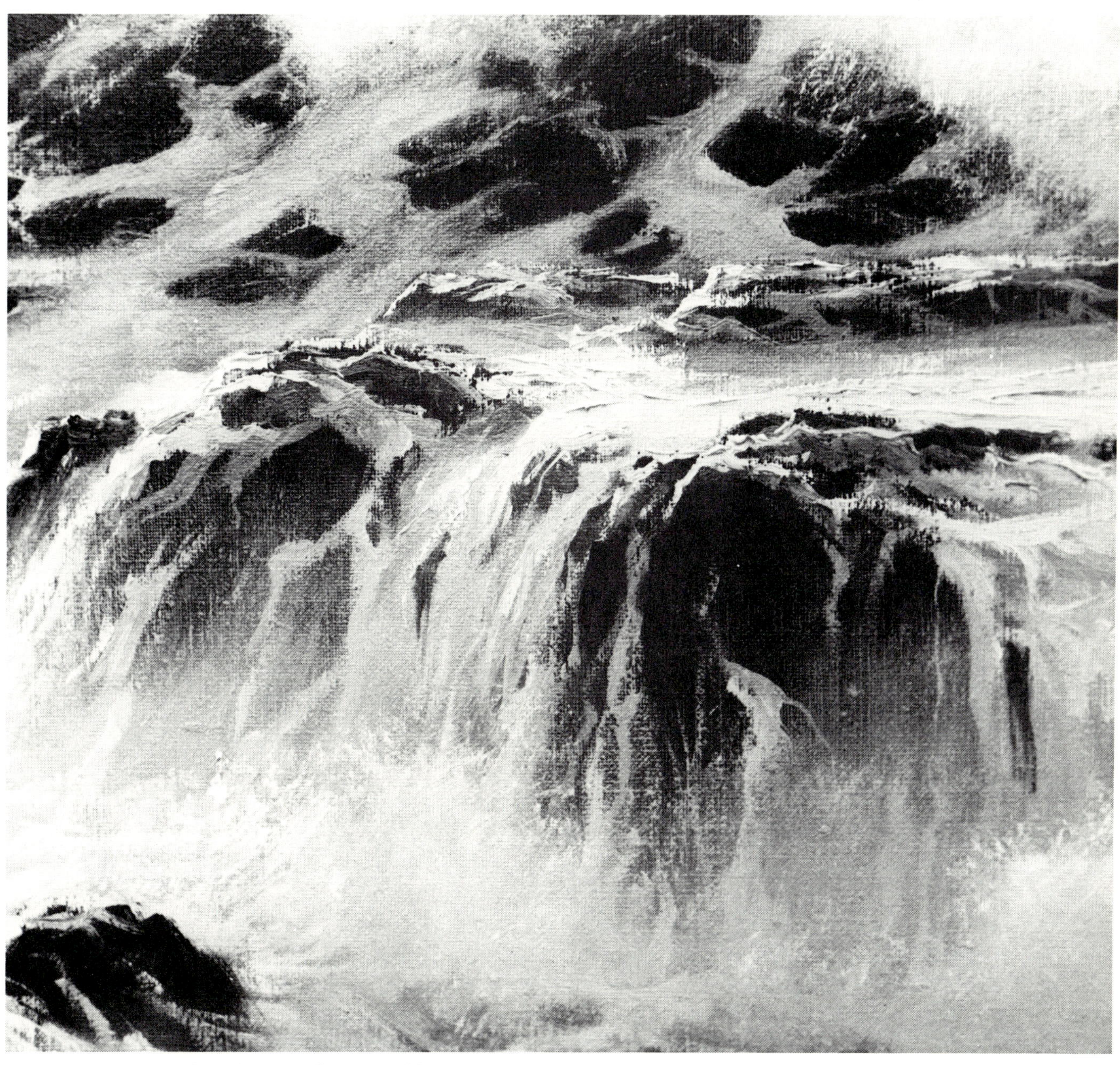

Figure 77. Spills and trickles combine to add interest to this detail.

DEMONSTRATION 26:
PAINTING A ROCK

Step 1. Painting this rock should give you practice in making both angular and rounded shapes. Work in a background and foreground in colors of your choice. For the rock, use equal parts of yellow ochre and purple or mix burnt sienna and blue to get a dark gray. Then lighten the mixture with a bit of white. This represents the basic color of the rock, which is middle-toned.

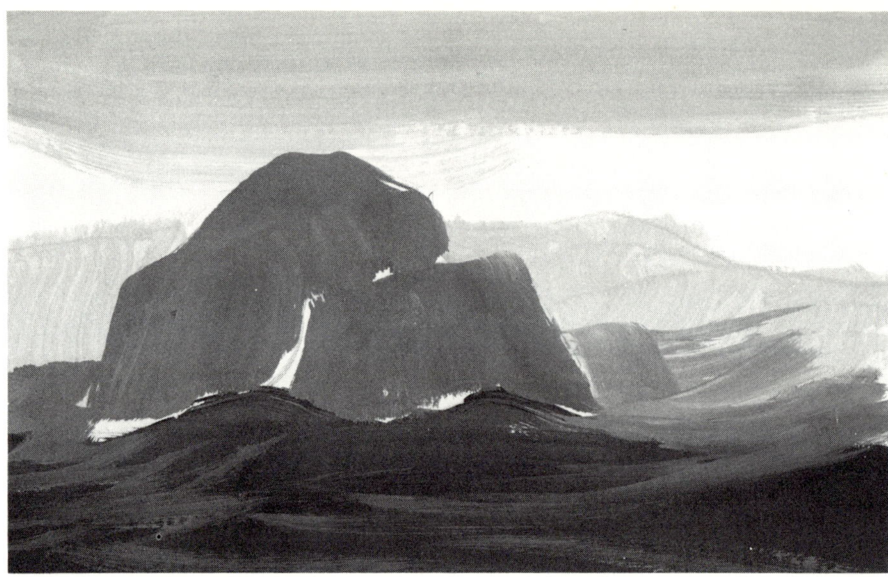

Step 2. Go back to your original dark mixture (without the white) for the rock, and work this dark tone into the areas of the rock that are in shadow. On the angular sections of the rock, make straight strokes. On the rounded sections, mix straight and curved strokes. These strokes represent the deeper shadows on the rock. Use the same mixture to add some reflections in the wet foreground.

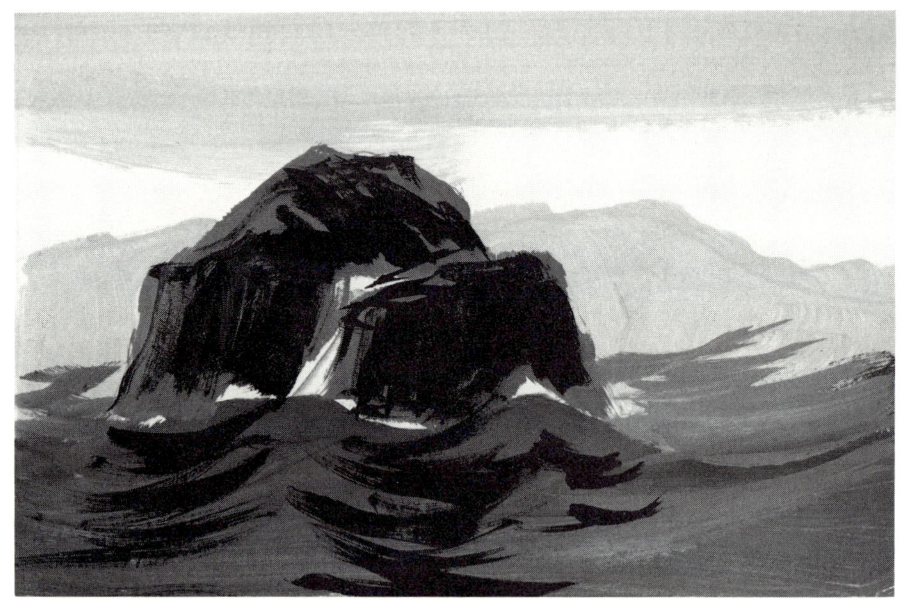

Step 3. Finally, reflect the sun and sky off the rock, keeping the shapes angular or rounded depending upon the strokes you use. Reflect the sun and sky into the foreground as well.

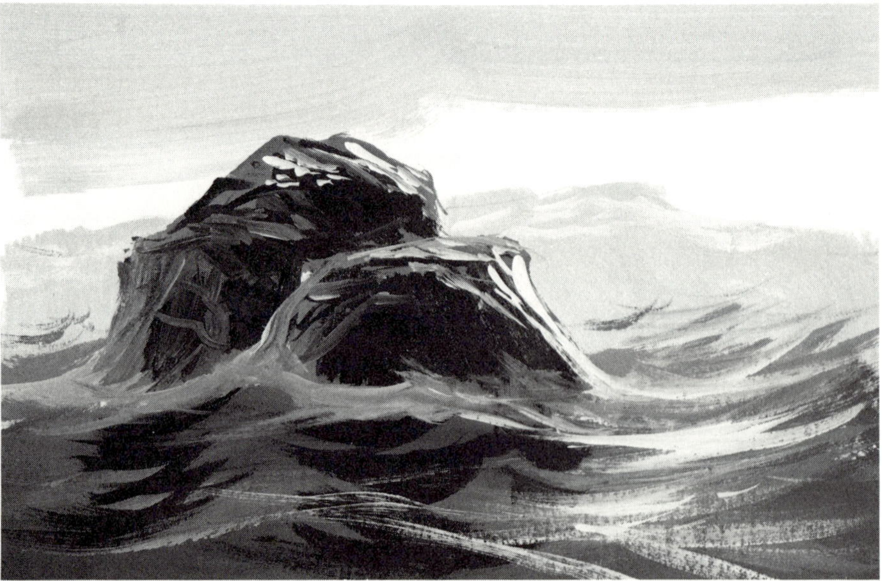

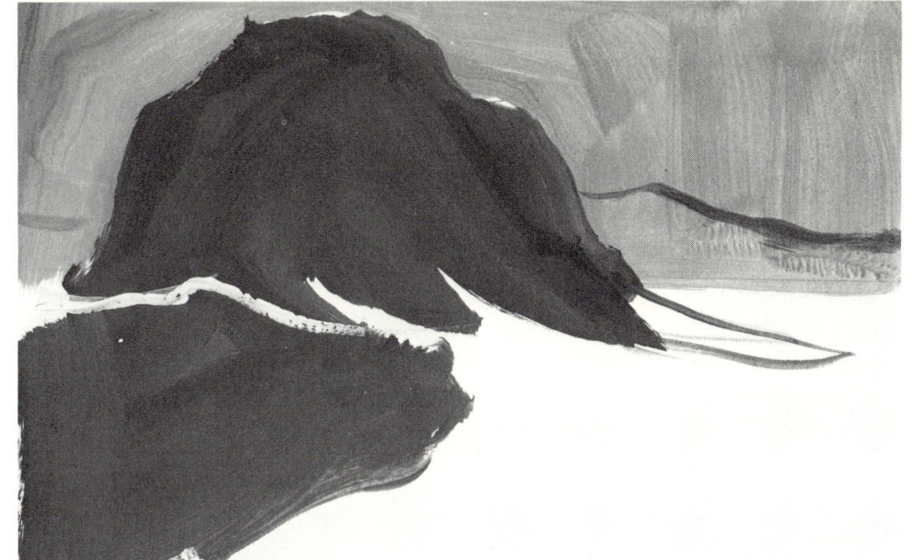

Step 1. Not much attention was paid to water against rocks in the last demonstration. However, anchoring a rock so it sits in the water is a common problem with students. All too often their rocks appear to float in the water. Begin this study by painting in a large rock and a background. Also paint some of the rock color where it would appear below the surface.

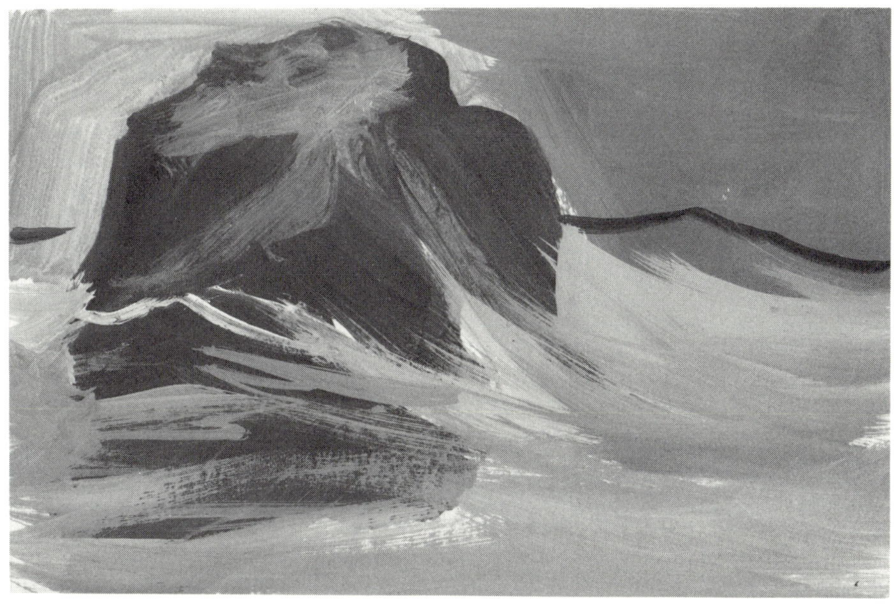

Step 2. Using a color for shadowed foam, sweep the foam up against the rock on the right-hand side. On the left, reflect the sky or allow only a small amount of foam to go over the section of rock that appears below the surface.

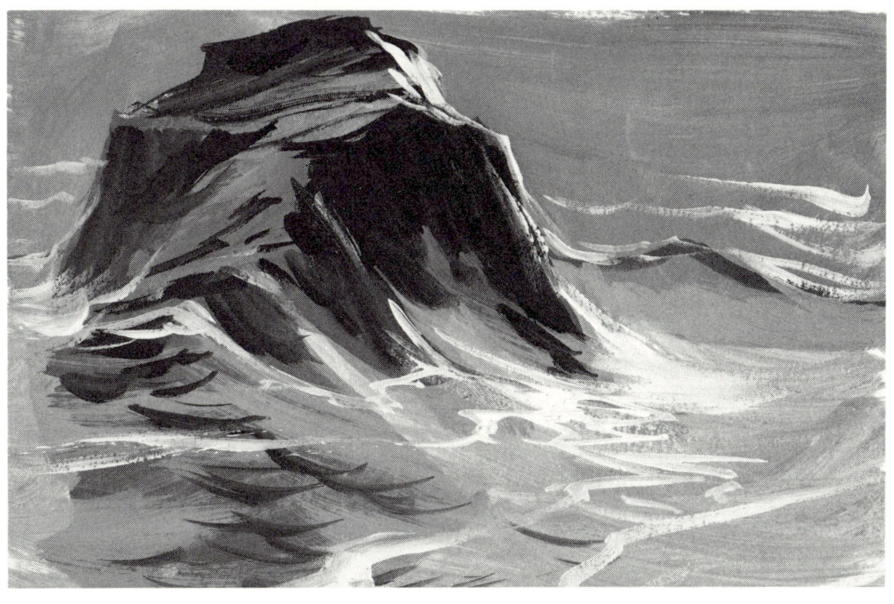

Step 3. Finish the background and the rock according to previous lessons (for example, Demonstration 21). In the foreground, add a few foam patterns and reflected light to complete the effect of water against a rock. Notice that on the right the water sweeps up against the rock; but on the left it swirls alongside. Always try to show a mixture of effects such as these.

DEMONSTRATION 28:
OVERFLOWING WATER

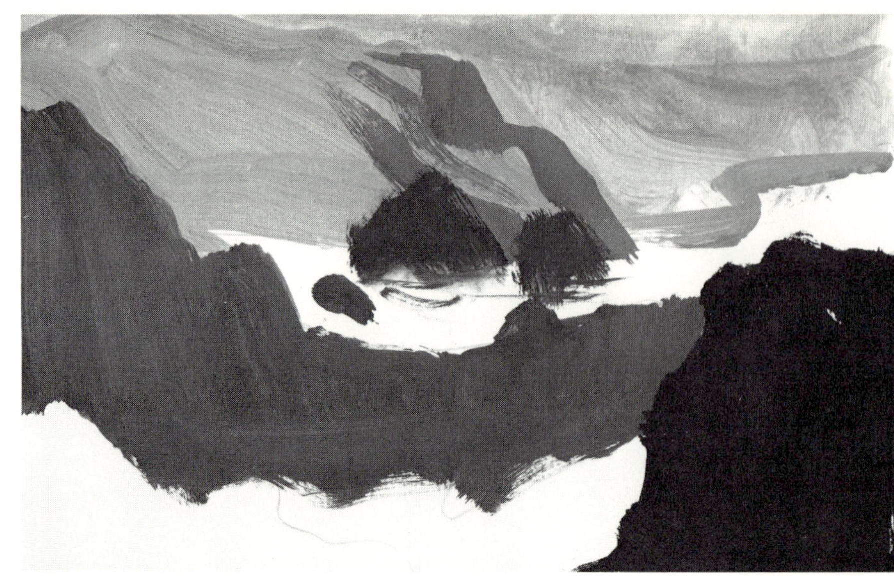

Step 1. Paint in a series of rocks, but leave a flat area unpainted where it will be reflecting the light of the sky. In this case, the middle rock extending across the painting has a flat top. This rock will eventually be covered with water that will also pour over the ledge.

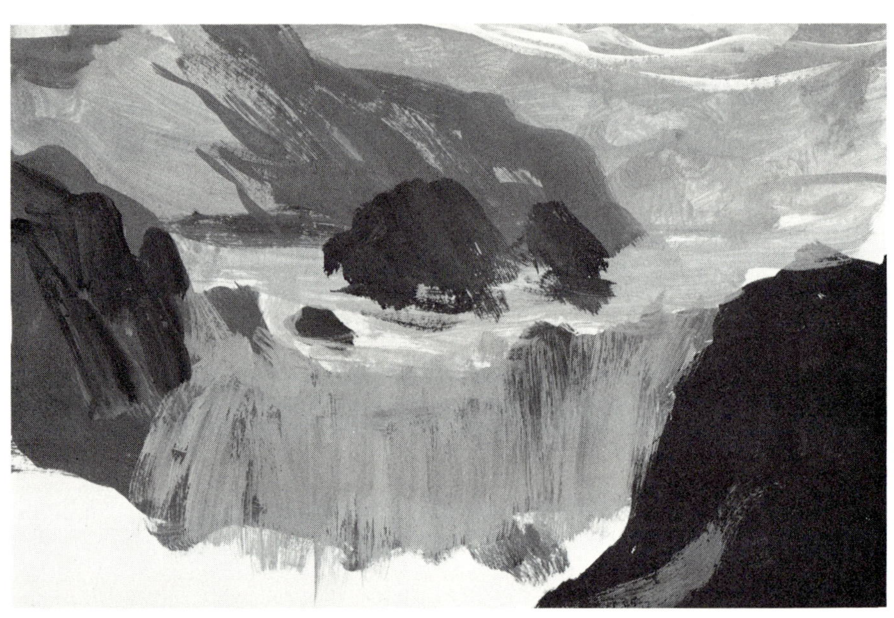

Step 2. Overflowing water is generally foamy after mixing with air, so think in terms of shadowed foam when preparing the colors for this. When painting water flowing over rocks, allow some rock color to show through, but use shadowed foam for the overflow area. Reflect the sky on the water that is flowing above the flat area of the rocks.

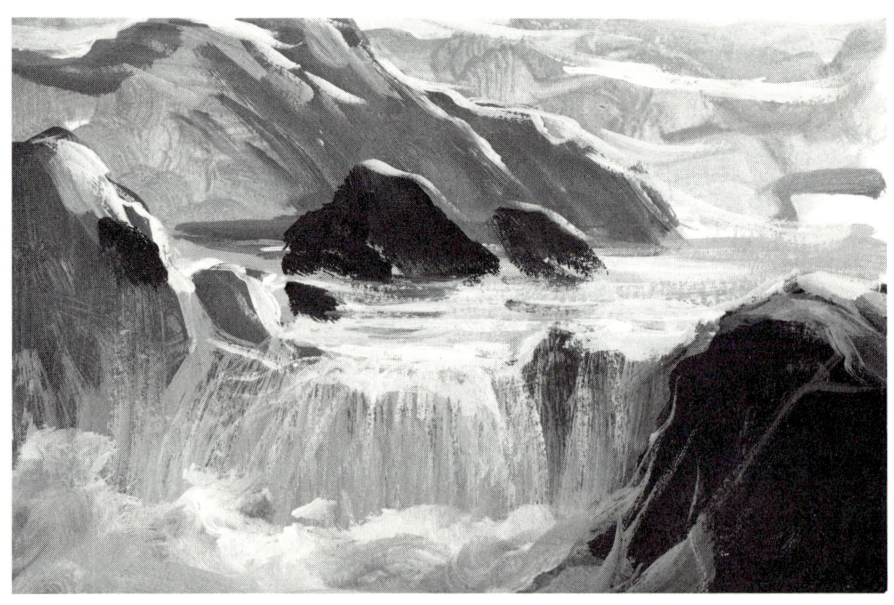

Step 3. As in most of these lessons, the addition of light and reflected light are the final touches. Notice here the use of light to give the impression of falling water. The overuse of this light would destroy its effectiveness.

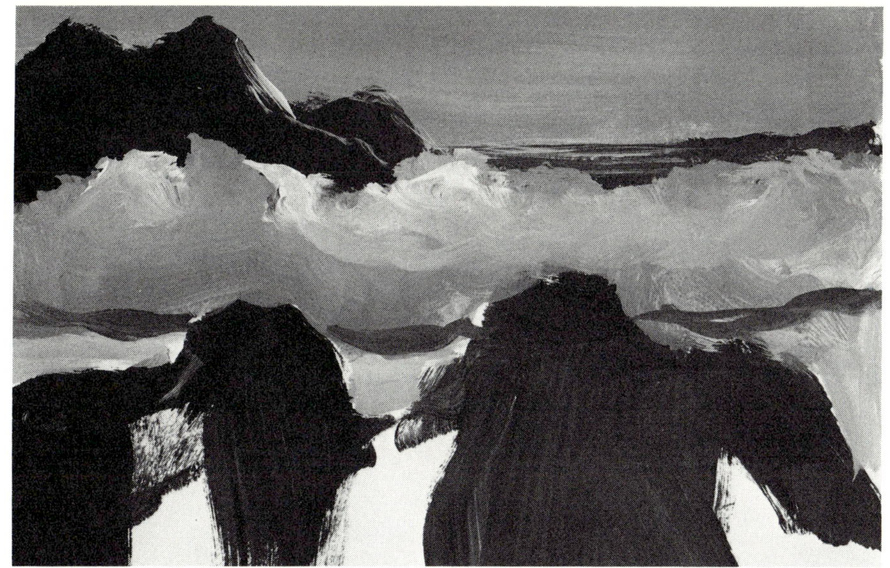

Step 1: Work in a background breaker and other objects for practice. Then paint in a rock form that has large gaps between segments. Leave these gaps unpainted. If the water that will spill over these gaps were to move slowly, then some rock color would have to show through. In this case, the drop is nearly vertical, so the falling water will be foamy from moving quickly.

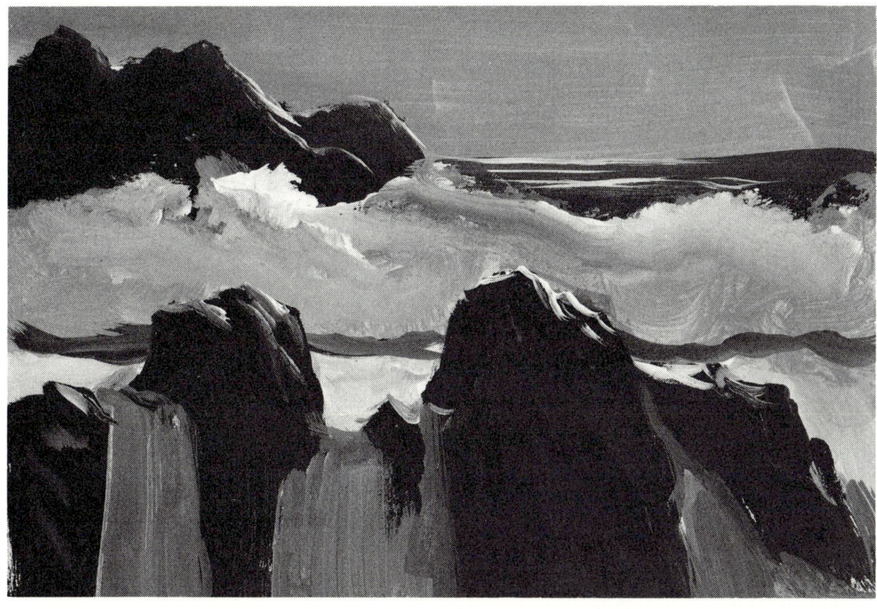

Step 2. Make up a light-gray shadowed foam by mixing either a green-purple (viridian/ultramarine-alizarin) or ultramarine blue-burnt sienna combination into white. Paint in the falling water without blending it with the rock color. Be sure your brushstrokes move downward as the water falls. Get the feeling of the water!

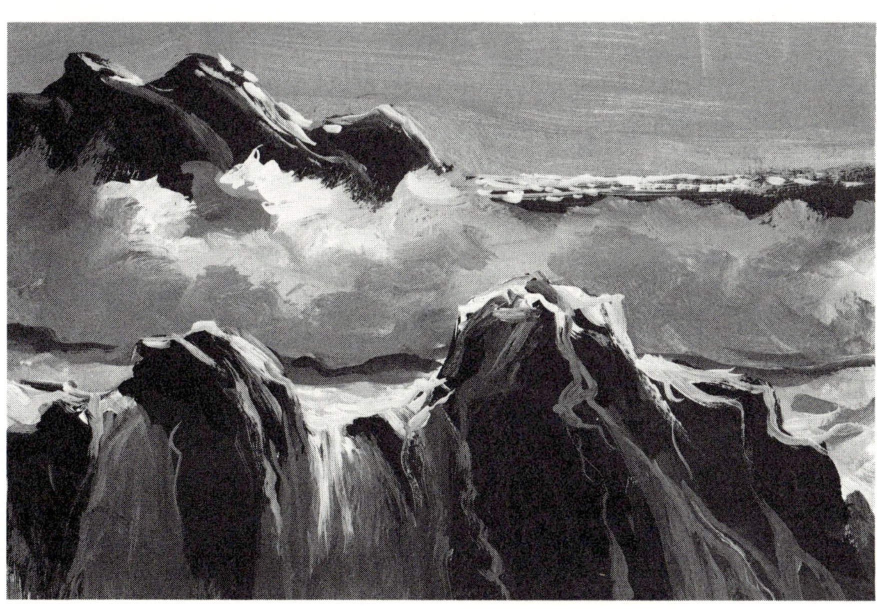

Step 3. Now add some trickles. They may start almost anywhere on the rock but should end up somewhere at the bottom, even though they disappear for a bit along the way. Both spills and trickles are best shown in light and shadow, both thick and thin. Whenever possible, use the trickles to show the contour of the rock face.

CHAPTER NINE

WORKING WITH SUNLIGHT

In Chapter Six I emphasized the point that the sea is a reflecting agent, both from below and above. From above, the sky as atmosphere casts its colors and values on the sea. Following that, but no less important, are the reflections of the sun and its spreading light.

A day without sunlight is gloomy and dull. Granted that an overcast day can be interesting, with subtle grays and even truer colors. But it lacks the glinting, sparkling effect that only sunlight can give. Use sunlight properly, and your paintings will come alive.

The use of sunlight in realistic painting is extremely important, but it's often omitted or misunderstood by students and even many professionals. Keep in mind that the sun carries color, and that these colors may change. Remember that sunlight influences the atmosphere which, in turn, influences the sea.

Think not so much in terms of color alone as of color influenced by color. And remember that color is carried by the sun's rays. Start with a basic color such as viridian for a wave. Darken it with the umber or sienna it would reflect from the ocean floor. Lighten it with the yellow, red, or orange from the sunlight. And finally, reflect the atmosphere on any portion that lies beneath the sky. When you're finished, you have realism in seascape, a technique you need never apologize for.

FRONT LIGHTING

The direction from which sunlight shines determines in part its intensity—even its color. Front lighting is morning light on the West Coast, and it can be a very warm color. I usually choose cadmium yellow deep or a yellow with a touch of alizarin in it for the sunlight.

Figure 78 was painted in front lighting. The major wave catches light from behind the viewer; the rocks are casting shadows as well as being in shadow. Notice the "echo" of light in the foreground. It isn't light enough to distract from the light-colored major wave, but it does subordinate the wave by spotting the lightest value in more than one place.

Front lighting can wash out color, because it eliminates so much shadow. In Figure 79, another example of front lighting, it was necessary to contrast the darkness of the rocks against the lightness of the foam, or the light foam would appear washed out under front lighting. The problem was solved here simply by placing the foreground in shadow while the breaker is fully lit. A contrast was formed by keeping the sunlit area so small.

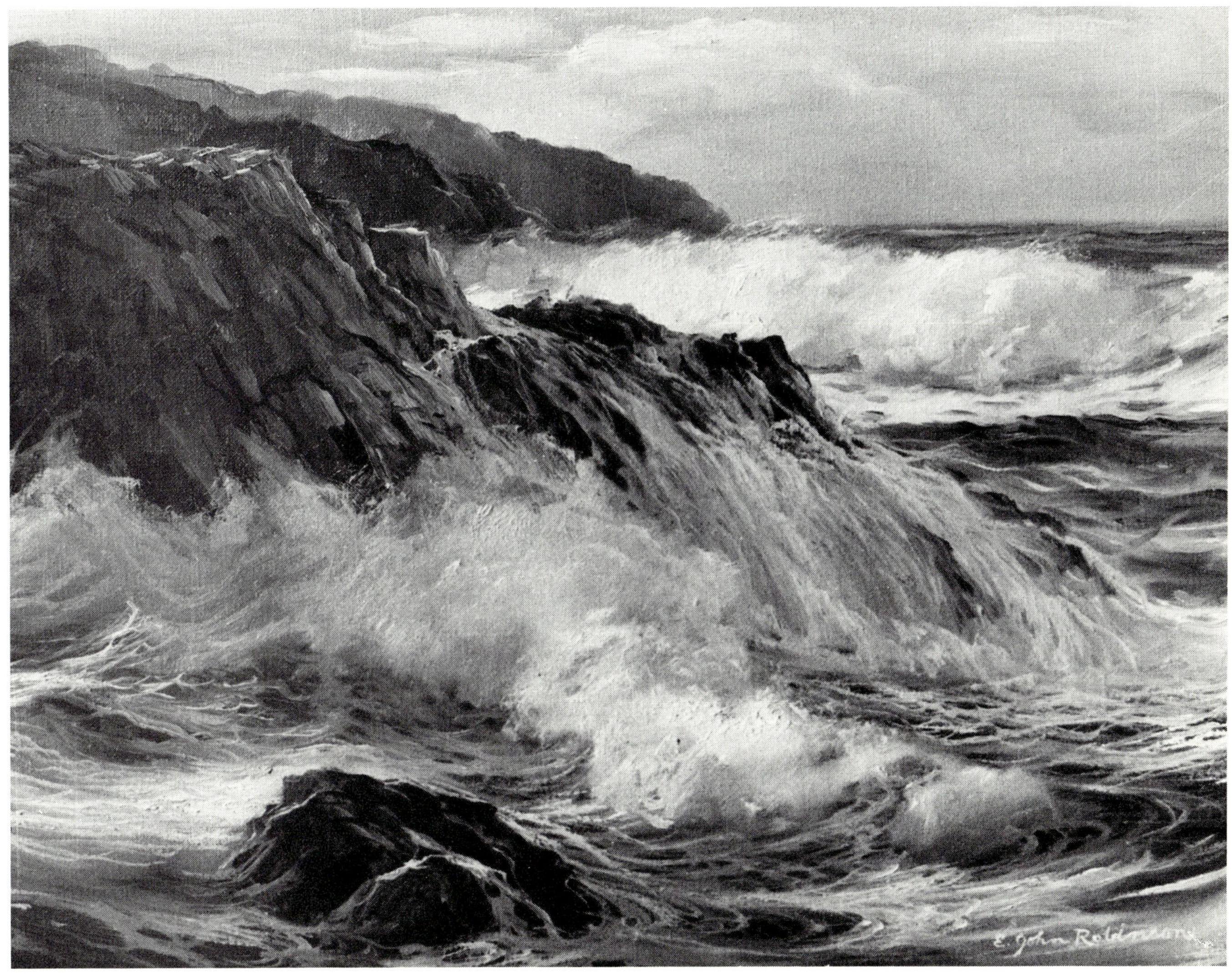

Figure 78. On the West Coast, morning means front lighting.

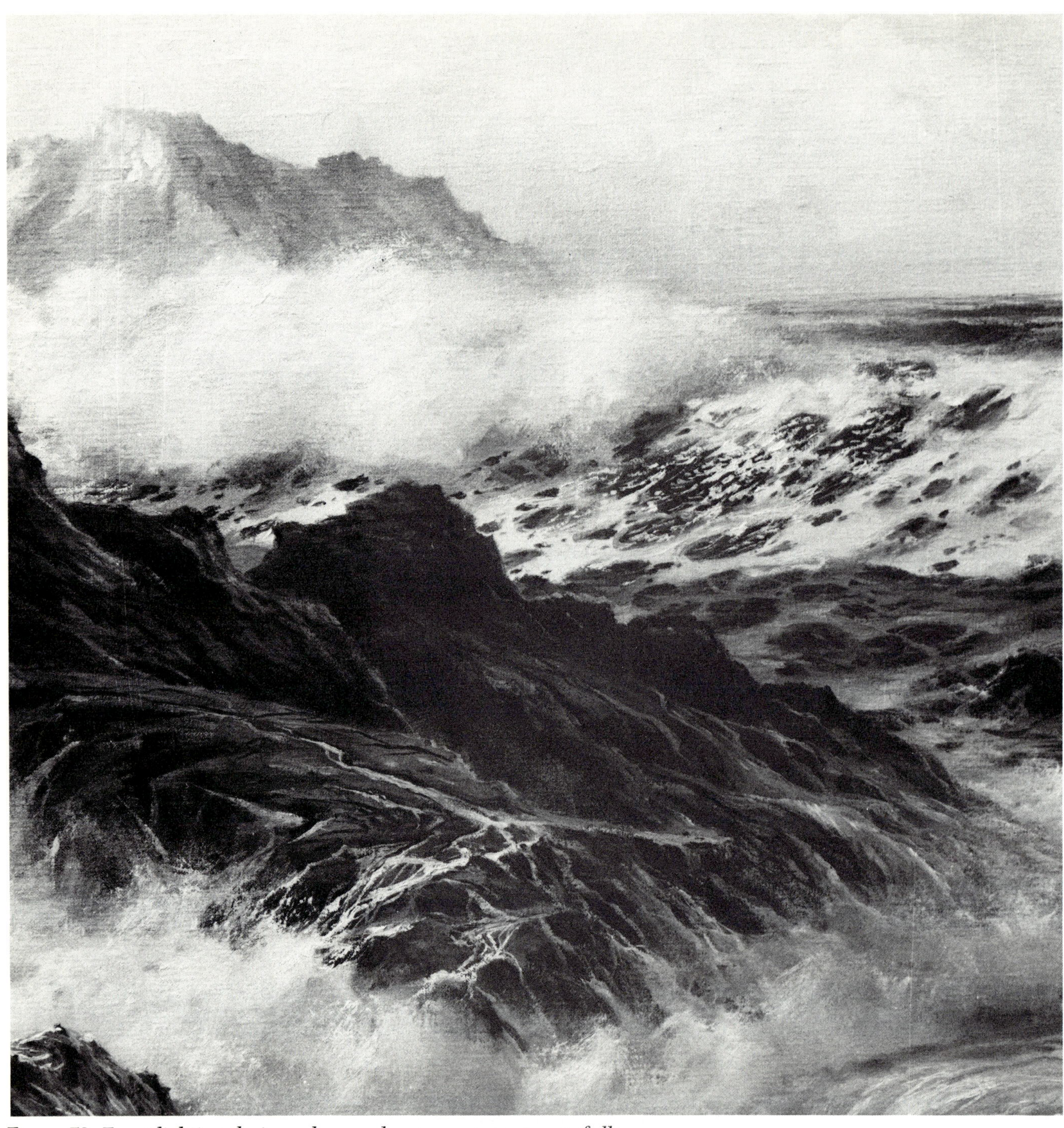

Figure 79. Front lighting drains color, so plan your contrasts carefully.

SIDE LIGHTING

When you place the source of light to one side, keep that area lighter and brighter than the rest of the painting. Notice in Figure 81 that the left-hand side is very bright, almost washed out in effect compared with the right-hand side. This was the intention of this particular composition, but it doesn't mean that all side-lit paintings must be the same.

The closeup view of a portion of wave (Figure 80) also shows lighting from the left. At the same time, the light glints off the clear wave face. The background rocks are in shadow.

Side lighting can give strong light-and-shadow effects similar to back lighting. The amount of contrast is up to you. You may choose to place the source of light high or low, make the sunlight warm or cool, and the intensity of light soft or brilliant. Whatever you decide, however, follow through with the same mood over the entire painting.

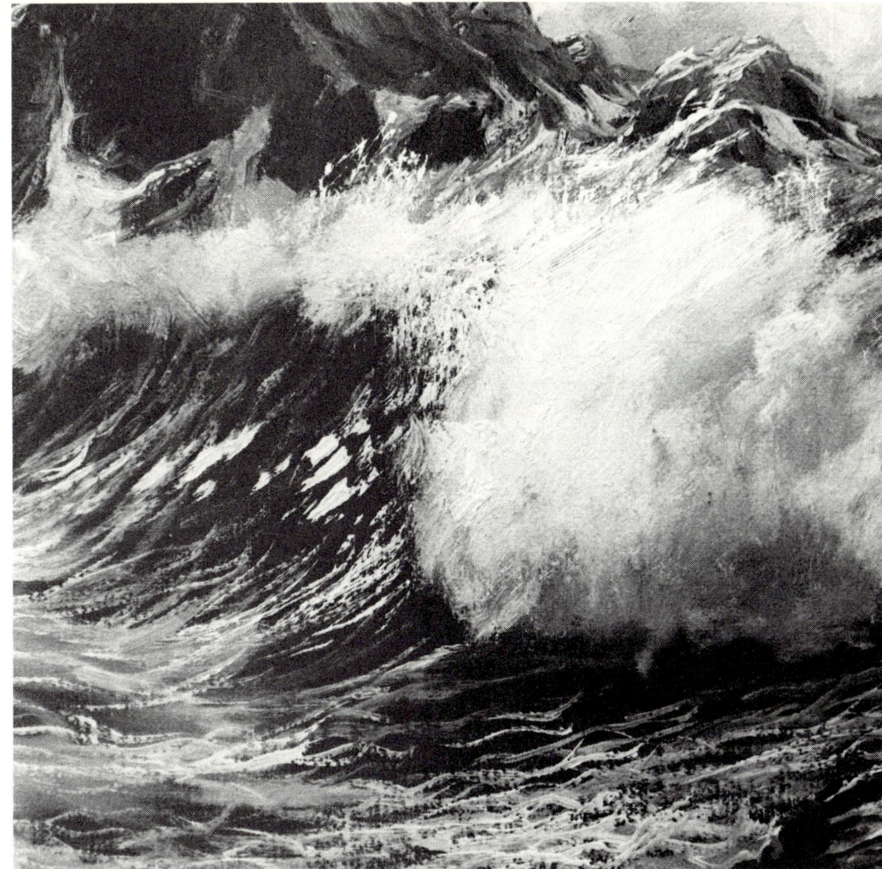

Figure 80. Strong light from the left is washing over the entire scene.

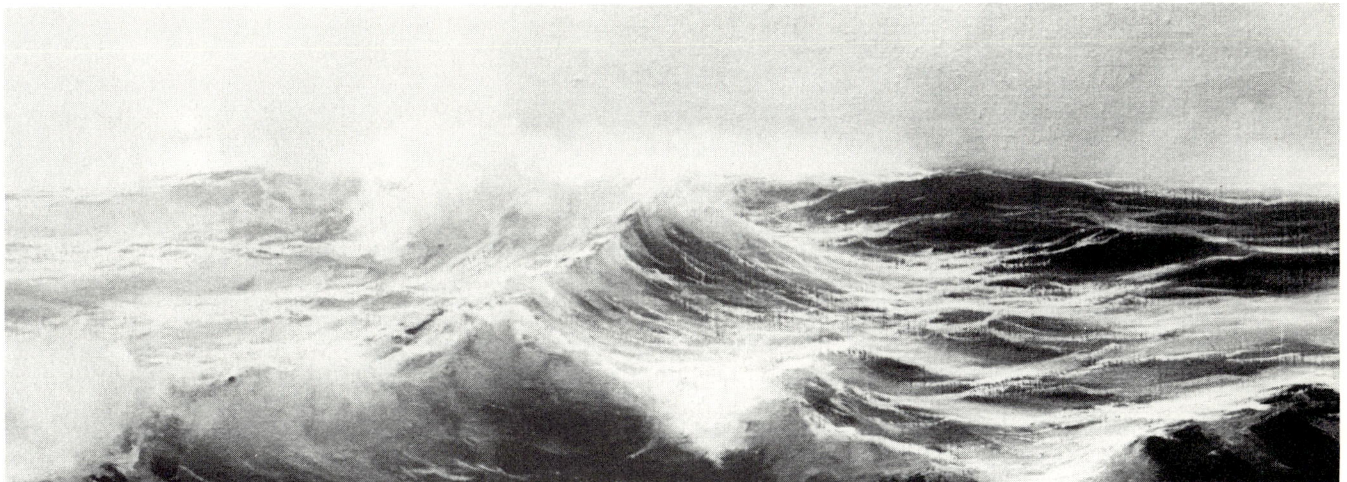

Figure 81. Side lighting strengthens light and shade on objects.

BACK LIGHTING

Most people draw, as they have since early childhood, by outlining the object. But in realistic seascape painting, outlining would be disastrous under almost any circumstances other than back lighting.

Although I love the glint of light on distant chops and the effects of glitter and glow, back lighting is my favorite lighting effect. Under its spell, waves become translucent and forms take shape with just a few brushstrokes of sunlight color. And it challenges my patience; it's not as easy as it looks!

Figure 82 shows a painting lit from the back, left-hand side. The background is faded by sunlight, but the areas receding from the light are highlights. The back, at the right, is drawn with sunlight. The major wave is a study of sunlit edges, and the foreground chops have been drawn with strokes of sunlight. In Figure 83 the wave is almost in halo but casts a long shadow before it. You will find a lesson on backlighting in Demonstration 30.

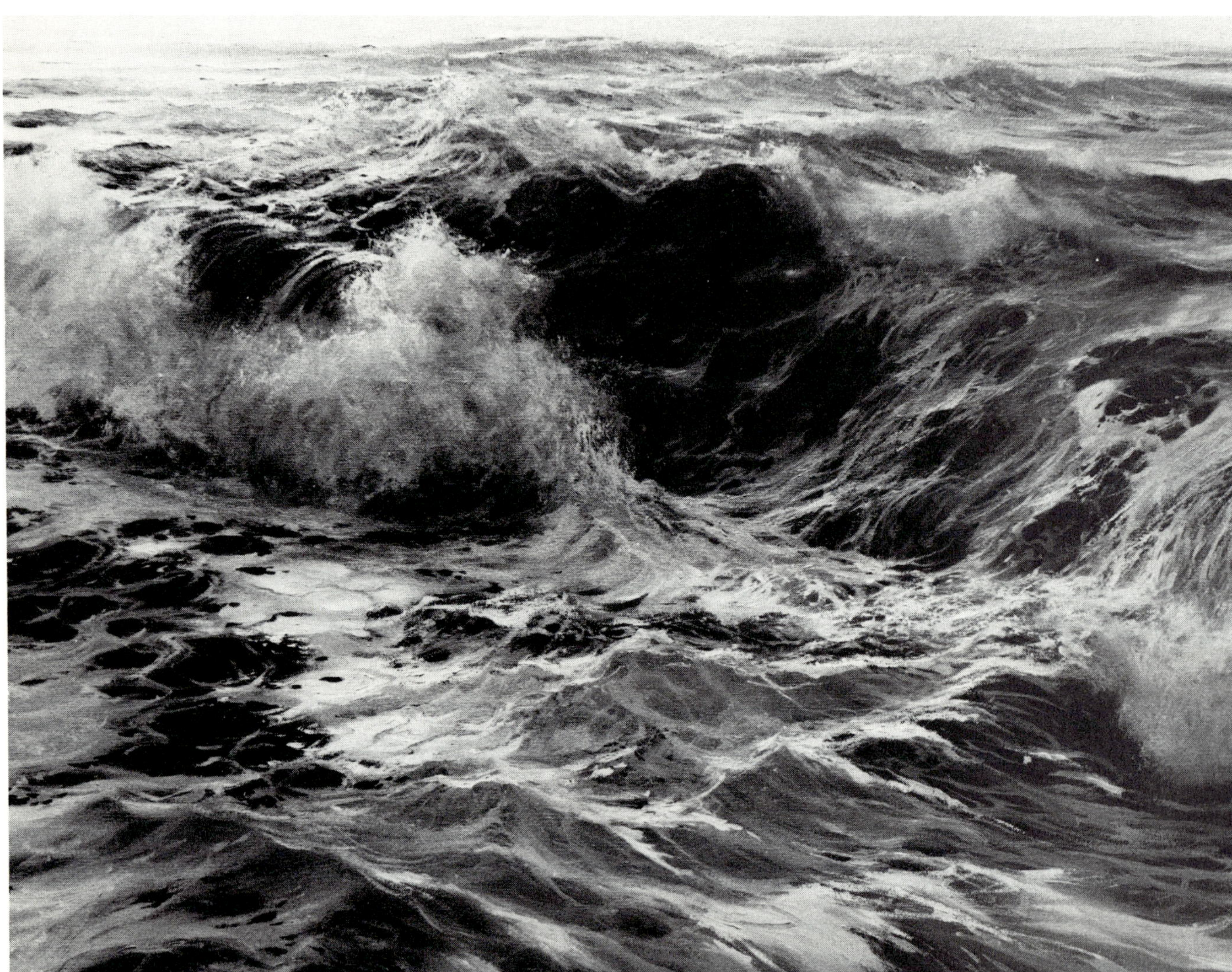

Figure 82. In this painting I let the sunlight define all form.

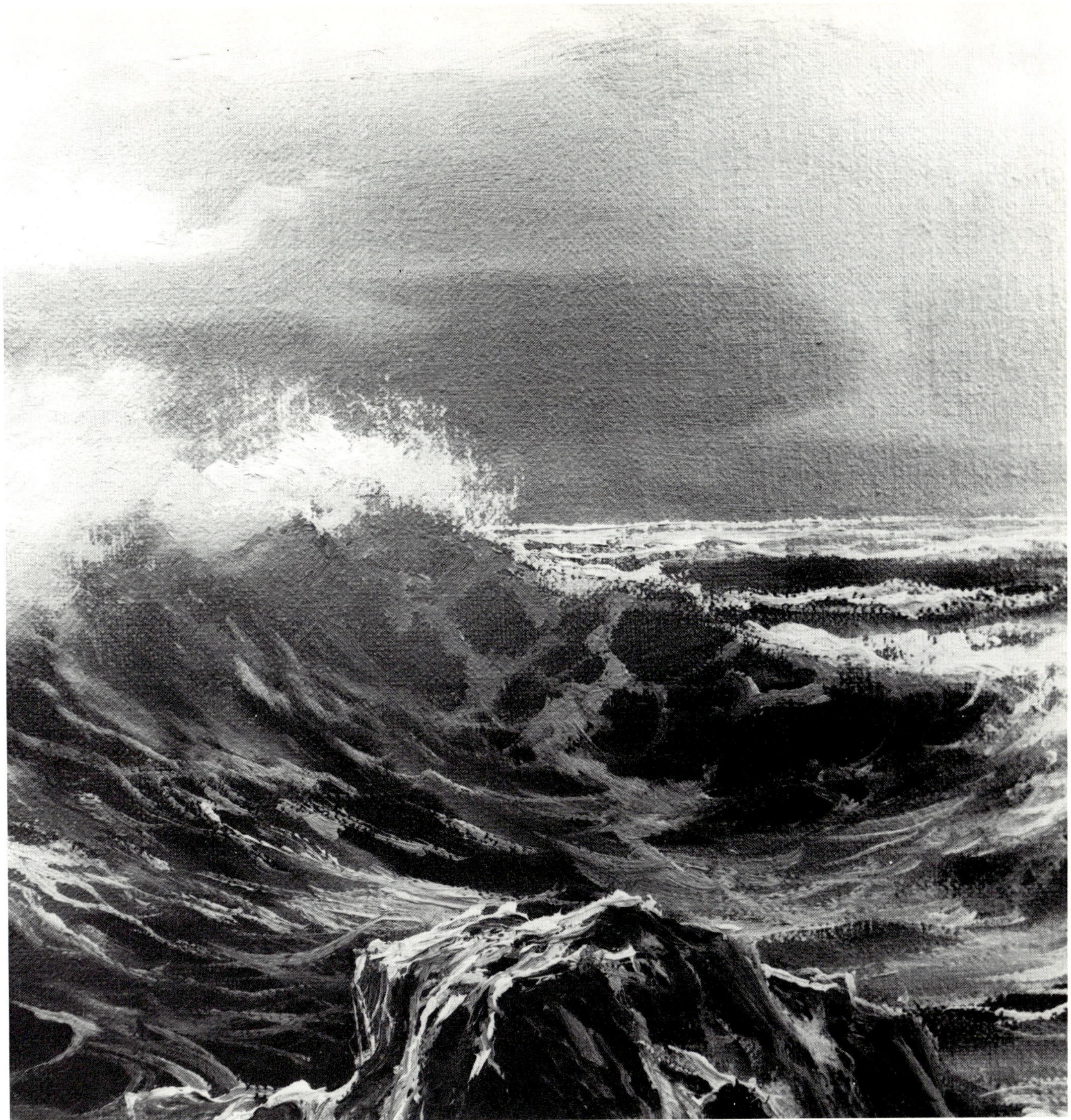

Figure 83. Shadows are at their longest when the light is from the extreme back.

DOWN LIGHTING

High noon produces down lighting. Like any other use of light, you must control how you display it. When you choose down lighting, work out ahead of time just how you want to use it. Avoid painting an entire composition of harsh light and shadow. Soften some areas or strengthen others, but remember that changing and comparing different areas in a painting help avoid monotony. (See Demonstration 31 for how to paint down lighting.)

In Figure 84 the sunlight is directly overhead and very bright, as is shown by the darkness of the wave shadow and brightness on the surface foam. I selected this effect for my sketch and carried it out. I could have softened the shadows on the wave and lessened the brightness of the sun on the sea. I could have diminished the background, or even the major wave, into fog, had I so desired. The choice always lies with the artist.

Down lighting has its effect on all objects. In Figure 85 notice that the trickles on the rock as well as the foam of the wave are lit from above. Whenever you start a painting, always determine the angle and direction of light first.

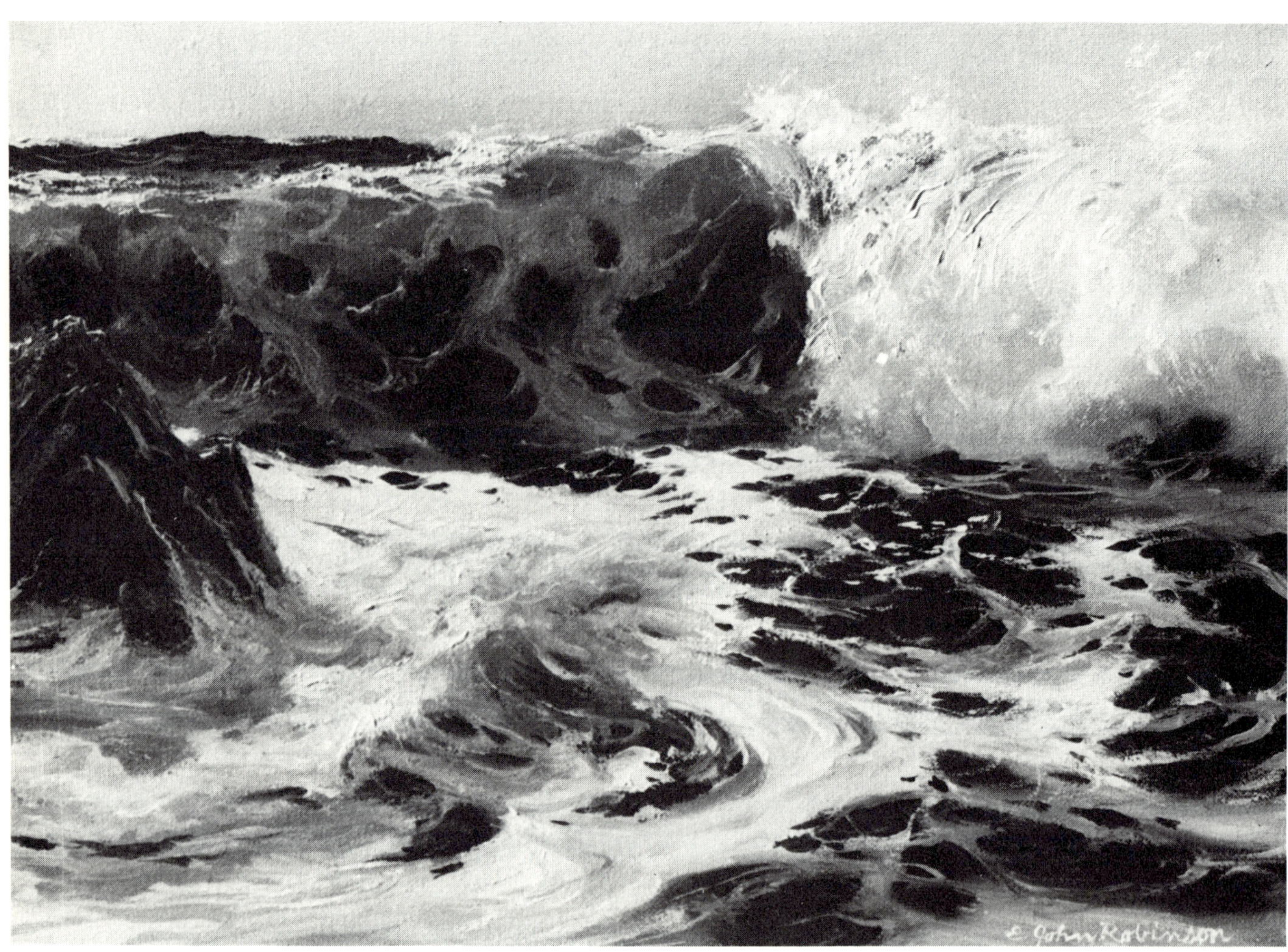

Figure 84. In this sketch the sun is directly overhead and the day is clear.

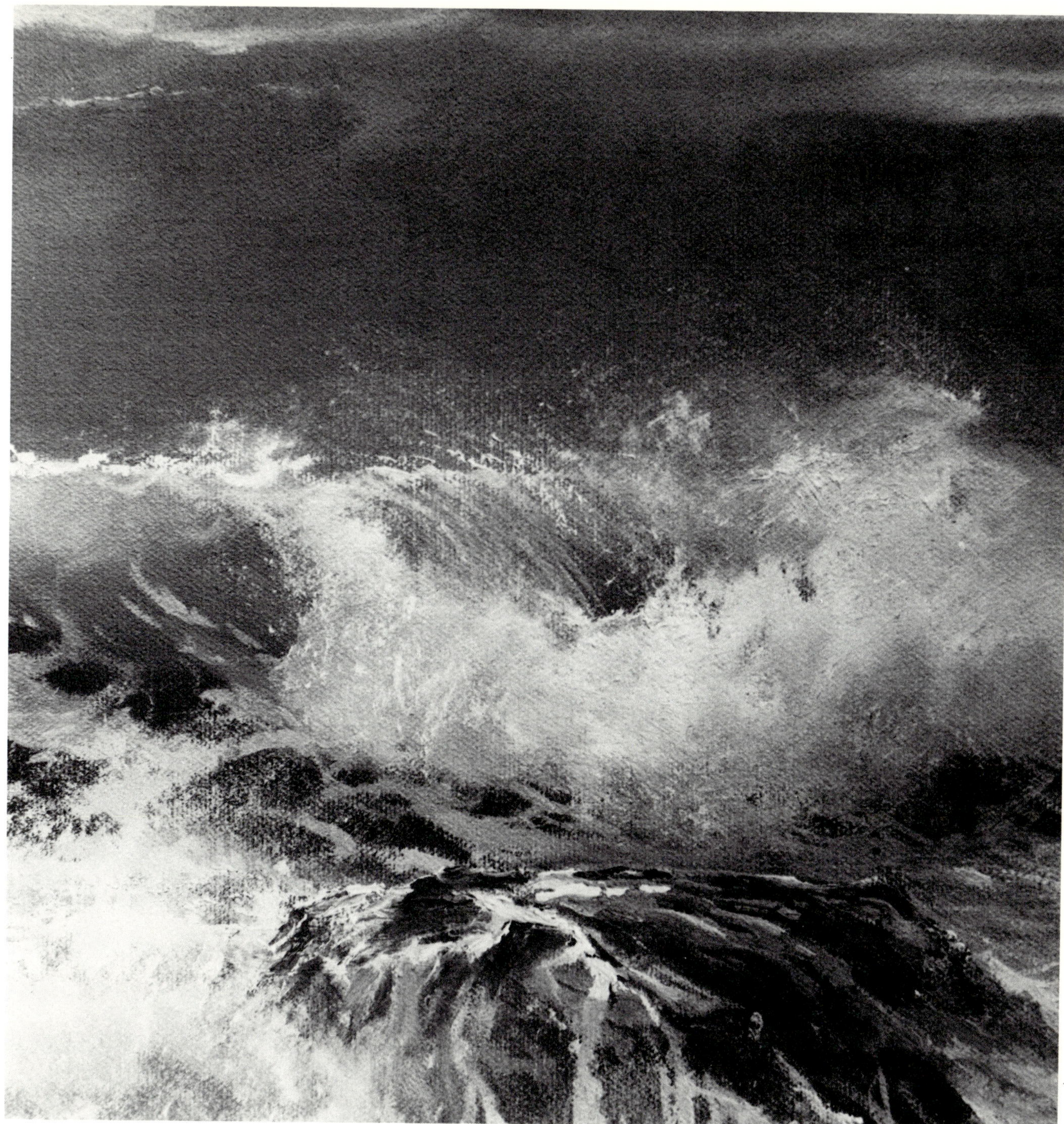

Figure 85. The entire sea—from foam to trickles—is bathed in a down light.

SPOTLIGHTING

I can think of no better way to show a center of interest than using the sunlight to spotlight one or two areas in a painting that I wish to draw attention to. The effect can get too obvious, however; so exercise some caution. And keep it subtle. Allow some light to strike in other places aside from the center of interest. Just be sure that the other spots are only echoes of the larger light and not obvious enough to distract from the main interest.

In most cases when spotlighting occurs, the atmosphere is overcast or cloud-covered, with a few holes where sunlight may penetrate. It's also possible to cast bluff shadows over a foreground such as in Figure 86 and allow a bit of light to play on the water. This is the use of mysterious light and it goes back to Rembrandt, and even earlier than that.

Apart from this, there's no natural explanation for why the lightest spot in this painting is where it is. It's there because I arbitrarily chose to put it there. I can only defend myself by arguing "artistic license" or that the sun peeked from behind a bluff. It doesn't matter. An artist must be authentic if he's a realist—but he can stretch things a bit, can't he?

The spotlighting in Figure 87 is more easily explained than that in the previous one. This is front lighting, but high rocks or bluffs have cast shadows and the rising wave picks up only a limited amount of direct sunlight. Notice that the light is echoed on a bit of foam in the background.

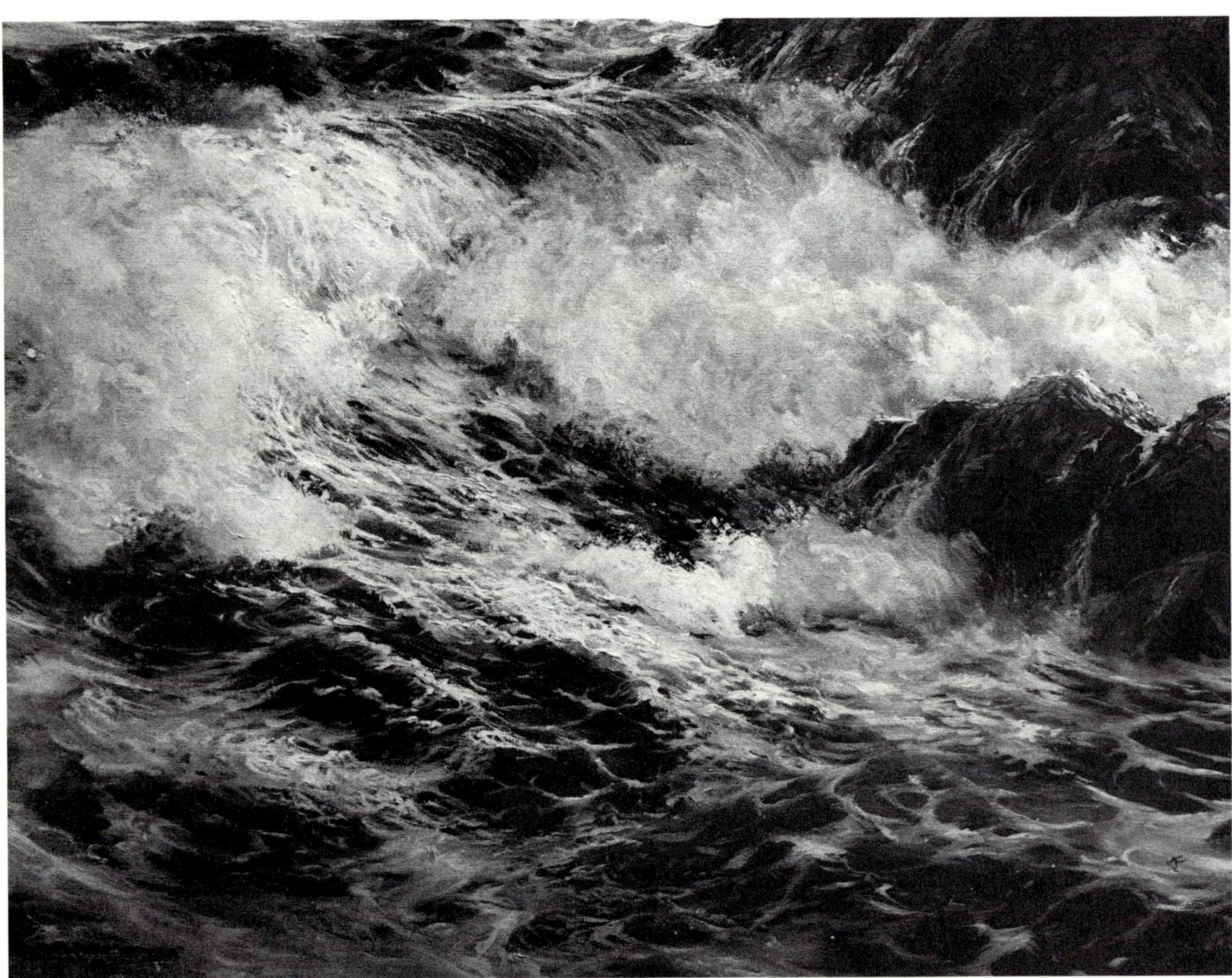

Figure 86. You may spotlight anything you wish in a painting.

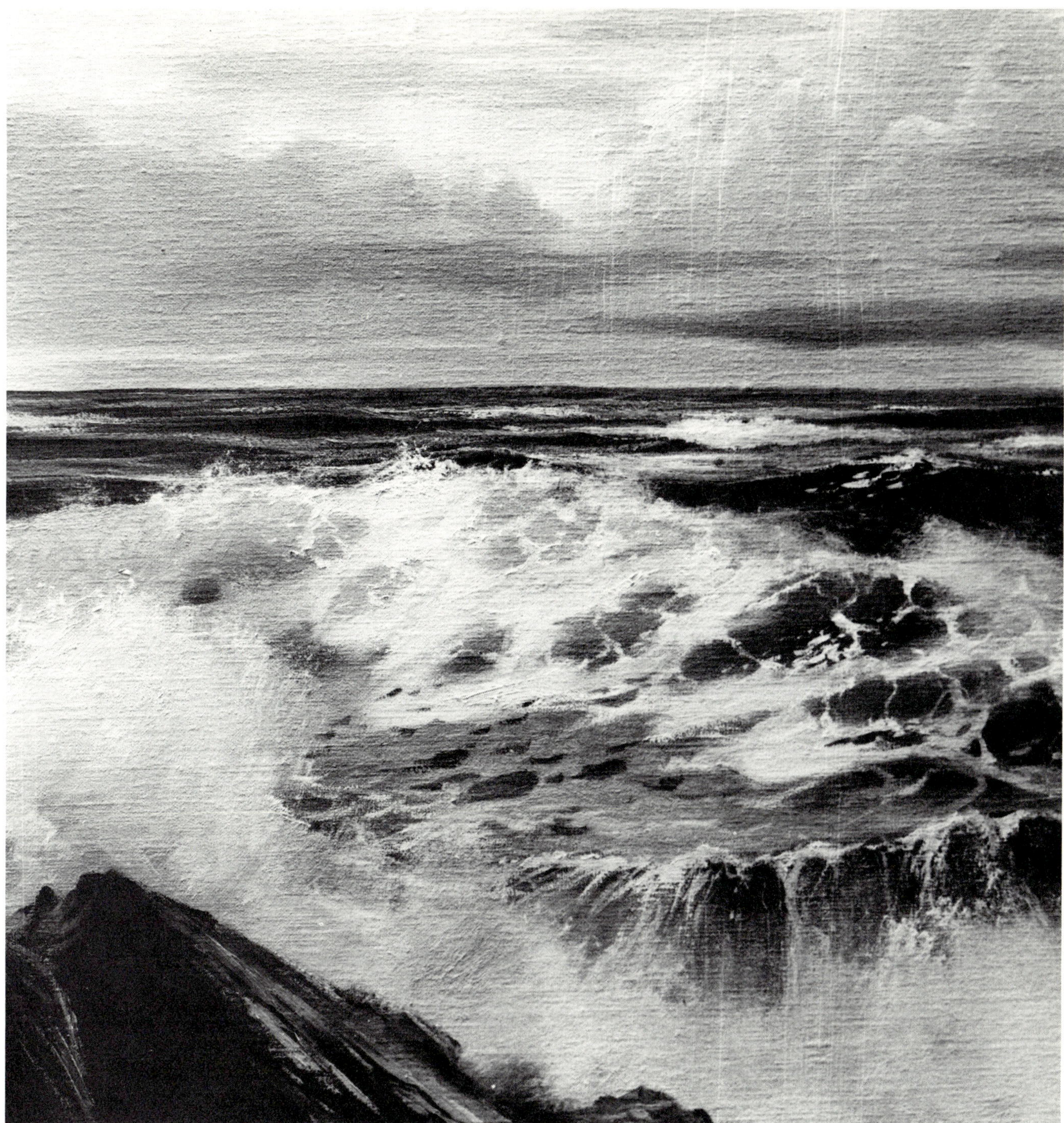

Figure 87. Spotlighting combines with front lighting for an interesting effect.

MISTY LIGHT

Misty light occurs when sunlight shines through an atmosphere of heavy moisture. This may occur in the distance with fog or moisture-laden air, or in the foreground when back lighting shines through water particles from foam spray.

I love misty light. It not only adds interest to a painting, but it almost makes the viewer put on dark glasses! We can't match the brilliance of the sun; we can only hint at it. But with a bit of trickery, our hints become stronger.

In Figure 88 the misty light is in the foreground, the result of light glowing behind an area of spray. This doesn't necessarily have to become the center of interest. On the contrary, it's a very good method of reducing the contrast in a particular area, thus making it less important, rather than more so. In Figure 89 the light fades everything in the background and some details on the right.

Remember, misty light requires back lighting; so don't try it under other conditions. When you paint it, mix your sunlight color, apply it to an area already painted, and blend it in. Use the dry varnish brush to soften the edges. No brushstrokes should be visible. Finally, put in a few crisp lines or glints of light, but keep them away from the center of the misty area.

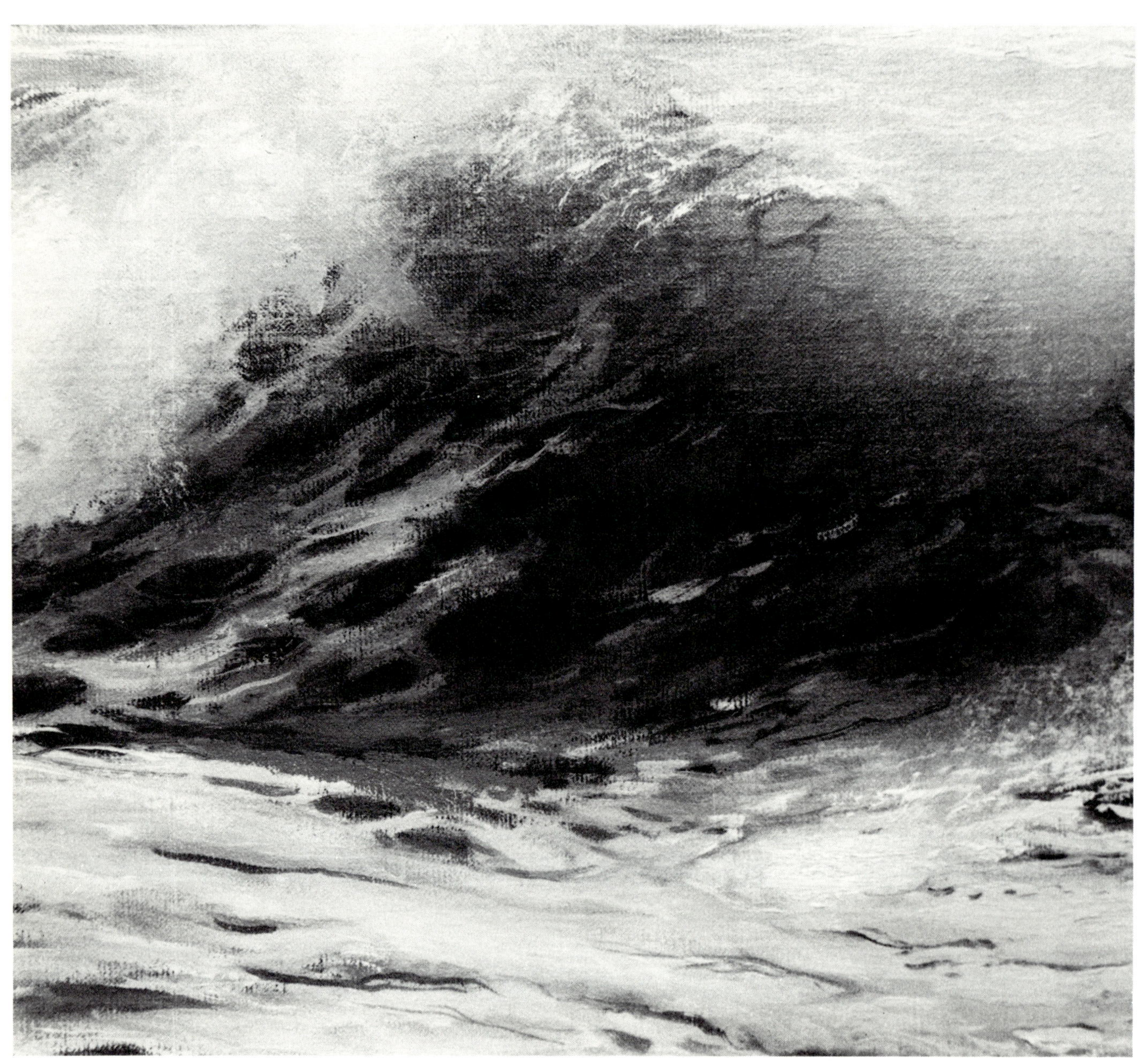

Figure 88. Misty light glowing behind an area of spray reduces contrasts.

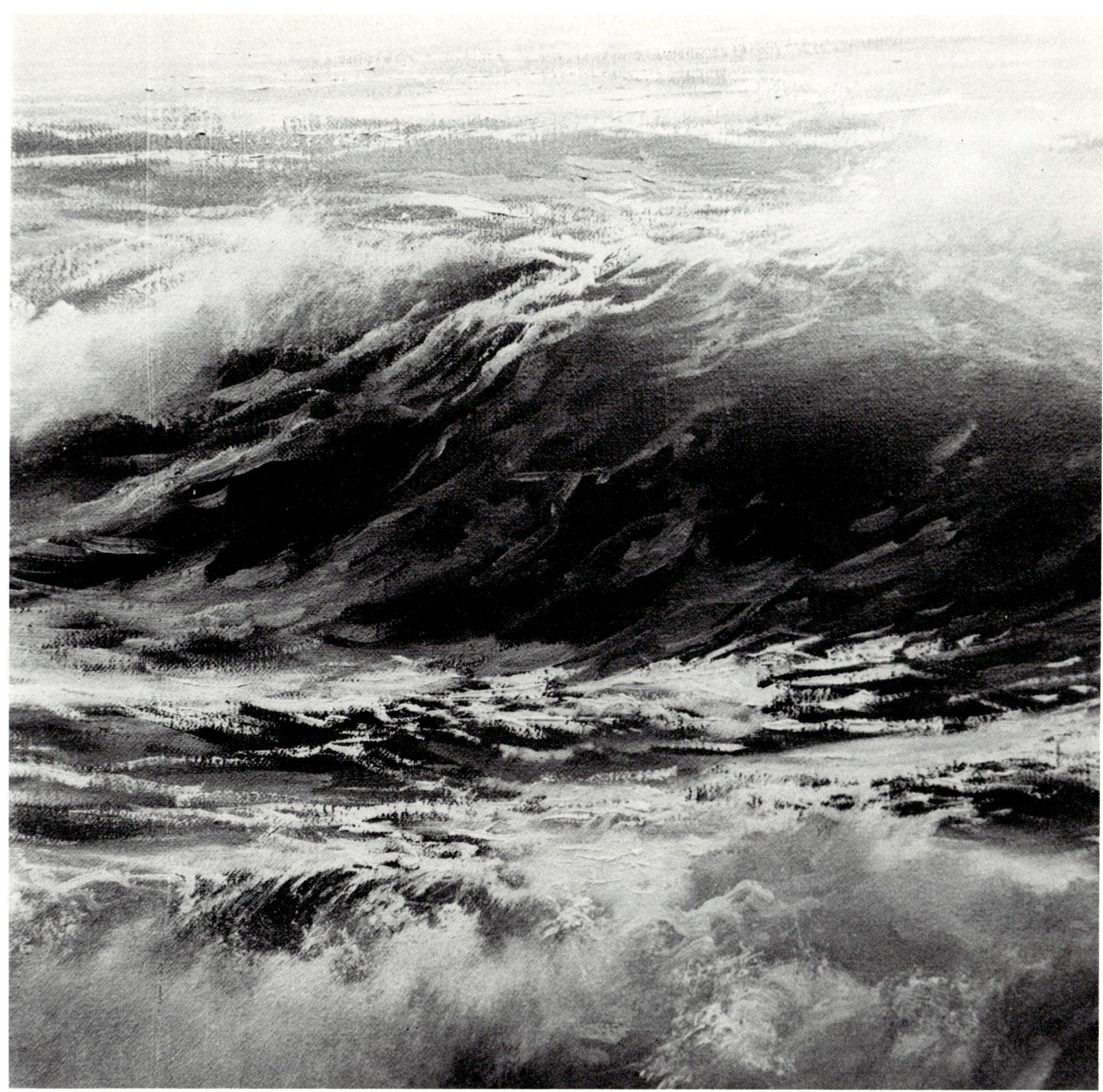

Figure 89. Details fade under a misty light.

DISTANCE WITH ATMOSPHERE

We can't separate sunlight from shadow, reflected light, and atmosphere. They're all the result of sunlight.

The atmosphere contains particles of dust and moisture that catch and reflect light (and color); their amount increases with distance. The more atmosphere you must look through, the less distinct objects will be. Therefore distant hills or headlands fade lighter and lighter under the influence of atmosphere.

Atmosphere is always the color of the sky, whether it's bright and clear or totally foggy. In addition, it's influenced by the color and placement of the sun. For example, if you chose a pale blue sky and a pale yellow sun, you'd lighten the blue sky nearest the sun with pale yellow. Applying this same principle to distance, use the color of your sky (atmosphere) to lighten any object as it recedes. (You can see how I paint atmosphere in Demonstration 32.)

In Figure 90 the headlands become lighter as they recede into the distance. They were a brown-green color up close, and were lightened gradually with the gray-blue mix I used for the sky. Each separate range had more atmosphere than the preceding one; hence more and more atmospheric color was used to lighten each receding headland.

Although Figure 91 contains a form of misty light too, the fading effect in the background is due to atmosphere. The atmosphere is nearly fog—it's thick enough to fade whatever lies beyond a few feet—but with sunlight coming through.

You'll find four more examples of using sunlight and atmosphere in the color section (Demonstration 15).

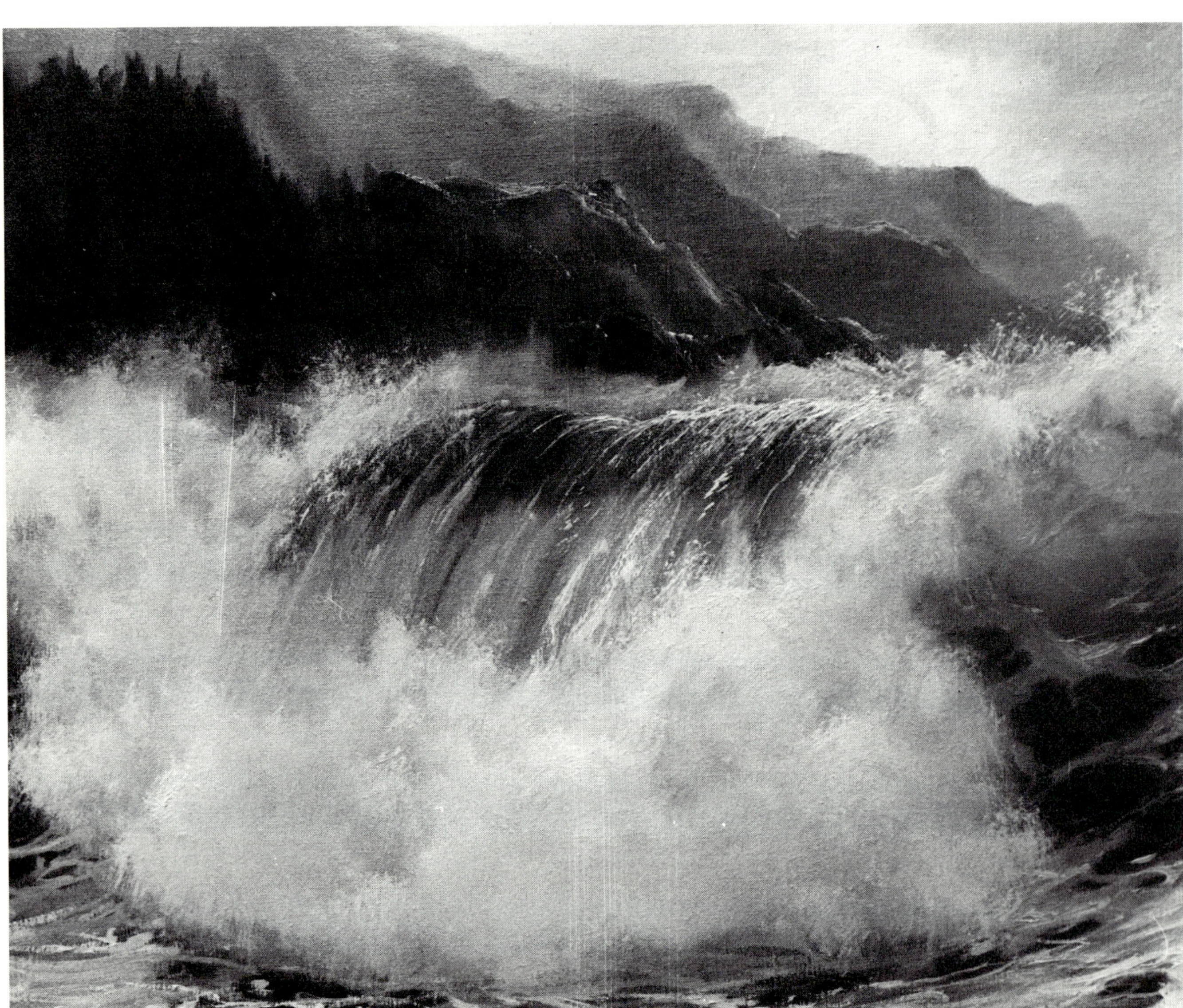

Figure 90. Distant headlands melt into the atmosphere.

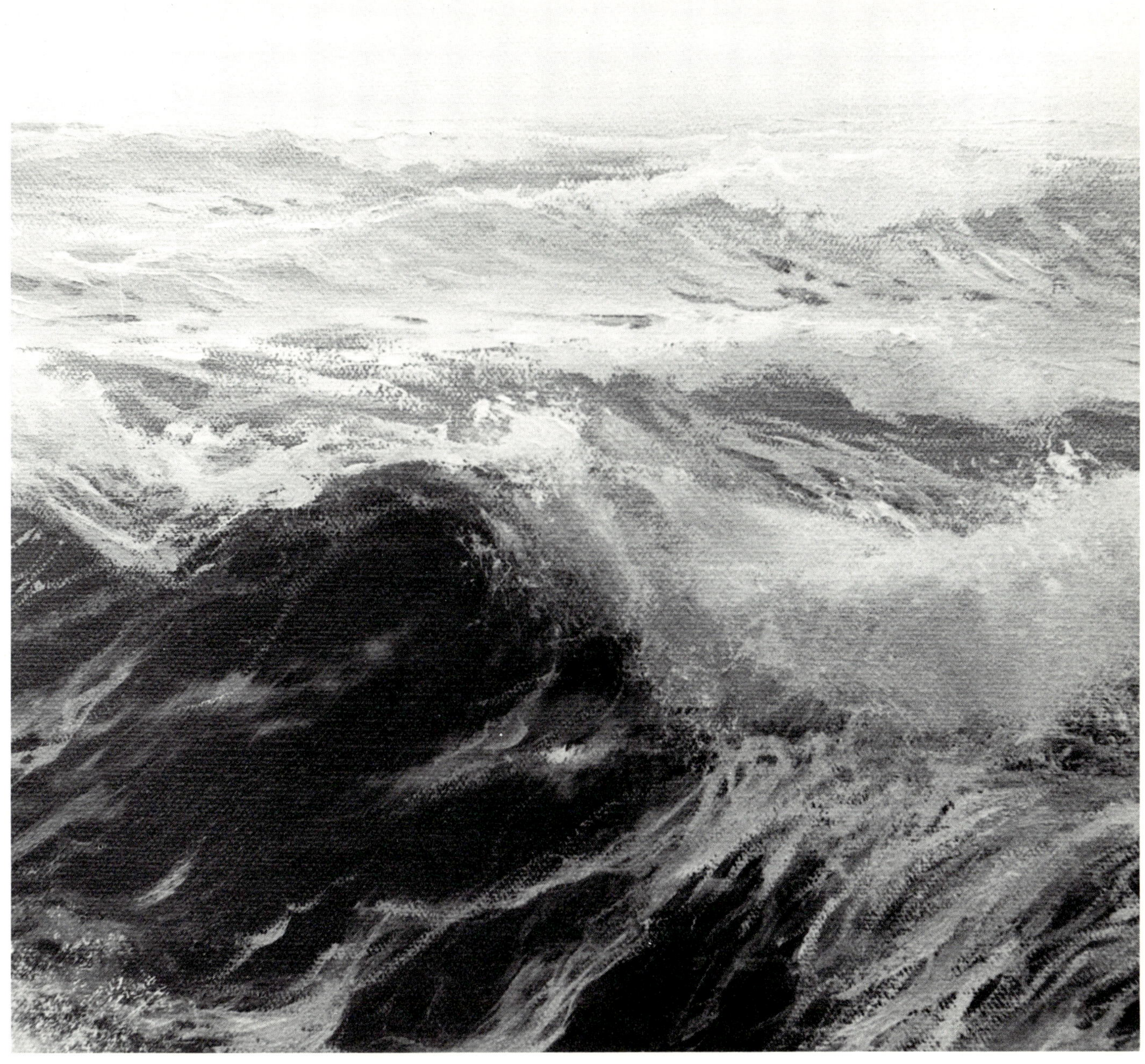

Figure 91. A combination of misty light and atmosphere softens all edges.

It should be clear by now that I believe the use of sunlight in a painting to be the most important thing to learn, with the one exception of the sea itself. Of course, you must first know the anatomy of the waves and rocks, but next you must learn how best to paint them. And this is where sunlight comes in.

I draw with sunlight, especially under back lighting conditions. I actually plan my compositions knowing that I can lighten or darken any area I please, secure in the knowledge that nature could show it that way. (See Demonstration 33 for a step-by-step lesson.)

A good example of this is in Figure 92. The light is from the back, but still fairly high in the sky, and sunlight dominates the composition as the main interest. Were the sunlit areas to appear elsewhere in this painting, the entire composition would be changed. Sunlight creates shadows, and together they create form and shape.

Figure 93 combines several sunlight effects due to the nature of the sea as a strong reflector of sky (atmosphere) and sunlight. First, the reflected light of the sun on the foreground; second, the misty effect caused by light coming through heavy moisture or spray; and finally, the contours of the wave face, picked out by a few tiny glints of direct sunlight.

Figure 94 is entirely drawn with sunlight. The distance is faded with atmosphere and back lighting, and all shapes are contoured with the highlight and reflected light of the sun.

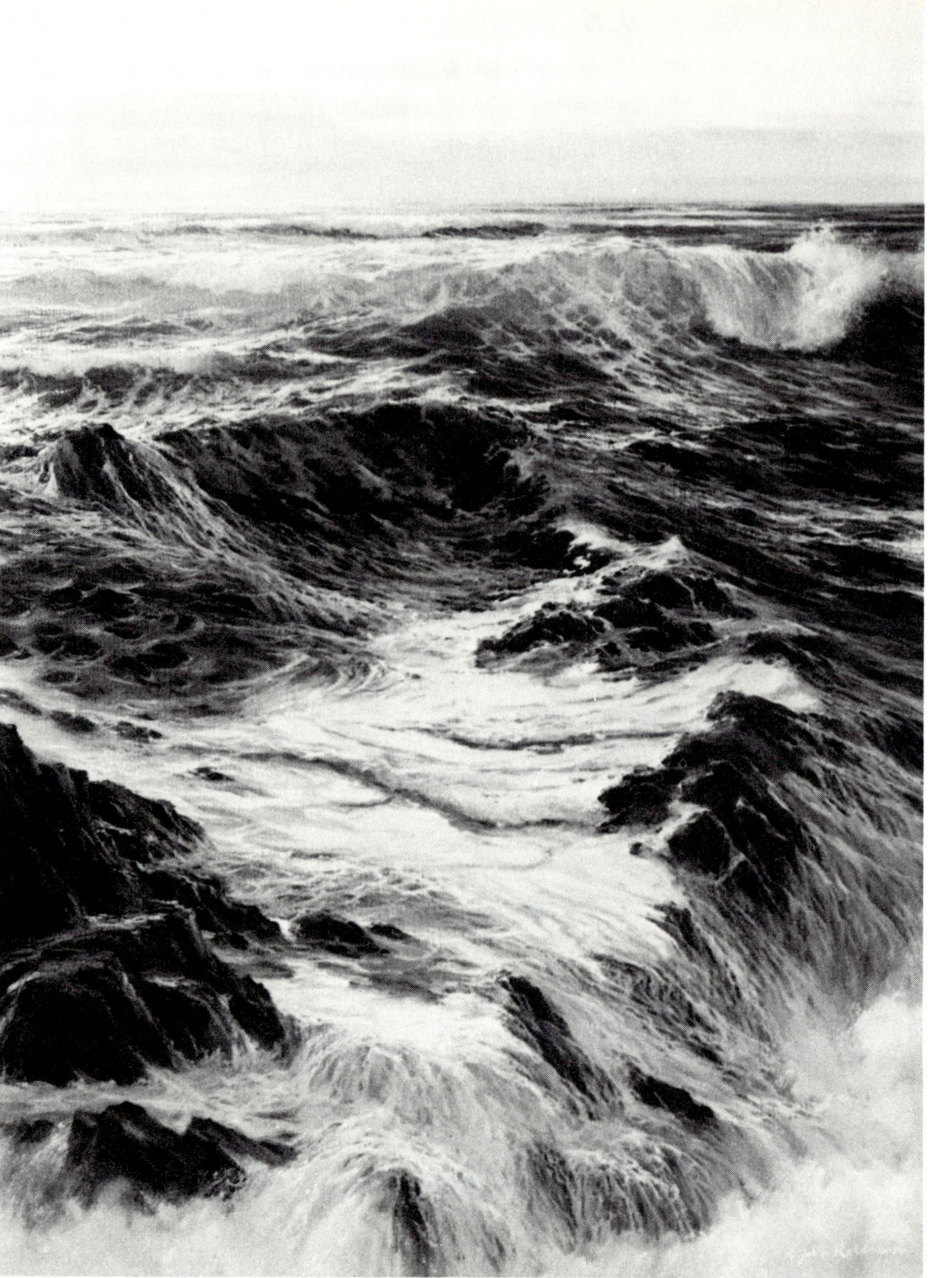

Figure 92. Sunlight contours all shapes and dominates this painting.

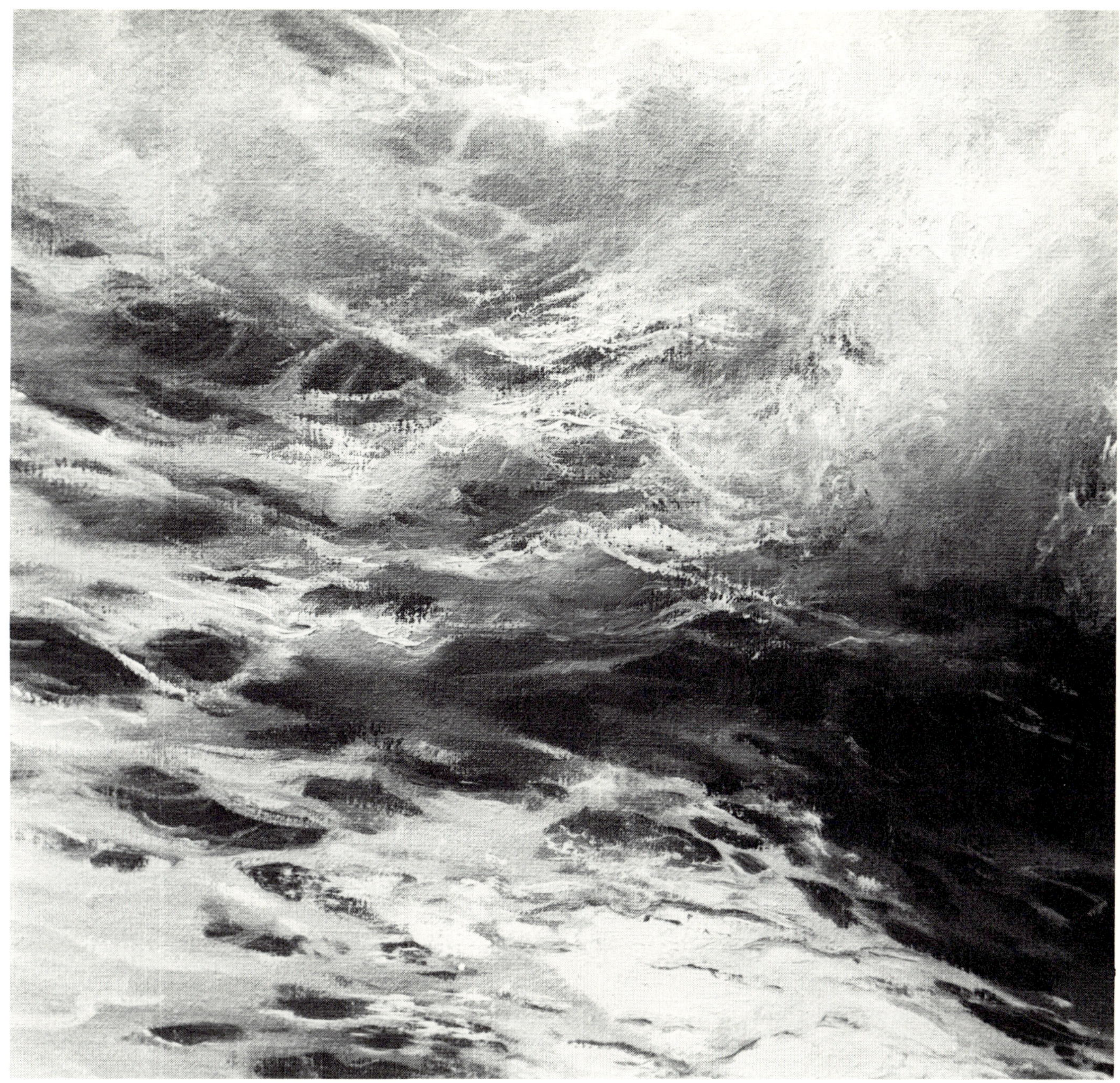

Figure 93. This closeup contains several different sunlight effects.

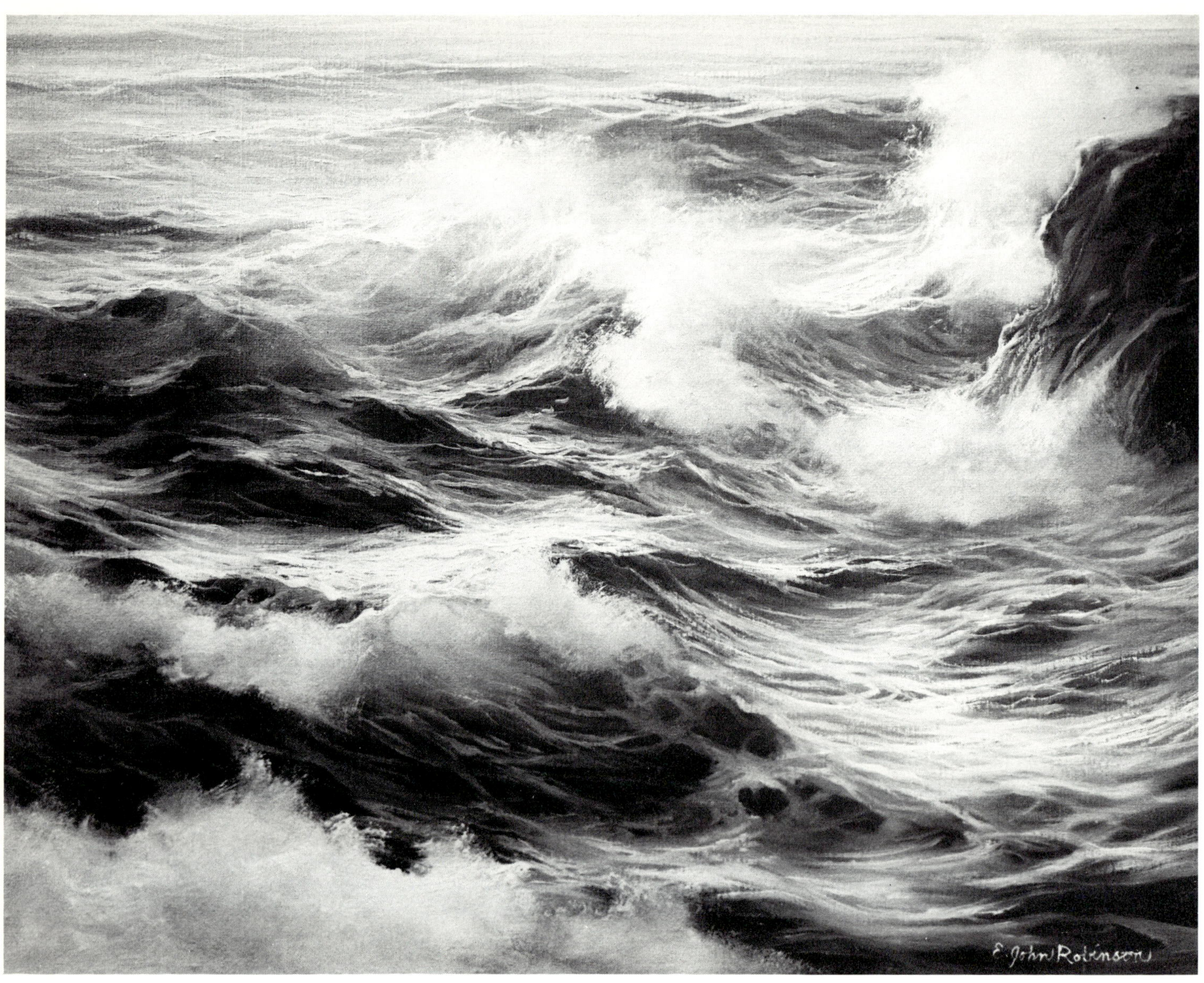

Figure 94. This entire painting is truly a drawing with sunlight.

REFLECTED SUNLIGHT

If the sun is overhead and the water angles correctly with it, the sun will be reflected directly into the viewer's eyes. But not all sunlight is direct. There's a great deal of reflected sunlight, sunlight that struck elsewhere and bounced to where you see it after being reflected from the sky and atmosphere; areas lit by the sky that have first been lightened by the sun. The use of reflected sunlight is merely another way to extend the colors and effect of the sun to influence the area below or within its range.

In Figure 95 I use both. The foreground is direct reflection; that is, the sunlight strikes the sea and is bounced directly to your eyes. The same is true of the glitter on the middle portion of the wave. The rest, however, is bounced light.

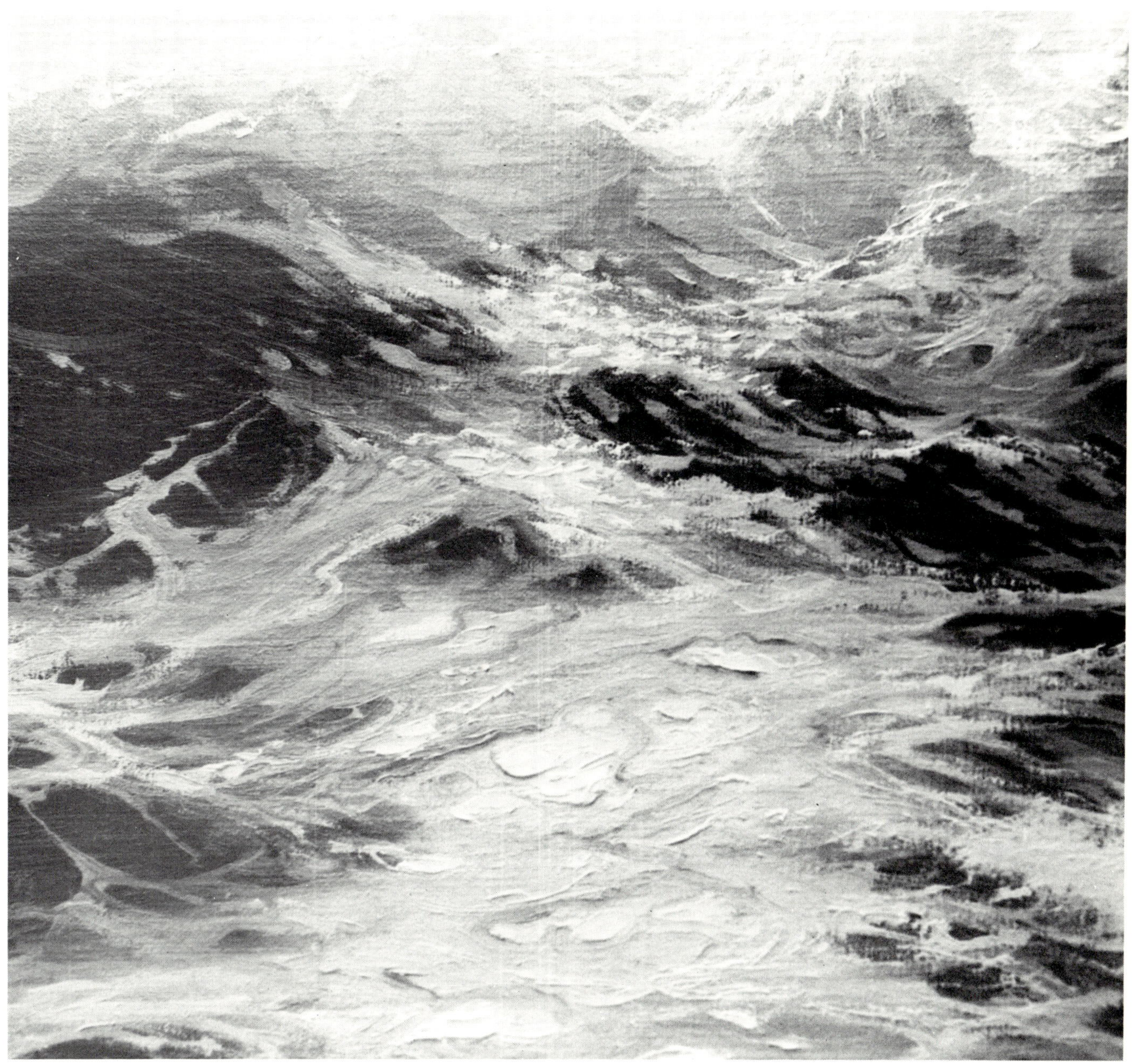

Figure 95. A few holes in the foam and a faded path of light reflect the sun.

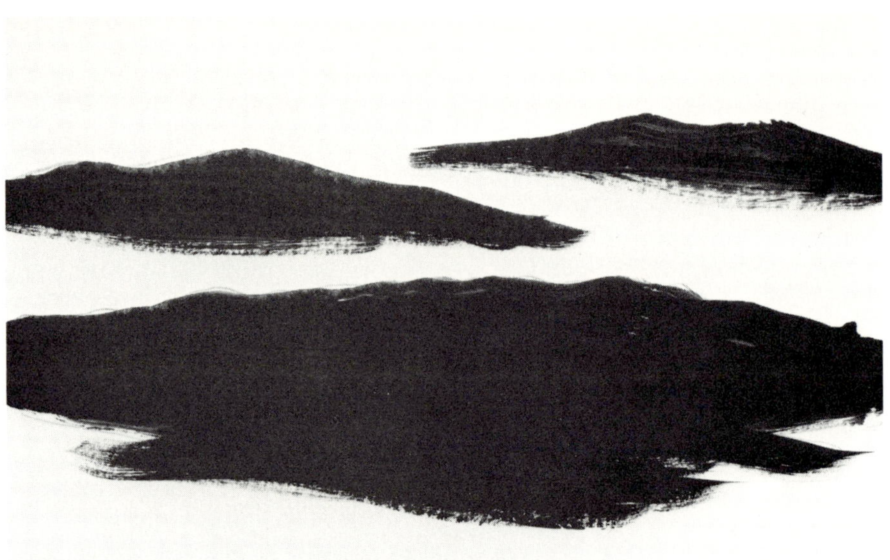

Step 1. Back lighting means simply that objects are lit from behind. Always determine the direction of light before you begin painting. To begin this lesson, paint in a foreground swell and a couple of background swells.

Step 2. The sky, or atmosphere, should be painted in next. Choose a gray or middle-toned blue and paint the sky as well as the troughs between the swells. Reflect the sky color at the base of the larger swells to show their sweep or contours.

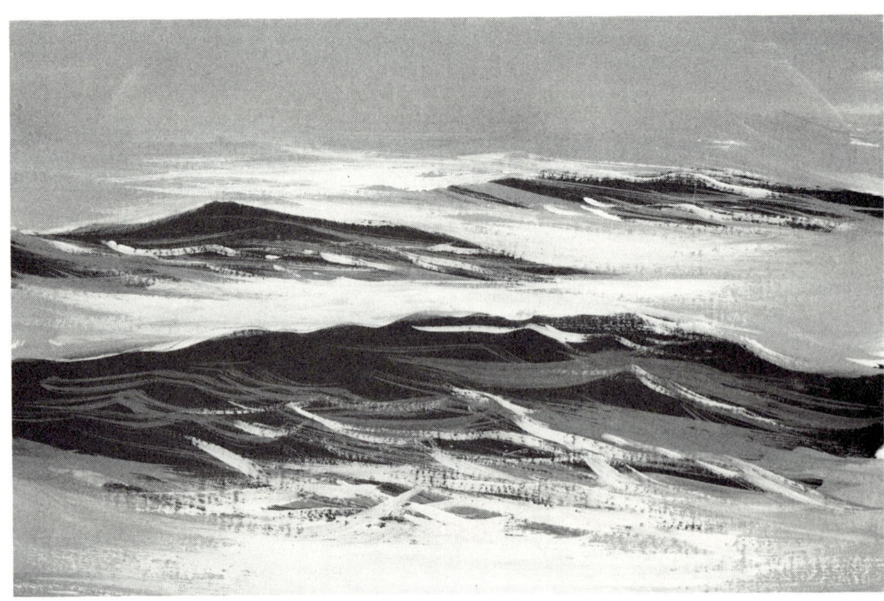

Step 3. Use the effect of the light sparingly. In the background sea there may be quite a scattering of glitter, but notice that the swells are outlined only at the top, while the rest of the swell is in shadow.

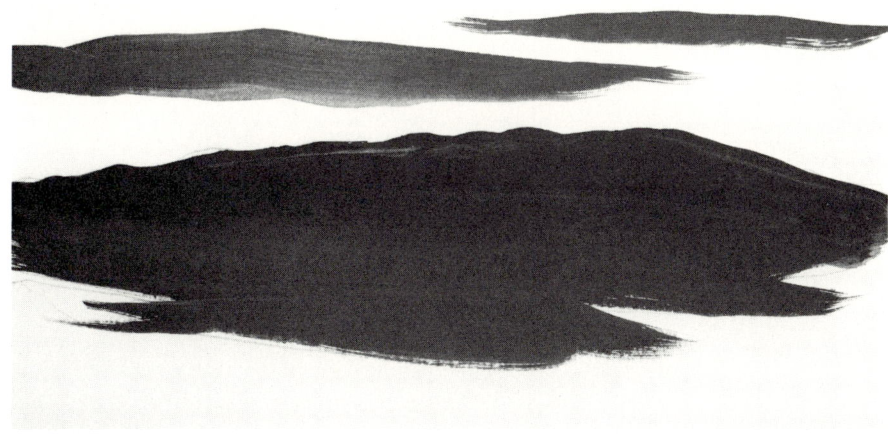

Step 1. Down lighting occurs when the sun is directly overhead or close to that position. Here the trough will be flooded with light. Start this study with the same composition you used for back lighting.

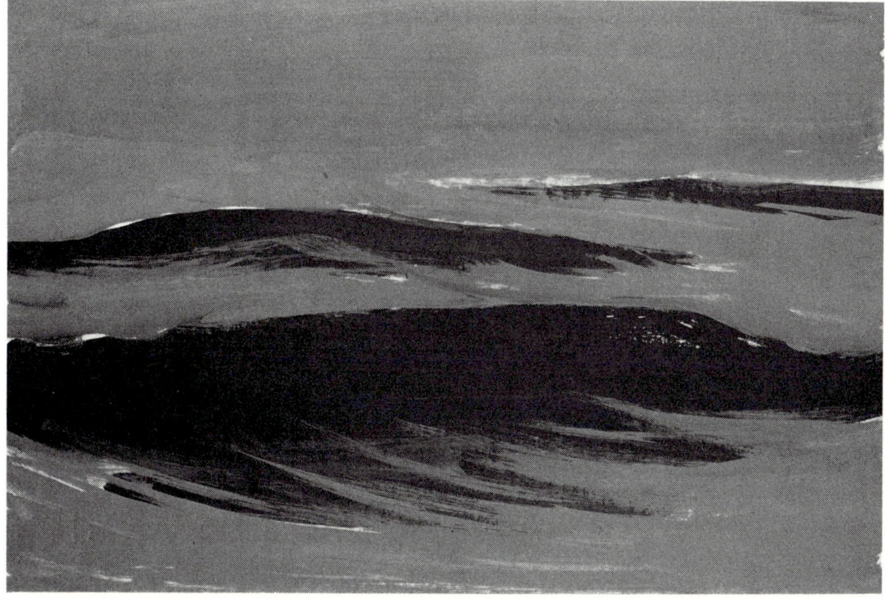

Step 2. Use any color scheme you wish at this point. But remember, the color of the sky must continue right down between the swells. Notice that I have reflected a bit more sky color on the waves, which has a tendency to flatten them more here than in Demonstration 30

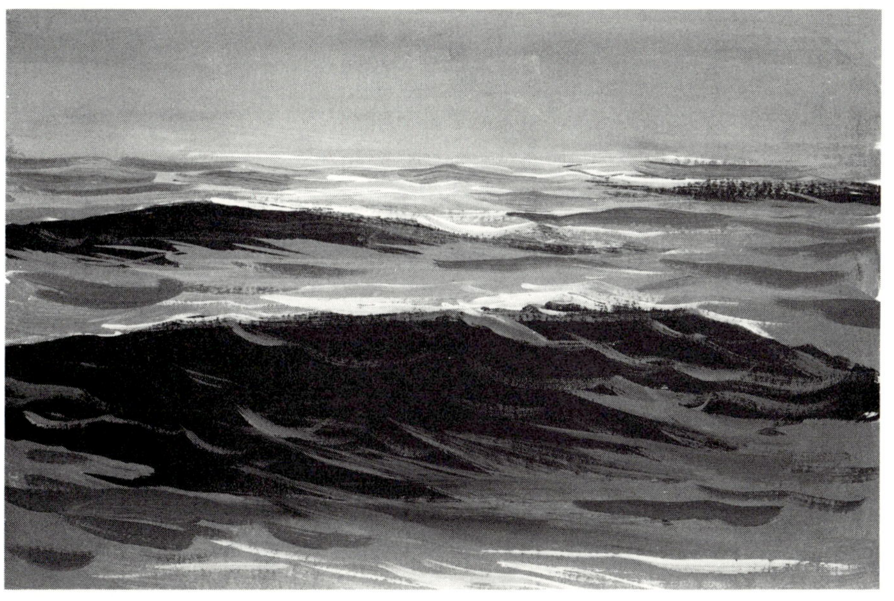

Step 3. Let the light shine! Mix a yellow-white mixture and fill the area between swells with reflected sunlight. Don't let it continue out on each side or you'll lose the effectiveness of bright lighting from overhead.

Step 1. Painting atmosphere really means working with a sky color or other mixture that influences the color of everything in sight. Block in a simple composition. Mix a gray blue and paint in the sky.

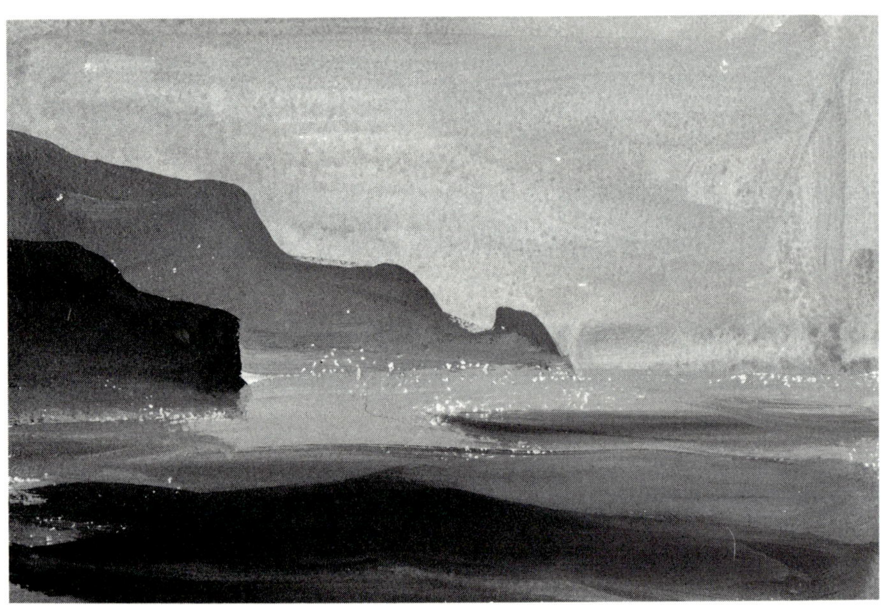

Step 2. Now mix a rock color such as burnt sienna and viridian and use it pure to paint in the middle-ground rock. To paint the distant headland, mix the sky color into the rock color. This is the influence of atmosphere. Now mix the color of your water and start with a dark value in the foreground, but gradually lighten it with the sky color as the scene recedes.

Step 3. Polish up this study by adding the sparkle of sunlight and reflecting some of the sky color onto the foreground waves. The final result should give the feeling of moisture-laden atmosphere with sunlight sparkling through.

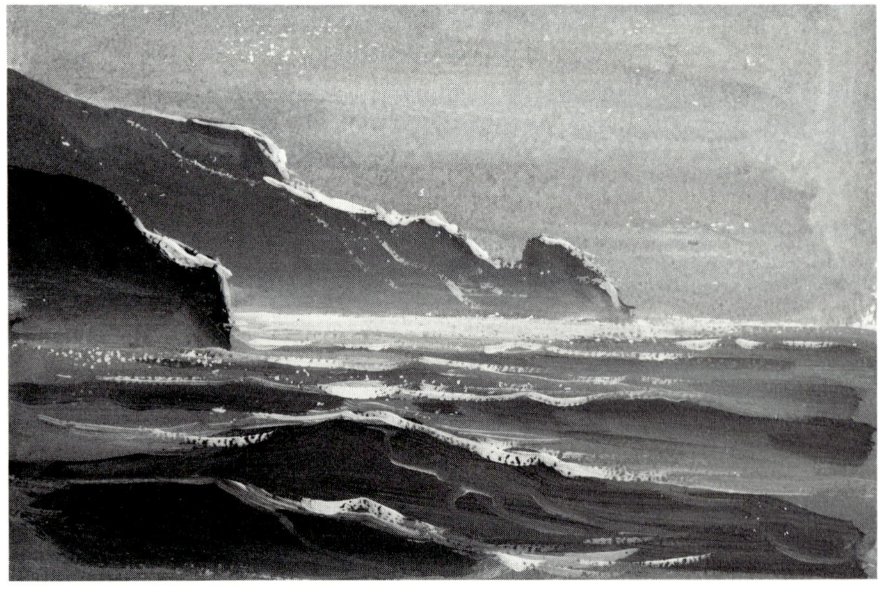

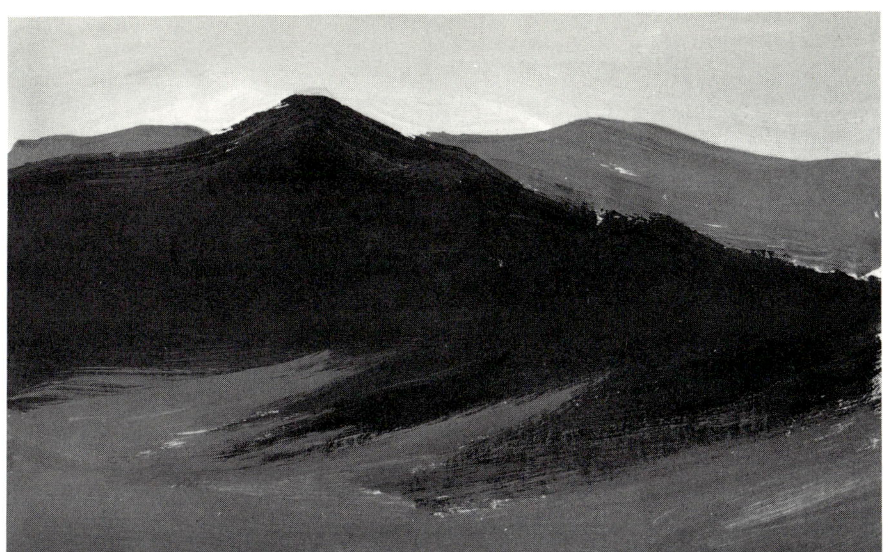

Step 1. This final lesson is intended to demonstrate how sunlight can change contours. Begin by painting two compositions like the one here. Make the foreground wave large and dark. Reflect the sky as you learned to do previously.

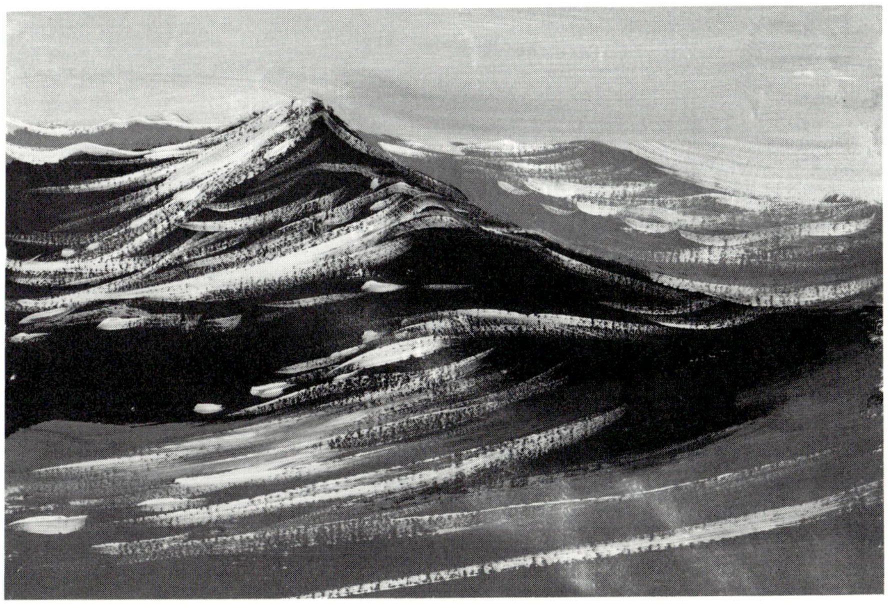

Step 2. In your first composition, reflect the sunlight by using long, sweeping strokes. This should give the effect of a rhythmic movement such as you'd also see in strong winds and moving seas.

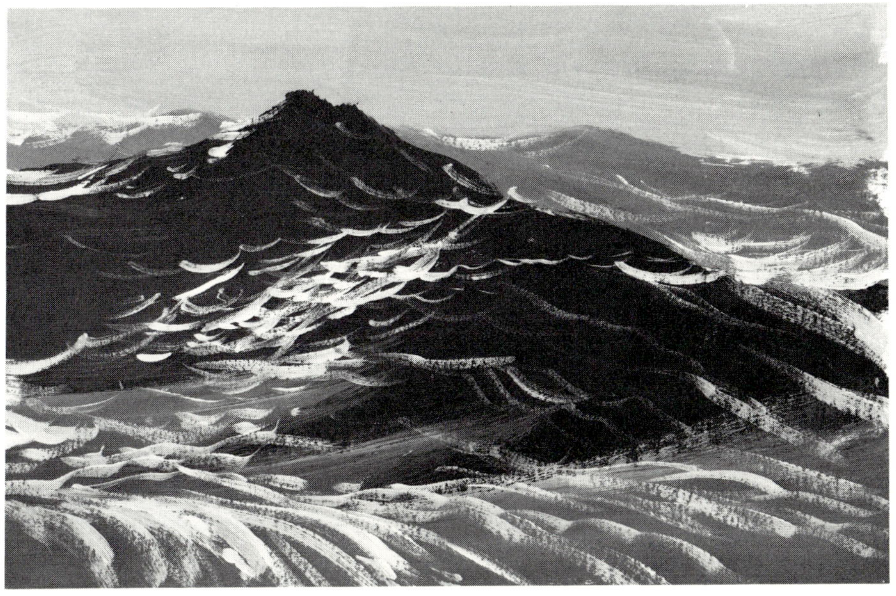

Step 3. In the second sketch, which should be the identical composition, use short choppy strokes to reflect the light. Keep the same basic contours on the main wave, but in the foreground change the strokes in order to move the water towards the viewer. Now compare the two sketches and see how important reflected sunlight can be to a painting.

CHAPTER TEN

PUTTING IT ALL TOGETHER

There's no magic formula for painting seascapes. Hard work, perseverance, and a desire to be different are the ingredients for success. Constant study, experimentation without the stigma of producing a masterpiece, and the knowledge that success is never really found because a newer problem has come up— all add up to a professionalism that brings a kind of success.

Study the paintings that follow, discover how they were composed of the lessons found throughout the book, practice these lessons, then paint, paint, paint! When you can compose your own paintings and use the knowledge you've gained from this and other books, you'll be a working artist.

A painting is an accumulation of knowledge and ideas put together to show a split-second moment in time. Put as much as you can into this image, but never put it in such a way that each idea fights with the others. Always feature a dominant mood, subject, or effect and play down the others so as not to distract. There are many paintings to be painted, many ideas to be discovered and tried. Don't try to put them all in one painting.

Whenever a problem arises, remember there's always an answer. Look for it in this book; and, if you're fortunate enough to have the sea itself for reference, look for it there.

PLATE 1. SPRING MORNING

This painting has a very simple composition: a major wave, little sky, and much foreground. The wave, with its brilliant sunlight and translucent water, is the center of interest, but the subtle qualities of the painting lie in the foreground. Notice the hidden rocks and seaweed in the depth of the water. Once a center of interest has been established, there should still be areas of secondary interest. Spring is a time of rebirth and freshness. I hope this painting reflects some of that feeling.

There's very little in the sky and background sea to study. See Chapter Four for information regarding the major wave; Chapter Nine for handling the sunlight on a wave; and Chapter Seven for the foam patterns, which are all linear. The entire foreground of this painting is a study in transparent water (Chapter Five).

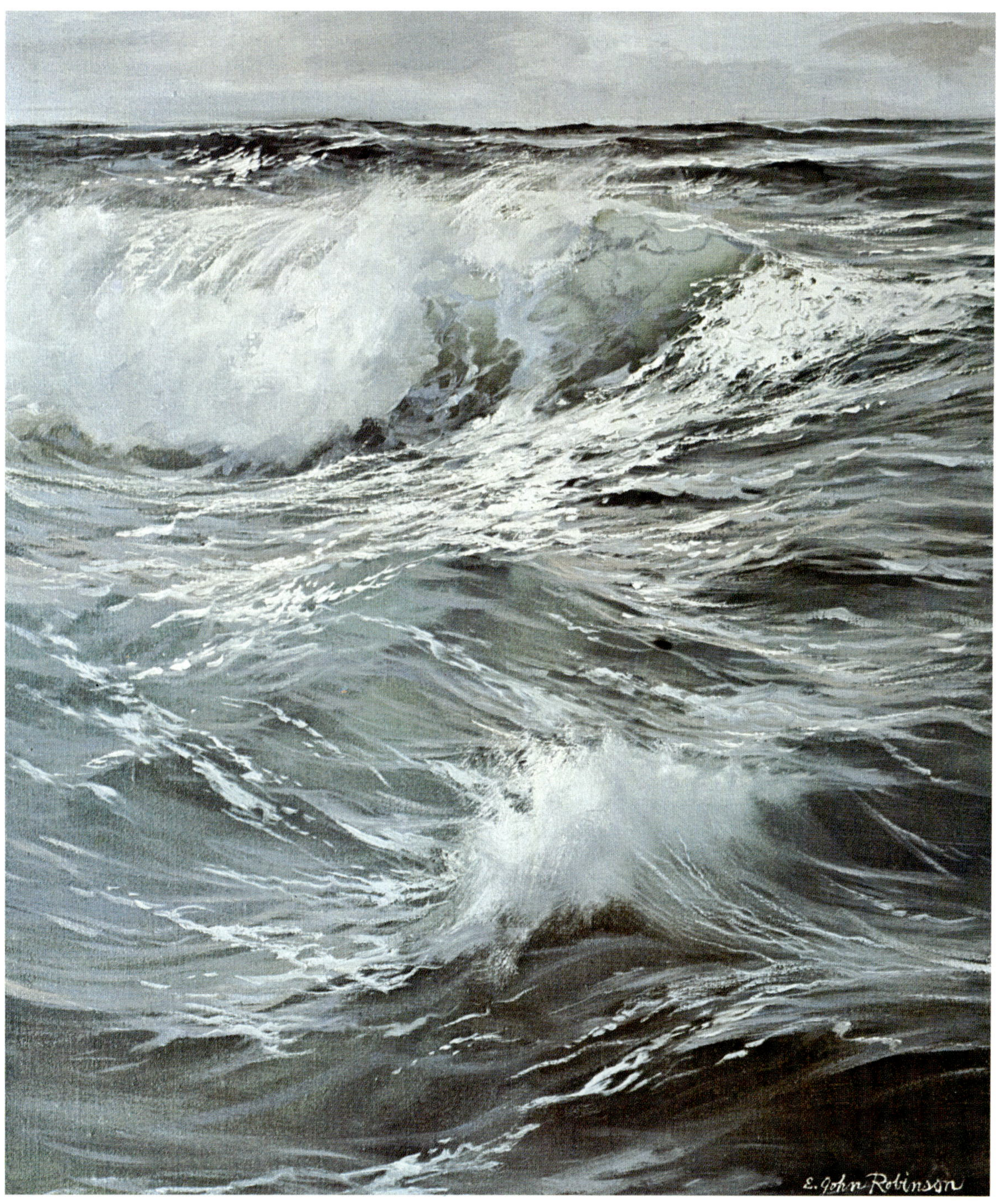

Plate 1. Spring Morning. Oil, 30″ x 24″/76cm x 61cm.

PLATE 2. NORTHWEST SHORES

This painting is a good example of how to control several areas of interest. The central wave is obviously the center of interest even though the sky, the headlands, and the foreground also attract attention. What keeps the interest from being divided is the amount of attention paid to the wave and the handling of edges. The edges of the clouds are soft and don't attract the eye, whereas the edges of the wave are well-defined, even harsh, and immediately catch your interest. Also, the wave has the one color in the painting that's not repeated, except for an echo of it in the distant swell.

"Northwest Shores" has a strong sky (Chapter Two). The background sea is mild; but the headlands fade with atmosphere (Chapter Nine). The major wave here is a good example of that discussed in Chapter Four. The roll, leading edge, and breaker foam are only variations of the basic ones taught. The foreground is a study of angular rocks (Chapter Eight) and linear foam patterns (Chapter Seven).

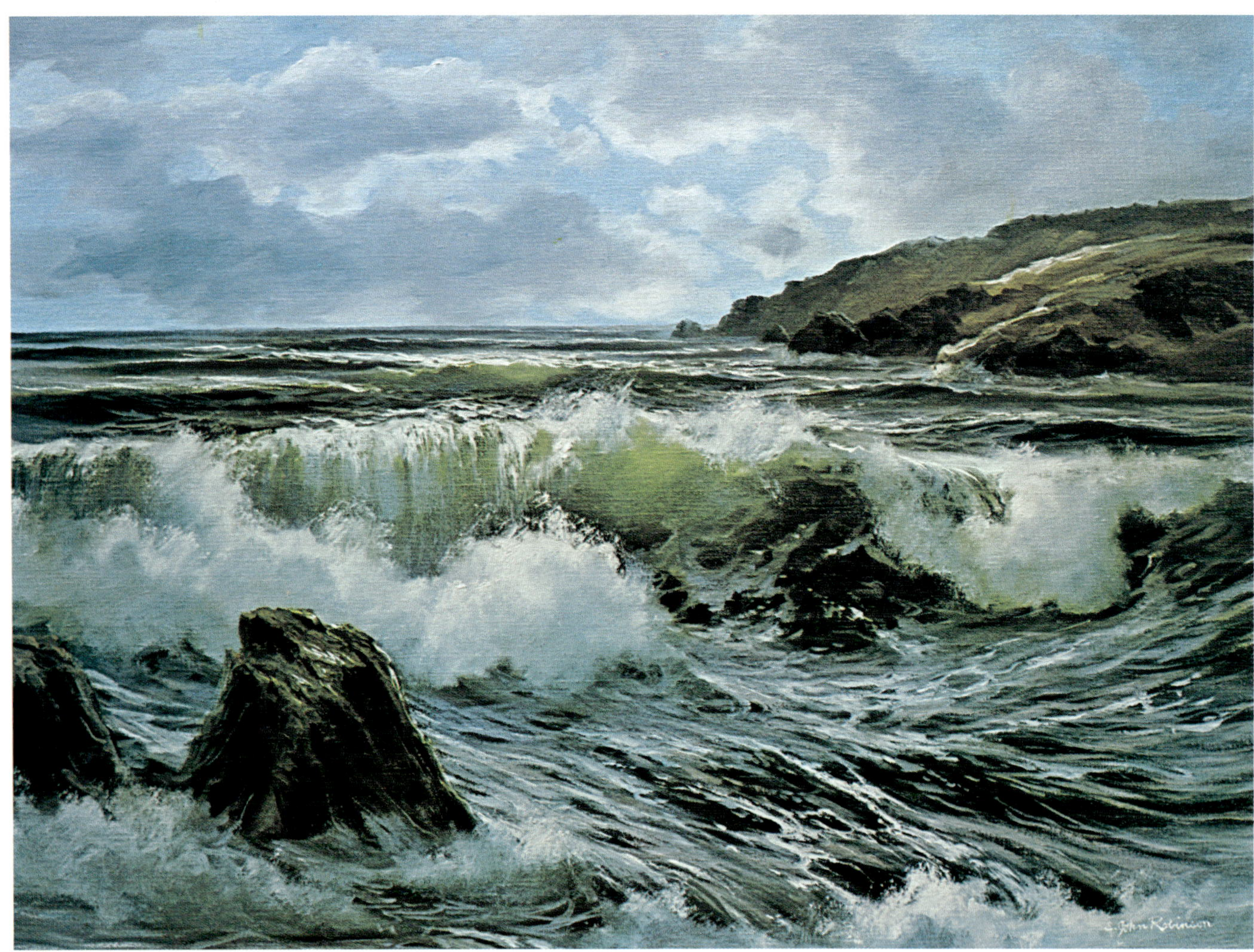

Plate 2. Northwest Shores. Oil, 30" x 40"/76cm x 102cm.

PLATE 3. OFF THE POINT

Here's an example of morning light on the West Coast. The sunlight reflects from a thousand tiny mirrors and dances among the foam patterns. Crystal water, shadowed foam, and brilliant sunlight are the building blocks of this painting. The sky is subdued and keeps its place far in the background. The rocks are dark and angular and oppose the coming wave. They cast their shadows and reflect the light of the surf. There's a promise of a day of changes, of subtle moods, and possible excitement.

Check "Spotlighting" in Chapter Nine; also, linear foam patterns (Chapter Seven). The sky and background are not dominant, but the cloud formation is a study of light and shadow and can be found in Chapter Two. Perhaps the most important part of this painting is the clear atmosphere (Chapter Nine) and the sparkle of light in the foreground (Chapters Three and Nine).

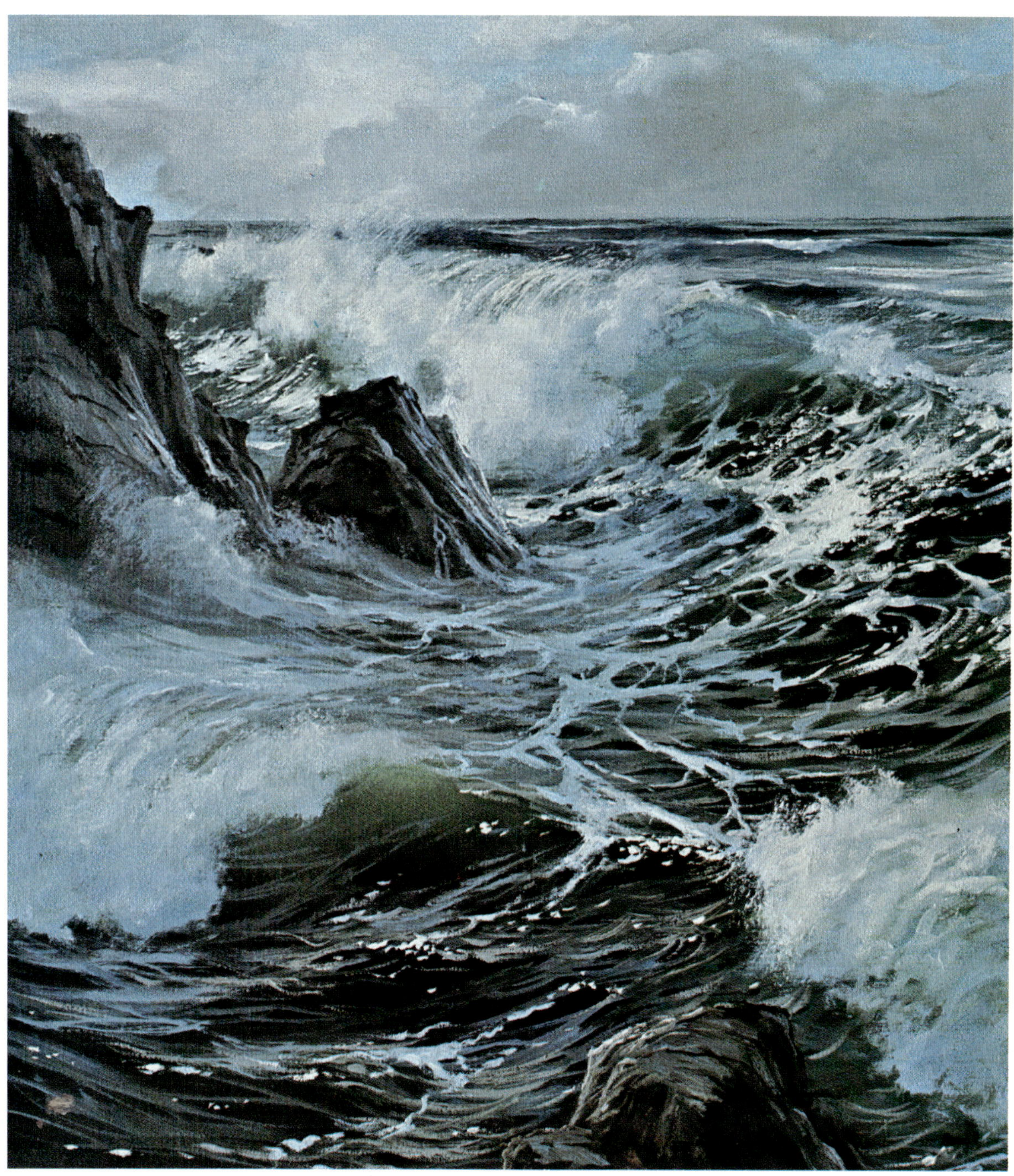

Plate 3. Off the Point. Oil, 30" x 24"/76cm x 61cm.

Sometimes an artist derives more satisfaction from the finished painting than he had anticipated while painting it. This one, for example. Perhaps it was my pleasure in using the effect of reflected sunlight or maybe it was in the unusual twist of the wave. I can't really say, but I think the painting reflects my enjoyment. I hope it encourages more.

This painting is made up of basics, just like the others. Keep in mind that you start with basic ideas and then expand on them. The dominant center of interest here is the glitter of sunlight (Chapters Six and Nine). The wave is a variation of a "granddaddy" wave and is an offshoot of that described in Chapter Four. The foreground of this painting is rather simple, with a couple of rounded rocks (Chapter Eight) and a few linear foam patterns (Chapter Seven).

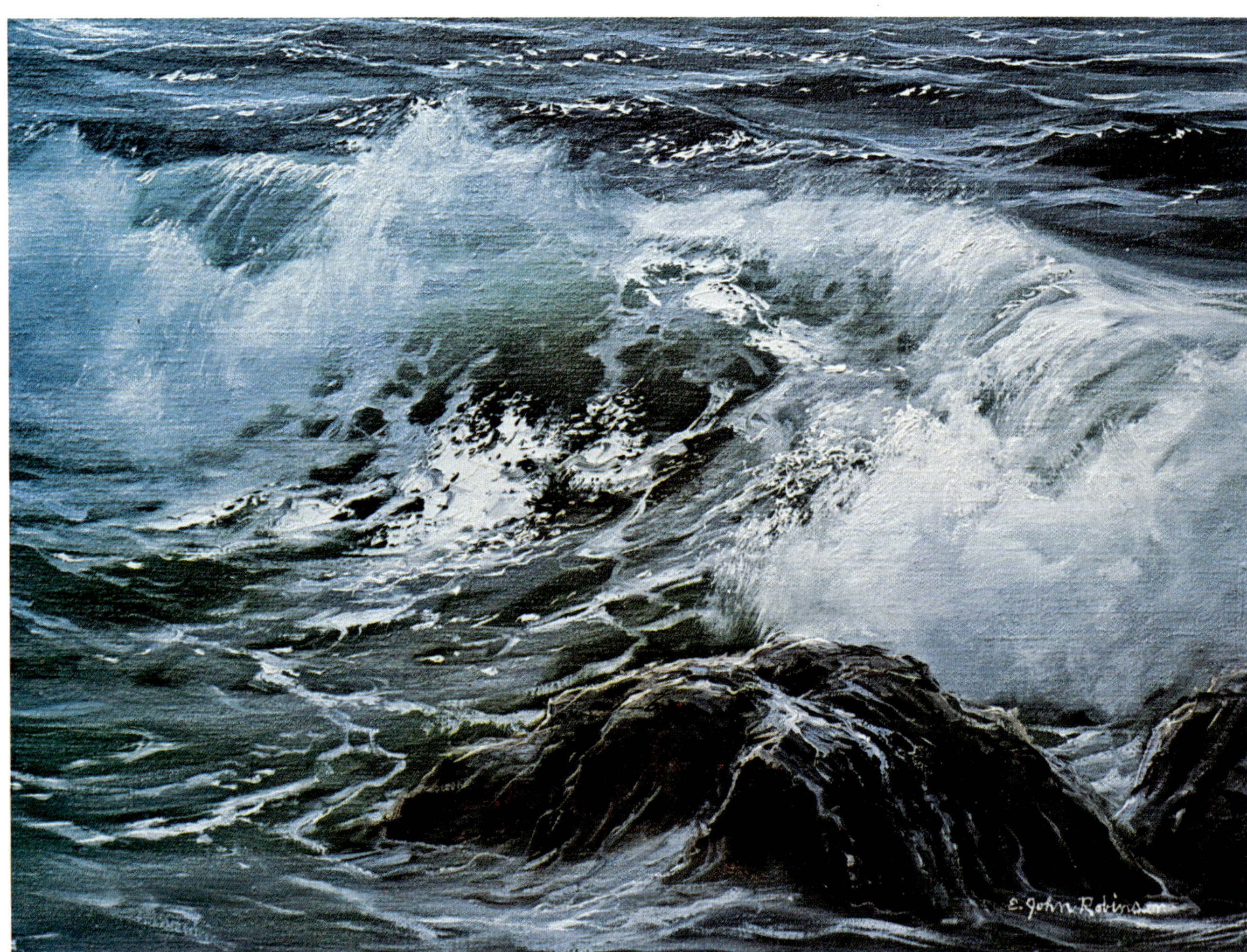

Plate 4. Mid Morning. Oil, 18″ x 24″/46cm x 61cm.

PLATE 5. HEAVY SEAS

When the ocean is agitated by storm or heavy winds, the surface is a mass of swells made up of minor swells which in turn are made up of even tinier swells called "chops." This painting portrays the choppy feeling, both in swells and troughs, and the glitter of dancing light. The more choppy the water, the more mirrors from which light will reflect. This painting suggests the aftermath of a storm or the announcement of a new one. At any rate, the dark swells in the distance are somewhat ominous.

This is a composite of several studies. In the background is a moody sky best described as rain squalls in (Chapter Two). The background sea is a good study of Chapter Three with its swells and glitter. The major wave is a variation of any basic wave, but notice that it's unique and unlike any other wave because of its treatment. Check Chapter Four for the study of waves, Chapter Six for the reflecting qualities of the sun—especially in the foreground, and Chapter Seven for the use of foam patterns.

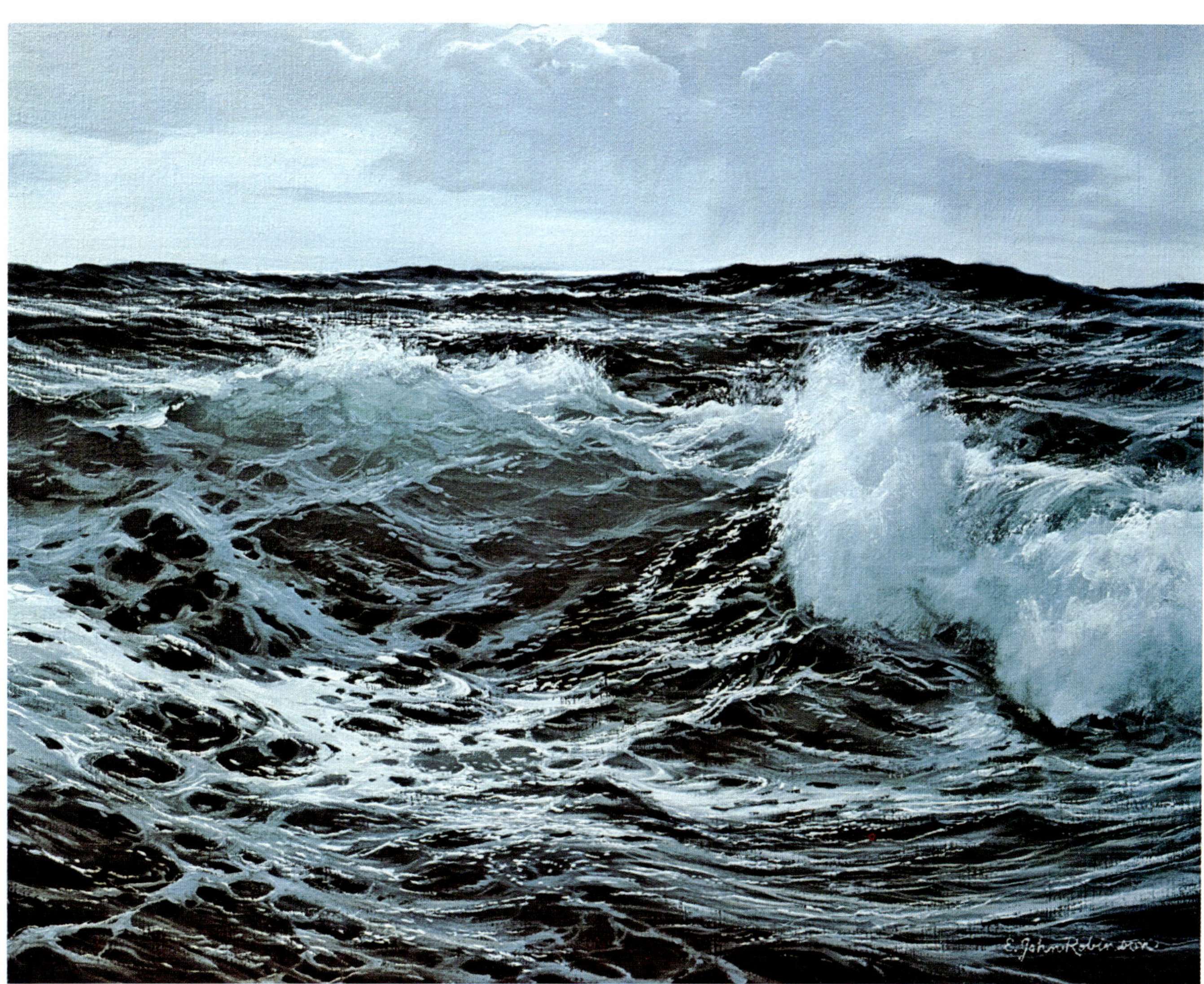

Plate 5. Heavy Seas. Oil, 24" x 30"/61cm x 76cm.

PLATE 6. MOVING SURF

The entire composition of this painting is designed to suggest movement. While the background is rather calm, it still has an undulating appearance and backs up the movement of the central wave and flowing foreground. The foreground floods over a submerged rock but is connected by foam patterns to the wave. The rising foam at the base prevents the feeling of water flowing right out of the painting. Atmosphere is also important in creating distance without distracting from the foreground.

This painting is primarily of a foamy surf (Chapter Seven). Next in importance is the wave, which takes a bit from the description of translucent water (Chapter Four) and mass foam (Chapter Seven). The foreground is a prime example of overflowing water (Chapter Five) because it is somewhat transparent, and because the water flows over rocks (Chapter Eight).

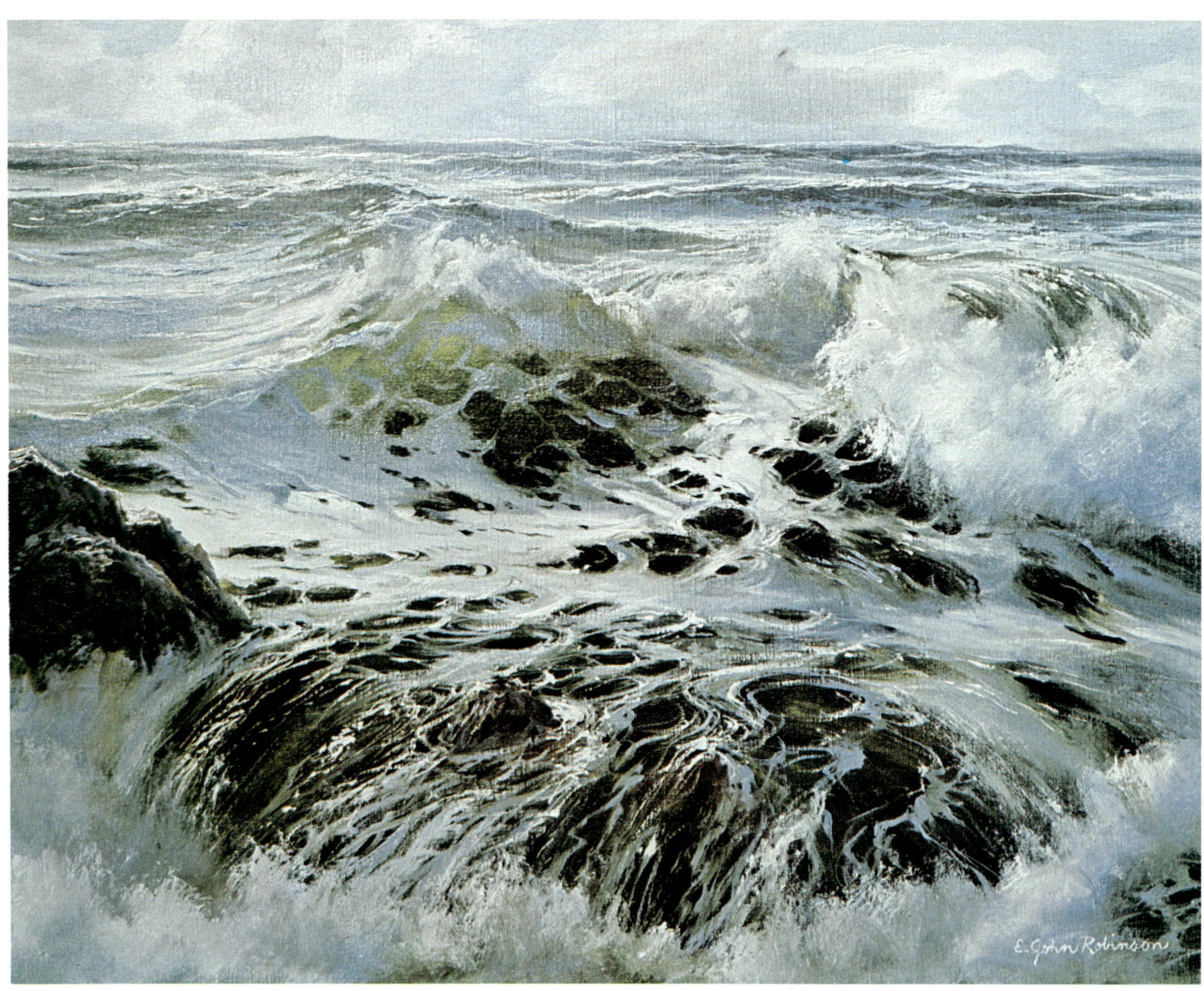

Plate 6. Moving Surf. Oil, 24″ x 30″/61cm x 76cm.

Sometimes a storm sends waves crashing to shore so frequently that the surf doesn't have a chance to recover, and the foam becomes a constant blanket. In this painting the foam is heavy enough to cover most of the water and only breaks away when the water rises high, as in a wave. When the entire surf is white foam, it can only be portrayed realistically with the use of sunlight and shadow.

This foamy surf is special because of its folding, "whipped cream" effect (Chapter Seven). The major wave has a touch of translucent water (Chapter Four), but is otherwise a study of the foamy surface. Even the sky is rather nondescript so as not to distract from the foreground surf.

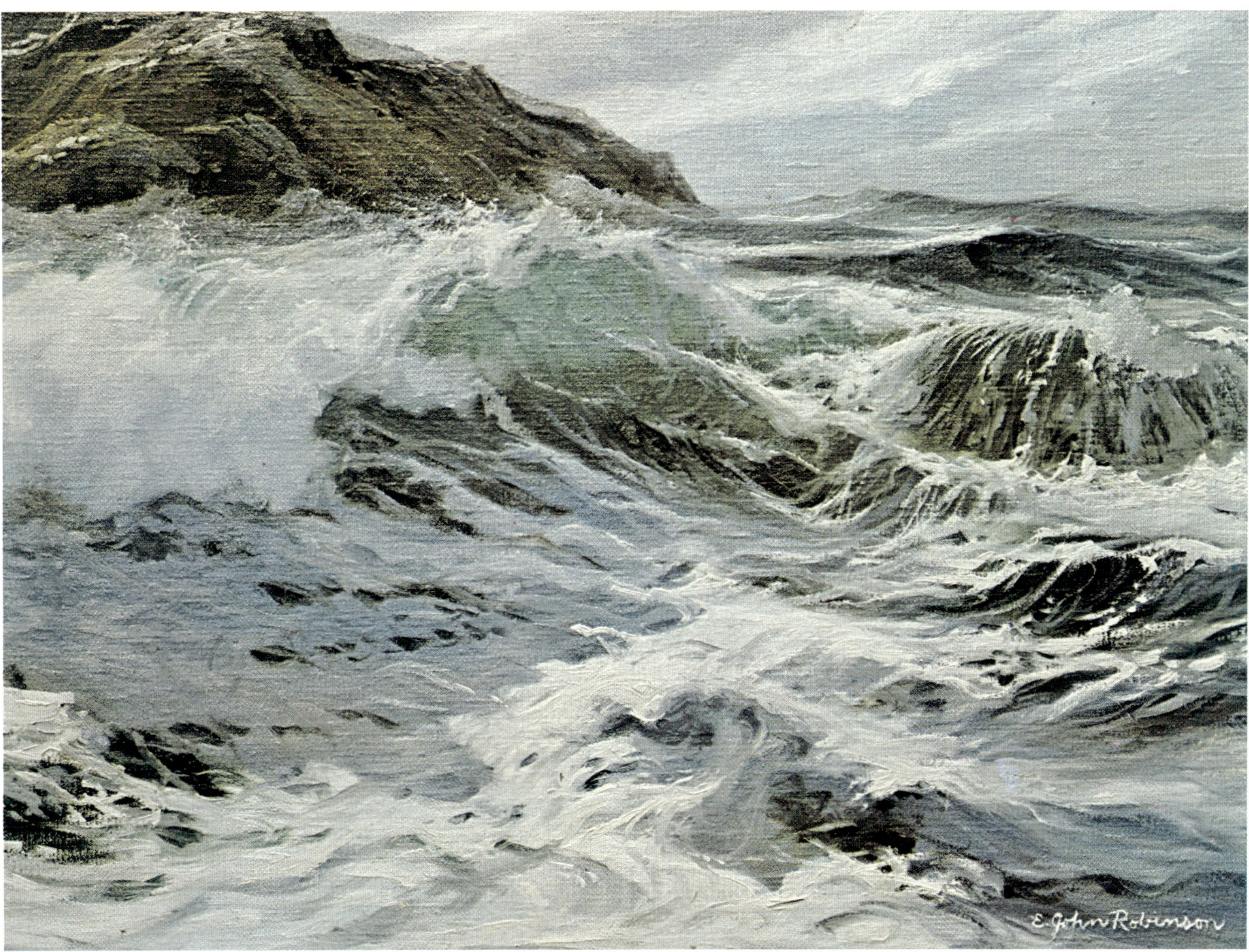

Plate 7. Yesterday's Storm. Oil, 18" x 24"/46cm x 61cm.

PLATE 8. OFF SHORE

Along the same theme as in Plate 7, this painting shows the folding effect of foam found in an agitated surf. Notice the drapery-like folds of foam and an effect not unlike wrinkled skin. The face of the wave itself is covered with foam. Again, the entire foreground is executed with nothing but light and shadow and a bit of water showing through where the foam is thin. Paintings such as this, while really studies, still present an artistry often lost in more carefully planned paintings.

The foamy surface here can be found in Chapter Seven under "the layered look" and "the whipped cream effect." This is an example of folding foam that can best be studied by painting drapery. For the reflection of sunlight, study Chapter Nine carefully. The entire forground is made interesting mainly because of it.

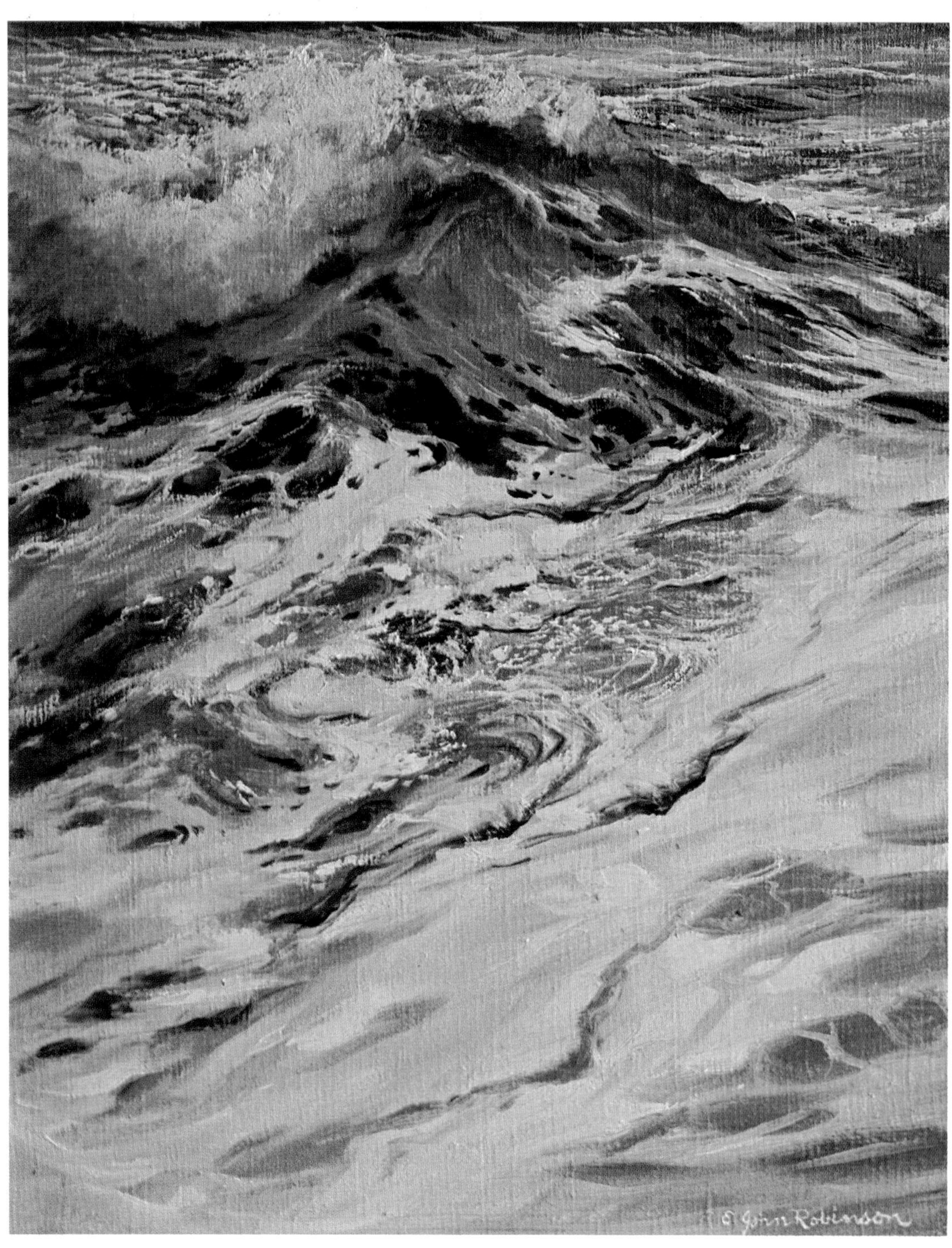

Plate 8. Off Shore. Oil, 24″ x 18″/61cm x 46cm.

PLATE 9. ISLANDS IN THE FOG

One of my favorite spots is the northern Oregon coast, where rocky tree-covered islands stand offshore. When the fog moves in, hiding some and revealing others, it presents a soft mysterious mood, a gentle quietude, unmatched anywhere in the world. I've matched the surf to this mood by creating a slowly breaking wave against a rather smooth surf. Even the rock lies prone and non-threatening.

The center of interest here is the major wave. Notice especially the treatment of the translucent part, the roll, the leading edge, and the foam (Chapter Four). The rest of this painting is a study of atmosphere and how it reflects off the sea. Check Chapter Nine for hints on painting fog and reflecting sunlight.

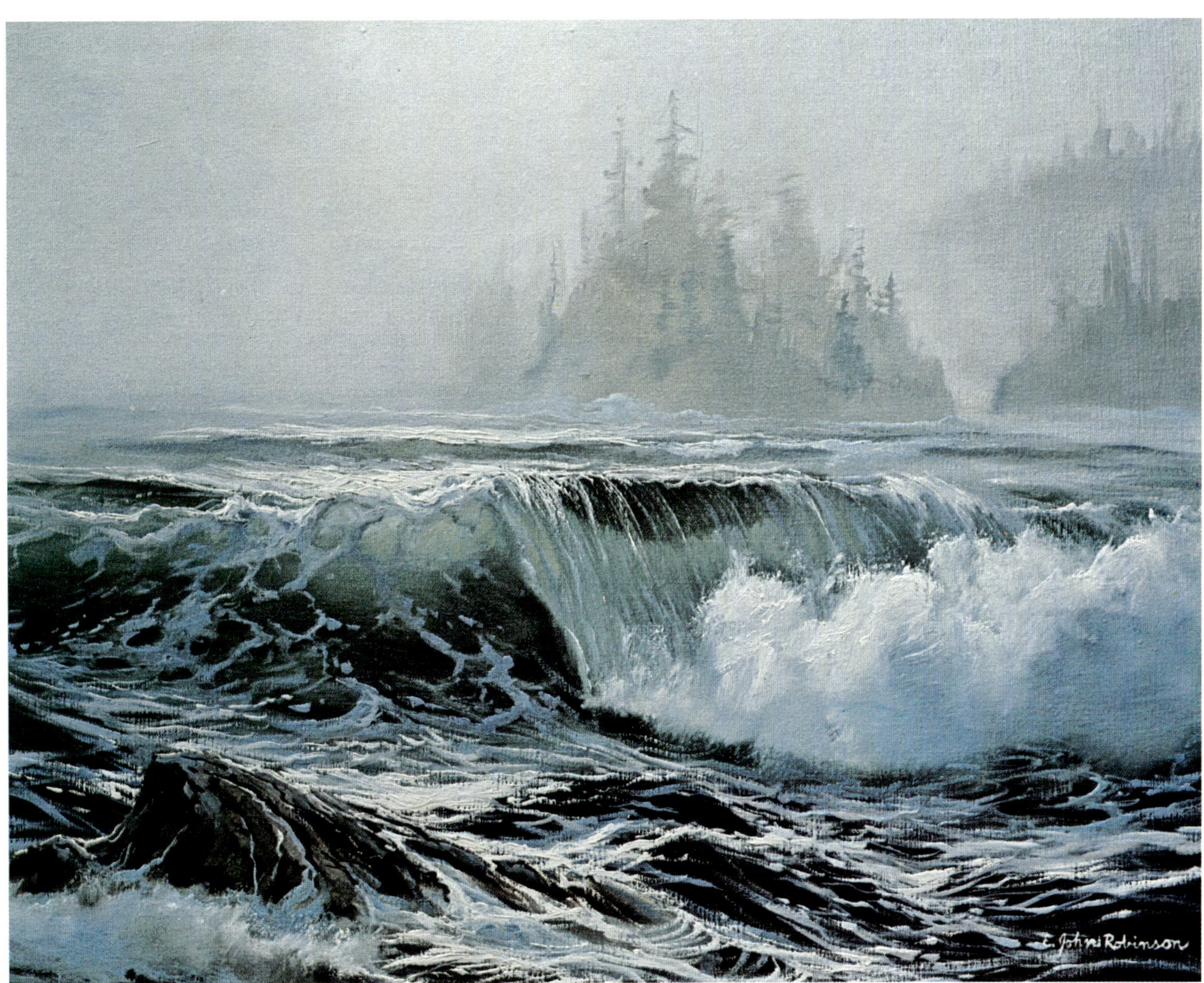

Plate 9. Islands in the Fog. Oil, 24″ x 30″/61cm x 76cm.

PLATE 10. OVERCAST

Whenever I paint fog or heavy cloud cover, I still like the effects of sunlight shining through, even if it's weak. If you hold a piece of white paper up to this painting, you'll find that the paper is several steps lighter than the lightest value in the painting. The painting still reflects sunlight though, and would be cold and uninteresting without it. Notice that the sunlight is a warm ochre-type yellow against the cold green water. The rocks remain neutral and serve mainly to reflect the sky.

Here's another painting with no sky, yet you know (immediately) the color of the sky and the sun. This is because the sea reflects those colors in the atmosphere (Chapter Nine). The major wave is mostly clear water, choppy, but not foamed up (Chapter Five). Also in Chapter Five is a study on tide pools, the water left high by the tides. Notice a variation of this in the foreground.

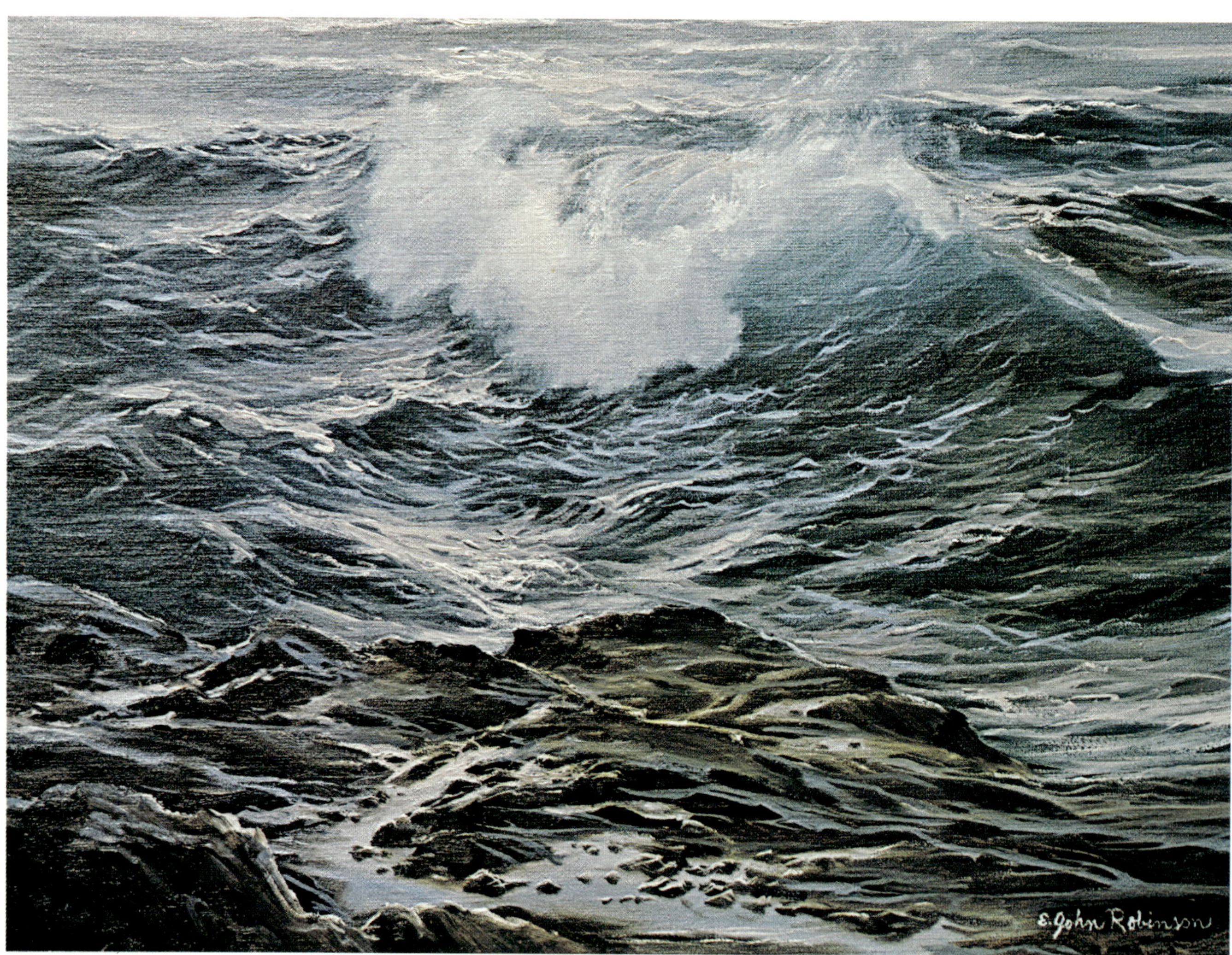

Plate 10. Overcast. Oil, 18″ x 24″/46cm x 61cm.

The time of least agitation of the surf is at low tide or just before it turns to flood tide. At this point the waves, especially low ones like this, seldom stir up much action. The foreground here is clear water, undisturbed by heavy froth. The transparent quality of the water shows submerged rocks and its color is influenced by seaweeds. The sun sparkles brightly, but the background sea suggests an approaching wind. Whitecaps are forming, and clouds are sweeping the sky. The mood will change.

You may find rounded rocks described in Chapter Eight and major waves discussed in Chapter Four, but the main themes of this painting will be found in Chapters Five and Nine. Chapter Five contains, first, a study of the transparent surface, which is so evident in the foreground of this painting. Second, in Chapter Five, is the study of reflected sunlight which appears here as glare and sparkle. The sky is played down to keep the composition simple. The linear foam patterns are few so as not to cover the transparent water. The entire painting is designed to help the viewer enjoy sparkle on transparent water.

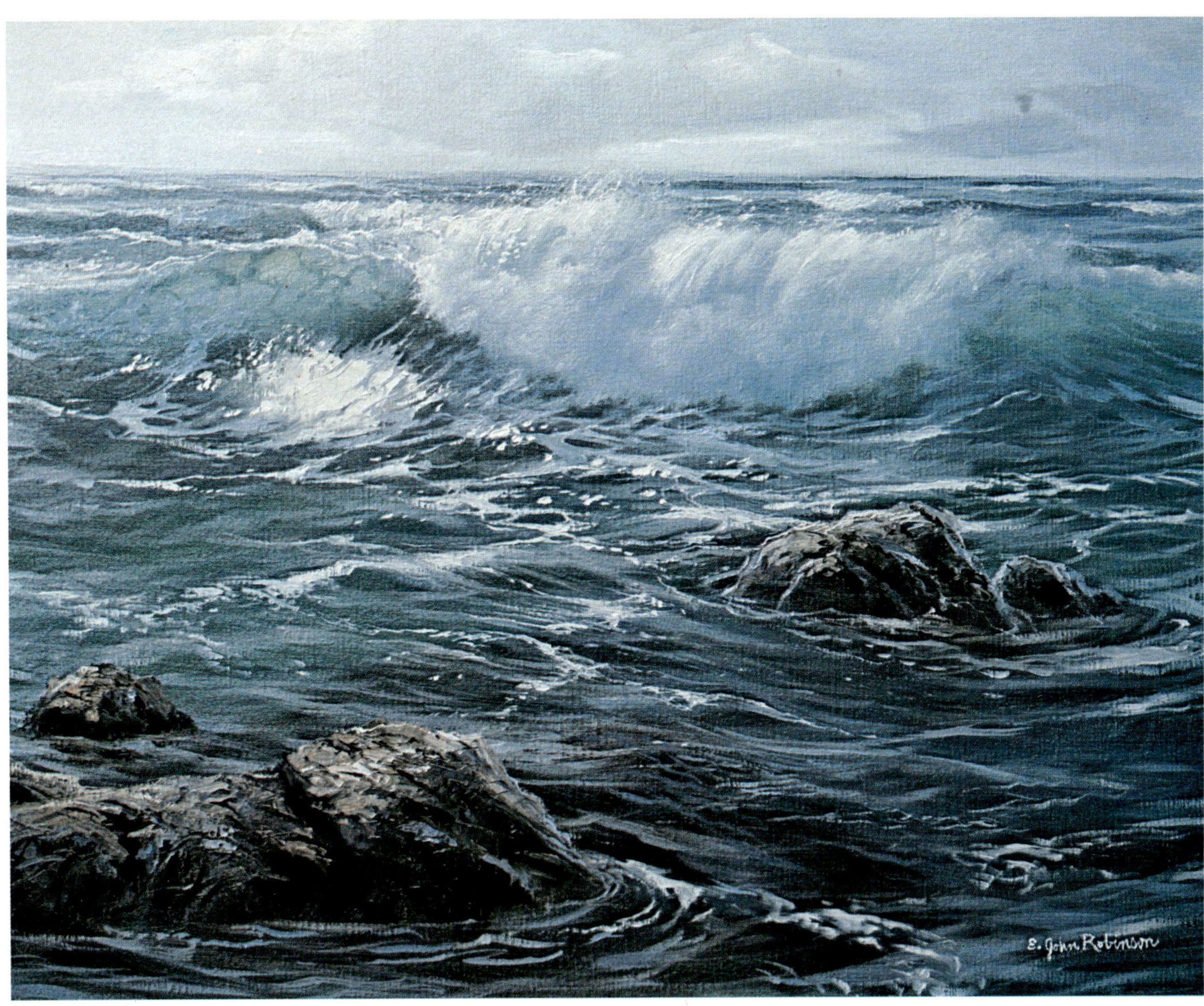

Plate 11. Low Tide. Oil, 24″ x 30″/61cm x 76cm.

I love November on the Coast. The temperature drops, the storms begin, and the sea changes from its summer laziness to unleashed energy. The swells rise to staggering heights, the wind blows, foam sprays and mingles with the air, and the sky transfers wind and rain to the moving energy of storm-tossed breakers. It's a time for most people to rest by the hearth, but for the seascape painter, it's a time to awaken, a time to learn.

Check Chapter Two, especially cumulus clouds, for a study of this sky. The background sea is nearly invisible, but note that the horizon line is broken (Chapter Three). The unique image of the major wave (Chapter Four) is due to special handling: the placement of sunlight and shadow, the leading edge, and the foam trails and glitter on the face. The rocks are not dominant but are the angular type described in Chapter Eight. Notice the reflection of the sun in the foreground surf (Chapter Nine), and the overall pattern of foam in the foreground (Chapter Seven).

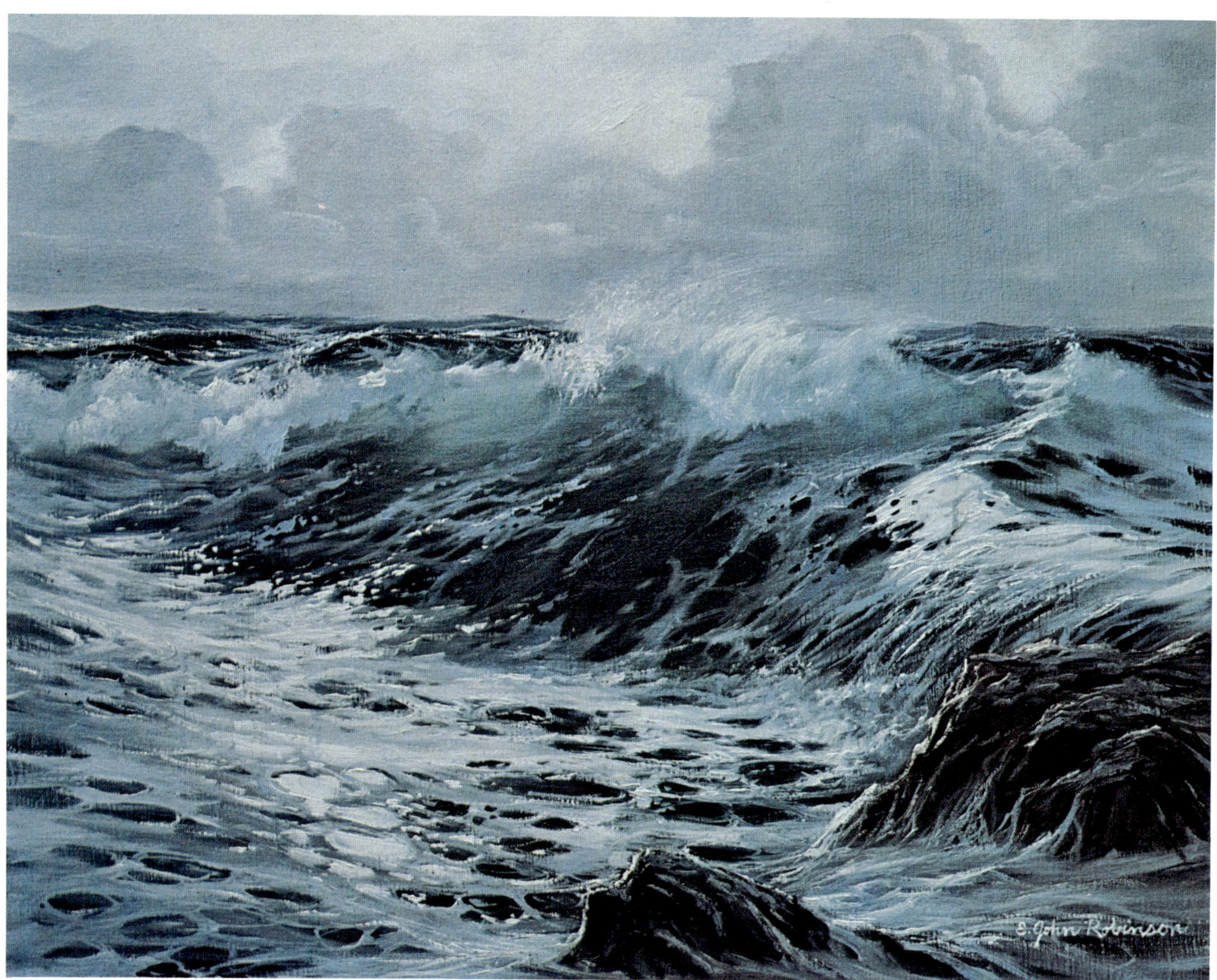

Plate 12. November Mood. Oil, 24″ x 30″/61cm x 76cm.

PLATE 13. SETTING SUN

A painter should look for the unusual to present to the viewer. In this case, the sun is setting just as a cresting wave breaks the horizon line. It's a rare moment—only occasionally can you can look into the sun without hurting your eyes—and this painting captures it perfectly.

I mentioned once before that I liked to look directly into the setting sun. Here's an example of that effect. Start with the cumulo-nimbus clouds (Chapter Two), then use the study for glow (Chapter Three). Place the sun right behind a rising wave. The wave itself is a study of linear foam patterns (Chapter Seven). The foreground is entirely reflecting (Chapter Six); it reflects the sky and the seas as well as the wave and foam.

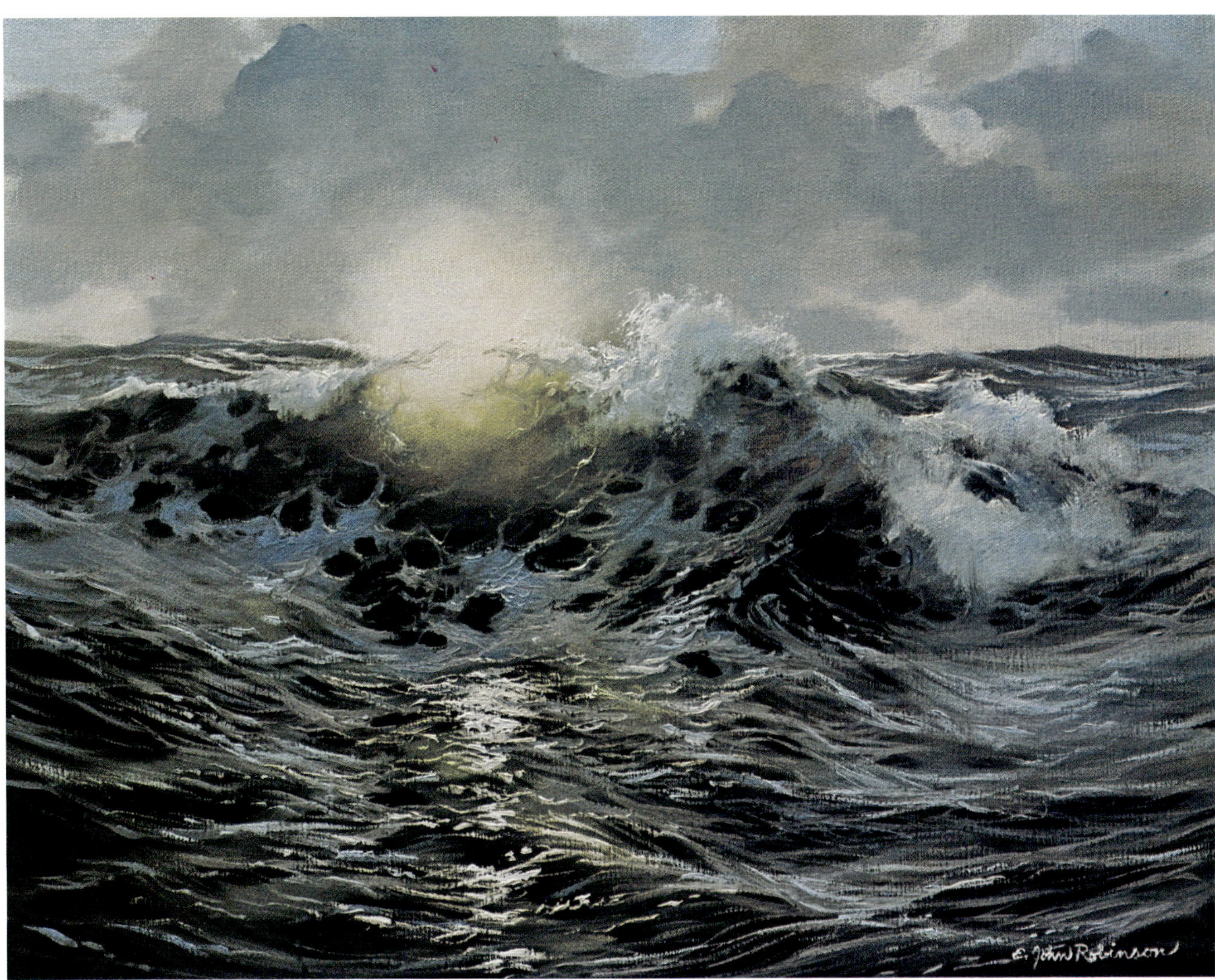

Plate 13. Setting Sun. Oil, 24″ x 30″/61cm x 76cm.

PLATE 14. AUTUMN TWILIGHT

Is it my imagination or are twilights in autumn more colorful than at other times of the year? In any case, the warmth in this painting is low-key, but strong enough to influence the background and the major wave. The foreground has little influence from the warm sky but is interesting in itself as clear water pours over a submerged rock. The quiet of the painting is based on long, steady rollers beneath the setting of the sun. There's no threat here—only tranquility.

This painting is quiet and maybe a bit somber. It's a good example of sunlight as some other color besides yellow. In this case it's mixed from raw sienna and white. The most important features to study here are the glow in the sky and the effect it has on the background sea (both in Chapter Three). The wave is another variation on a basic wave from Chapter Four, but the foreground combines reflecting sunlight (Chapter Nine) and clear water over the rocks (Demonstration 14 and Chapter Five).

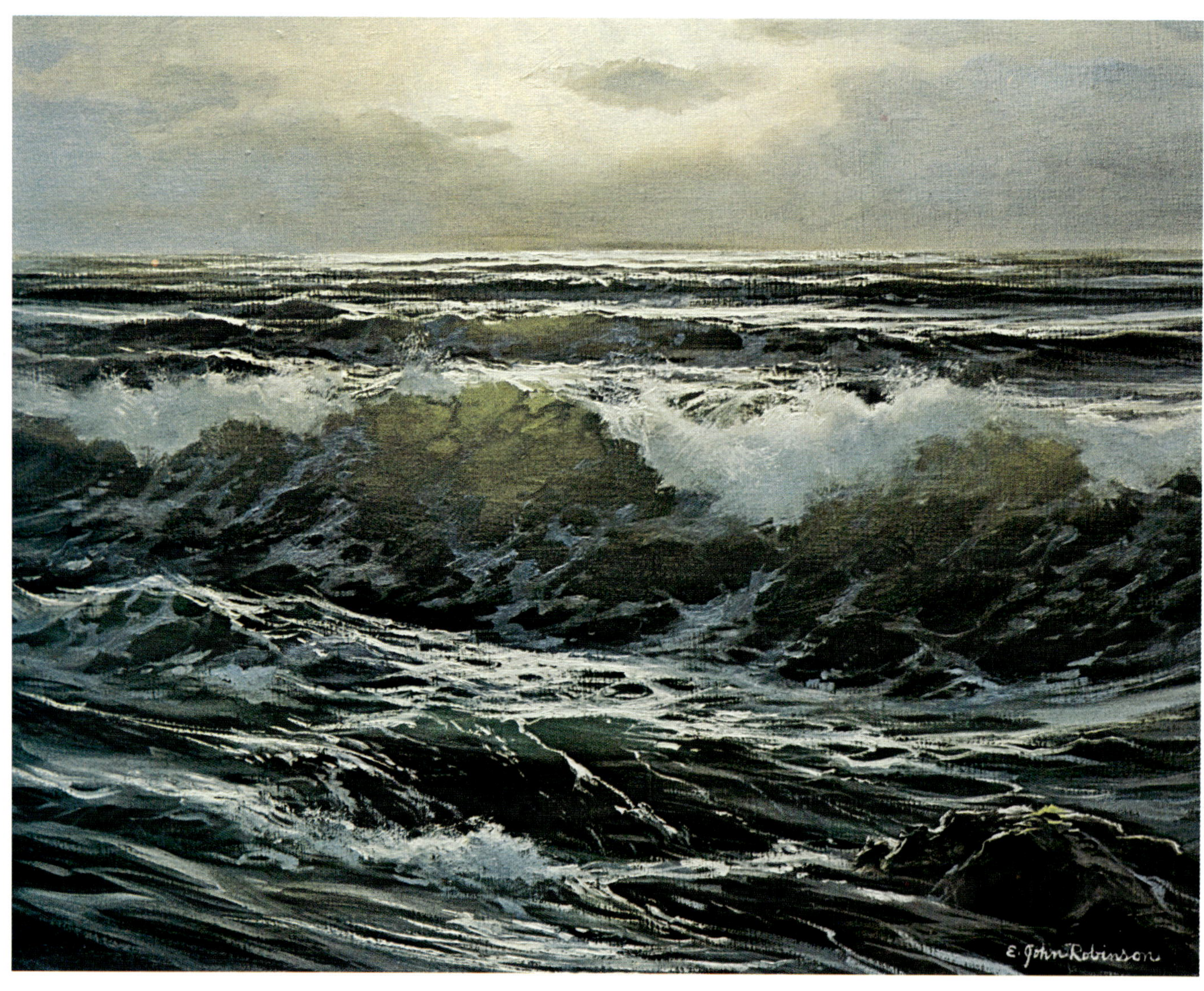

PLATE 15. SUMMER EVENING

There's more color and action in this painting than in Plate 14. This surf is moving and tumbling, the sun is high enough to sparkle over the action, and the rocks—with their sharp profiles—create an entirely different mood. There are many ways to portray a subject or even a mood. Explore them. You'll find each as interesting as the last and as important as the next. Creativity is the favored child of variety.

This is one of my few paintings that shows so much rock. In this case I felt it was necessary to the composition. Notice not only the way the water rushes over rocks, but the way it splashes up against them. Here are examples of almost all the studies of Chapter Eight as well as the transparent or clear water over rocks (Chapter Five). The background, major wave, and much of the foreground are a variation of glow, the spreading sunlight found in Chapter Three and shown step-by-step in Demonstration 15. In this case I used burnt sienna and yellow ochre.

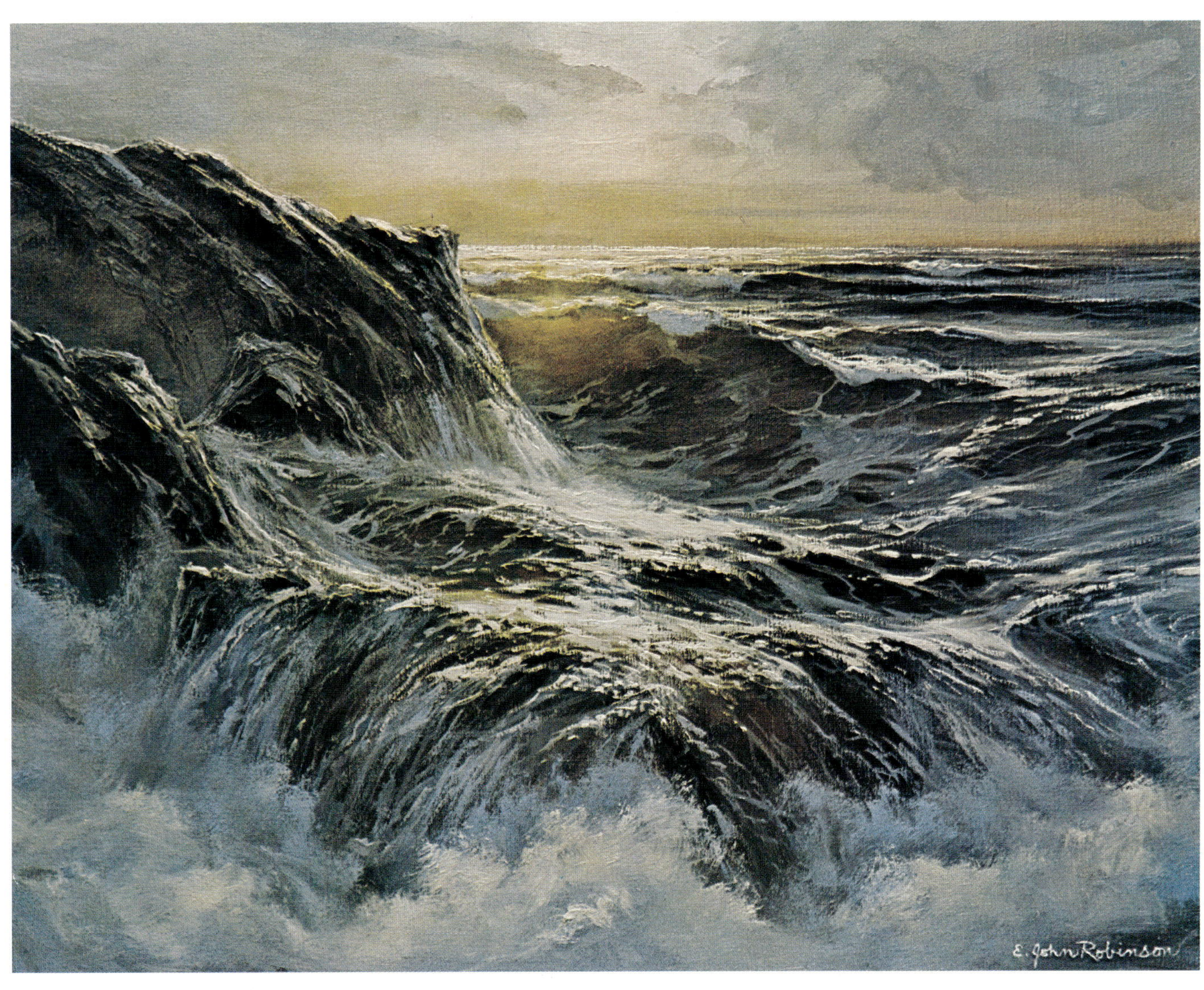

Somewhere there was a moment like this. It was a warm night, and the moon was full behind scattered clouds. The sea was choppy and glistened from the reflected light of the bright moon. There's no reference to land here, but the horizon lies a long way off and it's easy to let your thoughts move out and beyond. To me, it's much like staring into a fire—probably a primitive, but surely a human, mannerism.

I don't believe this is a typical moonlight, but it's a composite of effects mentioned in this book. The clouds are interesting only because they're backlit. The largest portion of this painting is the background sea (Chapter Three).

Pay special attention to the description of the ground swell in regard to the middle area of this painting. The major wave has no translucent portion but is a study in moon sparkle and shadows. The hint of foam patterns is kept low key so as not to distract by making the painting too busy.

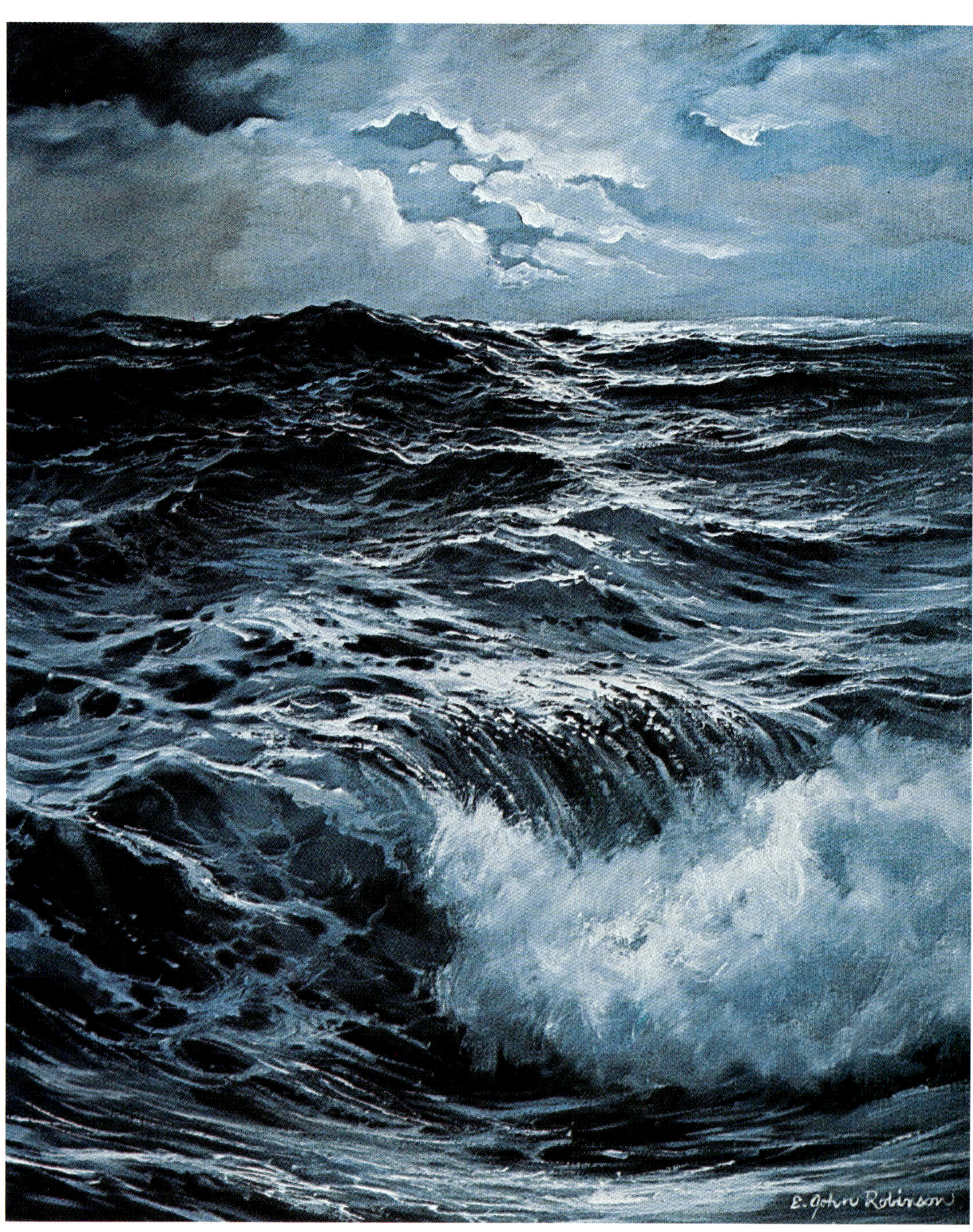

Plate 16. Moon at Sea. Oil, 30″ x 24″/76cm x 61cm.

CONCLUSION

Enthusiasm is quickly triggered by a book such as this; but I'm also aware that real frustration can emerge, as well. The knowledge I've shared with you in this and in *Marine Painting in Oil* has taken me many years to accumulate. Just because I write it down for you doesn't mean that you've mastered it.

Mastery is individual, it comes at different speeds for different people, but·it comes more quickly if you make yourself receptive. As I mentioned at the beginning, don't add the stigma of painting a good painting to a learning situation. Instead, learn on scraps that can be thrown away without a thought. I'm well aware of how difficult it is to "let go" of a painting that started out great but became a lost cause somewhere. Learn, and then apply your knowledge with some skill. The results will be better.

Also, study all the information you can find on the subject before you start a new problem. In other words, don't look at one of these ideas and start using it before you truly understand it. Read what I say, follow the step-by-steps, and practice the idea on scraps until you feel comfortable with it. Then apply it.

Please don't say, "I can't." Say, instead, "I can" or "I will" or "blankety-blank" or your pet phrase—and try again. You may have to try several times, which is another good reason to practice *before* you apply it to a painting.

Keep studying using this book, the sea, or a teacher. Your must be open-minded and capable of learning from all sources. Never be satisfied, but don't be too critical, either. Strive to improve upon yourself, and never mind what others are doing. And if you're criticized, weigh the remarks with an open mind. Even children can speak truths.

In the meantime, paint and enjoy the experience of learning, as I do everytime I look at the sea or touch a brush to canvas. There'll always be a new experience waiting just for you. Allow yourself the enjoyment of finding out. You deserve it!

BIBLIOGRAPHY

Bascom, Willard. *Waves and Beaches: The Dynamics of the Ocean Surface*. New York: Doubleday, 1964 (paperbound).

Hoopes, Donelson F. *The American Impressionists*. New York: Watson-Guptill, 1972.

Mathey, Francois. *Impressionists*. New York: Praeger, 1967.

Payne, Edgar. *Composition of Outdoor Painting*. Los Angeles, distributed by C. Palmer Payne.

Cooke, Hereward Lester. *Painting Lessons from the Great Masters*. New York: Watson-Guptill, 1972.

Pool, Phoebe. *Impressionism*. New York: Praeger, 1967. London: Thames & Hudson, 1967.

Sargent, Walter. *Enjoyment and Use of Color*. New York: Dover, 1923 (paperbound).

Special section on waves in *Oceans Magazine* (published by the Oceanic Society, San Francisco, Calif.), No. 5, September/October 1975, pp. 10-49.

AUTHOR'S BIOGRAPHY

E. John Robinson was born in Oregon and grew up on the rugged Oregon coast where he began painting at an early age. He started winning awards in elementary school and continued through high school with national honors in the National Scholastic contests in art.

Formal art studies began with a scholarship to the Cornish School of Allied Arts in Seattle, Washington, and he completed his studies at the California College of Arts and Crafts in Oakland, California. He received his masters degree from San Francisco State College, San Francisco, California.

Robinson's work is becoming more widely known each year. His paintings have appeared in *Oceans* magazine, on the cover of *Reader's Digest*, twice in the Fine American Art Calendar (Lezius-Hiles, Ohio), and are being reproduced by Frame House Gallery, Louisville, Kentucky.

His paintings are continuously shown at the Ruth Carlson Gallery, Mendocino, California, and the Zantman Galleries, Carmel and Palm Desert, California. In Oregon they can be seen at the Lincoln Art Galleries, Lincoln City, Oregon. In addition, over 1,500 of his paintings are in private collections throughout the country.

Mr. Robinson devotes full time to studying and painting the sea near his home in Mendocino, California. He no longer has the time to teach either public or private lessons but encourages students through his books.

INDEX

Edited by Bonnie Silverstein
Designed by Bob Fillie
Set in 11-point Laurel by Publishers Graphics Inc.
Color printed by The Lehigh Press, Inc.
Printed by Halliday Lithograph Corporation
Bound by A. Horowitz and Sons